Pacification

PACIFICATION

The American Struggle for Vietnam's Hearts and Minds

RICHARD A. HUNT

WESTVIEW PRESS

Boulder • San Francisco • Oxford

Copyright © 1995 by Westview Press, Inc.

Published in 1995 in the United States of America by Westview Press, Inc., 5500 Central Avenue, Boulder, Colorado 80301-2877, and in the United Kingdom by Westview Press, 12 Hid's Copse Road, Cumnor Hill, Oxford OX2 9JJ

Library of Congress Cataloging-in-Publication Data
Hunt, Richard A., 1942–
    Pacification : the American struggle for Vietnam's hearts and
minds / Richard A. Hunt.
        p.   cm.
    Includes bibliographical references and index.
    ISBN 0-8133-1182-9
    1. Vietnamese Conflict, 1961–1975—United States.   2. Vietnam—
Politics and government—1945–1975.   I. Title.
DS558.H86   1995
959.704′3—dc20
                                                                                                94-41893
                                                                                                CIP

Printed and bound in the United States of America

The paper used in this publication meets the requirements
of the American National Standard for Permanence of Paper
for Printed Library Materials Z39.48-1984.

10   9   8   7   6   5   4   3   2   1

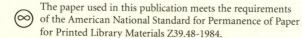

Contents

List of Illustrations   ix
Acknowledgments   xi
List of Acronyms   xiii

Introduction   1

1   **An Insurgency Begins**   4

The North Resumes the Struggle, 4
A House Built on Sand: South Vietnam Under Diem, 8
American Support of South Vietnam, 12

2   **Insurgency Unchecked, 1961–1965**   16

The Kennedy Administration and Vietnam, 16
Diem's Attempts at Pacification, 20
New Attempts at Pacification, 25

3   **The War and the "Other War," 1965–1966**   31

The Strategy of Attrition: Pacification Supplanted, 31
Doubts About Westmoreland's Strategy, 35
Reviving Pacification, 35
Limited Progress Under General Thang, 42

4   **Not by Force Alone: The U.S. Army in Pacification**   45

Civil Affairs, 45
Military Operations, 47
The Advisers: Liaison and Reporting, 59

5   **The Search for Solutions**   63

No One in Charge, 63
High Aspirations: Heads of State at Honolulu, 70

Retooling for Pacification, 71
Looking for Solutions, 74

6   Unifying American Support of Pacification   82

The Civilians' Last Chance, 82
The Creation of CORDS, 86
A New Start, 89

7   The Early Days of CORDS, May–December 1967   99

Project Takeoff, 99
Stronger Local Forces, Stronger Local Defense, 106
Battling the Communist Underground, 109

8   Leverage: CORDS's Quest for Better Performance   121

The Waning of Leverage, 122
The Revival of Leverage, 124
The Balance Sheet at Six Months, 130

9   The Tet Offensive and Pacification   133

On the Eve of the Offensive, 133
The Tet Offensive, 136
Disenchantment and Reappraisal, 141

10   What Next?   144

Project Recovery, 144
Taking the Offensive, 149
A Stronger Base, 152
Moving Toward Expansion, 154
Getting the South Vietnamese on Board, 156

11   Abrams in Command: Military Support of the APC   172

I Corps, 172
II Corps, 177
III Corps, 182
IV Corps, 188

12   The Impact of the APC   193

Whose Standards? 194
Mixed Results in South Vietnam, 195

The Numbers, 197
The View from Washington and Saigon, 202

13 New Directions   208

Looking for an Exit, 208
A New Commander, 211
Change in CORDS, 214
President Thieu's Pacification Plans, 215
The Communists Adjust, 217

14 One War or Business as Usual?   221

A Step Forward: Operation WASHINGTON GREEN, 222
A Step Backward: Operation RUSSELL BEACH/
    BOLD MARINER, 227
An Abrams Strategy? 232

15 The Phoenix Program: The Best-Laid Plans   234

Procedures, 235
Plans Gone Astray, 236
The F-6 and Binh Minh Campaigns, 242
The Army's Involvement: A Matter of Ambivalence, 244
Results, 247

16 The Ambiguous Achievements of Pacification   252

The Balance of Power in the Countryside, 253
Pacification Derailed: The 1972 Easter Offensive, 255
Underlying Doubts, 258
Building a Political Community, 263

17 The End of an Experiment   269

Advisers: Seeking the Best and Brightest, 269
CORDS Under Siege, 272
The Heritage of CORDS, 275

A Note on Sources   281
Notes   283
About the Book and Author   335
Index   337

Illustrations

Maps

1.1 South Vietnam administrative divisions   9

Tables

3.1 South Vietnamese forces available for pacification
     at the end of 1966   43

7.1 Increases in advisers for CORDS   108

12.1 HES rating for the end of the APC   198

Figures

6.1 OCO, December 1966–April 1967   84

6.2 CORDS staff   92

7.1 Communist structure of South Vietnam   111

Photographs

A navy corpsman carrying a South Vietnamese child   160

A member of the Viet Cong defecting   161

A member of a Popular Forces platoon after liberation   162

General William Westmoreland   163

Prime Minister Nguyen Cao Ky and General Nguyen Van Thieu
with President Lyndon Johnson   163

William Porter receiving orders from President Lyndon Johnson
and adviser McGeorge Bundy   164

Robert Komer with President Lyndon Johnson and adviser
Robert Nathan   164

Robert Komer and Ambassador Henry Cabot Lodge at a White
House meeting   165

Ambassador Ellsworth Bunker conferring with President Lyndon
Johnson and adviser Walt W. Rostow   165

President Lyndon Johnson with Robert Komer   166

President Lyndon Johnson meeting with Secretaries Dean Rusk
and Robert McNamara   166

General Creighton Abrams briefing the president and cabinet   167

Prinicpals of the MACV staff   167

Ambassador William Colby with a Revolutionary Development
Cadre team   168

Communist defectors at a *Chieu Hoi* lecture   168

Graduates of a Revolutionary Development Cadre training course   169

Civilian members of a People's Self-Defense Forces unit   170

William Colby at a school   171

Acknowledgments

Over the course of a project that has taken many years to complete, I have amassed numerous obligations to persons and institutions. My colleagues, past and present, at the Army Center of Military History have helped in ways both substantial and subtle. Eric Bergerud and Raffi Gregorian deserve individual thanks for their encouragement and insights into pacification. Thomas Scoville needs to be acknowledged for his pioneering work *Reorganizing for Pacification Support* and also for his energetic, farsighted efforts to ensure that the papers of the CORDS organization were preserved as an entity. These records are indispensable for the study of pacification. I salute the staff of the Lyndon Baines Johnson Library, particularly former archivist David Humphrey. Everyone at the library was unfailingly helpful and thoroughly professional. Their support made research there rewarding and pleasurable. At Westview Press, I am grateful to Peter Kracht, Mick Gusinde-Duffy, and Shena Redmond for shepherding this manuscript to publication and to Jan Kristiansson, my editor, for wielding her sharp pencil to bring consistency to my manuscript.

Numerous persons involved with the pacification program gave generously of their time. I greatly benefitted from the counsel of William Colby and Robert Komer, the first two chiefs of CORDS. Both patiently pointed out misperceptions and mistakes and helped clarify many issues. Komer proved especially helpful. He read chapter drafts with a sharp eye and improved their accuracy, providing in his inimitable style the insights of his experience. I appreciate the knowledge all those involved in pacification tried to impart and hope that, despite any interpretive differences, they will regard this book as a balanced account of the travails of an important and complex program. Errors of fact or judgment remain solely my responsibility, despite the valiant efforts of the many knowledgeable people who advised me. The interpretations expressed in this book are my own and do not represent those of any government agency, office, or department.

Finally, I am indebted to my wife, Nancy, my son, Ashley, and my daughter, Kathleen, who patiently bore my countless absences during the many weekends and nights I spent researching and writing this book. They endured a seemingly interminable process with grace, and their encouragement helped pull me through. For all these things, I am grateful to them and hope this book in some ways repays their sacrifice.

Richard A. Hunt

Acronyms

AAR	after action report
ACS	assistant chief of staff
AID	Agency for International Development
AIK	assistance in kind
APC	Accelerated Pacification Campaign
ARU	Armed Reconnaissance Unit
ARVN	Army of the Republic of (South) Vietnam
CAP	Combined Action Platoon
CG	Civil Guard
CIA	Central Intelligence Agency
CIDG	Civilian Irregular Defense Group
CINCPAC	commander in chief of the Pacific Command
CIO	Central Intelligence Office
CMH	U.S. Army Center for Military History
COMUSMACV	commander, United States Military Assistance Command, Vietnam
CORDS	Civil Operations and Revolutionary Development Support
COSVN	Central Office for South Vietnam
CPDC	Central Pacification and Development Council
CTZ	corps tactical zone
DepCORDS	deputy to COMUSMACV for CORDS
DF	disposition form
DIA	Defense Intelligence Agency
DIOCC	District Intelligence Operations Coordinating Center
DOD	Department of Defense
FBI	Federal Bureau of Investigation
FY	fiscal year
GNP	gross national product
GVN	Government of (South) Vietnam
HES	Hamlet Evaluation System
ICEX	infrastructure coordination and exploitation
ID	identification
JCS	Joint Chiefs of Staff

JGS	Joint General Staff
JUSPAO	Joint United States Public Affairs Office
LORAPL	Long-Range Planning Task Group
MAAG	Military Assistance Advisory Group
MACCORDS	Military Assistance Command, CORDS
MACDC	MACV Directorate of Construction
MACV	Military Assistance Command, Vietnam
MAF	Marine Amphibious Force
MALT	mobile advisory logistics team
MAP	Military Assistance Program
MASA	military assistance security adviser
MAT	mobile advisory team
MEDCAP	Medical Civil Affairs Program
MFR	memorandum for record
MHD	Military History Detachment
MHI	U.S. Army Military History Institute
MILPHAP	Military Provincial Health Assistance Program
NCO	noncommissioned officer
NLF	National Liberation Front
NPFF	National Police Field Force
NSAM	National Security Action Memorandum
NSC	National Security Council
NSF	National Security Files
NSSM	National Security Study Memorandum
NVA	North Vietnamese Army
OCO	Office of Civil Operations
ORLL	operational report lessons learned
OSD	Office of the Secretary of Defense
PAAS	Pacification Attitude Analysis System
PF	Popular Forces
PHREEX	*Phung Hoang Reexamination*
pow	prisoner of war
PPG	*The Pentagon Papers,* Gravel edition
PROVN	"Program for the Pacification and Long-Term Development of Vietnam"
PRP	People's Revolutionary Party
PRU	Provincial Reconnaissance Unit
PSDF	People's Self-Defense Force
psyops	psychological operations
RD	revolutionary development
RF	Regional Forces
RVN	Republic of (South) Vietnam
SAAFO	Special Assistant to the Ambassador for Field Operations

SACSA	Special Assistant for Counterinsurgency and Special Activities
SDC	Self-Defense Corps
Seabees	U.S. Navy Construction Battalion
SLO	Special Liaison Office
TAOR	tactical area of responsibility
TFES	Territorial Force Evaluation System
USAF	United States Air Force
USAID	United States Agency for International Development
USIA	United States Information Agency
USMC	United States Marine Corps
USOM	United States Operations Mission
US-VR	*United States–Vietnam Relations*
VC	Viet Cong
VCI	Viet Cong infrastructure
VN	Vietnam
VSSG	Vietnam Special Studies Group
WNRC	Washington National Records Center

Introduction

For decades, the problem of Vietnam plagued American strategists and policymakers, who viewed the struggle there as another front in the Cold War against the expansion of communism. From the Geneva Convention of 1954 that ended the French Indochina War to the fall of South Vietnam in 1975, the United States supported a panoply of military and political plans, among them various pacification programs, to shore up a succession of governments in Saigon. Broadly speaking, the Americans conceived pacification as a means to defeat a communist insurgency and help build a national political community in South Vietnam. The American-backed counterinsurgency efforts of the early 1950s that quelled the communist-led Huk movement in the Philippines helped generate a belief that the United States had a singular mission. As one historian expressed it, there were confident assertions in the Eisenhower years that "the American record authorized, if indeed it did not command, the United States to undertake nation building in Southeast Asia."[1] From the beginning of South Vietnam's existence as an independent nation in 1954 to the end of the war, the pacification program assumed many guises, but its steadfast purpose was to help realize the ultimate American and South Vietnamese goal of an independent, sovereign, and noncommunist South Vietnam. Pacification was an integral part of allied strategy to realize this goal.

This book examines the American role in pacification, which was largely one of providing advice and support for the program. America's involvement in the "other war," as pacification was sometimes known, was never as publicized as its participation in other aspects of the conflict, such as the U.S. Air Force (USAF) and Navy bombing campaigns or the "big-unit war" fought by U.S. Army and Marine Corps (USMC) units. But under Lyndon Baines Johnson, the United States enthusiastically embraced a unique nation-building mission in South Vietnam that had its origins in the same presidential impulses that gave birth to the Great Society and the April 1965 offer to North Vietnam of a billion-dollar economic development program for the Mekong River valley region on a scale to dwarf the Tennessee Valley Authority.

Pacification encompassed both military efforts to provide security and programs of economic and social reform and required both the U.S. Army and a number of U.S. civilian agencies to support the South Vietnamese. The Americans underwrote the program's costs and as advisers proffered technical, administrative, and military assistance. As financiers and advisers, U.S. officials could theoretically influence or leverage the South Vietnamese, but a number of factors, including fragmented American management and Saigon's insistence on exercising its sovereignty, circumscribed Washington's influence. Poor coordination and duplication of effort characterized American support of pacification. The unification of American military and civil support of pacification under a single manager, the U.S. military commander in South Vietnam, represented a watershed. How and why pacification programs succeeded or failed, how and why American support of pacification changed, and how the changes affected pacification are the themes of this work.

This book attempts to fill a void in the literature on the Vietnam War—the lack of a comprehensive study of American attempts to support the various South Vietnamese programs that composed pacification. Not another treatment of air and land operations or one more account of the American decision to intervene militarily in 1965, this book concentrates on an unfamiliar but crucial story: American support for the South Vietnamese effort against the communist politico-military campaign to defeat South Vietnam. Far too many books on Vietnam have ignored pacification or merely alluded to it in passing as the "war in the villages" or the struggle for "hearts and minds" before returning to matters of diplomacy or conventional military operations.

Unfortunately, some key participants in the pacification program have not published detailed accounts. Robert Komer, who was pivotal in mobilizing the American involvement in pacification, sketched out his approach to pacification in his monograph *Bureaucracy Does Its Thing,* and Edward Lansdale, who became a key American figure in the political war after he helped extinguish the communist Huk insurgency in the Philippines, treated pacification cursorily in his memoir *In the Midst of Wars.*[2] The exception is William Colby's *Lost Victory,* a passionate defense of the programs he once ran. A Central Intelligence Agency (CIA) official involved in South Vietnam since the early 1960s, Colby was in charge of American support of pacification from 1968 to 1971. A handful of studies have centered on particular facets of pacification, such as refugee resettlement or the Phoenix program.[3] Other accounts have analyzed events in a single province.[4] A number of first-person accounts by pacification advisers have examined the war through the prism of an individual's tour of duty.[5] Absent from bookshelves has been a discussion of the overall development of the program and its connection to national policy and military strategy.

The basic concepts of pacification emerged from the counterinsurgency doctrine of the late 1950s and early 1960s. That doctrine, espoused by limited-war theorists such as Charles Osgood, was designed to help the United States deal with conflicts at the low end of the spectrum of warfare, insurgencies, or wars of national liberation.[6] Counterinsurgency melded a wide array of civil and military programs to defeat revolutionary insurgent movements in poor or developing nations. On the civil side were programs of economic development, land reform, and broader participation in politics. On the military were the provision of security by police and paramilitary forces and anti-insurgent operations by mobile, lightly armed ground forces. South Vietnamese government officials, police and paramilitary units, and specially trained cadre teams sought to improve rural social and economic conditions and defeat communist, or Viet Cong (VC), forces. According to one practitioner, pacification tended to supplant counterinsurgency as the operative term in 1964–1965.[7]

Although none of South Vietnam's forty-four provinces could be said to represent the widely varying geographic and political conditions in the country, some were clearly more important strategically and politically, and also more difficult to pacify, than others. In these areas the struggle was its most intense. According to Department of Defense (DOD) statistics, ten provinces accounted for half the combat deaths: all of I Corps plus Binh Dinh, Kontum, Tay Ninh, Kien Hoa, and Dinh Tuong. The communists were in control of these provinces when they defeated the French. Not surprisingly, the communist clandestine organization, the so-called Viet Cong infrastructure (VCI), was also its strongest in many of them: Quang Nam and Quang Ngai in I Corps, Binh Dinh in II Corps, Tay Ninh in III Corps, and Dinh Tuong and Kien Hoa in IV Corps.[8] To achieve lasting results, pacification would need to cripple the Viet Cong movement in the tough provinces.

Thanks to the convergence of a number of factors, pacification began its most promising period at the end of 1968. Unified management of American support under the military, which occurred in 1967; increased support from the U.S. Army; the buildup of South Vietnam's local security forces; and the development of a comprehensive campaign provided the framework for the turnaround of the program.

The unification of American support of pacification offers a significant example for the future. The story of pacification in South Vietnam shows how the U.S. government broke the bureaucratic mold and merged civil and military programs belonging to separate agencies under a single manager running a single organization, Civil Operations and Revolutionary Development Support (CORDS), enabling him to devise an integrated program to counter all facets of the insurgent political and military threat. In a period of declining national security resources and increasing likelihood of American military force involvement in low-intensity conflicts or operations other than war (terms currently in vogue), joint service and combined civil-military efforts may likely become the rule. And the American experience in pacification, with its numerous pitfalls and painful and costly lessons, is certain to be instructive. Although rooted in the Cold War struggle against communism, the experience in South Vietnam was not the first or is it likely to be the last American attempt at nation building, but it is one that surely will reward further study.

1

An Insurgency Begins

The end of French colonial rule in 1954 resulted in the partition of Vietnam. North Vietnam's leadership sought to unify the Vietnamese under its rule. To accomplish this end, the leaders in Hanoi in the late 1950s turned to insurgency. Adhering to the tenets of revolutionary warfare of Chinese Communist leader Mao Zedong, as modified by Vietnamese leaders such as Truong Chinh, Ho Chi Minh, and General Vo Nguyen Giap, architect of France's defeat, Hanoi built a clandestine political organization throughout the South Vietnamese countryside. Combining political appeals, terror, and guerrilla warfare, the Viet Cong sought to destroy the local outposts of South Vietnamese president Ngo Dinh Diem's government and deprive it of its rural political and military base.

In the early 1950s, America devoted relatively little attention to South Vietnam. The problems of this small, distant land were relatively unimportant compared to the grave situations in Europe and Korea, which were perceived as vital to national interests, where the United States directly faced communist military forces. Concerned with the spread of communism in Asia, the American government bolstered the fledgling Diem regime with military and economic aid to help preserve South Vietnam as an independent and noncommunist nation.

The North Resumes the Struggle

During World War II, Vietnamese revolutionary Ho Chi Minh, the founder of the Indochinese Communist Party, formed the Vietnam Doc Lap Dong Minh Hoi (League for the Independence of Vietnam), or Viet Minh as it was commonly called, as a nationalist resistance organization. In August 1945, it briefly replaced departing Japanese occupation forces, establishing a short-lived Democratic Republic of Vietnam that claimed to represent all of Vietnam. After the French returned to power in 1946, the Viet Minh successfully waged insurgent warfare to end colonial rule but failed in its objective of attaining an independent and united Vietnam.

The Indochinese Communist Party (renamed the Dang Lao Dong Vietnam, or the Vietnam Workers' Party), led by Ho Chi Minh, continued to fight for a unified Vietnam after 1954. The party maintained close ties with Viet Minh cadres in the South. It also trained in the techniques of revolutionary war some ninety thousand southern-based Viet Minh cadres who had moved north following the partition of the country. They later returned south and merged with those who had stayed behind to form a new insurgent force, the Viet Cong.[1]

Between 1954 and 1956, the Dang Lao Dong discouraged armed activity in South Vietnam—restricting cadres to limited self-defense measures and directing them to develop a political movement in the villages.[2] Beginning in 1955, Diem's military and police forces, however, destroyed much of this communist political apparatus. By the end of 1957, several hundred suspected party members had been killed and an estimated sixty-five thousand arrested. The Army of the Republic of (South) Vietnam (ARVN) attacked the party's bases in the Plain of Reeds on the Ca Mau Peninsula and in War Zone D. Party membership dropped by a third from a base of five thousand. The official party histories consider these years the "dark period."[3] Internal dissension over Hanoi's policies further weakened the southern revolutionaries, and for a while the survival of an organized insurgent movement seemed questionable. The Saigon government may have been justified at the time in regarding the insurgents as a minor irritant.

Beginning in 1956, the southern insurgents, the Viet Cong, started building a political organization and forming local military units in Quang Ngai province, the U-Minh forest, and the heavily populated farming regions around Saigon and in the Mekong River Delta. The Viet Cong also rebuilt its base camps in the unsettled jungles close to the capital—War Zones C and D, the Iron Triangle, the Trapezoid, and the Ho Bo and Boi Loi woods. The key base area, War Zone D, forested and difficult to penetrate, was close to the Cambodian border, yet accessible to the lower delta and the central highlands. These remote bases allowed the nascent forces to develop and operate in secret. The following year, Viet Cong forces, which numbered thirty-seven armed companies, began small-scale guerrilla operations. Several hundred government officials were assassinated.[4]

Only in 1959 at the party's Fifteenth Plenum of the Central Committee did Hanoi, reacting to Diem's success against the communist movement and its perception of growing popular resentment of his rule, change strategy. The success of Diem's attacks forced the party to expand and protect its forces.[5] It began sending supplies and personnel southward and assumed more direct political and military leadership of the insurgency. It also ordered the insurgents to dismantle Saigon's administration in the countryside and step up attacks on government villages and outposts.[6] Through a combined military and political struggle, party leaders hoped to stop Diem's campaign against them and accelerate the disintegration of the Saigon government, gaining adherents to their movement from the numbers of South Vietnamese disaffected with his rule. Throughout 1959, the level of fighting increased. In response, Saigon moved forces against base areas and began to move people into new settlements, so-called *agrovilles,* from villages vulnerable to communist political action.

The following year, in December 1960, North Vietnam established the National Liberation Front (NLF) of South Vietnam, an umbrella organization that included the Viet Cong and representatives of other groups opposed to Diem. Like the original Viet Minh, this ostensibly broad-based organization was actually under communist control. Organized by a handful of persons affiliated with the Communist Party, the NLF drew its early membership from former Viet Minh, the Cao Dai and Hoa Hao sects, disaffected minorities (Cambodians and Montagnards), university students, some farmers in the delta, anti-Diem intellectuals, and others who, for one reason or another, opposed the Saigon regime. The NLF served several purposes. It allowed the party to attract a broad spectrum of dissident elements into the insurgency and exercise control of rival opposition groups. In setting up the NLF, the communists sought to make it the focal point for all antigovernment activity.[7]

The communists slowly transformed the NLF into a shadow government, with political cells extending from the village level, through district and province political committees, to a clandestine central authority. Communist Party members, however, dominated the upper echelons of the NLF's political apparatus, and the Politburo in Hanoi directed its policies, goals, and strategy. The party's success in establishing a united front with no visible ties to the communist government in the North gave the party enormous political and propaganda advantages. Under Hanoi's control, the NLF successfully projected the image of an autonomous and *indigenous* group. This widely held public impression had, William Duiker perceptively concluded, "momentous effects on the worldwide image" of the Viet Cong,[8] identifying it as a legitimate political alternative to the government of South Vietnam. The image of the front as a southern opposition group also enabled Hanoi to sow confusion about the nature of the struggle in Vietnam. Hanoi's effort to unify Vietnam could be attributed for propaganda purposes to an internal struggle among South Vietnamese political groups.

To establish this rival government, or infrastructure, inside South Vietnam, the communists relied on measures of repression and reform. They carefully blended a campaign of terror against government officials, a skillful organizational effort that unified the movement, and promises of reform.[9] Communist recruiting and organizational techniques at the local level were both simple and pragmatic. Communist organizers moved into a village, seeking to build popular support by promising to redress local grievances against landowners and the government. Cadres established local political councils that addressed specific grievances. Cadres worked through the local peasant leadership and sought adherents from a broad range of social and economic groups to solidify ties between the party and the peasants.[10]

Next came the crucial step, the use of violence—assassination or kidnapping of local officials—to uproot the government. According to one party member, the purpose of terrorism was to eliminate known opponents and intimidate the people.[11] The insurgents would execute unpopular officials in full view of assembled villagers as punishment for alleged crimes "against the people." In other instances the party publicly forced local officials to humiliate themselves by denouncing the government and confessing their "guilt." Staged confessions nullified an official's worth in the eyes of villagers. The party was more circumspect in dealing with popular officials, however, eliminating them secretly to avoid arousing public resentment.

Lacking adequate territorial security and police forces, rural government officials were especially vulnerable to such tactics. The loss of representatives in the countryside, Saigon's symbols of authority as well as sources of information on rural conditions, put the Diem government in the position of "legislating in a void," to use Bernard Fall's apt phrase. In this way the communists sought to break the ties between the peasants and the central government, creating the impression that Saigon had neither the will nor the ability to protect its own people.[12] The daily presence in the village of the party's political or military personnel was in marked contrast to the sporadic appearances of government officials or soldiers, so that a villager, even if he or she distrusted the revolutionaries, probably had little choice but to go along with them. The government's thinly spread forces were often not close or strong enough to protect the peasants from reprisals.[13]

Communist cadres drew rural settlements into a larger organization. Cadres trained some villagers in communist tactics and techniques, eventually assigning them missions outside their immediate locales and raising some to more responsible positions in the hierarchy. The cadres' recruiting program was successful. An analysis of interviews of captured enemy personnel concluded that most peasants supported the National Liberation Front because the cadres had approached and mobilized the villagers.[14] Control of a village gave revolutionary leaders tangible advantages. They exacted taxes in kind, usually rice, to help feed their military forces. The levying of taxes was a sure manifestation of the party's governing authority.

Control of villages also allowed the Viet Cong to build up guerrilla forces. They generally fell into two categories: full-time regulars and part-time paramilitary forces. Full-time forces consisted of both main force and local force units. Main forces were organized into divisions and regiments, which generally operated at the national and regional levels against regular units of the South Vietnamese armed forces. Local forces were less heavily armed and fought as smaller units. They were subordinate to communist political authorities in the provinces, districts, or cities where they were usually stationed and, like the main forces, had combat support and service components.

Part-time forces, operating as guerrillas, served in the villages and hamlets. The Viet Cong organized three types of part-time forces: combat, village, and self-defense militia. Combat guerrillas were formed into platoons, squads, and cells that conducted small-scale operations at the local level. Village guerrillas were lightly armed, part-time forces. Even without weapons, village guerrillas epitomized the party's control of a settlement. Self-defense militia were generally unarmed and partly trained personnel (mostly women, older men, and children) who functioned (sometimes involuntarily) as guards and low-level service troops, helping collect taxes, dig trenches, carry supplies, and construct simple booby traps and other obstacles.[15]

The Viet Cong's main forces, local forces, and guerrillas were mutually supporting. Main forces provided a shield for the work of lower-level units, and guerrillas assisted and supported main force operations against ARVN. A military headquarters at each echelon exercised direct operational command of soldiers and units at that level and administrative control of those below it. Military units at all levels were subordinate to the directives of a parallel political organization, the party.

The Politburo and the Central Committee in Hanoi exercised overall control of the war effort, issuing resolutions and directives to communist organizations and leaders inside South Vietnam. To control soldiers and cadres south of the partition, the communists established a separate southern regional office in the early 1950s, the Central Office for South Vietnam (COSVN). COSVN was disestablished after the 1954 Geneva Accords but reactivated as the fighting intensified in 1961 and 1962. This headquarters, which moved its location several times during the war, was always relatively close to Saigon. Below COSVN, the party organized echelons of command, which were political and not military, at region, province/subregion, district/city, and village and hamlet (see Map 1.1). COSVN controlled the territory south of Darlac and Khanh Hoa provinces, while Hanoi directly supervised the war effort in those two provinces and the area to the north. The provincial- and district-level Viet Cong administrations carried out a wide range of governmental tasks, from internal security to public health. The primacy of the party illustrated the importance that communist leaders attached to the nonmilitary aspects of their revolution. Arms served to eliminate opposition, a precondition to creating a new political order, a united Vietnam.[16]

In political organization and in military strength, the communists by 1959–1960 constituted a serious and growing threat to the Saigon regime's independence. As William Colby, the CIA station chief and adviser to President Diem noted later, the communists had issued no formal declaration of war in 1959 but had begun a long-term political struggle after carefully laying a solid foundation.[17] They had established inside South Vietnam an organization for building a political movement and military forces based on a strategy for physically and politically isolating the regime from the people.

A House Built on Sand:
South Vietnam Under Diem

South Vietnam lacked a unifying identity, a tradition of political community. Regional, ethnic, and religious antagonisms afflicted the region from its earliest days

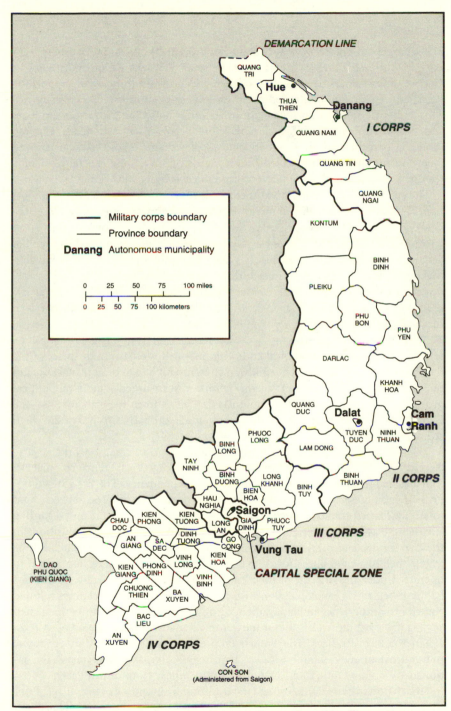

MAP 1.1 South Vietnam administrative divisions. *Source:* Central Intelligence Agency, "South Vietnam Provincial Maps" (Washington, D.C.: CIA, September 1967).

as a separate nation. Between 1954 and 1956, thousands of Roman Catholics fearing persecution left the North and settled in South Vietnam. Regarded by many in Cochin China as outsiders, the Catholic émigrés proved a bulwark of support for the Diem regime and controlled many leadership positions in the government. This ruling Catholic minority sought to govern a nation that in sheer numbers was overwhelmingly Buddhist. Sizable ethnic minorities, principally Chinese (about 6 percent); ethnic Cambodians called Khmers (about 3 percent); and primitive mountain tribes, called Montagnards, living in the central highlands (perhaps 4 percent of the population) lived uneasily with the Vietnamese.

The country was divided into four corps and forty-four provinces. South Vietnam's population of roughly 16 million persons was concentrated in two large areas. Two-thirds of the people lived in the southern part of the country, the region encompassing III and IV Corps (see Map 1.1), which also contained the capital, Saigon, and, to its south, the country's main rice-growing region, the sprawling Mekong Delta. The remaining one-third of the population lived along the narrow northern coastal plains of Hue, Danang, Quang Ngai, and Qui Nhon. Large expanses of territory in the rugged central highlands of II Corps and the western reaches of I Corps were sparsely populated.

After the Geneva Accords of 1954, the government in Saigon had to establish itself as the sole legitimate political authority in South Vietnam in the place of the departing French colonists. The southern government had to offer protection and political and economic support against communist insurgents and rival political groups. Opposition from the communists as well as from the armed sects—the Cao Dai, the Hoa Hao, and the Binh Xuyen—made the early survival of the Diem regime dubious.

The heritage of French rule hampered Saigon's effort to create a workable government. In the late nineteenth and early twentieth centuries, French colonial authorities had ill-prepared the Vietnamese for independence. The French had opposed Vietnamese self-rule and withheld the freedoms of press, speech, and assembly. French colons, expecting their rule in Vietnam to endure and regarding Vietnamese as inferior, monopolized the leadership and managerial positions in the civil service and ministries. French officials departing in 1954 left behind the fragile shell of a rigid bureaucracy that the Vietnamese were largely untrained to operate. Under the tutelage of their colonial masters, Vietnamese civil servants had imbibed the French obsession with formal bureaucratic procedures but had gained little experience in management or policymaking.[18] This unfortunate legacy made it even more difficult for the South Vietnamese to create and operate an effective administration. The French failure to share political and economic power drove many Vietnamese leaders to join anticolonial groups such as the nationalist Vietnam Quoc Dan Dang or the Indochinese Communist Party.

French practices had undermined the traditional autonomy of the village. Prior to the French arrival in Indochina, the village had served as the center of local politics. In each village, a council of notables had constituted an informal governing body and had the right to draft budgets and raise revenues from the rental of communal lands, tax surcharges, and the sale of licenses. Traditionally, villages were also responsible for law and order.[19] The French forced the villages to provide the colonial government with census data for imposing taxes and recruiting labor for French-controlled enterprises. The colonial authorities closely monitored local elections and the councils.[20]

France's economic bequest to South Vietnam was equally debilitating. Save for a small class of wealthy businessmen and landowners, most of whom were French educated, the Vietnamese acquired little of value from an economic system organized primarily to serve the colonial power. French companies owned large rubber plantations where Vietnamese toiled under oppressive conditions. Native workers were poorly paid and forced to live on the plantations in what amounted to confinement away from their families and ancestral lands. After the French departure, the Vietnamese elite essentially replaced the French managers and middlemen, thereby perpetuating the existing system rather than reforming it.[21] Beginning in 1874, the French government had opened large areas of land in the Mekong Delta, then a sparsely inhabited area, for rice farming. Wealthy urban entrepreneurs had slowly bought up tracts of farmland traditionally belonging to established villages and hamlets and had allowed farmers to till the land in exchange for the payment of a fixed percentage of the crop in rent.[22] The result was that large numbers of Vietnamese in Cochin China were either landless or tenants, despite Diem's land reform law of 1956, which limited the size of landholdings. Because most South Vietnamese peasants did not own the land they farmed, land reform became a potent political issue.

In 1954, the government of South Vietnam controlled only the cities and large towns. To govern, Diem had to extend his rule to the villages, where the bulk of the people lived. Pacification of the countryside was thus a key government program inextricably linked with the history of South Vietnam. In 1955, Diem appointed his minister of defense to oversee the activities of ARVN, police forces, and public administrators in gaining control of the rural areas. Diem labeled this operation *national security,* but the more familiar term *pacification,* which had been closely associated with the French, remained in common usage. Americans were involved as well. Edward Lansdale, a USAF general and CIA adviser who enjoyed Diem's confidence and had been advising him on pacification, headed the advisory element for this effort.[23] In June 1954, Landsdale had been reassigned from the Philippines, where he had been working with President Ramón Magsaysay on a similar program.

Saigon's military, which existed as a force independent of French control beginning only in 1954, had to be built practically from scratch. Few of the Vietnamese who had served with the French had done so in leadership or staff positions or had technical training. Units had to be organized, recruited, trained, equipped, and supplied, a process that even with U.S. funds and assistance would take years of effort.[24] In addition to a regular army, South Vietnam's armed forces consisted of paramilitary units. The Civil Guard (CG) and the Self-Defense Corps (SDC) (along with the police) were primarily responsible for protecting villages against

Viet Cong raids and constituted the principal local forces available to province and district chiefs. Like most elements of South Vietnam's force structure, the CG and SDC had antecedents in the colonial period. The Civil Guard, created by presidential decree in April 1955, drew members from defunct paramilitary organizations that had fought against the Viet Minh. After 1956, these poorly led and inadequately trained paramilitary forces had to protect the rural population after ARVN withdrew from rural areas to reorganize and modernize under the tutelage of American advisers. The CG and SDC were less well trained, armed, and paid than regular South Vietnamese soldiers, and, although they came to bear the brunt of insurgent activity, they represented the weak link in Saigon's internal security. Control of South Vietnam's military was centralized. From headquarters in Saigon, the Joint General Staff (JGS) issued orders to the commanding generals of the corps.[25]

By 1956, Diem, to the surprise of many observers, had taken promising steps toward building a healthy political base.[26] He had disarmed the sects and installed loyal province and district chiefs. South Vietnamese province chiefs were the highest-ranking political officials outside Saigon and were responsible for carrying out the central government's pacification plans. These chiefs were assisted by staffs composed of representatives from the Saigon ministries. Many province chiefs, especially in contested areas, were military officers loyal to Diem. The forty-four provinces, analogous to the *départements* of France and called sectors for military purposes, constituted extensions of the central authority. The province chiefs also served as sector chiefs. Each of the six autonomous cities (Saigon, Cam Ranh, Vung Tau, Dalat, Danang, and Hue) was equivalent in political status to a province. Provinces were divided into administrative units called districts, headed by district chiefs. Districts, essentially administrative units lacking a political constituency, were the lowest level at which representatives of the Saigon government operated.

Diem filled many high military and political posts with Vietnamese who had cooperated with the French and migrated to the South as the colonial authorities withdrew. Most of the émigrés from the North had little knowledge of the countryside or the problems that burdened the peasants. But such individuals formed the foundation of the Saigon government and, despite Diem's opposition in the 1930s to French rule, made it difficult for the South Vietnamese president to divorce his administration from the legacy of French colonialism.

American Support of South Vietnam

U.S. involvement in South Vietnam, at first modest, steadily grew after World War II, representing an expanding commitment on the part of successive American presidents. In 1950, President Harry S Truman began to send military supplies to assist the French in their struggle against the Viet Minh. Following France's withdrawal from Indochina, the administration of President Dwight D. Eisenhower enlarged the American role in South Vietnam. He set up a collective defense organization, the Southeast Asia Treaty Organization, to provide for the mutual security of countries in that region and also decided to give American military aid directly to the South Vietnamese.

American funds defrayed some of the cost of military pay and allowances, training, construction, and medical services. South Vietnam came to depend heavily on American economic aid. Between 1955 and 1960, American economic aid averaged nearly $222 million annually. That figure represented over 20 percent of South Vietnam's gross national product (GNP), which over those years averaged about $1 billion.[27] American assistance made possible economic development and touched most aspects of national life. American aid subsidized the nation's imports and supported school construction, agricultural credit and cooperatives, police training, industrial development, banking, taxation, and finance. American aid also constituted the financial footing of South Vietnam's independence.[28] The United States Operations Mission (USOM), the field office of the Agency for International Development (AID), administered the aid package.

In the late 1950s, the United States viewed North Vietnam's regular forces as the most significant threat to South Vietnam. Consequently, the small, 740-man American Military Assistance Advisory Group (MAAG) in Saigon, which assumed responsibility in 1955 for training South Vietnam's armed forces, prepared them to stop a conventional invading force by emphasizing large tactical military formations—regiments, divisions, and corps—and the gathering of conventional military order-of-battle information. MAAG's fixation on the threat of a massive overt invasion caused it to slight counterinsurgency doctrine, intelligence, and training.[29]

Support of police and local security forces was initially USOM's responsibility. Local security forces at this time consisted of the provincial-level Civil Guard and the village militia Self-Defense Corps. Both organizations belonged to the Ministry of the Interior and therefore did not benefit from the American Military Assistance Program (MAP), which set forth the amount and kind of weapons, equipment, munitions, and training support that the United States would extend to South Vietnam's military forces. Both organizations were relatively neglected. Only in 1959 did the U.S. government finally agree to help equip and train these local forces, which until then had depended on arms and equipment left by French and Japanese forces many years before.[30] Although the situation improved in 1960 when the CG and the SDC transferred from the Ministry of the Interior to the Ministry of Defense, making them eligible for American financial assistance, these paramilitary forces were, in the judgment of the official army history, "still unprepared, untrained, and unequipped" to cope with the insurgency.[31]

In 1960, Diem, concerned about the worsening situation in the countryside, asked that his paramilitary forces be strengthened and suggested that several of the better CG units be reorganized into territorial regiments to provide local security. Lieutenant General Samuel T. Williams, the MAAG chief, disagreed. Williams was reluctant to begin new programs that might detract from the buildup of conventional armed forces. Nevertheless, on Diem's insistence he supported a scaled-down version of the proposal, agreeing that U.S. Army Special Forces soldiers would conduct four-week training sessions in counterinsurgency warfare for a number of 100-man, special security companies. However, about 25 percent of the trainees failed to complete the course of instruction, and the MAAG abandoned the training program.[32]

That Washington saw no immediate danger from local guerrilla forces or communist political cadres was apparent from the counterinsurgency plan that Admiral Harry Felt, commander in chief of the Pacific Command (CINCPAC), began to develop in March 1960. It reached President John F. Kennedy's desk in late January 1961, when he signed it. The plan presumed that the Saigon government could both cope with the communists and improve its fortunes if it made reforms and had sufficient forces at hand. The counterinsurgency plan financed an increase of 20,000 men in ARVN, bringing total strength to 170,000, but provided only modest support ($12.7 million) for expanding the CG to 68,000. Under the plan's umbrella, agencies in Washington separately pushed their own programs with little regard for an overall strategy. The plan lacked a program for political action—a means of organizing the peasants in support of the government and counteracting the presence of the communists in the countryside. Absent a sense of crisis, no officials in Washington or Saigon questioned the plan's adequacy.[33]

In exchange for increased aid under the terms of the counterinsurgency plan, the Kennedy administration urged Diem to make certain reforms: Bring opposition leaders into his cabinet, give more power to the National Assembly, and reorganize the chain of command to reduce the authority of province chiefs over military forces.[34] Yet Washington had difficulty influencing South Vietnam. Although American leaders believed that government reforms were needed, they were unwilling to reduce or cut off economic or military assistance for fear of fatally weakening Diem's government and were often stymied by Diem's understandable desire to preserve his country's sovereignty. The South Vietnamese president did not want to be perceived as an American puppet and feared that American demands, such as land reform and a promotion system for the armed forces based on merit rather than political connections, would fray the ties of those loyal to him. At the same time, failure to reform his army and provide more responsive government put him at a disadvantage in competing with the Viet Cong for public support.

Diem's repression and authoritarian rule drove many anticommunist South Vietnamese to oppose him. Political reeducation centers to detain suspected communists or other dissidents, military tribunals to try suspects, and limits on freedom of the press were among the measures that estranged Diem's potential supporters. The behavior of government officials also served to weaken Diem's political base. Often officials and soldiers returning to villages liberated from the Viet Cong were accompanied by landlords, who reclaimed their property and collected back rents. In some cases government officials themselves were landlords. Such practices led many peasants to identify the Saigon regime with exploitation, particularly in light of VC "land reforms." Between 1956 and 1960, the communists had abolished the system of tenancy and distributed land directly to the farmers.

By the end of the 1950s, the liabilities of the Diem government outweighed its strengths. Even though Diem had defeated the sects and had begun to develop South Vietnam's armed forces with American funds and military expertise, South Vietnam's economy and armed forces were almost totally dependent on U.S. aid. That aid was insufficiently focused on the serious communist threat in the countryside; it concentrated on strengthening conventional forces, not those specially earmarked for guerrilla warfare. The lack of properly trained South Vietnamese local security forces, which otherwise could have competed with Viet Cong recruiting campaigns, proved a handicap for the Diem government. In practice, these forces tended to alienate villagers and, because they were ineffectual, often proved to be a source of weapons for the Viet Cong.

Diem's autocratic methods and reliance on family and northern émigrés to run the government undercut his efforts to establish a political base. He faced the additional handicap of having the communists label him as an American puppet, although he worked hard to formulate independent policies. Yet he was vulnerable to this accusation because he was so obviously dependent on the Americans, and the VC propaganda exploited this dependence.

The Viet Cong also capitalized on its superior organization, especially its continual contact with villagers. In contrast, the South Vietnamese government's presence extended only to the district level. A gap existed between government officials and the villages. Governmental communications tended to flow in one direction, from the top down, and villagers often resented Diem's officials. The communists were no less authoritarian than Diem, but they were better organized to mobilize the peasantry. Lacking firm political support and hampered by armed forces trained for conventional war, Diem faced an increasingly skillful and confident communist opposition that gained strength through military operations and its ability to cultivate the growing dissatisfaction with his rule. The need for local security would become more critical as the insurgency gathered speed.

2
Insurgency Unchecked, 1961–1965

When John F. Kennedy became president in 1961, he wanted to chart a new course at home and overseas, grandly pledging in his inaugural address "to pay any price, bear any burden … support any friend … to assure the survival and the success of liberty." In national security he hoped to move American strategy from heavy reliance on nuclear weapons and massive retaliation to a posture of flexible response, a capability to meet a range of threats from insurgencies or wars of national liberation to nuclear war. The Kennedy administration envisioned counterinsurgency as a way to assist its allies in defeating wars of national liberation and sought to cultivate greater proficiency in counterinsurgency within the U.S. Army. During his administration, advancing the doctrine and practice of counterinsurgency and stemming the VC insurgents became major challenges. Assuming office after Kennedy's assassination in 1963, Lyndon Johnson would face even more difficult choices in South Vietnam.

The Kennedy Administration and Vietnam

The flourishing Viet Cong insurgency in South Vietnam raised concern late in 1961 in Washington. The new president realized he had to do more than merely rely on the counterinsurgency plan drafted in the previous administration. In October 1961, he dispatched to Saigon a team of high-level military and civilian officials under Walt W. Rostow, head of the State Department's planning staff, and General Maxwell Taylor, the president's military representative and a leading theoretician of the doctrine of flexible response. In a personal charge to General Taylor, the president stressed "[that] the South Vietnamese had to be responsible for their independence and that social, political, and economic problems deserved the same amount of attention as military ones." Kennedy directed Taylor to devise a counterinsurgency plan to stop the deterioration in South Vietnam.[1]

The Taylor-Rostow Mission

Discovering the plight of the Diem government to be more desperate than he had expected, Taylor recommended on his return to Washington early in November that the president increase the number of American advisers in-country and (under the guise of providing relief to the flood-stricken Mekong Delta) send to South Vietnam several U.S. Army battalions of engineer, signal, and medical troops with enough infantry to protect them. These suggestions reflected Taylor's feeling that more direct and active military measures were needed in South Vietnam. Absent from the report was any consideration of village politics, of how to strengthen Diem's rural base. Taylor's recommendations addressed only the central South Vietnamese government.[2] President Kennedy decided to pressure Diem to broaden the political base of his regime, linking increases in American aid to reforms, but Kennedy deferred a decision on the troop question.

He did agree to send more army advisers in 1961 to South Vietnamese regiments, battalions, and provinces. The administration believed that the gradual dispersion of American advisers to smaller South Vietnamese units in the field would more directly help improve South Vietnamese military performance and give the American command a new source of intelligence.[3] This was a major change. Prior to that time, less than one hundred U.S. Army advisers had worked with the South Vietnamese at the command level and in ARVN training centers, hoping that their advice would filter down to units in the countryside. The president also authorized a slight increase in the U.S. Army's Special Forces, the troops that were expected to be the vanguard of the counterinsurgency effort. By early 1962, the army had stationed close to nine hundred advisers in South Vietnam and had begun to train commissioned and noncommissioned officers (NCOs) in a four-week course at the Special Warfare Center at Fort Bragg, North Carolina.

To help manage the growing amount of American matériel and advisory support, Kennedy authorized the formation of the Military Assistance Command Vietnam (MACV) in February 1962 as a separate headquarters subordinate to CINCPAC. Lieutenant General Paul D. Harkins was assigned as the first commander of MACV. As the senior U.S. military representative in the Republic of Vietnam, he was responsible for American military policy, operations, and assistance as well as for advice to the South Vietnamese on security, organization, and the employment of military and paramilitary forces. In addition, the new command controlled the expanded advisory program.

Providing specialized training for the advisers proved difficult. A lack of qualified instructors on active duty forced the Special Warfare Center's commandant, Brigadier General William P. Yarborough, to contract for Vietnamese-language instructors from a commercial firm. General Yarborough also found it hard to get Vietnam veterans temporarily assigned as instructors because the units to which they were assigned were disinclined to lend them even for a short time and the Vietnam conflict had a low priority. Up-to-date, reliable data were hard to come by. General Harkins turned down Yarborough's request for information on government- and Viet Cong–controlled areas of South Vietnam on the grounds that it was "most sensitive" and had "strong political intonations."[4] Harkins's reluctance was troubling. The soldiers at Bragg, many of whom would soon serve in South Vietnam, surely had a need to know the situation in the countryside.

By early 1965, the U.S. Army was posting officers in all South Vietnamese corps and division headquarters, thirty-one regiments, three brigades, ninety-three battalions, forty-four provinces, and numerous districts.[5] Army advisers assisted in nearly every aspect of South Vietnamese military activity, except territorial security, a critical element of pacification. Despite the growing numbers, only a few advisers were assigned to pacification, a mere 100–150 of the 1,820 in Vietnam at the end of June 1964.[6] Nevertheless, this represented something of an improvement since before 1963 only 5 advisers had been authorized to assist the Regional Forces and Popular Forces (RF/PF).[7]

The Fight for Counterinsurgency

Following the Taylor-Rostow mission, the president took other steps to focus government attention on pacification. To improve coordination among the U.S. government agencies, he formed in January 1962 an ad hoc special group for counterinsurgency composed of the heads of the Department of Defense, the State Department, the Joint Chiefs of Staff (JCS), the Central Intelligence Agency, the United States Information Agency (USIA), the National Security Council (NSC), and the Agency for International Development. Its purpose was to encourage American military and civilian agencies abroad to develop interdepartmental programs to deal with wars of national liberation. A small staff headed by Richard Bissell of the CIA performed most of the group's work.

The group was hamstrung. Two of the main players, the Departments of State and Defense, proved unwilling to yield substantive control over their respective programs in South Vietnam. Furthermore, agencies disagreed as to whether political or military measures deserved priority. Civilian agencies, such as State and AID, argued that programs to win political loyalty and to ameliorate living conditions had to be first because they were prerequisites for establishing local security. Others countered that it was impossible to win the loyalty of people susceptible to communist taxation, terrorism, and levies. These disagreements reflected uncertainty within the administration as to the nature of the Viet Cong threat and the appropriate response.

Despite a lack of authority, the counterinsurgency group stimulated some organizational modifications. The Joint Chiefs of Staff created the position of Special Assistant for Counterinsurgency and Special Activities (SACSA) to handle counterinsurgency worldwide as well as military support for South Vietnam. The State Department established the Directorate of Political-Military Affairs, which included counterinsurgency among its responsibilities.

President Kennedy set up new organizations to deal with insurgency and dispatched army advisers to South Vietnam, but the army seemed reluctant to embrace counterinsurgency. In November 1961, as part of his desire to augment the army's counterinsurgency role, President Kennedy asked the army to place a senior officer in charge of the program. In compliance with the president's wishes, the army appointed Brigadier General William Rosson to oversee counterinsurgency but without a separate staff, forcing him to rely on that of the deputy chief of staff for operations, who handled army operations and plans worldwide. The army leadership found little reason to pay special attention to counterinsurgent warfare. Army chief of staff, General George Decker, allegedly told President Kennedy that "any good soldier can handle guerrillas."[8] Like much of the army staff, Decker was unenthusiastic about specialized training for guerrilla warfare, favoring the development of balanced U.S. Army forces that could meet a range of threats rather than specialists trained in one kind of warfare.[9] The implication for Vietnam was that specialized training would not be emphasized for South Vietnamese ground forces either.

The chairman of the JCS, U.S. Army General Lyman Lemnitzer, supported Decker's position but went even further, advising Taylor prior to his mission to South Vietnam that the insurgency had developed beyond the capacity of police and paramilitary forces to control. Therefore, strengthening South Vietnam's regular military should take precedence over building up the police and irregular forces.[10] Lemnitzer's advocacy of regular over irregular forces was consistent with the army's focus under the Eisenhower administration on boosting South Vietnam's conventional forces. His approach also represented one side of a debate conducted during the war about the kind of forces needed in South Vietnam and the relative strengths and weaknesses of ARVN, on the one hand, and paramilitary and police units, on the other.[11]

Kennedy's strong advocacy of counterinsurgency posed a dilemma for the army. Counterinsurgency called in some respects for a reversion to a simpler form of combat, lighter weaponry, and constant small-unit patrolling. These requirements could have been met either by creating specialized forces or by modifying the tables of organization and equipment for existing conventional units. Rather than greatly expanding the Special Forces, whose specialty was counterinsurgency, the army assigned the counterinsurgency mission to existing combat divisions that were already charged with fighting in a conventional mode. Counterinsurgency was an added responsibility. Like the ARVN, U.S. divisions were better prepared by organization, training, and equipment to engage regular, rather than irregular, forces.[12] The army did little to alter its force structure to meet the special requirements of counterinsurgency.

Army doctrine was also slow to change. Although the 1962 version of the army's basic manual on combat, *Field Manual 100-5*, discussed unconventional warfare and operations against irregular forces, it generally neglected the requirements of a situation in which the army's role was to advise the forces of a host nation. Regarding local forces, the manual stated perfunctorily that "the maximum use is to be made of non-U.S. forces and personnel for all activities in which they may be profitably employed."[13] That was all. As late as February 1965, shortly before U.S.

forces entered South Vietnam, the army's Combat Development Command was still working on an advisory handbook and on plans for integrating counterinsurgency doctrine into service schools and training programs. Despite President Kennedy's desire, the army had not devised a coherent counterinsurgency doctrine before it sent troops to South Vietnam in 1965.[14]

Diem's Attempts at Pacification

From the start of his rule, Diem tried to strengthen his government's ties with the rural population. His programs began with high promise but soon led to disappointment. In 1956, an ex–Viet Minh commander who had turned against the communists, Kieu Cong Cung, initiated (with assistance from General Lansdale) a program to send small teams of cadres to help the rural populace by assigning them to periods of duty in the villages. The government built schools and medical dispensaries and dispatched teachers and health workers to rural settlements. The program ran aground after it enlisted Saigon-based civil servants as cadres to work, eat, and live with the peasants. Daily contact with the peasantry, it was hoped, would make these Saigon bureaucrats more sensitive to rural conditions. However, they tended to view such contact with disdain and considered transfer from the capital as a demotion. With Cung's death in 1957 and the growing influence of Diem's brother, Ngo Dinh Nhu, this program was transformed into a vehicle of government control, imposing additional obligations on peasants. The idea of improving rural conditions receded into the background.[15]

In 1959, Diem initiated a relocation program that was intended to protect peasants by moving them into strong rural settlements, or *agrovilles.* They were to contain schools, medical facilities, electricity, and other social services and offer training in new agricultural techniques. He also hoped to stabilize the government's authority in the face of increasing incidents of assassination and kidnapping of rural officials. Diem launched the *agroville* program on his own, informing the American Embassy only after it had started. Even though the U.S. government underwrote approximately 60 percent of nondefense budgetary expenditures, it exercised virtually no control over the program, having few advisers in the field.[16]

Many peasants endured the hardships of building the *agrovilles,* but few reaped the rewards. Vy Thuan, an *agroville* in Chuong Thien province, for example, had room for only one-fourth of the work force that had built it. The majority labored without recompense under arbitrary and demanding construction schedules set in Saigon. Government officials forced farmers to leave rice fields at planting and harvesting time to work on construction projects.[17] The Viet Cong mounted some small raids on the new settlements but most often employed terrorism and threats against government officials to intimidate people and impede work. Hampered by poor planning and riddled with mismanagement, the *agroville* program failed.

Agrovilles were but one of a series of flawed South Vietnamese pacification programs. In 1961, the Diem government inaugurated the strategic hamlet program, which was roughly based on a proposal by Sir Robert Thompson, head of the British Advisory Mission to Vietnam, who had helped plan the successful counterinsurgency campaign in Malaya in the 1950s. Thompson saw rural political instability as the primary threat to Saigon and regarded as wrong the American army's emphasis on having ARVN clear large VC formations from uninhabited territory such as War Zone D. In his view, the government could defeat insurgents only if it genuinely aided and protected the people. Thompson urged building a solid base of political support. He envisioned protecting rural communities with security forces (chiefly police and paramilitary forces) so that social and economic improvements could occur.[18]

Instead of surrounding hamlets with security forces, as Thompson proposed, Diem and Nhu devised the strategic hamlet program with a different emphasis— security would begin within hamlets. Fortified hamlets would protect the people.[19] Nhu, who directed the program, established three goals for it. First, the government would tie the people in fortified hamlets into a communications network, providing them with local defense forces to ward off guerrilla raids and stationing reaction forces nearby in case of emergency. Second, the program would strive to unite the people and involve them in governmental affairs. Third, the program would improve living standards.[20]

American officials had conflicting opinions about the strategic hamlets, reflecting fundamental differences over the best way to counter the Viet Cong movement. The head of the MAAG, Lieut. Gen. Lionel McGarr, objected to the concept because it downgraded the activities of conventional forces. In his mind, defended hamlets connoted a defensive posture of ground forces tied down in static positions and spending too much time on civic action projects.[21] The American Embassy held the opposite position, believing the military clearing operations advocated by McGarr were only a first step toward achieving security and winning political loyalty.

Diem had his own purposes. He saw the program as a means of getting assistance from the United States while keeping overall direction of the war effort in his own hands. He knew he needed American support but realized the danger of being perceived as an American puppet. Controlling the program enabled him to fend off critics and retain independence.[22] He continued to resist Washington's pressure for political reforms.

Disregarding American views, Nhu set ambitious goals. He wanted seven thousand of South Vietnam's fourteen thousand hamlets completed by early 1963 and another five thousand by early 1964. The remaining two thousand he expected to be swept along by example. Nhu exerted severe pressure on province chiefs to meet quotas and held them responsible, despite their lack of authority over local representatives of other agencies.[23]

Direct American aid was far from generous. The United States allocated a modest 10 million piasters ($285,714).[24] To support Diem's effort, American agencies, pushed by Ambassador Frederick Nolting, reorganized their assistance, forming in March 1962 the Inter-Agency Committee for Province Rehabilitation, with representatives from MACV, USOM, USIA, and CIA. However, no agency was designated as central manager.

In practice, the strategic hamlet program fell short. Its failings resembled those of the *agrovilles*. The government emphasized physical control of people. Cabinet officials, misunderstanding the peasants' needs, expected them to sacrifice time and money for the promise of future benefits. All too often government policies uprooted farmers and their families and forced them into enclosed settlements, which restricted their freedom.[25] The elections of local officials, an important part of the program, were characterized more by government control of the process than by voluntary participation.[26] A shortage of capable local leaders hindered efforts to obtain popular backing, as did the lack of integrated support from the various South Vietnamese agencies working in the hamlets.

Nhu's grandiose plans led to overexpansion, creating far more hamlets than Saigon's military forces could protect or cadres administer.[27] Rufus Philips, an AID officer in charge of American support of the strategic hamlet program, felt that Nhu's heavy-handed pressure forced local officials to supply him with meaningless data on the numbers of strategic hamlets.[28] In 1962, the South Vietnamese government designated some twenty-six hundred settlements in I, II, and III Corps as completed strategic hamlets. The actual meaning of "completed," a MACV report ruefully admitted, varied widely from hamlet to hamlet in terms of quality of defenses and percentage of population under government control.[29] In other words, MACV was uncertain about how many viable strategic hamlets actually existed.

Because the central government exerted such pressure to show gains, official reports and statistical data coming from the field were generally unreliable. Reports also heavily emphasized quantitative data, focusing on tangible items that could be counted: the number of hamlets constructed, linear feet of barbed wire used, weapons distributed, length of training, and so on. These reports, while of some use for management purposes, shed little light on the intangibles at the root of the conflict: the balance of political power in the countryside or the political loyalties and views of the peasantry. Pressure to meet unrealistic goals encouraged hasty performance of superficial aspects of the program, such as erecting fences, which often sufficed in official South Vietnamese documents to reclassify officially an existing settlement as a strategic hamlet.[30]

The program was plagued with problems. In Phong Dinh province southwest of Saigon, makeshift defenses (in some cases only rows of bamboo stakes) and inadequate weapons left inhabitants with scant protection. The guards in many areas possessed no rifles or knives, only eight-foot poles with ropes for hitting VC cadres and tying them up. The province chief in Long An complained of inadequate government support, even though he was able to mobilize one-fourth of the province's population to construct hamlets.[31] The strategic hamlet program encountered problems outside the delta as well. In some coastal villages of central

Vietnam, the Viet Cong was so well entrenched that it had no reason to fight. Relative calm often resulted from an accommodation between local members of the Viet Cong and villagers.[32]

Jeffrey Race, author of a study of Long An, rendered a harsh verdict on its strategic hamlet program: "The strategic hamlets, ... as the testimony of even government officials showed, were a terrific annoyance, through controls on movement which interfered with making a living, through demands for guard duty which interfered with sleep, through the destruction of homes and fields."[33] His conclusion was unfortunately valid for other parts of the country. The U.S. Embassy made essentially the same assessment: "Most Vietnamese view the strategic hamlet as a security measure, not as an element of revolution."[34] General Harkins criticized the execution of the program as superficial because it left enemy hamlets and salients in government-run areas. He urged Diem to expand the program more logically in order to consolidate his hold on the countryside.[35]

The communists initially limited their opposition to disseminating propaganda that compared the strategic hamlets to prisons and inserting agents provocateurs to stir up popular resentment. By the summer of 1963, however, they had shifted tactics, directly attacking hamlet fortifications and severing radio links between hamlets and nearby reaction forces. The new approach soon bore results. Whereas in late November 1963 Harkins was still able to inform General Taylor that he knew of no strategic hamlets under the actual control of the Viet Cong,[36] by July 1964 an American and South Vietnamese survey was reporting that only 30 of the 219 strategic hamlets completed in Long An province, for example, still remained under governmental control.[37]

Contemporaneous with the strategic hamlet program, the Diem government undertook two other pacification initiatives: one to encourage defections from communist ranks and the other to arrest, kill, or capture key members of the Viet Cong through a combination of intelligence and police operations. In April 1963, while hopes were still high for the strategic hamlets, Diem began, at the urging of Ambassador Frederick Nolting and Sir Robert Thompson, the *Chieu Hoi*, or "Open Arms," program. Under its provisions, the government offered clemency to insurgents willing to lay down their arms. Despite the obvious potential for weakening the government's adversary, *Chieu Hoi* led a precarious existence from the start. The program's budget was small, and authorized funds often went unspent. For a while *Chieu Hoi* even had no identity as a discrete program; it was merely a directorate headed by an ARVN captain within the Ministry of Psychological Warfare. Poor training and low wages of government cadres plus frequent communist attacks against *Chieu Hoi* reception centers made it difficult to recruit ralliers and cadres. Inadequate coordination between *Chieu Hoi* field representatives and Saigon ministries and between American and South Vietnamese agencies also hampered operations. In 1963, the program achieved modest success, with eleven thousand communist soldiers or cadres defecting. The number of ralliers fell precipitously to five thousand the following year.[38]

Even with a problem-ridden start, American defense analysts considered the program "cost-effective." It was cheaper, according to Pentagon computations, to gain defectors than to seek out and kill enemy soldiers. Analysts calculated that during the program's first two years, costs averaged about $14 per returnee. Moreover, the Americans saw defectors as contributing to South Vietnam's economy and their inclusion in South Vietnamese society as helping mend social and political rifts caused by the fighting. Despite such advantages, the South Vietnamese government felt ambivalent about the *Chieu Hoi* program, accepting it as a way of draining enemy manpower but not embracing it as a constructive process of amnesty and national reconciliation. The Americans felt that the Diem government was failing to exploit the psychological advantage of offering a new and fresh start to defectors.[39] But the Americans may have underestimated the difficulties of Saigon absorbing former adversaries into a fragile South Vietnamese society during war.

If the *Chieu Hoi* program was the carrot, the organizations created to dismantle the VCI were the stick of Diem's pacification policy. These institutions were of two kinds: police forces and intelligence organizations. Elements of the South Vietnamese National Police, which was established in 1962, tried to capture members of the Viet Cong clandestine government. The special branch of the police was responsible for maintaining internal security and gathering intelligence against the Viet Cong; the combat police, for stopping armed terrorists; and the regular police, for handling traffic and civilian criminal offenses and operating checkpoints to disrupt the movement of Viet Cong personnel and supplies. Both the CIA and AID supplied advisers and trained South Vietnamese police forces. ARVN provided security for police operations against the infrastructure and supported the counterintelligence work of other elements of the South Vietnamese armed forces.[40]

The South Vietnamese, with American assistance, tried to improve their intelligence collection by establishing new organizations. At the national level, the CIA helped establish in 1963 the South Vietnamese Central Intelligence Office (CIO), whose missions were to penetrate Viet Cong organizations, serve as a national clearinghouse for the analysis of intelligence, and provide coverage of the communist movement in the countryside for the central government. This organization would coordinate, CIA station chief William Colby hoped, the work of existing intelligence agencies against the communists.[41] Yet the lack of a budget, poor cooperation from other South Vietnamese intelligence agencies, and an insufficient number of personnel specifically trained in intelligence (only 88 out of 350) prevented CIO from making much headway.[42]

New organizations also appeared at the local level. With American financial assistance, the South Vietnamese established in 1964 Province Intelligence Coordination Committees to coordinate and monitor military and civilian intelligence about the VCI within each province. Unfortunately, many committees existed only on paper, and the coordination they were supposed to engender among South Vietnamese organizations was an all-too-rare occurrence.[43] Also in 1963, census grievance teams were organized. Although the census teams actually collected population statistics, their main purpose was to gain the confidence of villagers and develop sources of information on local communists.[44]

During Diem's rule, the potential benefits of these programs to the government's anti-insurgency effort went largely unrealized. Reforms in intelligence collection and police operations were too often hampered by indiscriminate, brutal interrogation methods that yielded little information and by a shortage of trained professionals to staff the new organizations. Diem's pacification programs failed to stem the insurgency, and his rule, which became more arbitrary and repressive, enjoyed less and less popular support. Dissatisfied with the lack of success against the Viet Cong and alarmed at the regime's apparent loss of popular support throughout 1963, the Kennedy administration concluded that South Vietnam needed new, more effective leadership to prosecute the war and tacitly encouraged an anti-Diem coup, which succeeded in November 1963.

In the political turmoil that followed the coup, national direction of pacification came to a halt, and provincial and district officials hesitated to act without guidance from Saigon. Early in 1964, the government officially abandoned the strategic hamlet program. That was inevitable. A South Vietnamese survey had disclosed that only a small percentage of the hamlets still remained in friendly hands.

Exploiting the weakness in Saigon, the Viet Cong quickly increased its holdings in the countryside. Outside the towns, Saigon's control of territory and people significantly slipped. By March 1964, the government was estimating that the Viet Cong dominated 50 percent or more of the *land* in twenty-two of forty-four provinces. In some, the enemy controlled almost all the territory: 80 percent in Phuoc Tuy, 90 percent in Binh Duong, 75 percent in Hau Nghia, 90 percent in Kien Tuong, 90 percent in Dinh Tuong, 90 percent in Kien Hoa, and 85 percent in An Xuyen. Overall, the Viet Cong dominated 30 percent of the territory and over 15 percent of the people of South Vietnam.[45]

New Attempts at Pacification

A new South Vietnamese government led by General Nguyen Khanh, faced with erosion of rural support, published in February 1964 a revised pacification plan that the American Embassy and MACV had helped formulate.[46] Called *Chien Thang*, or "Will to Victory," it envisioned the steady expansion of the government's presence like an oil spot spreading from secure to contested and insecure areas. The U.S. Army provided support, under MAP, to paramilitary and military forces involved in the new operation.[47]

Chien Thang set out to avoid repeating the errors of the strategic hamlet program: forced relocation of people and an obsession with quantity. Plans for public works and other improvements at the local level required full consultation with the local citizenry. Resettlement of people would occur only in accordance with community desires and would be planned well in advance. To put the plan into effect, the Khanh regime established a new chain of command that consolidated control of pacification under the military and focused the program on the Saigon area and the delta.[48] The government assigned ARVN units to outlying, unpopulated zones and tried to concentrate their energy on clear-and-hold operations, such as opening roads and waterways and providing population security, that supported pacification.

On paper the plan represented a marked improvement over earlier pacification efforts, but its execution was faulty. Military support was lacking. MACV reported that 86 percent of ARVN operations in April still aimed at destroying enemy units, a mere 4 percent provided population security, and only 10 percent sought to open roads. ARVN units did not stay in any area long enough to offer sustained protection for pacification projects already under way.[49]

Government cadres were supposed to recruit laborers and win the allegiance of the people. But the government allowed cadre programs to multiply (twenty-seven different types existed) and lost sight of the original notion of a small, dedicated elite. It sent too many cadres into rural areas without training them sufficiently or ensuring that they were fully committed to South Vietnam's cause. Consequently, the potential of the cadre program went unrealized.

Chien Thang also failed to coordinate the contributions of the civilian ministries and paid scant attention to the role of the CG and SDC, which were supposed to provide local security. The plan also neglected to tie together psychological operations (psyops) with the ongoing *Chieu Hoi* program,[50] so the number of defections proved disappointing. Brigadier General William DePuy, operations officer, or J-3 for MACV Commander General William C. Westmoreland, contemptuously dismissed the *Chien Thang* plan as innocuous and vague about the roles and missions of forces, village and hamlet defense, and the respective roles of the province chief, district chief, and village chief.[51]

In May 1964, as the *Chien Thang* program was faltering, the embassy and MACV proposed another initiative, known as *Hop Tac*, or "Victory." *Hop Tac* also represented an attempt to employ the oil spot concept in the region around the capital.[52] As General Westmoreland, one of the chief advocates of *Hop Tac*, reasoned, if the Americans and South Vietnamese could not succeed here, where could they?[53]

In contrast to earlier pacification schemes, MACV, not the civilian agencies, was executive agent for American support of *Hop Tac*. This represented a precedent for involving the U.S. military in pacification. Westmoreland called on Major Robert Montague, who had served as an adviser in the delta, to assist at the staff level in getting the program started. *Hop Tac* foreshadowed the military's later role in pacification support, in which Montague was also involved. To monitor South Vietnamese progress on pacification and develop reliable American data on the situation in the countryside, MACV in July 1964 made U.S. Army advisers responsible for preparing overlays and reports every month on the status of security in their provinces. MACV devised the new system because it distrusted

South Vietnamese reporting, and Secretary of Defense Robert McNamara and Director of the CIA John A. McCone wanted narrative reports that analyzed statistical data from the field.[54]

With the backing of the embassy, Westmoreland persuaded the Khanh government to establish a *Hop Tac* council to coordinate the activities of South Vietnamese military units and civilian agencies involved in the plan. This council had a limited role, which disappointed MACV and the embassy. It was subordinate to the military, lacked control over the ministries, and was required to use the military chain of command to disseminate its instructions, which were more prescriptive than directive in nature. The council lacked executive powers, being limited to conducting studies and undertaking liaison. Westmoreland felt particularly frustrated because he had hoped to make *Hop Tac* a balanced civil-military effort and the council a joint American–South Vietnamese working committee for increasing U.S. influence on the pacification program.[55]

A critical failing of both *Hop Tac* and *Chien Thang* was the continued inability of paramilitary and police forces to provide local security. Main force Viet Cong and North Vietnamese Army (NVA) units openly challenged the government inside South Vietnam and encountered little trouble in overcoming lightly armed, poorly disciplined, and partially trained South Vietnamese territorials: the Regional and Popular Forces.[56] Protecting people from the interference of VC guerrillas and cadres greatly depended on a substantial upgrading of these territorial forces as well as on the continued presence in a populated area of regular ARVN troops. But RF/PF strength failed to reach authorized levels, even though the MAAG had supported the territorial forces since 1960.[57]

The military strength of ARVN formed an unsteady bulwark. All twenty-seven ARVN battalions assigned to support *Hop Tac* were understrength. On average, only about 66 percent of the authorized strength of each unit was present for duty, and even that figure was deceptively high because a few units were significantly above the mean. The ratio of authorized to present-for-duty strength underscored the low state of training, readiness, and morale. Insufficient troop strength was a major obstacle for *Hop Tac*.[58]

Other problems bedeviled the South Vietnamese military. ARVN failed to cooperate fully with police units operating checkpoints on roads and canals. For that reason, police efforts to control population movements, keep commodities out of communist hands, and apprehend Viet Cong suspects suffered. To support *Hop Tac*, the government diverted ARVN battalions to the capital region from other areas, such as Binh Dinh province, leading to a decline in pacification when the battalions moved away. Even in *Hop Tac* provinces, frequent changes of unit commanders, inadequate numbers of mobile forces, and weak local governments hampered operations to provide security.[59] General Westmoreland concluded that the high levels of the government were so concerned about possible coups that few South Vietnamese officers gave *Hop Tac* more than minimum attention. Khanh himself held crack airborne and marine brigades in Saigon to quell any attempt to overthrow his regime.

In part, the lukewarm performance of the South Vietnamese leadership and rank and file was attributable to South Vietnamese attitudes toward the war. Some South Vietnamese had already been fighting since the end of World War II. In the judgment of the MACV director of support for *Hop Tac,* Colonel Daniel Richards, the war had become "a way of life" for the South Vietnamese "rather than something to finish off quickly so they can get on to other more desirable pursuits." Government cadres exemplified Richards's point. They usually worked from 9 A.M. to 5 P.M. and took long lunch breaks, in contrast with members of the Viet Cong, who lived and worked among the people.[60]

The bleak prospects for pacification were readily apparent. Robert Thompson concluded after a trip to South Vietnam in 1964 that the government had failed to carry out pacification and that security had deteriorated steadily to the point where the government's survival was at stake. Secretary McNamara; Ambassador Taylor; McGeorge Bundy, President Johnson's national security adviser; and the chairman of the JCS, General Earle Wheeler, shared Thompson's views.[61] The JCS would not consider as even reasonably accurate Saigon's evaluation that between 1962 and 1964 pacification was at a "standstill."[62] Setbacks in pacification especially disturbed the secretary of defense. During a visit to South Vietnam in May 1964, McNamara had complained to General Harkins that he could neither understand nor get a satisfactory explanation of how the Viet Cong continually attacked and overran hamlets that the government and MACV listed as secure.[63]

In January 1965, the Saigon government reported that pacification had improved in the *Hop Tac* provinces, a claim that lacked credibility. Chau Hiep hamlet, located in eastern Gia Dinh, the province encircling the capital, was alleged to be secure when the Viet Cong struck with a full battalion. The attack succeeded because understrength ARVN and paramilitary units had failed to clear and hold the areas surrounding the town. On the basis of such incidents, Lieutenant General John Throckmorton (Westmoreland's deputy), for one, was openly skeptical about South Vietnamese reports, charging that *Hop Tac* did not exist as a meaningful operation. Between August 1964 and May 1965, MACV counted nearly five hundred separate attacks or acts of terrorism, sabotage, or propaganda in Gia Dinh alone, a period when official figures gave provincial South Vietnamese forces an implausible strength advantage over the communists of 483 to 1.[64]

Despite American misgivings about *Hop Tac,* MACV wanted it to become the prototype for pacification plans throughout South Vietnam because it had been more successful than anything else to that point in coordinating the civilian and military aspects of pacification and served at least to force the South Vietnamese to take action. Although MACV persuaded the ARVN command to draft *Hop Tac*–type plans for the other corps areas, the program formally ended in 1965 after General Khanh fell from power.

Pacification losses were even more serious in light of the ominous changes the communists made in fighting the war. Late in 1964, they began building military strength for what Westmoreland believed was an attempt to finish off South Vietnam with a "conventionally organized general offensive."[65] Hanoi had decided to improve the arms of the guerrilla units and organized the first division-sized Viet Cong forces. The size of communist local forces also grew because the failure of pacification granted enemy recruiters wider access to South Vietnam's manpower. In addition, Hanoi sent the first regular NVA units to join the battle in South Vietnam.

North Vietnam's moves forced President Johnson in December 1964 to reassess overall American policy. He instructed Maxwell Taylor, who had replaced Henry Cabot Lodge as U.S. ambassador, to push the South Vietnamese to take a number of actions: Bring the armed forces and police to authorized strength; replace incompetent officers and commanders; clarify and strengthen police powers of arrest, detention, and interrogation of Viet Cong suspects; clarify and strengthen the authority of the province chiefs; and broaden and intensify the civic action program to convince the people that the government desired to help them. Unmistakably, this was an agenda for the South Vietnamese, and the president wanted Taylor to make it clear to them that future American assistance was contingent on making progress.[66] By these instructions to Taylor, Johnson also indicated the importance he attached to pacification.

Although it was President Johnson's preference in December 1964 merely to assist the South Vietnamese, a basic change in American objectives had already taken place, setting the stage for more active U.S. military involvement in Vietnam. As set forth in National Security Action Memorandum (NSAM) 288, the new policy committed the United States not merely to assist the South Vietnamese but also to *maintain* a noncommunist government in South Vietnam. In rather sweeping language, NSAM 288 linked South Vietnam's security with that of the United States. The new policy also signified America's determination to increase its support of the regime in Saigon—in effect to do what was needed to keep South Vietnam noncommunist.

In January 1965, neither Westmoreland nor the South Vietnamese could answer the question, How could a weak and unstable central government carry out a national pacification program? *Hop Tac,* which Westmoreland actively supported, offered little encouragement. One South Vietnamese who would later play a prominent role in pacification, General Nguyen Duc Thang, then the J-3 of the JGS, wanted the South Vietnamese high command to take over pacification because the civilians running the program had performed so poorly.[67] But the problem with pacification went deeper than the shortcomings of its civilian leaders. Some Americans, among them William DePuy, who as MACV J-3 would help Westmoreland devise his military plans, believed that the VC had gained the upper hand psychologically, having captured most of the emotional issues, such as social justice and freedom from oppression.[68] The Saigon government had lost the mystique of revolution to the communists, making it even more arduous for the government to gain political support. With the numerous coups following Diem's overthrow, Saigon's political legitimacy was suspect. How could pacification be carried out in the absence of legitimate and stable authority? How could Saigon capture the banner of revolution and justice when many of those in positions of command in the South Vietnamese military had opposed the Viet Minh and held the current civilian government in contempt and when the government was dependent on American assistance? In February 1965, Westmoreland confided to DePuy that pacification would get nowhere given such fundamental problems, and he was right.[69] By that time, the political and military situation in Vietnam was nearly totally inimical to pacification. It would be fair to conclude that pacification was on its deathbed.

By early 1965, the United States had abandoned hopes of confining its involvement in South Vietnam to counterinsurgency. The Kennedy and Johnson policy of helping the South Vietnamese fight the communists through economic and military assistance had not worked. South Vietnam's pacification plans had collapsed. Despite the glimmers of hope—for example, from the new *Chieu Hoi* program—the overall pacification effort, notably the strategic hamlet program and its lackluster successors, had failed to stem the insurgency. NVA units entered South Vietnam, and VC forces were growing and their hold on the countryside tightening. South Vietnam's poorly run programs suffered further from insufficient and ill-coordinated support from the United States. American leverage was ineffective in reforming programs, owing to a combination of reluctance to assume control of the South Vietnamese and Saigon's resistance to proposals that made it appear to be a puppet of the United States. The pacification program remained riddled with problems in mid-1965, when the massive American employment of regular forces began. The need to prevent a likely communist military victory would temporarily put aside the search for solutions to the shortcomings of pacification.

3

The War and the "Other War,"
1965–1966

The arrival of North Vietnamese and American combat forces in the summer of 1965 transformed the nature of the war in South Vietnam. By the end of the summer, the enemy's combat strength, which had steadily increased in 1964 and early 1965, reached an estimated 221,000, including 55 NVA battalions and 105 VC battalions.[1] At the end of July, President Johnson announced plans to deploy forty-four more army and marine battalions, increasing American military strength in South Vietnam to 175,000 by the end of the year. The president had decided to send regular U.S. Army units and not to mobilize any reserve units. It was no longer just a struggle to defeat Viet Cong insurgents. A war between conventional North Vietnamese forces that had entered South Vietnam and American ground forces, the so-called main force war, was superimposed on the continuing political struggle for the countryside. MACV changed from a staff originally concerned with advisory duties to a headquarters, dubbed "Pentagon East," that increasingly concentrated on operations. As U.S. Army and Marine Corps units arrived in 1965, pacification became known as the "other war," a patronizing usage that stigmatized the program's status as a noble but failing endeavor that was no longer the main event.

The Strategy of Attrition:
Pacification Supplanted

When President Johnson sent the first American combatants to South Vietnam in the spring of 1965, his immediate goal was to stave off the almost certain military defeat of ARVN and preserve the Saigon government. Although Johnson issued no directives to MACV commander, General Westmoreland, on how American troops should operate to sustain the country's independence, he did limit the U.S. commander's options, imposing restrictive rules of engagement. Fearing a wider war, the president prohibited ground operations against communist sanctuaries in Laos and Cambodia. Seeking to maintain South Vietnam's freedom rather than to subjugate North Vietnam, Johnson also banned U.S. conventional ground operations inside North Vietnam, despite that country's role as a de facto belligerent. The president also closely supervised the bombing by the air force and navy of selected targets in North Vietnam, which had begun in February, hoping through military pressure to force Hanoi to agree to peace talks.

Sizable additional forces, and the president's restrictions on engagement, meant that a new strategy was in order. The static operational concept, devised in the spring, of using U.S. troops to secure American bases no longer made sense. Westmoreland concluded that the communists had decided to start the climactic third stage of guerrilla warfare (mobile warfare by battalions, regiments, and divisions), with the NVA units coming into South Vietnam and the Viet Cong's strengthening of its forces from village guerrillas to main force regiments. He hoped to find and destroy enemy formations inside South Vietnam before they could endanger population centers or flee to their cross-border sanctuaries. The mobility and firepower of American units enabled Westmoreland to station them in base camps and firebases away from population centers and near probable infiltration routes to engage enemy forces in remote areas. U.S. Army helicopters, UH-1Ds, which first arrived with the newly activated 1st Cavalry Division in the fall of 1965, provided air transport for combat troops and allowed American commanders to quickly concentrate soldiers in scattered bases against an enemy formation.[2] In Westmoreland's view, this concept of operations, based on superior firepower and mobility, was tested successfully in the Ia Drang in November, as helicopters, tactical fighters, and heavy bombers provided combat support to elements of the 1st Cavalry battling NVA units in the remote jungle.

To make use of reinforcements, Westmoreland devised a three-phase concept of operations in which pacification had a distinctly subordinate role. His primary concern was to contain the enemy's spring-summer offensive of 1965 with the relatively small number of U.S. troops on hand. The offensive in the central highlands, led by at least three NVA regiments, overran border camps, besieged district towns, and, Westmoreland feared, threatened to cut the nation in two. His plan called first for averting South Vietnam's defeat by using his initial increment of American soldiers primarily to clear logistical base areas and protect military installations for the arrival of subsequent units. Because General Westmoreland felt that the threat posed by North Vietnamese and Viet Cong main force units in 1965 was so severe, he did not include American support of ongoing pacification efforts in the first phase. In the second phase, beginning in 1966, Westmoreland expected, with the twenty-four additional battalions that would then be at his disposal, to go on the offensive and "resume and expand pacification operations" in priority areas: the capital region, certain delta provinces, most of I Corps, and Binh Dinh and Phu Yen provinces in II Corps. In the final phase, he envisioned victory at some unspecified time after 1968 as the incremental attrition of enemy strength would make the war too costly and force the enemy to seek a negotiated settlement.[3]

As Westmoreland's strategy evolved by 1966, it sought to wear down communist forces through the exercise of superior firepower and mobility, a concept patterned after the Ia Drang battles of November 1965.[4] Westmoreland found attractive the proposition that a crossover point could be reached where the enemy would lose forces at a higher rate than it could field replacements. The general's concept of attrition was less a detailed plan of procedures and objectives than a general framework for operating that delegated wide latitude to subordinate commanders. With an emphasis on attacking the enemy, attrition provided little incentive for subordinate commanders to deploy their forces to enhance population security.

Westmoreland rejected in 1965 what he regarded as the defensive strategy of using American forces to protect populated enclaves, a strategy suggested by army chief of staff General Harold K. Johnson and embraced by Ambassador Taylor.[5] Westmoreland and his staff regarded the enclave concept as "an inglorious, static use of U.S. forces in overpopulated areas" that would leave them positioned in vulnerable beachheads and allow the enemy to hold the initiative on the battlefield.[6]

He chose to focus on pursuing the enemy away from population centers, even though guerrilla units seriously threatened the inhabited areas of the countryside. The insurgents registered gains in the central coastal provinces and resisted government efforts to curtail their influence in the delta and the provinces around Saigon. In large parts of the country, government control was restricted largely to areas surrounding district and province capitals and the major roads and waterways during daylight. The embassy estimated in April 1965 that 23 percent of the population was under Viet Cong control.[7] The country was already cut, not in half as Westmoreland feared, but into many discrete pieces, some controlled by the communists and some by Saigon.

To be an effective strategy, attrition required that American and South Vietnamese forces possess the initiative on the battlefield, controlling the frequency and location of fighting. Success would rest on the ability of American forces to find and defeat the enemy. Early operations, however, established a pattern of frustration. In June, the 173d Airborne Brigade, commanded by Maj. Gen. Ellis Williamson, attacked Viet Cong bases in War Zone D but made sporadic contact and withdrew after a few days' stay in the enemy's stronghold. In November, the soldiers discovered evidence of the enemy's hasty departure—abandoned camps, tunnels, and caches of food and supplies.[8] Enemy forces, immune from direct ground attack in their sanctuaries, could menace many areas simultaneously, forcing the Americans on the defensive. Westmoreland recognized this problem, informing the Mission Council in January 1966 that fully one-half of U.S. troops were tied down securing base areas.[9] Aware of the difficulty of engaging the enemy, Westmoreland reported to the Mission Council in August 1966 that the enemy still "has not exposed himself significantly to date; the MACV J-2 estimates that roughly sixty percent of enemy forces have not yet been committed."[10] Westmoreland's method of operation failed to take the battlefield initiative away

from the enemy. Analysts in the Office of the Secretary of Defense (OSD) confirmed this finding in 1967, publishing it in the *Southeast Asia Analysis Report,* a
semiofficial periodical.[11]

By 1966, it had become increasingly apparent that the VC main forces and the
NVA units tended to evade the Americans and South Vietnamese, drawing them
away from populated areas. Like any intelligent adversary, the VC and NVA concentrated their attacks against weaker forces, primarily the paramilitary forces deployed among the population to provide local security. The preponderance of enemy actions were small in scale and relied heavily on terrorism, sabotage, and
attacks by indirect fire. The brunt of the fighting in terms of frequency of engagement and percent of casualties thus fell (in spite of the increasing number of U.S.
combat personnel) on the poorly trained, inadequately equipped, and badly led
paramilitary forces.[12] The communists zeroed in on this vulnerable target because
its decimation would destroy Saigon's hold on the countryside, making domination of the rural population easier.

The presence of fresh combat forces from the United States and the demonstrated weakness of ARVN in coping with the enemy's main force threat was in
large measure the basis of a joint American–South Vietnamese decision in mid-
1965 that further removed U.S. forces from pacification. Vietnamese pride was
also a factor. In July, General Thang expressed his displeasure and that of Gen
Nguyen Chanh Thi, I Corps commander, to General DePuy about the growing
pacification role of the U.S. Marines, which was conducting clear-and-hold operations in populated areas. General Nguyen Huu Co, who was both chief of the
JGS and minister of defense, had also raised this issue with McNamara, averring
that pacification should largely be undertaken by the South Vietnamese.[13] The
allies thus agreed to let U.S. troops shoulder the burden of engaging regular enemy battalions and regiments, while the ARVN would primarily seek out large
guerrilla units, thereby supporting the local forces that provided close-in security
for populated areas.[14]

Westmoreland and the South Vietnamese command believed that ARVN was
better suited to work among and protect the indigenous population than were
foreign-born troops. Yet since they perceived ARVN as demoralized, they had little choice but to have fresh, well-armed American troops engage the enemy's regular forces. As more American troops entered the war, the American role in the
main force war continued to expand, except in the delta, where ARVN was responsible.[15] No American ground combat units were assigned to fight in this
heavily populated region until 1966.

Command-and-control arrangements between U.S. and South Vietnamese
forces reinforced the concept that the forces of each nation remained separate entities with distinct missions. In April, Westmoreland turned down the notion of
encadrement, of placing American officers and cadres in charge of South Vietnamese units, because of the language barrier and the requirement for additional
logistical support. Westmoreland feared a loss of South Vietnamese morale if
ARVN units were put under U.S. control. He also rejected the idea of joint command of American and South Vietnamese forces. Not wishing to seem to operate

as a "neocolonial" power, the American commander preferred informal command-and-control arrangements that were established through coordination and liaison. The tactical area of responsibility (TAOR) concept was used to coordinate operations between adjacent units. Each unit had its own TAOR, within which the unit commander controlled military operations. One side effect of these coordinating arrangements was to reinforce the autonomy of South Vietnamese armed forces, making it more difficult for the Americans to persuade the South Vietnamese to undertake reforms.[16]

Doubts About Westmoreland's Strategy

Westmoreland's concept of operations and the growing responsibility of American forces to fight the war for the South Vietnamese worried policymakers. As early as October 1965, McGeorge Bundy, and his brother, William Bundy, the assistant secretary of state for the Far East, feared Westmoreland's operational plan meant that the Americans would take the dominant fighting role and relegate South Vietnam's soldiers, whose ability was critical to the long-term survival of the government, almost to a cameo role.[17] McNamara feared the MACV commander's plan would lead the American public to conclude that the war had become largely a U.S. enterprise.[18] Maxwell Taylor, ambassador to South Vietnam from July 1964 to July 1965, warned that Westmoreland's concept would mean sharp increases in American casualties relative to those of the South Vietnamese. He believed it was a mistake to reserve ARVN for secondary combat missions and a large share of the static defense. Such an outcome would create the damaging impression, he advised McNamara and Wheeler, that this U.S. ally could do little to defend its own country.[19]

Despite reservations about the division of combat roles between American and South Vietnamese forces and the perception that indigenous forces were relegated to a less demanding assignment, the president and his advisers were reluctant to override Westmoreland's judgment on how to fight. Throughout 1965, Washington acceded to his requests for additional forces that would allow him to carry out his strategy.[20] The White House was nonetheless convinced that military strategy alone could not accomplish the administration's policy of helping South Vietnam develop the strength to defend itself. The sharpened focus on the military aspects of the war and the fear that pacification was being pushed into the shadows as more American soldiers arrived in South Vietnam troubled members of the president's inner circle—Dean Rusk, Robert McNamara, and McGeorge Bundy—as well as Johnson himself.[21]

Reviving Pacification

In March 1965, at the start of the troop buildup, the president recognized that pacification needed more American support and wanted to redress the imbalance between the other war and an expanding military conflict.[22] The appropriate mix between the other war and the war of attrition remained a presidential concern throughout the Johnson administration.

As American combat troops were entering Vietnam in 1965, the Viet Cong was continuing to consolidate its rule in many areas of South Vietnam and improve its logistical support. Free movement of goods and people at night was estimated to be possible in only nine of South Vietnam's provinces. In I, II, and III Corps, many district and provincial capitals were inaccessible except to an armed convoy with air cover. By the end of 1965, the U.S. Mission could discern no gains in pacification in about 60 percent of the provinces and concluded that a national integrated program had scarcely advanced beyond the planning stage.[23] The pacification program had sunk to its nadir. Two years of chronic political instability following the overthrow of Diem had left their mark. Governments were formed that lacked political support and were in turn overthrown by other ineffectual regimes. With each coup, the new rulers replaced key ministerial officials in Saigon, disrupting central direction and administration of pacification programs. Concomitant shakeups of corps and division commanders made it more difficult to provide continual protection for the rural population increasingly threatened by the Viet Cong.

At a time when American military intervention relegated pacification to a lesser role in the conduct of the war, the South Vietnamese, with financial and advisory help from the United States, strove to revive the program. A number of developments made a revival possible. Growing numbers of U.S. Army forces, which actually exceeded 180,000 by the end of 1965, made unlikely South Vietnam's military defeat. The Saigon government itself, long vitiated by factional fighting, attained a measure of stability under the military rule of Premier Nguyen Cao Ky and Chief of State Nguyen Van Thieu, who came to power in June 1965. One official, Major General Nguyen Duc Thang, a Ky ally, led the rebuilding effort. Appointed by Ky in October 1965 as minister of revolutionary development (RD), Thang gained control of most South Vietnamese agencies involved in pacification, becoming in 1966 secretary general of the Central Revolutionary Development Council, a cabinet-level body of representatives from the Ministries of Youth, Agriculture, Public Works, and RD. No single South Vietnamese official since Diem's brother Nhu had exercised such broad authority over pacification.[24] At this juncture, no American official exercised comparable authority over American support of pacification, which was administered by several independent agencies, primarily MACV, AID, and CIA.

In January 1966, Thang merged a number of existing cadre organizations into a new program called the Revolutionary Development Cadre. Recruited from the areas where they were assigned, cadre members trained at the National Training Center at Vung Tau,[25] where Thang sought to inculcate anticommunist ideology and transform recruits into revolutionaries and agents of social change.[26] RD Cadre teams were composed of fifty-nine men and women between the ages of twenty-one and twenty-nine. In each hamlet the cadres were assigned a staggering array of tasks: restore local elected government, assist in community self-help or government-subsidized development projects (such as repairing roads, buildings, and bridges), provide medical treatment to the ill, and aid farmers in getting credit. Teams would also issue identification cards to citizens, recruit people for the armed forces, organize and train self-defense groups, uncover and arrest members of the Viet Cong, and conduct political rallies.[27] The teams would begin work after enemy combatants had been driven away. Half the team would serve as a security force; the other half would initiate development projects.

The problem of providing security for the teams grew during 1966 as enemy attacks on them increased. In addition to launching more strikes, the Viet Cong stepped up its propaganda efforts to discredit the cadres' credibility with the populace and intensified proselytizing.[28] As worrisome as the Viet Cong threat to the RD program was the loss of cadre members for other reasons.

Unfortunately, government personnel policy was a strong disincentive to serving in the RD Cadre, failing to exempt team members from military service. Time spent in service on a cadre team did not even reduce the obligated tour of active duty in the armed forces. Civilian agencies also recruited from the ranks of the teams. Desertion was another cause of attrition; service with the RD Cadre could be arduous, requiring hard work under dangerous conditions. Cadres also deserted because they were assigned away from their home district or misused in non-RD tasks.[29]

When the figures for discharge and desertion were added to the number of casualties, losses for the RD Cadre were alarming. In the first six months of 1966, the cadre lost 814 members; in the second half of the year, the number climbed to 1,997. In the first half of 1967, losses nearly doubled again, reaching 3,861. Between January 1966 and June 1967, the average number of cadre members serving in the field increased from 15,000 to over 21,000; however, the loss rate more than tripled over the same period, going from 11 to 36 percent of the average number of cadres on duty.[30] The number killed or captured by the communists remained fairly constant. What accounted for the increased losses was the rising number of cadres who were discharged or deserted.

The cadres' most formidable task was to overcome the government's lack of credibility. According to a "roles and missions" study undertaken by the embassy, peasants had become inured to the government's rhetoric and were acutely sensitive to its actual deeds: military units failing to provide security or to support outposts under attack, soldiers stealing livestock or crops, village leaders charging unauthorized fees, and RF/PF units helping collect back rents. Poor security, a lack of commodities, a dearth of able and dedicated local officials, and central government apathy toward projects that it did not fund all hampered development. So great was the alienation that the peasantry, according to the study, concluded that the VC would win after U.S. forces departed because government soldiers would be unable to dislodge guerrilla forces or uproot the Viet Cong's covert organization. To be sure, that conclusion was based on impressionistic evidence, but no American involved with pacification disputed its underlying premise: that little rapport existed between Saigon's officials and the people of the country-side.[31] General Thang, aware of the antipathy between the government and the people, ruefully admitted that in Binh Dinh province the South Vietnamese preferred to have South Korean and American troops, rather than the ARVN 22d Division, protect them.[32]

As in the earlier strategic hamlet program, government workers concentrated on the easiest and most visible tasks, well digging and the like. Many cadre teams, with a mere twelve weeks of training, were scarcely qualified to train local self-defense groups, let alone transform the social, political, and psychological environment of the villagers. Not all cadre members shared General Thang's dedication or sense of the program's significance.

Even with a promising start, the cadre effort could not be expanded to all of South Vietnam owing to limited personnel, a scarcity of training facilities, and attrition. Better protection of the cadre teams might have lessened casualties, but attrition primarily stemmed from desertions and discharges. There was a continuing need to train replacements just to maintain the authorized end-strength. To train enough cadres for all of South Vietnam would have taken years. Greater numbers by themselves could not have offset the alienation between government and people.

Other pacification initiatives supported by the United States benefited from more resources. Until 1965, *Chieu Hoi* had only one American assigned to it full time. In 1966, the United States greatly increased its financial support to about three-fourths of the cost, added advisers, and expanded the staff supporting the program. In addition, Washington appointed Ogden Williams, a high-ranking AID official who had served in South Vietnam in the 1950s and the early 1960s, to oversee American support and gave him a mandate to make *Chieu Hoi* more effective. He arrived in July with two assistants. The Saigon government, for its part, agreed to reorganize the *Chieu Hoi* Ministry and assign staff workers in all provinces. The government also increased the number of South Vietnamese armed propaganda teams, composed of ralliers who entered communist areas to persuade known Viet Cong members to defect to the government's side. The teams augmented the psychological operations of RD Cadre units and helped publicize the RD program. By 1966, the teams numbered nearly two thousand.[33] By the end of 1966, *Chieu Hoi* had become a vital element of the pacification effort. With the number of ralliers nearly doubling from 10,018 in 1965 to 20,242 the next year, the program had begun to take off.[34]

South Vietnamese police forces, which had a part in providing local security and apprehending members of the infrastructure, grew significantly thanks to increased American funding and advisory support. Between 1964 and 1966, the strength of the police nearly doubled, from 33,500 to almost 60,000. Under AID auspices, the police operated a radio communications network linking villages and hamlets with police units and teletype/telegraph hookups from Saigon to regional police headquarters. AID also supported training centers for the National Police. In addition, the government sought fifteen thousand recruits for the National Police Field Force (NPFF), a separate police branch. Created in 1965, this lightly armed and highly mobile force was to provide local security after the departure of ARVN forces. It was to remain until regular police forces were able to maintain law and order.

The Regional and Popular Forces, intended to sustain local security, evolved in 1964 from the CG/SDC and grew steadily in size. The RF's authorized strength jumped from 92,000 in October 1964 to 141,000 in August 1966. During that same period, Popular Forces increased from 159,000 to 176,000.[35] In a series of reorganizations between 1964 and 1966 that MACV pushed, the government integrated the RF/PF into the South Vietnamese armed forces under the command of the Joint General Staff to improve the paramilitary's deployment, training, and logistical support. Newly created administration and logistic support companies were designed to maintain RF/PF units in the field. RF/PF staffs were absorbed into province headquarters and made an element of the ARVN staff. JGS also assumed responsibility for training but soon relinquished that function to an RF/PF directorate. Paramilitary units trained at one of six centers and served four-year tours of duty. MACV had advisory responsibility.

The RF and PF were riddled with problems. The rosters of these territorial forces were frequently padded with "ghost soldiers"—fictitious or deceased members—so that military and provincial officials could skim off the extra funds. Such corruption harmed morale and made it difficult to obtain an accurate assessment of the territorial forces' strength. Since PF platoons were employed in clear-and-hold operations and provided close-in protection for settlements, shortfalls in personnel proved particularly inimical to pacification. The PF suffered higher casualty rates than the RF or the regular army.[36] The paramilitary forces would require more managerial attention and greater funding if they were to become effective.

In addition to paramilitary units, the Saigon government hesitantly encouraged the formation of local self-defense groups, which would serve as village militia. In 1966, the minister of interior was in charge of these units. The RD minister was also involved because RD cadres helped train self-defense groups. AID and MACV both urged Saigon to set standards for the issuance of weapons and citizen participation. By the end of 1966, American efforts were bearing some fruit. Prime Minister Ky authorized the formation of self-defense groups in government-secured new life hamlets. All citizens, children and women as well as men, were to be enlisted in the units to ensure broad civilian participation.[37] Rural insecurity limited the militia's growth, however, since units could be established only in villages under government control. Limited training funds and instructors and a scarcity of surplus weapons also impeded the development of militia forces. Yet a more basic problem hampered expansion of the militia: The government did not yet feel comfortable with the idea of arming the civilian population, fearing the weapons might easily fall into communist hands.[38]

Military operations of American and South Vietnamese forces also hampered pacification by generating refugees. In the judgment of a major study on war victims, allied operations were the principal cause of refugees in South Vietnam.[39] This occurred in several ways. Artillery and air strikes in preparation for an operation frequently fell on populated areas, forcing people to flee. Prior to some operations, U.S. units evacuated civilians from their homes into camps to minimize casualties. Chemical defoliation of suspected communist base areas also caused people to move when the drifting spray damaged crops. In the course of operations, friendly forces sometimes attacked inhabited villages in pursuit of the enemy. On other occasions, enemy soldiers hiding in settlements fired at friendly forces hoping to provoke retaliatory fire that might kill or wound or destroy property or crops and thus alienate people.

The creation of refugees, or uprooted persons, did not begin with the arrival of American combatants. It was a long-standing problem of large magnitude. Under the strategic hamlet program, between 1961 and 1964 an estimated 873,700 persons were relocated. CORDS later estimated the number of refugees who left their homes and evacuees who were forced to move in 1964 and 1965, largely before the buildup of U.S. ground forces, at 510,000.[40] After 1965, the growing intensity of the fighting increased the number of uprooted, which jumped to an estimated 980,000 persons in 1966.[41] Around 1.2 million people in South Vietnam were refugees at one time or another between 1965 and 1967, according to some sources.[42] Accurate statistics on the refugee population were hard to obtain, in part because South Vietnam's figures included only persons who registered for assistance. The government had no estimate of the number of homeless who were cared for by friends and relatives and therefore had not sought public assistance. Other families, seeking better economic opportunities or a safe haven, voluntarily left the embattled countryside to take up residence in relatively safe urban areas.

Finding safe areas for the uprooted, who needed temporary government shelter, proved difficult when fighting created new refugees and the communists attacked the areas where refugees were to be resettled. Rather than being able to return safely to their villages, refugees were forced to squeeze into already crowded havens in protected areas, further straining an already inadequate system of care. Refugee camps were usually dismal warrens located on marginal land or wasteland far from any labor market.[43] AID officials evaluating camps in I and II Corps found malnutrition, poor schooling, insufficient rice allowances, and poor sanitary facilities.[44] The lack of employment or self-help opportunities in the camps and the sometimes arbitrary resettlement practices complicated the plight of the refugees.

In 1965, two understaffed and underfunded government agencies sought to alleviate the growing refugee problem. The Ministry of Social Welfare received, registered, and temporarily housed the homeless and provided them with cash payments for one month. Resettlement was the task of the Ministry of Rural Reconstruction. It granted resettled persons an allowance of 3,500 piasters (around $35 at official exchange rates) and a six-month supply of rice. The sheer numbers of homeless people—most of whom were women or persons too young or too old to work—plus the strain on the government's capacity to handle an expanding refugee population mandated an increase in American aid and involvement.[45]

With American urging, South Vietnam's government in April 1966 created a new agency specifically to improve its handling of refugees, the Special Commissariat for Refugees, and empowered its head, Dr. Nguyen Phuc Que, to oversee refugee programs formerly run by other South Vietnamese agencies. Because more American funds were available, Dr. Que was able to raise the daily relief payment to ten piasters per person, still a modest sum. He also tried to alter the prevailing official South Vietnamese attitude from treating refugees as burdens to seeing them as potential supporters. It was his policy to help refugees regardless of political affiliations. He sought to persuade province chiefs and military commanders to take a more benevolent attitude toward refugees, arguing that if the government failed to help people, this would generate enmity toward the regime.[46] Under his direction, the commissariat also undertook to provide primary education and limited vocational training in the refugee centers and to build classrooms. The commissariat did its best to help registered refugees but was constrained because many province chiefs held less enlightened views than Dr. Que.[47]

Washington viewed an elected national government as a necessary step in building a political community and as an aid in establishing a mandate for a noncommunist national government. The Johnson administration also recognized that a democratically elected civilian government would help quell criticism in the United States that the Saigon regime was unrepresentative and authoritarian. Heeding recurrent American calls, Thieu and Ky pledged to convene a constituent assembly in 1966 to draft a new constitution and hold national elections for legislative and executive offices after the constitution was approved.[48] The move to establish constitutional government was also an attempt to win an anticommunist plebiscite. The regime viewed elections as a way of obtaining public ratification of its policies and leadership, an official legitimacy it felt the Viet Cong lacked.[49]

Between March and June 1966, pressure from Buddhists and other noncommunist groups for a return to civilian rule and greater civil liberties culminated in open rebellion by the Buddhists and dissident military elements after Ky relieved Lieut. Gen. Nguyen Chanh Thi, the powerful commander of I Corps. The turmoil in Hue and Danang, which was quelled by the dispatch of ARVN units, revealed the fragility of the government's popular base and caused Ky to speed up the timetable for the constituent assembly, which was convened in September. Elections for the new president and legislature were scheduled for the summer of 1967.

After communist terror in the early 1960s had nearly wiped out a generation of local officials, General Thang made restoration of local government one of the tasks of the RD teams, and two laws enacted in December 1966 facilitated the RD Cadre's attempts to involve villagers in local political and economic affairs. The first law sought to reinstate the village as the basic administrative unit, placing villages under the authority of an elected village council and an appointed village administrative committee.[50] The council, which was responsible for implementing the central government's policies, met several times a month, could make decisions about village construction plans, and could authorize expenditures under half a million piasters, or about $6,250. The second law dealt with the role of the administrative committee, which carried out the decisions of the council and managed village affairs in four areas: security, propaganda, social welfare, and agriculture.[51] The committee chairman enforced the laws and regulations and oversaw the functions of other government agencies.

Unfortunately, Saigon's organizations in the countryside circumscribed these new local bodies, weakening the effect of the new legislation. One American report on village government concluded that RD teams seldom coordinated their work with the village chief or with other groups of cadres. Instead, the teams dealt mainly with higher-level officials at the hamlet and district levels or followed plans devised in Saigon, effectively nullifying the attempt to stimulate local involvement in politics.[52]

Limited Progress Under General Thang

Following his appointment in 1965 and early 1967, General Thang was a proselytizer, a planner, and the most influential advocate of pacification within the government. He frequently visited province chiefs to make manifest the government's interest and encouraged them to keep the cadre teams hard at work.[53] During this period, the South Vietnamese improved their organization for pacification, instituted the RD Cadre program, moved to establish a popular political base through local and national elections, and improved refugee care. Thanks to U.S. financial backing and ARVN's support of the cadre teams, sizable numbers of South Vietnamese were working on or supported pacification (see Table 3.1) at the end of 1966.

Despite Thang's energy and leadership, pacification was beset with numerous problems that seemed endemic to the government's operations. Cumbersome administrative procedures in the provinces slowed the movement of materials and the issuing of directives to the districts. Low pay and poor training undermined the dedication of local officials and made them susceptible to corruption. In Bien Hoa province, local authorities pressured the cadres to give most of the fertilizer and credit allocated to the province to the authorities' relatives and friends. Cadres refusing to cooperate were allegedly threatened with assassination. Budgeted funds reached the provinces slowly. Monies earmarked for 1965 programs, for example, reached provincial officials' hands only in June, at the end of the fiscal year (FY), and then were allocated parsimoniously. As a result, provinces such as Chau Doc could not work on the current year's plan. In addition, shortages of AID construction materials and military supplies also dogged Thang's efforts.[54]

TABLE 3.1   South Vietnamese Forces Available for Pacification at the End of 1966

Force	Authorized Level (in 1,000s)
ARVN and marines (part time)	281
Regional Forces	133
Popular Forces	189
Police Field Forces	4
RD cadres	35[a]
National Police (in provinces)	20[a]
Self-defense forces	21[a]

[a]Estimated.

Source: Memo, Montague to Komer, sub: RVN Forces Available for Pacification, 9 September 1966, CMH Chron files.

In spite of increased attention to pacification by the Americans and South Vietnamese and the growth in funds and personnel, progress in protecting the people from Viet Cong political or military pressure, the key to pacification's long-term success, remained poor. The U.S. Mission reported that 552 hamlets were raised to secure status in 1966, little better than half the government's goal for that year. By December 1966, Saigon was claiming control of 4,700 of the 12,000 hamlets in South Vietnam and ten of its sixteen million people, but U.S. officials doubted the accuracy of those numbers.

The pressure local officials felt to attain goals set by Thang's ministry undermined genuine pacification. Only several days before General Thang's inspection tour to Long An, provincial officials hastily began work on construction projects to demonstrate that progress was being made.[55] Local Vietnamese officials labeled Loc Tien hamlet in Can Giouc district as pacified—even though it was surrounded by communist bases and villages and government agents were afraid to remain there overnight—because the cadres had routinely completed all the tasks required to certify a hamlet as pacified.[56] The Long An province chief on December 15, 1966, ordered a district chief to make "secure" three additional hamlets by the end of the year so that the province's program would look better in government reports.[57]

The most serious failing was the lack of appreciable gains in weakening the grip of the clandestine Viet Cong political and military apparatus on large areas of the countryside, a fact recognized equally in the provinces and the White House. In August 1966, the Mission Council heard General Westmoreland discuss the tenacious strength of the communists in the Binh Chanh district of Gia Dinh province—ten minutes by jeep from the capital—and the government's failure to identify and eliminate the infrastructure. To Komer, then a presidential aide, the enemy's hold on the villages was symptomatic of the failure of pacification.[58]

The program benefited from the leadership of General Thang, restoration of political stability in the capital, and constant allied military pressure against enemy main forces, but these developments had not by the end of 1966 proved decisive or been translated into a viable program for strengthening Saigon's political base. The Viet Cong had suffered no crippling loss of strength or control of the countryside. No answer had yet been found for the overriding question, How could pacification be improved and the insurgents stopped? A new force, the RD Cadre, was not the answer. What alternative resources were available for pacification? What other forces could the government enlist in the other war?

4

Not by Force Alone:
The U.S. Army in Pacification

Following the 1965 buildup, the U.S. Army became more involved in pacification. It supported the other war in three interrelated ways. Involvement in civil affairs—that is, in efforts to improve rural living conditions—was one. A second, the use of American forces to help provide security, complemented the first, although attrition of the enemy's battalions and regiments absorbed the preponderance of the army's resources. A third was the work of advisers, who carried out liaison with South Vietnam's civil and military authorities responsible for pacification.

Civil Affairs

U.S. Army civil affairs teams helped construct public works and assisted refugees. The teams coordinated their efforts with AID as well as with local government officials. In addition, army medical teams provided care for civilians.[1]

The buildup of U.S. forces gave civil affairs a sharper focus. Before 1965, U.S. Army civil affairs mobile training teams assisted ARVN in developing construction projects for villages and organized two experimental South Vietnamese civil affairs companies. Confronted with the growing number of displaced persons, MACV requested in the summer of 1965 the deployment of sixteen civil affairs refugee teams to help tactical units provide refugee assistance. Each team comprised a leader, a civil affairs specialist, a medical doctor, a medical NCO, a construction officer, and a counterintelligence officer. MACV delimited the army role in civil affairs to tactical situations, placing the teams under the operational control of tactical units and headquarters. Four teams were sent to I Corps, nine to II Corps, and three to III Corps. The 41st Civil Affairs Company arrived in Nha Trang in December to provide administrative support.

In 1966, the army sent two additional civil affairs companies to Vietnam. The 29th Company was deployed to Danang in June 1966, and the 2d Company went to II Field Force in Long Binh in December 1966. These units became involved in a variety of small-scale projects, such as the construction of schools, hospitals, and wells; the improvement of crops; and the provision of public health programs. Many projects were related to refugee care, whereas others were initiated unilaterally without reference to any larger program.

As with other aspects of pacification, coordination was essential but difficult to achieve. In the area of refugee assistance, the South Vietnamese and AID, in addition to the U.S. Army, were involved. The Saigon government retained overall responsibility for the refugee problem, and AID was accountable for American refugee assistance and provided most of the supplies and construction materials. Army refugee teams had to work closely not only with AID and South Vietnamese officials but also with army G-5s and S-5s (staff officers in charge of civil affairs) and district and province advisers, each of whom also had a role in caring for the refugees. The lack of a comprehensive policy for the care and control of refugees made coordination more difficult.

With organic construction equipment and specially trained personnel, U.S. Army engineer units made a significant contribution, viewing assistance to the people of South Vietnam or projects designed to enhance the image of the government as part of civil affairs. Engineer groups and battalions repaired war-damaged dispensaries and schools; constructed new hospitals, orphanages, fishing piers, water supply systems, and electric power systems; and helped distribute construction supplies for South Vietnamese self-help projects. In 1966, army engineer troops began to reopen highways and rebuild bridges, primarily to move units, supplies, and heavy military vehicles. But restoring and upgrading the road system and keeping these lines of communications open benefited pacification as well, improving access for farm products and finished goods. The engineers contributed to South Vietnam's economic development.[2]

Army personnel also carried out a separate medical civil affairs program (MEDCAP). Developed from a joint proposal by the embassy and MACV in 1962, MEDCAP teams in the following year began to provide outpatient care for South Vietnamese civilians living in rural areas. The teams worked with their ARVN counterparts in a settlement for a short period of time, established temporary health stations, and trained the South Vietnamese in medical techniques. Initially, 127 army medical personnel were assigned to the teams. Over time, medical personnel came from all the military services in South Vietnam, although the army continued to administer the program.[3]

As the American military commitment grew, the army also aided Vietnamese hospitals. Under the Military Provincial Health Assistance Program (MILPHAP), which commenced in 1965, the army sent groups of physicians and medical technicians to South Vietnamese provincial hospitals. By early 1966 teams operated in six provinces and by 1970 were present in twenty-five of South Vietnam's provinces. Augmenting the South Vietnamese hospital staff, the teams assisted in clinical, surgical, and medical care at South Vietnamese installations. Unlike the

MEDCAPs, which moved, MILPHAP teams constituted a relatively fixed source of support for local public health care programs.[4]

Although civil affairs programs would have benefited from even greater U.S. Army involvement, they were no real substitute for the efforts of South Vietnamese officials. Civil affairs projects were easily undone by inadequate South Vietnamese follow-up efforts, corruption, or resurgence of VC activity. Civil affairs programs, clearly essential to the goals of pacification, required a secure environment. By themselves, these programs were insufficient to cope with the Viet Cong, which employed a mixture of military force, terrorism, and a sophisticated political apparatus to impose control.

Military Operations

The army's operations in support of pacification ranged from joint operations with South Vietnamese forces to experiments linking military operations and civilian assistance programs under a single manager. In some operations, army units sought to keep communist forces away from rural settlements and buck up South Vietnamese forces providing population security. In others, U.S. ground forces helped relocate inhabitants from villages in enemy-controlled areas to new settlements or camps run by the government in an attempt to sever the guerrillas' hold over the population. Still others sought to assist government military and police units in apprehending members of the Viet Cong infrastructure. From these varied approaches emerged a keener appreciation of the limits of the American military role in the war for the villages and a clearer recognition of the need to harmonize the civil and military approaches to pacification.

The question of what kind of operation constituted military support of pacification was to a large extent semantic. Throughout the war, there was no clear-cut demarcation among the various kinds of ground operations: search and destroy, clear and hold, and pacification support. Many operations contained elements of all three types. To further confuse the issue, some officers disingenuously argued that any operation that weakened enemy forces by definition aided the other war. The real criterion in deciding whether an operation aided pacification was to what extent it reduced communist control or enhanced the government's position in the countryside. Did operations contribute to security and economic development? What contribution did American units make in the war for control of the villages?

County Fair Operations

County fair operations combined civic affairs projects to garner political support with cordon-and-search operations to provide security. The object was to focus on one village, search for members of the infrastructure, gather intelligence, and try to gain the sympathies of the populace. After American units cordoned off a village to prevent suspected Viet Cong insurgents from escaping, ARVN soldiers entered the village. They usually segregated village males from the rest of the population and detained for further interrogation men without valid identification cards, draft dodgers, or persons whom South Vietnamese police or intelligence officials suspected were involved with the communists. While the ARVN soldiers interrogated suspects, American and South Vietnamese civil affairs teams provided medical care for the villagers and conducted political indoctrination. On some occasions an army band would entertain the villagers, or civil affairs personnel might run a lottery with prizes or hold a barbecue.[5]

An operation conducted in June 1966 in Tan Phuoc Khanh, a village in War Zone D about thirteen miles north of Saigon on the eastern border of Binh Duong province, typified what happened during a county fair operation. Elements of the 5th ARVN Division and the U.S. 1st Infantry Division conducted this county fair, which was part of a larger operation, LAM SON II. While the U.S. division provided security, an RD Cadre team began organizing local elections, taking a census, and working on small construction projects. Some villagers welcomed the government's presence, telling cadre workers during the operation that if the settlement were safe from Viet Cong harassment, more people would live in it.[6]

Despite a friendly reception from the villagers, province advisers reported that the operation was faltering. When an ARVN battalion from the 5th Division replaced the American unit, the people complained to the American advisers, saying the behavior of the South Vietnamese soldiers antagonized the populace. The villagers preferred the Americans and wanted them to return.[7]

The operation failed to produce the lasting security from communist harassment that the villagers wanted. The joint task force spent just three days in Tan Phuoc Khanh trying to uproot an infrastructure that had become entrenched over a period of years. By the end of 1967, enemy incidents in the vicinity of the village had increased dramatically. Without the protection of the U.S. 1st Division, enemy main and local force units threatened the village, which was then guarded by fifty-seven cadres and thirty-eight PF and seven RF soldiers. After a Viet Cong company overran the village watchtower in November, the government sent an RF platoon to Tan Phuoc Khanh, only to withdraw it about a month later. One of the hamlet chiefs resigned in December because he feared for his life. The VCI remained active in the village, taxing people, dispensing propaganda, and gathering intelligence. At the end of December, the province chief believed the Viet Cong was infiltrating new recruits back into village local force units. After visiting Tan Phuoc Khanh, two American field evaluators from MACV protested that the village's official rating as "secure" was false.[8] They were right.

If American and South Vietnamese forces had stayed, they would have had a better chance of providing lasting security, but friendly forces departed to secure another settlement and left only pacification cadres behind. In Tan Phuoc Khanh, then, it was only a matter of time before the communists returned and undermined ongoing programs. The relative scarcity of American soldiers, the weakness of ARVN, the depth and extent of the Viet Cong's hold on the countryside, and General Westmoreland's desire to be on the offensive produced the continual movement of friendly units from one troubled area to another.

County fair operations often manifested Americans' ethnocentrism and insensitivity about what they as foreigners could actually accomplish. Having U.S. Army troops help, heal, and entertain villagers was in no way detrimental to pacification, but American goodwill and civic action could not win by proxy popular allegiance to the Saigon government. A fundamental difference separated American humanitarian assistance programs that provided temporary amelioration from the South Vietnamese pacification effort of trying to establish lasting security and ongoing political ties between the villages and the government in Saigon. If the South Vietnamese were to believe in their government, that government had to establish its own credibility. American armed strength could drive Viet Cong forces away from villages or force them underground and might prevent the military defeat of South Vietnam, but it could not be a surrogate for the South Vietnamese government.

The U.S. 25th Division in Hau Nghia and Long An

The continual movement of units made it difficult for the army to provide lasting security, especially in areas where the communists' political organization and guerrilla forces were firmly entrenched. The Communist Party had been active in Hau Nghia since the 1930s, and over several generations many families had served with first the Viet Minh and then the Viet Cong. Hau Nghia supplied rice to the Viet Cong, and enemy supply routes from Cambodia to communist bases in the Mekong Delta and the Plain of Reeds cut through the province. To deal with the area's insecurity, the government designated Hau Nghia a special tactical zone to coordinate ARVN activities against Viet Cong units and in 1964 made it a separate province.[9] In 1964 and 1965, virtually the entire province was vulnerable to attack. According to American advisers, the Viet Cong could interdict at will any road in Hau Nghia, overwhelm any government outpost, or mount assaults against province and district capitals. In October 1965, the communists staged a multi-battalion operation against Duc Lap, a settlement one mile from the province capital, causing the government to withdraw the South Vietnamese rangers stationed there. Lacking protection and fearing further destruction, many towns-people left Duc Lap.[10] The Viet Cong kidnapped and assassinated local officials and dissuaded other qualified persons from taking government positions in Hau Nghia. Pacification programs languished and government cadres were inactive, in part because the ARVN battalion in Trang Bang sat idly guarding its base camp, providing no security.

The U.S. 25th Division went to Hau Nghia primarily to help protect Saigon's western flank. In January 1966, the division's 2d Brigade arrived in the province. The division established its headquarters in late March at Cu Chi, one of the least pacified districts in South Vietnam. The irony of this site was revealed later: The division placed its headquarters right on top of an extensive hidden tunnel system housing the local Viet Cong command.[11]   ·

Initially, the division's operations, primarily search and destroy, disrupted VC military activity, kept VC units on the move, and inflicted heavy, although by no means irreparable, losses on the communists.[12] According to one of the division's battalion commanders, Lieut. Col. Boyd Bashore, American firepower gave friendly forces an advantage over their foe. From his perspective, the Americans needed to employ all available artillery, tanks, and aircraft and mount operations only within their range. Engaging the enemy with small units in counterinsurgency fashion, rifle versus rifle, would in his view take away that advantage. In the first six months of 1966, the security of Hau Nghia improved markedly.[13]

Progress tapered off in the second half of the year as the Viet Cong modified its tactics to cope with superior American firepower. VC units avoided contact or moved into "pacified" hamlets, inviting armed retaliation, in which case the hamlet's population bore the brunt of the destruction. Local South Vietnamese forces were no barrier to the entry of guerrillas. The province's Regional Forces tended to confine themselves to defending their own bastions. Viet Cong local force battalions also operated in company- or smaller-sized units, making it harder for larger American and South Vietnamese formations to locate and engage them in combat.

The American style of combat proved ill-suited in dealing with the insurgents. American operations were generally sporadic brigade- or battalion-sized sweeps lasting several days, permitting the VC to lay low and recuperate if hurt or return to an area after U.S. troops had moved on. A brigade's tactical area of operations normally encompassed several districts, making it difficult for U.S. troops to provide continual security for any single location. Moreover, many of the 25th Division's units also operated in neighboring Tay Ninh or Binh Duong provinces, reducing the U.S. soldiers deployed in Hau Nghia. With the forces it brought to bear, the U.S. 25th Division was unable to eliminate Viet Cong main forces in the province. Even if units of the 25th division had remained in Hau Nghia for longer periods of time, they risked making local forces dependent on their continued presence. American forces could not compensate in the long run for the deficiencies of South Vietnam's armed forces, which had so far proved incapable of protecting the populace.

A second test of U.S. Army support of pacification occurred in Hau Nghia's southern neighbor, Long An, a critical province in the upper Mekong Delta. Containing some of the richest rice lands of South Vietnam, the province produced twice as much rice as it consumed and shipped part of the surplus crop to Saigon. Long An was the delta province closest to the capital, and two of the major highways from the rice-growing regions of the upper delta to Saigon passed through it. Since the days of the strategic hamlet program, Long An had been the focus of command attention. It had been part of the *Hop Tac* plan, and General Khanh and Ambassador Lodge viewed it then as a harbinger of the future of the country.

Despite the government's efforts, pacification foundered. The Viet Cong continued to recruit, tax, and indoctrinate. ARVN did little to control the flow of information and supplies to the enemy, the police had little success in uncovering communist political operatives, and cadres had great difficulty in developing local governments in the rural areas. Hamlets were inadequately protected, because, as AID adviser Earl Young lamented, local security forces were understrength and slow to respond to calls for help.[14] Although the government's eight thousand armed men in the province (including regular soldiers from the ARVN 25th Division and police) outnumbered the VC units, South Vietnam's forces were on the defensive and provided little security for the populace.[15] Government cadres were naturally reluctant to visit insecure settlements. On Christmas day 1965, the communists mortared the outskirts of the provincial capital, Tan An, and frequently flew their banner over many villages, even those near district headquarters. The communists blocked the same stretch of National Highway 4 at regular intervals.[16]

In June 1966, General Westmoreland proposed stationing a U.S. Army battalion from the 25th Division in Long An as an experiment to see how well American troops could fight in a heavily populated delta area. Up to that time, they had operated mainly where relatively few people lived. Representing a basic change in the deployment of U.S. forces, Westmoreland's recommendation met with opposition from the embassy. Ambassador Lodge feared that American operations in heavily populated areas could alienate local people. Deputy Ambassador William Porter and political counselor Phillip Habib worried that rice production and the local economy could suffer if American forces and firepower enlarged the scale of fighting in the fertile delta. At the root of their concern was the possibility that the war in the delta, like the war in the rest of South Vietnam, would become an American struggle, with indigenous forces playing an ancillary role and the imbalance between military campaigns and civilian programs of political and economic development becoming further skewed.[17]

Westmoreland did his best to reassure the civilians in the embassy that American firepower would be carefully controlled to minimize danger to the people in the countryside. He was convinced that U.S. troops, which the province chief had requested, would enhance security by keeping enemy forces off balance and helping open roads and canals so that more rice reached the marketplace. American military forces, Westmoreland argued, would also boost South Vietnamese morale.[18] In his view, Long An presented an opportunity for a military victory. If the communists chose to escalate, they would, in Westmoreland's words, be "putting themselves into the meatgrinder."[19] Killing one thousand Viet Cong troops could, he thought, break the VC movement in the province. In Westmoreland's eyes, the primary role of American troops was furtherance of the attrition strategy, although their presence in Long An would contribute indirectly to pacification. With a crying need for better security and a plea from South Vietnamese authorities for American forces, Westmoreland had good reason to deploy U.S. Army forces to the province, which he did. As the commander of American forces, it was within his charter to reassign troops within South Vietnam.[20]

Civilian protests made this a potentially divisive issue, and Westmoreland made sure that he kept the Mission Council fully apprised. At his request, Maj. Gen. Frederick C. Weyand, the division commander, briefed the council on his division's concept of operations, reassuring it of the importance he, as a division commander, attached to pacification. He hoped to subordinate ongoing military operations as much as possible to the ends of pacification. He also hoped to integrate South Vietnamese forces—from police to ARVN—into his operations and exploit all intelligence jointly by establishing intelligence coordinating centers. Weyand also pledged to deploy forces in company and platoon formations and refrain from large sweeps to minimize the number of persons displaced by the fighting. He agreed to fire artillery only in daylight hours into nonsettled areas when the province chief permitted it. Such tactics would hold down civilian casualties and property damage, but they relegated Westmoreland's hope of grinding up the Viet Cong to a lower priority. In September, General Weyand moved a battalion from the U.S. 25th Division into Long An.[21] Weyand's concern for the South Vietnamese people and for the enhancement of pacification assuaged Ambassador Lodge as well as Secretary McNamara. In October, Weyand briefed the secretary. A believer in the importance of the other war, McNamara was pleased with Weyand's stress on pacification.[22]

To harmonize military and civilian operations, Lodge asked Weyand to include RD Cadre teams in his plans so they could move quickly into villages that the American units had cleared. Lodge's request could not be met. In the fall of 1966, the province had only six RD teams. With less than one month's notice of the battalion's actual deployment, Porter was unable to arrange for additional teams. Thus, the Americans and the South Vietnamese were not in a position to take full advantage of the expected improvement in security that the American battalion would bring.[23] Deploying an American unit in Long An raised anew the problem of coordination between the military and the civilians.

At the end of 1966, General Weyand felt that the experiment had succeeded to the point where MACV could send additional American troops to the delta and Long An. The embassy, however, remained skeptical. From its perspective, U.S. Army units in the province had done little to improve security. Only two hamlets were secured in September and two in October. The major accomplishment of American forces was to recapture the district capital of Rach Kien, which the government had abandoned in October 1965. Porter noted that in reaction to the American battalion's presence, enemy forces increased from thirty-two hundred to about six thousand.[24]

The move into Long An resulted in no breakthroughs. The efforts of the 25th Division were insufficient in quelling either the Viet Cong movement or the doubts of American civilian officials regarding the effectiveness of U.S. Army operations in improving the South Vietnamese pacification program. Rather than confronting the army, as General Westmoreland hoped, enemy forces tended to avoid direct engagements.[25] The civilians understood that the use of American military force would not by itself bring pacification.

To Lodge, the experience of American forces in Long An underscored the need for a consolidated civilian and military effort. To test the feasibility of unified direction, in November he assigned the Mission Council coordinator, U.S. Army Colonel Samuel V. Wilson, as the leader of the entire American provincial advisory team. As a Green Beret and part of the Mission Council, Wilson had unique credentials. As leader, Wilson reported to Ambassador Porter on RD affairs, to Westmoreland on military issues, and to Lodge on the general situation in the province. The actual scope of Wilson's authority was left somewhat vague. The ambassador expected civilian and military advisers in the province to respond to Wilson's directions and the battalion commanders to consult with him on combat operations. Lodge also hoped the South Vietnamese would heed the American example and tighten their command-and-control arrangements.[26]

Colonel Wilson carried out a widely publicized pacification campaign in Long Huu village in Can Douc district. This rice-farming and fishing village of eleven thousand people was situated on a triangular-shaped island in the southeastern corner of Long An. Although far from the primary land routes to Saigon, Long Huu was located between two rivers that flowed to the capital. Long Huu had been under Viet Cong control since 1965, when the communists overran the last government outpost. The communists used Long Huu as a logistical support base and transit point for units operating out of the Rung Sat Special Zone, essentially the river approach to Saigon. The island's rice and fish provided food for enemy soldiers, and the communists relied on the population for taxes and recruits. The party never established overt control because it knew its cadres would be at a tactical disadvantage if American or South Vietnamese forces ever occupied the island.[27]

Colonel Wilson and district chief Major Tran Truong Nghia felt that the lightly guarded village could be easily defended after it was retaken. According to Major Nghia, the people of Long Huu, 60 percent of whom belonged to the anticommunist Cao Dai sect, wanted the government to return. He envisioned the village as a foundation for the expansion of pacification in the district, even though the land directly north of it remained an extensive, entrenched Viet Cong base.[28]

Wilson, the South Vietnamese district chief, the MACV subsector adviser, and the commander of the U.S. 199th Infantry Brigade formulated plans to capture the village. The operation would test Wilson's theory of "bloodless" recovery of communist-held territory and his idea of "*chieu hoi* in place." His plan was to surround the enemy with overwhelming force, leaving no hope of escape, and convince troops to defect rather than fight. Defectors would be directly reintegrated into the local community rather than transferred to a distant *chieu hoi* center for interrogation and retraining. The aim was to reconcile the ralliers with those loyal to the government. As province team leader, Wilson was able to convince the commander of the 199th Brigade to change his plan from a search-and-destroy operation with preattack artillery barrages to a search-and-clear sweep of the entire island, which, it was hoped, would minimize damage to homes and crops.[29]

On March 7, 1967, the operation began. Pamphlets were dropped before a battalion of the U.S. 199th Brigade and the ARVN 2d Battalion assaulted the island. The landings went smoothly, and the island was captured without a fight. After the operation, only one U.S. company remained, and it, along with the ARVN unit, patrolled the island. Government workers from various agencies—social welfare, information, refugees, health, psychological warfare, police, public administration, agriculture, education, and *chieu hoi*—started programs to help the villagers and win their loyalty. Premier Ky and Ambassador Porter visited the newly pacified village, and by virtue of the attendant media publicity Long Huu became a showcase of pacification.[30]

Over time, Long Huu was shown to be less than a glittering success. Forewarned of the operation, most VC cadres had left the island beforehand, but they then gradually returned. The infrastructure never departed, nor was it disturbed by the allied assault. The American force stayed for a short time, leaving the island's defense in the hands of two ARVN companies, one RF company, and one PF platoon. When the South Vietnamese regulars withdrew during the summer, the paramilitary units redeployed to the vicinity of the village seat, Ap Cho, conceding the rest of the island to the enemy, which without hesitation reestablished control. In September, some South Vietnamese civilians moved to Ap Cho from Viet Cong areas because they wanted to avoid the continuing air strikes, artillery barrages, and combat operations, not because they were pro-government.[31]

Although the island's people welcomed the government's arrival in March, shortly afterward they found reason to complain. Agricultural cadres did not help carry out the agrarian development plan. Most government representatives moved to other villages. Misbehavior by RF soldiers alienated villagers; stealing fruit and chickens did little to win popular sympathies. Allegations of rape and the actual rape of a village girl by a government official provided additional fuel for Viet Cong propagandists. In the judgment of U.S. advisers, South Vietnam's own propaganda arm, the Vietnam Information Service, did nothing effective to counteract the communist vitriol. While on the island, ARVN soldiers were openly hostile to the *hoi chanh,* the defectors from Viet Cong ranks. Of the 103 people alleged to have defected, 71 were in fact captured. Only 32 were actually induced to surrender. The political training course for the ralliers lasted only a week instead of the promised month, and the new village government was composed of Diem-era appointees or wealthy landlords, who used the PF to help collect back rents and taxes.[32] The government bungled the opportunity to pacify Long Huu.

Short-term accomplishments were modest. In Long Huu, VC forces were temporarily displaced by American and South Vietnamese soldiers, but the island was not pacified. The deployment of a U.S. Army battalion to Long An province led not to the breakup of the communist movement but to the stationing of additional U.S. forces. Improved security in the province through mid-1967 corresponded directly with the presence of military forces. In effect, the Long Huu operation yielded no lasting political change. Despite the infusion of funds and troops, Long An remained in mid-1967 under enemy control. Because Long An was a showcase province, the government pressured local officials to show on paper satisfactory results. Major General Le Nguyen Khang, the commanding general of III Corps, pushed the province chief to certify as pacified hamlets some that AID regarded as insecure.[33]

What was the impact of the single manager or team leader concept in Long An? That idea was not immediately copied in other provinces because the Americans believed few persons matched Colonel Wilson's expertise in planning military operations and administering economic aid programs. The civilians were averse to impose on other provinces a management concept that disturbed existing bureaucratic and command arrangements. They remained opposed to an arrangement that would interject the military into civilian fields and that would in their view complicate relations between American military and civilian officials. The absence of a breakthrough in Long An reinforced the mission's reluctance.[34] Yet the two-month single manager trial impressed Komer, then a special presidential assistant for the other war. Arguing for stronger central control of pacification, Komer used the trial in Long An to lobby the chief executive. He told Johnson that the trial in Long An demonstrated that unified management helped the Americans motivate the South Vietnamese (Colonel Wilson, for example, had been able to force the removal of two corrupt provincial officials) and that U.S. and South Vietnamese military support of pacification was the key to improved security. Better direction and coordination of American civilian and military assets were, for Komer, the principal lesson of the single manager experiment.[35]

Operation FAIRFAX

U.S. Army efforts to support pacification in Gia Dinh, a province abutting Saigon, fared no better. In 1966, the communists threatened to take over parts of the province, notably the districts of Thu Duc and Binh Chanh, where the infrastructure was especially strong. They burned schools and frequently attacked outposts. In Binh Chanh district, they overran a police station and were poised to overwhelm the district headquarters. South Vietnamese forces were understrength and the government cadres disorganized. In virtual control of the district, the Viet Cong could approach Saigon from the west and southwest and cut the roads from Long An to Gia Dinh. Gia Dinh was also one of the provinces where the government had launched the abortive *Hop Tac* program of 1964–1965.

To bolster government defenses and destroy VC guerrillas and infrastructure, the allies launched Operation FAIRFAX/*Rang Dong*, a combined American–South Vietnamese offensive that began in December. The commander of II Field Force Vietnam, Major General Johnathan O. Seaman, assigned one U.S. Army battalion each to Binh Chanh, Thu Duc, and Nha Be districts in Gia Dinh. The South Vietnamese employed three ARVN battalions, each linked to an American unit. According to the plan, U.S. and South Vietnamese forces operating jointly for the first time in the war would within two months restore security to the point where the South Vietnamese could manage the province themselves. Events did not work out that way.

The effort to dismantle the infrastructure in Gia Dinh was beset with poor co-ordination. The American adviser handling the Provincial Reconnaissance Units (PRUs) failed to inform the district adviser or the U.S. Army battalion commander when or where they would operate, raising the possibility that the battalion's plans might interfere with the work of the counterinfrastructure teams clad in traditional Vietnamese peasant pajamas. Five separate South Vietnamese intelligence nets operated in Binh Chanh district. Each agency kept its information to itself. On the American side, intelligence was likewise compartmentalized by agency.[36] The existence of multiple intelligence channels on the American side made it difficult to exchange intelligence information in a timely fashion. The lack of unified collection and dissemination of intelligence sapped the anti-infrastructure effort.

Police units were badly deployed, limiting their effectiveness against the underground. One-third of the Police Field Forces protected the district interrogation center and were unavailable for operations. The police's blacklists of infrastructure members proved a handicap, often containing outdated and vague information.

As late as May 1967, security had not yet improved to the point where U.S. forces could move on, nor was that likely to occur in the short term. Guerrillas and political cadres simply slipped away from areas subject to military pressure, as they had done at Long Huu, and waited for the troops to depart before returning. FAIRFAX failed to break the web of interpersonal relations and institutions that allowed the infrastructure to function in Gia Dinh. The communists continued to collect taxes, recruit, gather intelligence, and inflict with mines and booby traps heavy casualties on the Americans and South Vietnamese. The infrastructure remained a formidable political rival to the government in the shadow of the capital. The conduct of the insurgency depended on the VCI. John Paul Vann, then chief of the American civil assistance program in III Corps, recognized this. In the spring of 1967, he concluded, "The VC infrastructure in Binh Chanh has been in position long enough, and is well organized enough to withstand any number of sweeps throughout the area."[37] The operations of American ground forces achieved a stalemate. In Binh Chanh, as in many other districts, they held the Viet Cong at bay but did not defeat it. If the Americans were to leave Gia Dinh, a South Vietnamese intelligence officer predicted in May 1967, "the VC will attack Saigon within a week."[38]

Operation CEDAR FALLS

Poor coordination between American civilians and military hurt a larger operation in support of pacification, CEDAR FALLS. In January 1967, while FAIRFAX was continuing in Gia Dinh, General Seaman launched a multidivision assault in the nearby Iron Triangle, an enemy base area just north of Saigon and close to the enemy strongholds of War Zones C and D. For over twenty years, the Iron Triangle had been a headquarters, staging area, and supply point for communist forces. Although sparsely populated, the Iron Triangle as well as the two war zones was strategically important. The enemy bases were situated between the cross-border sanctuaries in Cambodia on one side and the population and rice crops of the capital region and delta on the other. By sweeping the Iron Triangle, General Seaman hoped to disrupt enemy operations and perhaps capture North Vietnamese and COSVN plans.[39]

Seaman's concept called for sealing the entire area of operations, clearing it of civilians (most of whom were regarded as Viet Cong supporters or sympathizers) stripping away natural concealment, and destroying enemy installations and tunnel complexes. During the operation, the whole region was declared a specified strike zone, allowing field commanders discretion to call in air strikes and use artillery without obtaining further clearances. The U.S. 25th Division manned a blocking position on the western side of the Iron Triangle from the Boi Loi Woods to the confluence of the Saigon and Thi Tinh Rivers, and the 1st Division secured the northern end. General Westmoreland approved the operation.

Intelligence analysts expected any organized defense to come from the vicinity of Ben Suc, a settlement of about three thousand people thirty miles northwest of the capital on the Saigon River. Maj. Gen. William E. DePuy, commander of the 1st Infantry Division, wanted to seize and evacuate the village before the Iron Triangle itself was encircled so American firepower could be used freely without the risk of incurring civilian casualties. Relocating and assisting the villagers were the responsibility of the Office of Civil Operations (OCO) and South Vietnamese provincial officials. Three Police Field Force platoons would question all males in the village aged fifteen to forty-five, and an ARVN battalion would search for enemy weapons, supplies, and tunnels.

Fearing that communist agents in the government and armed forces might compromise the operation, the Americans closely held the plans for CEDAR FALLS. They briefed South Vietnamese paramilitary forces, the ARVN 5th Division commander, the American civilian province representative, and the Binh Duong province chief only *after* the operation was under way. The province chief had no time to plan for relocating refugees, even though it was his responsibility. John Vann, the only AID official to be part of the early planning, was expressly forbidden to coordinate with South Vietnamese authorities or to stockpile supplies at the site of the refugee center in the town of Phu Cuong in advance of the operation. He had to store them secretly in a nearby warehouse. Not surprisingly, the evacuation of Ben Suc was delayed. It took the province chief two days to obtain enough boats to move some twenty-eight hundred people, their personal belongings, and livestock: 247 water buffalo, 225 cattle, and countless chickens and pigs. Even with help from trucks from the 1st Division, the move took days to complete. Shelter at the Phu Cuong center was lacking because South Vietnamese agencies had received word of the operation only hours before the villagers began to arrive. The 5th ARVN Engineer Battalion and elements of the U.S. 1st Infantry Division erected shelters over the next several days with materials furnished by OCO and the division. There was a good deal of complaining by the new refugees, owing to their poor reception, their absence from their land, and the enforced idleness at the camp.[40]

Concerns over security, while understandable on military grounds, exacerbated relations between civilian AID officials and the 1st Division. Major General DePuy wanted to run the refugee relocation and assistance effort because he was convinced that Vann's agency and the South Vietnamese would "louse up" the operation. When DePuy visited the temporary camp at Phu Cuong, he blamed Vann and OCO for the unsatisfactory conditions: no charcoal, insufficient shelter, and inadequate sanitation. Vann in turn complained about the restrictions that limited his ability to prepare for the refugee movement. He felt his agency had done well in setting up a camp under severe handicaps and in handling six thousand people, twice as many as had been expected. General Seaman personally had to mediate the acrimonious dispute and vetoed DePuy's plan to take over the center.[41]

Attentive primarily to the enemy's military threat, military planners overlooked the political and public relations problems associated with the forced removal of South Vietnamese civilians from their homes. The American press publicized the relocation as brutish. Uprooting civilians, many of whom were already unsympathetic or even hostile to the government, would gain no support for Saigon but possibly additional recruits for the enemy.[42]

The operation also strained relations between the American military and the Saigon government. South Vietnamese authorities apparently had no voice in the decision to evacuate and destroy several villages—actions that clearly denigrated the government's sovereignty. Chief of State Thieu personally expressed to General Westmoreland strong disapproval over the evacuation of Ben Suc, urging that in the future protective forces move to where people lived instead of relocating people to protected areas. General Westmoreland agreed in principle but maintained that he had insufficient forces to defend Ben Suc during the operation.[43] The more likely explanation was Westmoreland's priorities. Major General Phillip Davidson, Westmoreland's chief assistant on military intelligence (J-2), sagely observed that while Westmoreland "pontificated about the importance of pacification, he devoted his energies and interest to operations like CEDAR FALLS ..., not to clearing and holding the insignificant hamlets and villages around Saigon."[44]

Besides the cost in adverse publicity, friction between U.S. civil and military agencies, and strained relations with the South Vietnamese government and people, CEDAR FALLS resulted in no lasting military or political control of the Iron Triangle. During the operation, American and South Vietnamese soldiers and police uncovered an extensive tunnel complex at Ben Suc consisting of a hospital, training school, large rice cache, and thousands of uniforms. Yet according to Brigadier General (later General and Chief of Staff of the Army) Bernard W.

Rogers, assistant division commander of the 1st Division, neither the South Vietnamese nor the Americans had sufficient forces to continue operating in the Iron Triangle or prevent the enemy from returning. Two weeks after the operation, he reported the area was "again literally crawling with what appeared to be Viet Cong."[45]

The Advisers: Liaison and Reporting

During the troop buildup, U.S. Army advisers increased in numbers. Between June 1965 and June 1966, the number of military advisers serving in the field rose from about thirty-five hundred to more than five thousand, an increase of over 47 percent. Many were involved in pacification. In 1966, about 34 percent of military advisers served in the provinces, in the districts, or with the RF and PF, working directly with South Vietnamese pacification officials. Advisers with mobile training teams and intelligence units also contributed to the effort to weaken the insurgents. The American advisers serving in ARVN divisions, regiments, and battalions that supported the RD Cadre or provided local security also helped the pacification effort.[46]

The steadily growing number of military advisers was in addition to the sizable number of civilian advisers, many of whom had pacification-related duties. In 1966, AID had hundreds of advisers in the provinces and districts working in economic development, health and social welfare, public administration, agriculture, and police programs.

The buildup changed the status of the military adviser. After U.S. combat units arrived, advising became a less desirable assignment than commanding a line unit. Advisory duty was considered outside the mainstream career pattern, and officers assigned as advisers increasingly came to perceive such a tour of duty as detrimental, hurting their chances for selection to schools and promotions.[47] The army's primary mission was combat, and that arena was where most ambitious officers sought to build their careers.

Advising, whether with South Vietnamese paramilitary organizations or province or district officials, was extremely challenging duty. The adviser had significant responsibilities, serving as a conduit between the American command and his South Vietnamese counterpart, reporting to his superiors on local conditions, and attempting to get his counterpart to improve the pacification program. The adviser also tried to ensure that his counterpart used American funds and materials honestly and productively. The adviser was also handicapped. He had no formal authority over the South Vietnamese and in practice could often exercise little leverage over the performance of his counterpart, who might be senior in rank, age, and experience. Sometimes the South Vietnamese officer stationed at the province or district was uninterested in his job, viewing duty in the field as a form of punishment, an exile from a headquarters or staff assignment that offered greater safety and quicker promotion.[48] In addition to these drawbacks, the adviser was an outsider. It usually took Americans several months to overcome language and cultural differences, and in many cases xenophobia, before beginning to understand the local military situation and the nuances of South Vietnamese military as well as civilian politics. The adviser had to work patiently for months to establish rapport with his counterpart but might be reassigned just as he was becoming effective.

Advisory duties were broad in scope and could encompass such functional areas as command, administration, intelligence, training, field operations, and logistics. The military adviser helped plan military operations and prepared after-action reports. He helped train paramilitary forces, cooperated with the efforts of other American information- and intelligence-gathering agencies, and expedited the flow of funds and matériel provided by USOM and the U.S. Army. A military adviser in a province or district also had to coordinate his activities with those of the province representative, an AID official who administered American support of nonmilitary programs such as police training and economic development. There was a manifest need for American advisers, if they were to be their most effective, to speak with one voice. If military and civilian programs overlapped or goals were in conflict, then the various advisers could be working at cross-purposes.

Coordination between civilian and military advisers in the provinces proved difficult. AID advisers were particularly distressed by the absence of a clear delineation of military and nonmilitary responsibilities and inadequate procedures to reconcile overlapping programs or differing priorities. A provincial coordinating committee, composed of the province chief, the sector adviser, and the province representative, did some coordinating and monitored the expenditure of American funds in the province, but the committee was short-lived. None of these advisers was empowered to take charge of the local support effort. Without a single coordinator at the province level, it was hard to develop a concerted policy on ways to influence South Vietnamese officials.[49]

Difficulty in coordinating civil and military programs extended to the district level also. In 1964, the army began to assign officers as district advisers. In addition to working with the army officers advising ARVN, the district adviser coordinated his activities and support with the plans of the AID representative and local government officials. As in the provinces, two separate American hierarchies—civilian and military—supported different aspects of pacification and advised the South Vietnamese at the lowest echelon of the Saigon government. Within the military hierarchy, the advisers with ARVN often disagreed with the advisers stationed at the provinces and districts.[50]

The army's involvement in pacification, essential in many ways to the conduct of the other war, achieved little more than limited and temporary gains. Civil affairs teams helped the refugee population, and army engineers assisted with construction projects, but these efforts were small in scale and clearly inadequate to the numbers of war victims and the amount of property destruction. Insufficient coordination between the Americans and the South Vietnamese and between U.S.

civil and military officials impeded allied efforts to disrupt the infrastructure. Gains made in conducting county fair operations and in moving troops into enemy strongholds such as Hau Nghia and Long An provinces proved transitory. Improved security too frequently directly correlated with the presence of American soldiers. They improved security where they were while they were there. But there were not enough, or ever would be enough, American troops for every unpacified part of South Vietnam.

The American ground strategy created a paradox: The U.S. Army was fighting on behalf of an army and a government that it tended to treat as if irrelevant. The U.S. Army supplanted ARVN in the main force war and in CEDAR FALLS relocated South Vietnamese citizens. The political objective of the war (an independent, self-sufficient South Vietnam) and the relative American neglect of the South Vietnamese government and military contradicted each other. U.S. Army commanders often failed to grasp that how they fought the war—uprooting people, creating refugees, and failing to dislodge the infrastructure—was linked to the attrition of government authority in the countryside. The numerous tactical successes of 1965–1966 were not transformed into lasting gains for the government. All too often the military conduct of the war was divorced from the goals of American policy as set forth in NSAM 288.

The big-unit war continued to overshadow pacification. Although U.S. Army operations were at times closely tied to pacification, the army considered that assignment to be subordinate to its primary mission: wearing down the enemy's large units. As Major General Julian Ewell, commander of the U.S. 9th Infantry Division, put it, "I had two rules. One is that you would try to get a very close meshing of pacification … and military operations. The other rule is the military operations would be given first priority in every case."[51]

General Westmoreland did think about increasing the army's involvement in pacification. At the end of August 1966, he informed the White House of his intention in the coming months to deploy his forces so as to help maximize the amount of territory cleared of enemy units and the number of people living in secured areas.[52] But the president's advisers, fearing Westmoreland's proposal would give the South Vietnamese an opportunity to step aside and let the Americans take over yet another aspect of the war, had other ideas. Rather than accept as sufficient Westmoreland's intention to orient more military operations to the mission of pacification support, Rostow and McNamara concluded that radical changes in the organization of military and civil resources and concrete working plans for pacification, "region by region," were needed before results could significantly improve. The underlying goal was to get the South Vietnamese to improve their conduct of pacification. The president agreed, telling Rostow to send "something to Westy so he will not *assume* that we have approved."[53]

The administration understood that Americans could not serve as surrogates for South Vietnamese officials or government-run programs. The critical variable in pacification was the ability of the South Vietnamese themselves. To be effective, the government had to follow up military operations with reliable services and dependable security. The key ingredient of successful pacification was an indigenous government that ably served and protected its citizens. The Americans might help as advisers, but that effort was weakened by the diffusion of advice by program and agency. No agency or body of advisers served to integrate the efforts of the civilians and soldiers.

5

The Search for Solutions

The arrival of American forces stabilized the military situation, but pacification, all observers recognized, was in trouble. By early 1966, pacification's problems could no longer be ignored. President Johnson was increasingly concerned about management of American support of the other war. Although he seemed content to allow General Westmoreland to run the ground war in Vietnam and Admiral Ulysses S. Grant Sharp, CINCPAC, to control the bombing campaigns as separate but coordinate spheres, he grew less comfortable with the division of military and civilian responsibility for pacification support. At the beginning of February, after meeting with Senator Robert Kennedy and his brother, Senator Ted Kennedy, and talking with newspaper columnists, McGeorge Bundy warned the president that "the time for us to act on organization for pacification is now. … We need to grab this issue before it grabs us." Bundy proposed that he visit Saigon to confer with Lodge about putting "pacification on a par with the political effort for peace and the military effort to turn back the aggression."[1] Johnson, as it turned out, had more in mind than having his assistant visit South Vietnam.

No One in Charge

Although the development of the RD Cadre, the growth of the police and RF/PF, and the modifications of the *Chieu Hoi* program were sources of encouragement to American officials, American support for these individual efforts was fragmented. Although each program was arguably necessary to help pacify South Vietnam, no one person or office was in charge of American support of pacification. AID handled the police, the refugees, and the *Chieu Hoi* program. The CIA was the primary adviser to the RD Cadre. MACV exercised jurisdiction over support for the RF/PF. No mechanism seemed at hand to ensure that the added resources for police, RF/PF, *Chieu Hoi,* and RD Cadre would be used efficiently in pursuit of a common strategy.

Lack of coordination and centralized direction had long characterized the American effort in South Vietnam, despite a general understanding that the ambassador headed the "country team," which consisted of all in-country U.S. agencies.[2] The American ambassador in Saigon presided over a large and unwieldy apparatus. He had to deal with an American military commander who was relatively autonomous within his jurisdiction as well as with the semi-independent heads of three civilian agencies—AID, USIA, and CIA—with responsibilities that included more than pacification support. Each agency maintained staffs in South Vietnam substantially larger than that of the ambassador. Each agency had its own channels of communication to its headquarters in Washington and carried out a wide range of programs. For programs and budgets, these agencies looked to Washington for guidance. Each agency operated under statutory authority granted by the U.S. Congress and was accountable to that body for its expenditures. The relationships among parent organizations in Washington magnified the disunity. Short of the president himself, no single agency, task force, or individual controlled American policy and operations in South Vietnam.

American support of pacification, involving more agencies of the U.S. government than any other program in South Vietnam, represented the epitome of this disunity. No single office in South Vietnam took pacification as its central task or was willing to subordinate its interests to allow another to take full responsibility for the entire program. In the minds of some U.S. officials, insufficient coordination of advice and support reduced American effectiveness in dealing with the South Vietnamese. The primary way the Americans could directly bolster pacification was to consolidate American support.

American agencies in South Vietnam had attempted to improve coordination. In Saigon, a committee under Deputy Chief of Mission David G. Nes was briefly established in early 1964 to coordinate American civilian and military programs. Before it even had a chance to operate, Ambassador Lodge summarily disbanded it, believing the new body usurped his and the mission's responsibilities.[3]

Trying to coordinate support in the field proved equally frustrating. In 1964, a provincial coordinating committee, composed of the province chief, the sector adviser (U.S. Army), and the province representative (AID), administered U.S. financial support of pacification projects. All three members had to approve in writing all expenditures of American funds in the province. This procedure, dubbed the "troika signoff," was a powerful tool both for combining civil and military efforts and withholding monies from corrupt or ineffective South Vietnamese officials. Yet this procedure was discarded after James Killen became director of AID programs in South Vietnam. Seeking to strengthen the administrative capabilities of the South Vietnamese by having them make decisions about the allocation of resources, he ended the troika signoff in June 1965.[4] Rather than have local advisers exert pressure on government officials, Killen wanted the South Vietnamese to improve their procedures and assume responsibility for decisions. By this step, he eliminated an important mechanism for coordinating the programs of AID and MACV advisers. Neither the MACV sector advisers nor the AID officials working on provincial operations were pleased with Killen's decision, which reduced their ability to influence provincial officials.

In July 1964, President Johnson gave the American mission an unusual opportunity for achieving unity when he appointed General Taylor as ambassador to replace Lodge. A former chairman of the Joint Chiefs of Staff, Taylor commanded respect from the armed services and seemed the ideal man to mesh military support with civil programs. Johnson granted him "full responsibility" for the American effort, including the military, and authorized him to assume "the degree of command and control" that he deemed appropriate.[5] In the view of Johnson adviser Robert Komer, the president intended that Taylor become a "proconsul" with the kind of broad powers Prime Minister Winston Churchill had granted General Sir Gerald Templar to deal with the Malayan insurgency in 1952.[6]

Taylor used the Mission Council, which he established in July 1964, to coordinate programs. Comprising the ambassador, his deputy, the embassy's political and economic counselors, and the heads of the other American agencies, including the military commander, the council met weekly under Taylor's chairmanship. Although the council set policy, Taylor sanctioned individual agencies' appealing council decisions to Washington, a practice that reinforced the ultimate independence of each organization. As ambassador, Taylor refrained from acting like a proconsul.[7]

During the spring of 1965, Taylor approved Westmoreland's suggestion of appointing a single manager for American programs in three provinces (Dinh Tuong, Binh Thuan, and Darlac). Under this plan, the embassy designated a single official, called a team chief, to head the province advisory effort. Civilians were appointed in two provinces; a military officer, in Dinh Tuong. The experiment, which lasted from June 1 to August 31, proved inconclusive, partly because there was no unified management at higher levels. Province managers continued to receive instructions from their own agencies and to view pacification from their agency's perspective. AID officials tended to dwell on refugees and schools, the military focused on the status of indigenous forces, and the CIA fretted about cadre programs. MACV felt uncomfortable with civilians heading province advisory teams, and some civilians in turn were dismayed at the idea of military officers managing civil programs. In September 1965, the embassy scrapped the experiment, deeming the three-month test inconclusive.[8]

The absence of unity in the Mission Council evoked a number of proposals by Washington officials to strengthen pacification support in South Vietnam at what Bundy in February 1965 called "the margin between military advice and economic development."[9] Rather than outlining a new overall strategy for pacification, the proposals stressed ways to make existing programs run more efficiently. In March, Bundy's assistant on South Vietnam, Chester Cooper, suggested setting up a multiagency task force under a single manager in South Vietnam so U.S. agencies could improve coordination of existing programs.[10] The Washington-based Vietnam Coordinating Committee, an interagency body for pacification support, wanted that manager to serve as chief of staff to the ambassador. A member of JCS, Maj. Gen. Rollin Anthis, USAF, went further in advocating that civilian agencies cede responsibility for pacification support to General Westmoreland,[11] an idea the civilians found unpalatable. According to this argument, which General Lemnitzer had made in 1961, the military should absorb internal security assistance programs from USOM because counterinsurgency forces, such as the police and paramilitary, were no longer able to handle the Viet Cong.

Cooper pushed for improvement at home as well. In March, he advocated the creation of a new position in Washington: "a Lord High Needler and two, possibly three, additional disagreeable but able assistants" to jump-start stalled programs, spark new ideas, and resolve interagency disputes over programs, goals, or resources.[12] Cooper's proposal for centralized management in Washington, which he submitted to McGeorge Bundy, was aimed at disrupting the bureaucratic status quo and required the president's backing. No agency would voluntarily cede control of its program to a rival or to a pacification "czar." Moreover, each would argue with some cogency that experience gave it an irrefutable advantage in continuing to manage its own programs. Unfortunately for a more unified support effort, Cooper's proposal came at an inopportune time. Forced to concentrate on deploying forces to remedy the deteriorating military situation and desiring to unify the administration behind the current Vietnam policy, the president could ill-afford to act upon Cooper's idea at the time.

Meanwhile, Bundy remained more concerned with the status of the embassy than with White House organization. He feared the embassy was too heavily preoccupied with the military situation to be "geared to a full steam operation" with the South Vietnamese cabinet on nonmilitary programs.[13] The coming end of Maxwell Taylor's tenure as ambassador, he believed, provided an opportunity to set in place a fully coordinated American program of military *and* nonmilitary activities under the leadership of a new ambassador who, in Bundy's view, understood the political nature of the situation in South Vietnam. He suggested the president replace Taylor with Lodge as soon as practical[14] because Lodge considered the other war the "heart of the problem" and would give it more attention.[15] Moreover, as a prominent Republican he would add bipartisan support for Johnson's Vietnam policy. The president agreed, and Lodge returned as ambassador in August 1965. To get the other war moving, the White House asked the new ambassador to develop a pacification plan with "a system of priorities and a definition of clear objectives."[16]

Ambassador Lodge proved to be a strong booster indeed for the other war, stimulating vigorous debate about how to carry out pacification. His cables and statements, which frequently called for a new strategic emphasis, represented a massive endorsement of pacification; his weekly messages to the president dwelled on pacification perhaps more than any other subject.[17] His rhetoric, however, was not always specific about concepts or concrete about how to organize and implement pacification programs, which the administration wanted. "Countersubversion/terrorism or pacification or counterinsurgency—I am not overly concerned with what we call it," he told his senior officers shortly after returning to Vietnam.[18] Yet despite his aloofness about distinctions and details, he contributed to changing the mood in Saigon about how to prosecute the war.

Johnson deliberately gave Lodge a mandate as sweeping as Taylor's: "to exercise full responsibility for the work of the United States government in South Vietnam."[19] But Lodge was no more inclined than Taylor to become proconsul. In his words, he viewed his responsibility as "tactfully and persuasively braiding together" the various strands of the pacification program without altering any existing command by the American military. Lodge did not view himself as a chief executive imposing his will on other agencies or members of the country team but as a kind of mediator, resolving disagreements "by persuasion."[20] He had little interest in establishing a more integrated organization to support pacification. The new ambassador saw Saigon's pacification effort as primarily civilian and planned to limit his liaison with MACV.

Although Americans regularly advised the RD Ministry, Lodge refrained from establishing a focal point for U.S. support of the cadre program. Mark Huss, an AID official in the embassy, was in almost daily contact with the ministry, but General Lansdale also met periodically with General Thang. AID and CIA provided funds, training, and advisers. MACV, through its district advisory teams, helped arm the cadre teams.[21] Each agency pressed its claim for becoming executive agent for American support of revolutionary development. Not wishing to usurp any agency's prerogatives, Lodge did not "prescribe any formal coordinating procedures." Nor did he set up a formal coordinating body at the provincial level.[22] Lodge showed little inclination to strengthen American support of pacification at the margin between military advice and political-economic development.[23] The White House's hopes for a better-run pacification program went unfulfilled.

As a part of his effort to boost pacification, Lodge asked General Lansdale to return to South Vietnam as his assistant and "executive agent" to provide liaison between the U.S. Mission and the South Vietnamese officials responsible for pacification. Almost from the start, Lansdale found himself in a difficult situation. Lodge gave him little latitude, effectively limiting what he could do. Lodge also expected Lansdale to take care of routine administrative duties within the embassy. American agencies were uncomfortable about Lansdale dealing with the ambassador on issues that traditionally fell within their purview. Lansdale's relations with high South Vietnamese officials, some of whom were personal friends, also annoyed Lodge, Deputy Ambassador William Porter, and Philip Habib, who ran the political section in the embassy. Lansdale found himself in a vulnerable position, having no independent operating authority, no funds, and, most significantly, no Washington constituency to back him up.[24]

In October 1965, after the administration had decided to send American combatants to South Vietnam, Chester Cooper argued again for a single executive empowered to manage American nonmilitary programs. He once again suggested to Bundy that the president appoint a deputy special assistant to the president for South Vietnamese affairs who would report to the national security adviser and have a decisive voice in allocating funds for all nonmilitary activities, including intelligence. Cooper also wanted this official to exercise responsibility in the areas where civil and military functions overlapped.[25]

Although the president approved no changes in organization, he and Bundy continued to discuss the idea of unified management. Bundy believed that the U.S. goal of sustaining a noncommunist South Vietnam required a greater investment in pacification.[26] The president and Bundy had been cognizant since the end of 1964 of the growing imbalance of the war effort. The administration remained apprehensive about nonmilitary programs, which took a back seat to the big-unit war. Bundy ruefully conceded to President Johnson in December 1965 that the United States "did not have a complete and fully developed political, economic, and social program to match the major new military deployments proposed for 1966."[27] Even in 1965 at the start of the buildup, money for military assistance (hardware, gear and clothing, and ammunition for the South Vietnamese) already outstripped economic aid by $28 million; the figure for military help excluded the cost of American military operations.[28]

Secretary McNamara shared Bundy's frustration, believing that military actions by themselves were no substitute for effective South Vietnamese government influence in the countryside. In several memoranda to the president in December, McNamara forcefully argued that the effort to secure the countryside was stalled and that successful pacification was the key to Saigon's long-term health.[29] McNamara acknowledged that as of the end of 1965, the White House had found no solution to the disparity between the military and civil sides of its policy.

Action was taken at a level below the Oval Office to remedy poor coordination of the American support effort. Deputy Assistant Secretary of State for Far Eastern Affairs Leonard Ungar proposed a conference of working-level members of the Saigon mission and U.S. agencies in Washington concerned with South Vietnam. Lodge readily agreed and sent Deputy Ambassador Porter as his representative. The conference took place January 8–11, 1966, at Warrenton, Virginia, about thirty-five miles from Washington.

The participants concentrated on the organization of U.S. Mission support for pacification but reached no agreement on what needed to be changed.[30] Advocates of tighter management were Washington based, such as White House staff member Chester Cooper and Maj. Gen. William Peers, SACSA for the Joint Chiefs of Staff. Bundy privately sought the president's approval to try persuading Lodge to give Porter greater responsibility for pacification, to make him "the field commander for pacification in the same way that Westmoreland is the field commander for the war." This role was necessary, in Bundy's view, since pacification was "absolutely equal in importance" to the fight against organized enemy units.[31] AID administrator David Bell, Undersecretary of State George Ball, and Secretary McNamara also supported this appointment.

All Saigon representatives wanted to keep their separate command channels and links with the ambassador. Each also wanted to keep his field programs intact. Despite a lack of unanimity on how to reorganize pacification support, the conferees agreed that pacification required a central managerial nucleus and that it ought to be located in the embassy.[32]

While the conference was in session, the president, continuing to grapple with the issue of better top-level organization for pacification,[33] set a new condition. He insisted that personnel or organizational changes be carried out only with the support of Ambassador Lodge.[34] Such a condition, which was reasonable in bureaucratic terms, would likely complicate any contemplated reorganization. By retaining Lodge's support for the Vietnam policy, President Johnson wanted to mute any possible political criticism of the war on the part of the Republicans or Lodge, who was expected to be a presidential candidate in 1968.

In contrast to Washington's growing interest in reorganizing was the embassy's laissez-faire attitude. Returning from the Warrenton meeting, Porter downplayed Washington's moves. The embassy, in his view, would continue to support pacification as currently organized.[35] With the president deciding to move only with Lodge's support and with Porter resisting new arrangements, the likelihood of change seemed slight. Yet as events turned out, Porter's position would prove to be short-lived, for Washington pressed unrelentingly for reorganization as a way to improve pacification and push it out of the shadow of the big-unit war.

At bottom, the organizational malaise stemmed from the way the Americans bifurcated the war effort into civil and military components: splitting military responsibility for the war from civilian responsibility for pacification and segregating military and civil programs under separate chains of command. The organization of the American government's effort led agencies to emphasize one aspect of the struggle depending on their charter. The division of the war effort, however rooted in bureaucratic logic, created problems. The military had assets that could support pacification. By contrast, the communists deliberately fused the armed and the political struggle.

The U.S. Mission lacked access to or control of South Vietnamese security forces. Pacification officials in the early 1960s tried to compensate for the absence of local security forces by creating new forces to clear and hold territory—for example, the Police Field Force and the various cadre teams, which then had to compete with ARVN for manpower. If the military had the resources, then one way to end the bifurcated effort was to make the military responsible for pacification.[36]

The need to involve the military in pacification was acknowledged within the army. In October 1965, the U.S. Army deputy chief of staff for operations, Lieut. Gen. Vernon P. Mock, argued that pacification "encompasses all the civil, military, and police actions required to eliminate organized VC activity." Offensive operations by American units to destroy the Viet Cong were "but a part of the total pacification program. It is important to keep these military actions in their proper perspective rather than considering them as the complete effort required to accomplish our objectives in Vietnam."[37]

High Aspirations: Heads of State
at Honolulu

Johnson's impatience manifested itself when he hastily arranged a personal meeting in February 1966 with South Vietnamese leaders Thieu and Ky in Hawaii to discuss the other war. According to Chester Cooper, although the president had had the idea of a conference on pacification "under consideration" for months, serious planning started just hours before the meeting was announced to the press. Returning to the White House from lunch on Tuesday, February 4, he had a rude reception. As Cooper recalled, "I got back at about 2:30, and I found that Bundy was raising hell looking for me. And I went down to his office, and he said, 'For God's sake, where the hell have you been? Don't you know we're going to be meeting in Honolulu on Saturday? ... There's going to be a public announcement of this at 3:00, and get the hell back to your office and prepare an agenda.'"[38]

Scheduling the meeting for February 6–8 was no whim. The sessions would take place right after the January 31 end of a thirty-seven day pause in the bombing of North Vietnam and just after Senator William Fulbright, chairman of the Foreign Relations Committee, began Senate hearings on the administration's war policy. The president hoped the conference would deflect public attention from the renewed bombing and the attacks of congressional critics. The Honolulu sessions deliberately focused on finding solutions for South Vietnam's social, political, and economic problems. Distressed by the short, hard lives of the South Vietnamese people, the president was moved to help them. He wanted American technology and know-how mobilized to help the South Vietnamese government improve health care, crop yields, and education so that people would have a reason to believe in and support the government. Johnson consciously wanted the conference to emphasize the nonmilitary aspects of the war; therefore he did not hold the sessions at the most convenient Hawaiian site, the U.S. Naval Base at Pearl Harbor. He hoped the high-level meeting between the heads of state and cabinet officers of the two nations would allay public and press criticism that his administration's policy overly concentrated on military issues and military solutions.[39]

The Declaration of Honolulu that emerged from the conference set a lofty tone. In this document, the Johnson administration promised to help the Saigon government end social injustice, improve living standards, and build democracy throughout South Vietnam. These goals were not dissimilar to the aims of Johnson's Great Society programs. The South Vietnamese government, for its part, pledged to hold elections, improve the health and education of its people, provide greater military protection for pacification workers, and care for refugees.[40] Johnson proclaimed that he was impressed "with the apparent determination of Thieu, Ky, and other Vietnamese Ministers to carry forward a social policy of radical and constructive change."[41]

At the end of the meeting, he admonished the conferees:

Preserve this communique [the Declaration], because it is one we don't want to forget. It will be a kind of bible that we are going to follow. ... You men who are responsible for these departments, you ministers, and the staffs associated with them in both governments, bear in mind we are going to give you an examination and the finals will be on just what you have done. ... How have you built democracy in the rural areas? How much of it have you built, when and where? Give us dates, times, numbers. ... Larger outputs, more efficient production to improve credit, handicraft, light industry, rural electrification—are those just phrases, high-sounding words, or have you coonskins on the wall?[42]

With that rhetorical flourish, the president concluded the conference. Bundy had hoped that the sessions would "get the gospel of pacification carved into the hearts and minds of all concerned, both here and in Vietnam."[43] The president succeeded. His efforts at Honolulu shoved pacification back into the public spotlight and were an important milestone in the campaign to boost the other war.

Retooling for Pacification

In a less visible way at Honolulu, Johnson also discussed American organization for pacification. That issue could not have generally been far from his mind, thanks to Bundy's continuing pleas that Johnson strengthen his team in Saigon and gain Lodge's approval to make Porter field commander for pacification.[44] Following the conference, Bundy went to South Vietnam and reported that embassy officers agreed that Porter was qualified to run nonmilitary programs. Bundy reminded Johnson that his "personal insistence on a strengthened effort" would be critical in persuading Lodge.[45] The president heeded this call and made Porter the focal point for pacification support in Saigon.

Dissatisfied with Lodge's oversight, President Johnson reminded the ambassador in mid-February that Porter was to pull together the Saigon mission's pacification efforts and that Lodge was to announce publicly Porter's role to demonstrate that the administration was following up on pledges made at Honolulu. The president had been considering making Porter "field commander for pacification" since the January Warrenton conference. With the president's prodding, Lodge proclaimed Porter's "new" role at the end of February. This step was the precursor of far-reaching changes.

The White House came to view Porter as someone who could compensate for some of Lodge's managerial shortcomings. Returning from Saigon, Bundy wrote a long memo for Johnson about the new arrangements and Lodge's leadership. In a frank assessment, Bundy concluded that Lodge had "little taste for the hard work that lies between a general assertion of purpose and a concrete administrative achievement" and that he was the "very model of a man who needs staff support." Porter, "shrewd, cool, strong, experienced and determined," was now deemed "indispensable." Bundy saw the new arrangement in Saigon as a triangle with Lodge at the apex. One line of the triangle went from Lodge to

Westmoreland, the other from Lodge to Porter. Porter would receive guidance from Lodge and the president, have authority over agency heads, and work to improve coordination between AID and MACV.[46]

In contrast to Bundy, Lodge and Porter had their own conception of Porter's position. If Washington thought of Porter as a commander, he thought of himself mainly as a coordinator. Lodge promised to relieve Porter of all routine duties so he could concentrate on pacification but also made clear that Porter would continue to be a subordinate and that Lodge would remain personally involved in pacification.[47] To be effective in this new role, Porter needed Lodge's help in clarifying his relations with others in the embassy. In 1965, Lodge had brought Lansdale to Saigon as special liaison officer to the government, and in that capacity Lansdale consulted with South Vietnamese officials on the RD Cadre program and other nonmilitary programs. There were obvious overlaps between Porter's and Lansdale's responsibilities. It was unclear in February just how Lodge planned to reconcile their respective roles. Porter's new assignment might be interpreted as a sign of the administration's disappointment with Lansdale's efforts.

Being under Lodge's thumb was not Porter's only difficulty. He had to deal with numerous independent agencies in Washington. No single manager was empowered to run pacification support. The White House staff had raised the issue of who should manage Washington's support of pacification several times in 1965. After the Honolulu conference, the president was ready to act.

Bundy was instrumental in framing the issue for the president, arguing in a February 16 memorandum that no one could provide executive support for Porter in Washington because that person did not exist. No single agency, committee of assistant secretaries, or even the president himself, Bundy concluded, could provide that support. The kind of man who preferred "action to excuses and management to contemplation" met Bundy's specifications for a czar for the other war. Johnson, who usually made no comments on memos, termed Bundy's "excellent" and asked Rusk, McNamara, and Bundy to submit to him by February 18 a list of candidates for director of nonmilitary operations under the president.[48]

Before Bundy left the White House at the end of February to run the Ford Foundation, he was involved in the selection of "Mr. Vietnam." As is customary, he advanced several names but recommended the president appoint to that position his deputy special assistant for national security affairs, Robert W. Komer. It would be "the best possible use of Komer. He has a very unusual combination of energy and experience, and his abrasiveness (which can be more accurately described as brashness) would be a positive asset in this particular assignment." Bundy saw other advantages. Komer was Porter's preferred candidate and was known as "President Johnson's man."[49] Significantly, Bundy offered no negative comments and also pushed Komer's name forward as a candidate for national security adviser. Komer subsequently held that position on an interim basis for six weeks until Walt Rostow came on board.

Brushing aside a State Department recommendation to place Washington's direction of pacification support in that department, Johnson acceded to Cooper's earlier proposal to locate a Lord High Needler on the White House staff.[50] (Bundy and McNamara also opposed State's proposal, fearing it would keep Mr. Vietnam several layers down in the bureaucracy and make it difficult for him to gain access to the president.) With this official in the White House, he would have the needed clout when dealing with cabinet members, such as the secretary of state or defense, in resolving interagency disputes.

On March 28, Johnson appointed Robert W. Komer as special presidential assistant for supervising pacification support from the White House. In contrast to most special presidential assistants, who were appointed to advise and coordinate, Komer felt he had received a broader mandate from Johnson: authority to direct, coordinate, and supervise in Washington U.S. nonmilitary programs for peaceful construction in South Vietnam—the entire other war.[51] Indeed, Komer's powers were substantial. He was authorized to draw support from the secretaries of state, defense, treasury, agriculture, health, education, and welfare; the administrator of AID; and the directors of the CIA and USIA. His authority extended as well to military affairs insofar as they affected the other war. Komer had responsibility for military resources in support of civil programs and for proper coordination of pacification with the deployment of combat forces and the conduct of military operations. The mission in Saigon was also to support him. Komer had direct communications with Porter. The president made it clear that Komer's authority was not just pro forma, announcing that Komer "will have direct access to me at all times."[52] Johnson wanted results, exhorting Komer to "keep those reports coming and let's list some achievements later."[53]

Wishing to manage the other war and not a large staff, Komer handpicked a small group of people experienced in pacification to work for him. Lieut. Col. Robert Montague, who had worked with Westmoreland on *Hop Tac,* was his executive officer. Ambassador William Leonhart served as deputy. Under them were Richard Holbrooke, formerly Porter's special assistant; Charles Cooper and Richard Moorsteen from the Rand Corporation; Al Williams from the Budget Bureau; and Peter Rosenblatt from the White House. Komer also replaced the Vietnam Coordinating Committee with an advisory committee that periodically met with him.[54] Komer set out to solve problems, prodding officials in Washington and Saigon. Forceful, persistent, and intolerant of bureaucratic delays, he earned the nickname "Blowtorch" from Lodge, who did not always appreciate Komer's tactics.

To ease congestion in the port of Saigon, which delayed the delivery of supplies and equipment for the pacification program, he persuaded the president to have the U.S. Army take over unloading operations from AID. Komer had concluded that AID lacked the experience and ability to handle the mammoth logistical problems of war, something the U.S. Army was trained to do. He had complained to Porter that he was baffled by AID's inability to account for most of the goods in the supply pipeline or to provide usable data for levies on the military, telling him that "McNamara wants facts so he can issue orders."[55] Komer had warned that the White House could ill-afford to wait eighteen months for AID to devise an efficient port operation. Under the new arrangement, the army brought in heavy cranes and a transportation battalion to operate the ports and cleared up the backlog. A pleased president exclaimed, "Bob, keep it up and keep it hot."[56]

Looking for Solutions

Encouraged by the RD Cadre's promise, Porter and Komer wanted to expand it. They desired in mid-1966 to open a second training center, doubling the number of cadres trained each year from nineteen thousand to thirty-nine thousand.[57] Other Americans took a dim view. Given the size of the adult population under Saigon's control, General Westmoreland feared a major expansion of the RD would come at the expense of the Popular Forces, leaving fewer security forces to protect the villages. In Washington, Assistant Secretary of Defense for International Security Affairs John McNaughton and General Earle Wheeler agreed that a larger cadre program might diminish the territorial forces.[58] The CIA, which oversaw the RD program, likewise doubted that South Vietnam's demographics could support expansion.[59] The pool of available South Vietnamese roughly correlated with the population over which the government ruled. Various South Vietnamese military and civilian agencies competed for the limited supply of skilled or trained people from this pool. The Johnson administration, faced with congressional opposition to a larger CIA budget to fund the expansion and doubts about South Vietnam's labor pool, vetoed a second training center.[60] Komer and Porter lost this battle but won another.

Both Ambassador Porter and Komer believed that with enhanced security, the cadres teams would be less vulnerable to attack and become more effective. Porter and Komer wanted South Vietnam's military to increase its support of the cadres and made that goal a high priority in dealings with Saigon officials. General Westmoreland also pressed the JGS chief to increase the amount of military support for the program.[61]

With this combined push from the Americans, the government agreed. At a Manila conference in October 1966, Prime Minister Ky announced that half of ARVN's battalions (about fifty) would provide security for priority areas where RD teams operated. By the end of 1966, the government had designated individual ARVN battalions for special missions, mostly clear-and-hold operations that sought to move enemy forces away from populated areas and secure them so that government cadres could work safely in the villages.[62] Ky also agreed to incorporate the idea into the 1967 pacification plan. By March 1967, ARVN had purportedly committed fifty-three maneuver battalions to the program, although probably fewer battalions actually provided support. ARVN and RF/PF units began to receive training in revolutionary development in addition to their normal instruction. Saigon could take this important pacification step because American ground forces had assumed responsibility for most of the main force war.

Ky's decision displeased some ARVN officers. They had come to resent being relegated to what they considered a less important role, pacification support, while the armed forces of their allies, the Americans and South Koreans primarily, concentrated on combating the enemy's large units. Being assigned to pacification duty made many ARVN company and field grade officers feel subordinate to the very forces that had come to South Vietnam ostensibly to assist them.[63] The United States pushed its ally to carry out an important pacification role, but it was not one that the South Vietnamese took on voluntarily. Not surprisingly, ARVN's support of the RD was often pro forma.

As the president's senior pacification official, Komer bent his major effort at improving American support. With more resources and better management, the Americans would be in a better position to help the South Vietnamese establish a viable pacification program. Much of his thinking was influenced by an army study undertaken in 1965 at the request of Chief of Staff General Harold K. Johnson. Titled "The Program for the Pacification and Long Term Development in Vietnam," or PROVN, the study was completed in March 1966. In looking at U.S. conduct of the war, it could find "no unified effective pattern" to American actions. With regard to pacification, the study concluded that poor interagency coordination hampered American support. Among many recommendations, PROVN advocated greater prominence for pacification within the framework of the allied war effort and unequivocal authority for the ambassador as the single manager of all U.S. activities in South Vietnam.[64] After several months as special assistant, Komer acknowledged that "most of my ideas have been borrowed liberally from the people and studies which impressed me—especially the PROVN Study."[65]

In the spring and summer of 1966, Komer and his assistants made several trips to South Vietnam on behalf of the president. These visits convinced him that the civil side of the war continued to suffer because of apathy at high levels in Washington agencies and poor organization and management in Saigon. Porter's staff was too small to accomplish what Washington expected, and Lodge burdened Porter with virtually all the administrative functions of the deputy chief of mission. The agencies in South Vietnam were unwilling to change their programs in the direction Porter wanted.[66] Komer wanted the chief executive to "prod Lodge and Porter into real action on pacification" and "keep the pressure on Saigon." Komer further argued that Porter ought to work full time, as Johnson had intended, on nonmilitary programs so he could tighten coordination of American political programs and mesh more closely civil and military programs.[67]

Instead of insisting that Lodge put Porter in charge of pacification, Johnson backed off. He requested that his ambassador submit "action proposals" on strengthening the "management structure" of the Saigon government *and* the U.S. mission to "clarify and focus pacification responsibilities at Saigon and in the provinces and districts." Presumably Lodge should have already taken such steps, so the president's charge could be seen as a sign of dissatisfaction. Nevertheless, Johnson refrained from direct criticism of the management by a Republican ambassador who was widely acknowledged to be an expert on pacification. The president, who earlier had enthusiastically urged Komer to keep the pressure on American agencies, warned him in August to "say or do nothing that reflects on Ambassador Lodge."[68]

An unwavering advocate of more funds and personnel for nonmilitary programs, Komer was convinced practically from the first of the need to increase the U.S. Army's involvement in pacification. In Vietnam, it had the largest pool of technically skilled manpower (engineers, logisticians, and advisers) and a large budget, and all elements of the organizaion were trained specifically to operate in wartime. More military officers serving as pacification advisers, easier access to army engineers to build roads and army logistics to provide arms and equipment, and greater reliance on army units to provide population security were in his mind possible methods of boosting American support for the other war.[69]

In frequent communications with Porter, Komer repeatedly urged the mission to levy support requirements on the military and to cadge resources from MACV. On one occasion Komer even suggested that Porter take a general officer, Lieut. Gen. Bruce Palmer, as his deputy.[70] For his part, Porter resisted pleas to bring the military further into pacification. He wanted and got a civilian deputy and countered Komer's many missives by proposing to civilianize advisory functions. In a nice reversal of roles, he asked for Komer's help in recruiting good civilians in sufficient numbers to eliminate the need for MACV advisory action in civil affairs at all levels. On the issue of the military's role in pacification, the two men were on a collision course. Porter wanted to push the military out of the way; Komer wanted it at center stage because of what it could get done.[71]

The disagreement seemed to intensify during the summer, with Komer's complaints about AID becoming more heated. There is, Komer wrote Porter, a tendency "at your end to regard our White House operation as properly confined to expediting requests from Saigon for people or supplies. ... This is not the conception the President had in mind in setting up our operation, nor the way I intend to play the game." In a second letter to Porter the same day, Komer continued in the same tone. Warning that he had to be blunt about the situation, because they were jointly responsible for changing it, Komer fired another salvo: "*The civil side is a mess.* Compared to our military operations, it's still farcical."[72]

At about the same time that relations between Porter and Komer had reached a low point, Komer drafted a very influential memo and circulated it to a few top officials in Washington and Saigon. Entitled "Giving a New Thrust to Pacification," the memo was a blueprint for far-reaching American organizational changes that synthesized Komer's ideas on American support for pacification, and sought to keep alive the notion of reorganization.[73] The memo came at a favorable moment. In August, Lodge revealed that he planned to leave his post in the spring of 1967 to enter the Republican primaries, and this news gave Komer an opportunity to raise the question of better management in Saigon and greater military involvement in pacification.[74]

The heart of Komer's memo contended that better management of existing re-sources offered the best way of enhancing the government's position in the coun-tryside. Komer proposed three alternatives. The first would give Deputy Ambas-sador Porter full operational control over all U.S. pacification activities, merging U.S. civil and military advisers at each level into a team under one chief. A direct chain of command would extend from the ambassador to the district senior ad-viser. The second alternative would retain existing separate civil and military command arrangements but strengthen management by placing a senior deputy for pacification in MACV and giving Porter a unified field operations staff. He would control U.S. civilians involved in pacification support at all levels. Komer's third alternative would assign civil *and* military pacification support responsibil-ity to General Westmoreland. The MACV staff would be restructured to include an integrated civil-military staff under a civilian deputy to the commander. A sin-gle manager would head an advisory team at each lower echelon. This alternative, the most radical, was his preference. Komer recommended Porter for the position of civilian deputy.

Komer's ideas found a mixed reception. McNamara and McNaughton both fa-vored placing pacification under MACV. Rostow also believed reorganization of American military and civil resources was in order. The mission apparently did not take the idea of reorganizing seriously, making no counterproposals or con-tingency plans.[75] General Westmoreland evinced little enthusiasm but directed his staff as a matter of routine to draft a contingency plan.

Sensing a more favorable climate in Washington, Komer began in Septem-ber an active campaign to shift pacification responsibility to the military. McNaughton and Komer worked out the tactic of having McNamara officially propose that the military take over responsibility for pacification support. McNamara circulated a draft memorandum for the president and sought the con-currence of other government agencies. The idea was to force civilian agencies to react to the idea of having the military manage American support of pacifica-tion.[76]

React they did. The State Department adamantly contended that the other war ought to remain in civilian hands. Placing pacification under the military would create the impression that "pacification had become a civil affairs/military gov-ernment matter, with all the overtones of the U.S. taking over in an occupied country."[77] Porter urged that Washington make no decision until the mission had made its own recommendations. He thought McNamara's proposal impractical and stressed that those with the most experience in pacification opposed military control most strongly. In his view, the military was less competent in civil matters and lacked the requisite political sophistication. In addition, he argued, the turn-over rate among military officers in South Vietnam was so rapid that "they have only a limited, recent knowledge of the situation and are handicapped in develop-ing rapport with the Vietnamese."[78] He warned of a serious reaction from Lodge if the administration made a quick decision.

In the face of unyielding opposition from the State Department and the embassy as well as AID and the CIA,[79] the president postponed a decision but decided to keep open the military option. To gather additional information, he sent Secretary McNamara, Undersecretary of State Nicholas Katzenbach, General Wheeler, and Komer to Saigon early in October. The civilians in Saigon misperceived the drift of events, believing that pressure for reorganization had abated. Rather than return to South Vietnam to brief the presidential party, Porter remained in the United States on personal business and let his new deputy, Ambassador Henry Koren, who had little time to prepare, discuss pacification. Komer called the experience a "fiasco" and felt it strengthened McNamara's desire to place pacification under the military.[80] Reflecting on the visit, General Westmoreland agreed with Komer's assessment:

> McNamara feels it is inevitable that I be given executive responsibility for American support of the [pacification] program. He is convinced that the State Department officials do not have the executive and managerial abilities to handle a program of such magnitude and complexity. I told McNamara I was not volunteering for the job but I would undertake it if the President wished me to do so, and I felt we could make progress. He stated that if this does not work after approximately three months, I could expect to take over.[81]

The trip had a significant impact on McNamara. In a lengthy memorandum to the president after the trip, he argued, as he had in 1964, for the centrality of pacification to the success of the administration's Vietnam policy. He concluded that the president needed to gird for a longer war because large-unit operations, bombing, and negotiations would not lead to a satisfactory conclusion of the struggle by the end of 1968. Progress in pacification, "more than anything else," would persuade the enemy to negotiate or withdraw. McNamara believed that a revived pacification program offered Johnson a way to conduct the war over the long term with lower risks and costs to the American people. The administration could not tolerate the continued failure of pacification, which McNamara called the talisman of ultimate American success or failure, and so he proposed consolidating the management of civil programs under a civilian. He set no grandiose goals for the proposed organization, merely that it produce within sixty days a realistic pacification plan for the coming year. (Lodge had been asked for such a plan in September 1965.) The principal benefit of the change, the defense secretary hoped, would be to shock the South Vietnamese out of their present pattern of behavior and get them to carry out the pacification program more effectively.[82]

On returning, Katzenbach proposed that Porter continue in charge, albeit with a military deputy to assist him. Katzenbach agreed with McNamara and Komer in recommending that the president put the embassy on notice. All three favored warning Lodge and Porter that the president would seriously consider placing pacification support under General Westmoreland if after a trial period of 90–120 days, the civilians had not pulled pacification together. The undersecretary of state's position signified that resistance to military management had weakened in the State Department. Komer believed that this latest test of civilian control was doomed. Rostow was inclined to agree but felt the administration could "afford a trial period to see if we are wrong."[83] In the aftermath of this trip, a consensus emerged within the administration that the military ought to take over the other war.

The president approved the recommendation that Porter remain in charge and informed Ambassador Lodge on November 4 that if this civilian effort failed, General Westmoreland would be made responsible.[84] On November 16, Johnson sent another reminder to a seemingly reluctant Lodge, telling him, in effect, to get on with the job as instructed. Writing personally to the ambassador, the president strongly and clearly expressed his preference: "Getting the U.S. military more heavily engaged in refocusing ARVN on the heart of the matter [pacification] is one reason why we have seriously considered charging MACV with pacification. I hope *you* will *ponder* whether this is not in the end the best way to achieve the aim you seek. I genuinely believe it is."[85]

The president's words deserve scrutiny. Aside from the barely veiled threat of a military takeover, Johnson carefully delimited the scope of the American military's role. The Americans would become not surrogates for the South Vietnamese but catalysts in getting them to do a better job on pacification. He also urged stronger management of the civilians from Lodge: "We depend on you not to let your people spend too much time in arguing details but to make them get on with the job." And in a handwritten note at the end of the letter, Johnson pleaded, "Make them all follow your orders." The president ordered Komer to *"Rush Double Rush"* the letter to Lodge.[86] In spite of Johnson's exhortation, Lodge was reluctant to draw up plans and did so only after Rusk, McNamara, and Komer reiterated Johnson's desire for rapid action.[87]

The president's decision led to the creation in Saigon of OCO, which would serve as a transition to a single manager for American support. Lodge announced the reorganization on November 21, establishing the new office as a kind of corporate subsidiary to the ambassador. Lodge's pronouncement brought to a close months of internal debate over the embassy's management of pacification support. Lodge still did not seek a deputy to relieve Porter of administrative chores, despite the president's repeated requests that Porter work full time on pacification support. That continuing burden and Lodge's absence for a month of home leave made it virtually impossible for Porter to spend much time shepherding the new organization.[88]

The decision to give Porter greater powers discomfited Lansdale, who complained directly to Lodge that the Special Liaison Office (SLO) was now "marking time out of the play." Although Lodge claimed he wanted the SLO to continue as senior liaison to General Thang, he refused to give Lansdale specific duties, saying only that he wanted the SLO "to help." What concerned Lansdale was not just his own loss of influence but also the drift of events. In his view, the massive advisory presence developing around Thang's ministry weakened him by creating an image of the RD leader as an American puppet. Lansdale criticized Komer as well for "attempting what McNamara had in 1961, run the tactics of Vietnam from 10,000 miles away."[89] Komer thought that Lansdale's operation needed to be better integrated within the mission. The establishment of OCO signified a diminished role for Lansdale's operation.

Advised by General Wheeler and General Johnson, Westmoreland speedily strengthened his headquarters' ability to support pacification.[90] On November 7, he established the Revolutionary Development Support Directorate, naming Brigadier General William A. Knowlton, secretary of the MACV staff, as director. The directorate would prepare MACV for the likelihood of taking over pacification support. If that occurred, it was expected in South Vietnam that Major General Weyand, commanding general of the U.S. 25th Division and highly regarded by military and civilians alike, would replace General Knowlton.

Yet even as OCO was being born, the mission was continuing to misread Washington's intentions. "I have never accepted the idea," Porter cabled Komer on November 10, "that these new arrangements must produce within 90 to 120 days or else." Komer responded pointedly, "Let me assure you that the president takes 90–120 days or else very seriously."[91]

Throughout 1965 and 1966, the president's personal interest in the other war was critical to its renewal. President Johnson committed himself to improving social and economic conditions both in the United States and South Vietnam. Economic and political development, aspects of pacification, were analogous to his cherished domestic Great Society legislation, and that was one reason Johnson attached importance to pacification. The chief executive had other reasons. Buoyed by the arguments of Bundy, McNamara, and Komer, Johnson regarded pacification as central to the ultimate resolution of the war—a viable South Vietnam— and a way to lessen American involvement and losses. In his November 16 plea to Lodge to strengthen South Vietnamese pacification, the president eloquently reminded the ambassador that more of "our boys" would "be gone" the longer the Americans carried the burden of the war.[92]

The impulsive decision to hold the conference at Honolulu in 1966 publicly and dramatically manifested his long-standing concern with the other war. Yet that same impulsive decision also revealed a leader hoping to counter criticism of his war policy with grand public gestures instead of immediate decisive steps toward resolving the underlying diffusion of managerial responsibility for the other war. In 1965 and 1966, he seemed not completely sure of how to realize greater emphasis on pacification, which in this period was largely a civilian undertaking. His alternating the ambassadorship between Lodge and Taylor, his hesitation in moving to military control of pacification support, and his reluctance to replace or offend Lodge seemed symptomatic of an underlying uncertainty. He wanted a balance of civilian and military efforts but made changes only reluctantly. The scope of American military and civilian involvement in South Vietnam had grown so extensively by early 1966 that the president could ill-afford to postpone basic decisions about how to run the war. His initial instinct was to find the "right man" who could solve the pacification problem rather than make organizational changes. He turned first to Taylor and then to Lodge to manage the country team. Disappointed, he then called on Porter and Komer, hoping by these appointments to get tighter control of the other war. By November 1966, when he wrote Lodge, the president was ready to make deeper changes.

Why the obsession with management? Management and organization problems were notions familiar to Americans in government and the military and were seemingly acultural, comprehensible to Vietnamese and non-Vietnamese alike. Management problems could be fixed with improved efficiency, reorganization, or the application of more resources. Management problems were amenable to U.S. strengths: technological superiority; its reservoir of trained leaders, managers, and experts; and abundant financial resources. Underlying issues, such as forging effective working relations with the South Vietnamese and developing an effective joint strategy that weakened the communists as well as built up the Saigon government, were less tractable to American strengths. The issues at the heart of the difficulty in South Vietnam would prove intractable in the long run.

6

Unifying American Support
of Pacification

The Office of Civil Operations was set up at a time when the president had come close to making the military responsible for pacification support. Headed by Ambassador Porter, OCO was accountable for integrating the mission's civil support of pacification. In terms of personnel and funding, the office remained essentially the offspring of AID, which supplied 54 percent of the budget, 78 percent of the people, and 54 percent of the commodities. The parent office in Washington provided administrative support. The second largest contributor, the CIA, furnished additional financing but a far smaller percentage of personnel and commodities. Nevertheless, OCO, containing nearly one thousand American civilians and directing programs costing $128 million, was far larger than any of its antecedents in South Vietnam.[1] Two members of Komer's White House staff, Richard Holbrooke and Lieutenant Colonel Robert Montague, on temporary duty to help Porter in Saigon, were largely responsible for designing the structure and operational concepts of the new office.

The Civilians' Last Chance

OCO unified the functions of the civilian agencies. It had authority to direct all American civilian staffs in Saigon concerned with pacification support and all American civilian programs outside Saigon. American civilians in the provinces were linked in a single chain of command, reporting to Porter. For the first time since the American buildup, American civilians in the field looked to one office in Saigon for guidance.[2] A notable exception was the intelligence-collecting activities of the CIA. In addition, OCO was to coordinate with the various agencies other civilian programs not dealing with pacification.

OCO consisted of six program divisions: refugees, psychological operations, new life development (provincial RD programs and programs for youths and sports, Montagnards, and social welfare), RD Cadre (to include training and census grievance teams), *Chieu Hoi,* and public safety (police) (see Figure 6.1). Responsibility for those programs shifted from their erstwhile parent agencies to OCO. Senior officials working on pacification were located together and in daily contact, a boon to cooperation. The civilian agencies now had a focal point for dealing with MACV, which enhanced their ability to coordinate with the military in planning for pacification support.[3] Since August, Brig. Gen. Willis D. Crittenberger had served as Porter's military deputy, but that link between MACV and the embassy bore meager results because, as Komer put it, Crittenberger was passive and Porter did not give him anything to do.[4]

At each subordinate level—region (corps), province, and, eventually, some districts—responsibility for civilian operations fell under one official who reported through the chain of command to OCO's director. The staff in each region was modeled on that in Saigon. Each province adviser was in charge of a team of six subordinates. Lodge hoped that granting the senior provincial adviser authority to write the efficiency reports of other civilian advisers, regardless of their parent agency, would help unify the advisory program. OCO also assigned an American official to serve as tactical area coordinator to each ARVN division involved in supporting pacification.[5]

Unification was not total. In general, the various agencies retained authority for funding the programs they had previously controlled. Logistical support remained with the parent agencies, not OCO. Porter lacked authority to transfer funds from one program to another, an impediment that hampered the reprogramming of money and resources to deal with unexpected problems. For instance, the CIA station chief retained veto power over planning, programming, funding, and operating the RD Cadre assistance program.[6]

As head of an organization with a life expectancy of around ninety days, Porter quickly needed to fill key positions. He selected the deputy director of the Saigon office of AID, L. Wade Lathram, as staff director, yet he had hardly settled into the job when, like Lodge, he left on a month's home leave. Porter wanted new directors for each corps and new representatives for each province, but he did not think there were enough senior civilians of the requisite caliber then in South Vietnam to fill all these slots. Many able civilians were anxious to return to their families and reluctant to extend their tours. In mid-November, Porter enlisted Komer's help. Komer directly asked Secretary Rusk, AID administrator William Gaud, CIA director Richard Helms, and USIA director Carl Rowan each for a list of twenty officers who would qualify as senior civilian representatives at the province and corps level, stressing that OCO's success depended on filling these positions quickly with talented people.[7]

Unfortunately for OCO, appointments were made slowly. Porter and Lathram selected the last of the senior province representatives only in mid-January. Near the end of January, Ambassador Leonhart regarded OCO and its regional headquarters as still "skeleton organizations." OCO had not yet requested that Washington agencies begin recruiting for 175 important positions on the Saigon and regional and provincial staffs.[8] The selection of John Paul Vann, the controversial

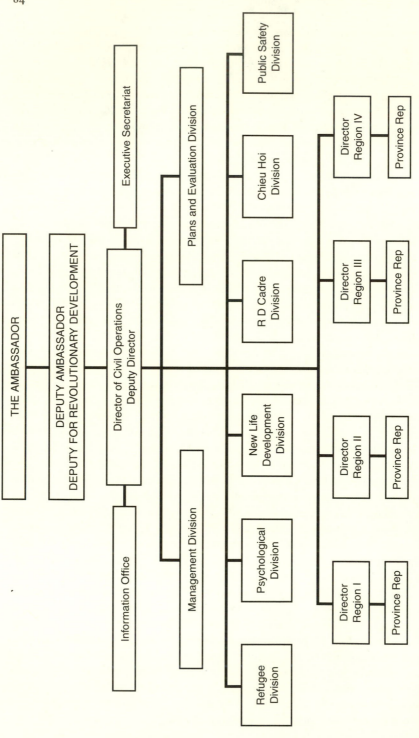

FIGURE 6.1 OCO, December 1966–April 1967

Source: Thomas Scoville, *Reorganizing for Pacification Support* (Washington, D.C.: GPO, 1981), p. 57.

former army adviser who had served in the delta in the early 1960s, as regional director for III Corps signified that OCO was serious about obtaining strong leaders committed to pacification, but time was OCO's implacable enemy. Not until February 1967 did OCO fill the 4 regional directorships—close to the end of the projected ninety-day life span allotted the fledgling office. Late in February 1967, about one-third of the authorized positions, many of them managerial posts, still remained vacant. OCO, like many other American bureaus in South Vietnam, never reached its full complement.

Obtaining highly competent people from civilian agencies that had just relinquished control of some of their programs, moving those people to South Vietnam, and familiarizing them with the special problems of the other war were difficult tasks. Finding and training suitable replacements for departing people also proved hard to accomplish. Many qualified civilians were reluctant to serve in South Vietnam because they perceived such an assignment as disadvantageous to their careers. Resolving personnel problems quickly while making visible progress within the allocated trial period verged on the impossible.

Understaffing was not the only problem OCO faced. Its authority and resources did not go far enough. The civil side of the war would continue to suffer unless it could call on the U.S. and South Vietnamese military, which Komer estimated had 80 percent of the assets. Integrated civil-military pacification plans, which were one way to get military support, lacked substance and were not binding. The 1967 combined campaign plan failed to make specific commitments of ARVN battalions or designate U.S. forces to perform pacification tasks.[9] Komer complained that Westmoreland operated independently of Porter and Lodge, making Porter's job impossible. At the end of January, Komer gave the president his assessment of OCO. "Porter can't be fairly charged with managing a pacification enterprise that is necessarily mostly military. The 90-day trial period will shortly be up without much more happening than consolidation of the civil side under Porter (long overdue, but not enough)."[10] Komer urged Johnson to get Taylor's and McNamara's views on what else needed to be done.

OCO, undeniably an improvement over previous organizations for pacification support, had no realistic chance of achieving the kind of results that would have assuaged its influential critics—Rostow, McNamara, and Komer. The root problems that the pacification program sought to overcome—insecurity and political indifference to the Saigon government in the countryside—were hardly amenable to quick fixes. The president and others recognized that. OCO consolidated civilian pacification support, but it could not really address the pivotal security question. That would have required added time to strengthen territorial forces and, most likely, more extensive involvement by American soldiers in clearing and holding populated areas. OCO failed to stem the inexorable drift toward military responsibility for pacification support. Komer continued to urge the chief executive to integrate the civil and military aspects of pacification under the auspices of MACV.[11] OCO had done little to deter the president from wanting to make the military the executive agent for pacification.

The Creation of CORDS

At the end of January, President Johnson began to plan additional changes. Both he and Komer viewed the single manager experiment in Long An province, which had begun the preceding November, as an important precedent. The president had Rusk, McNamara, and Westmoreland read a report on the experiment because it showed how "the Americans can start energizing the Vietnamese ... and how getting ARVN and the U.S. military involved in the security business is essential to results."[12]

Johnson's focus remained on making the U.S. military responsible for pacification support so it could help South Vietnamese officials do a better job. In February, Johnson went so far as to propose the appointment of General Westmoreland as ambassador, an idea that he must have known would invite strong dissent. By this appointment, the military commander would automatically gain control of civil programs. Predictably, the State Department objected. Undersecretary Katzenbach believed it unwise to enhance the U.S. military's position in South Vietnam while South Vietnamese authorities were under pressure to civilianize their government. He also thought such an appointment would confuse Defense and State command channels and complicate communications between Saigon and agencies in Washington. Katzenbach preferred that Lodge's successor be a civilian with "extraordinary political sensitivity."[13]

The president disagreed, telling Secretary Rusk on March 2 that he had decided to give "General Westmoreland the over-all task of Ambassador while maintaining his military command" and thus centralize American support of pacification. He wanted Ellsworth Bunker, a highly regarded diplomat, to serve as "Ambassador at Large, in Saigon, assuming responsibility for our political policy under Westmoreland's direction." Johnson asked for Rusk's help in persuading Bunker, who was then seventy-two years old, to take the assignment. Rusk dutifully discussed the matter with Bunker on March 4.[14]

The president's decision proved unworkable. Rusk quite properly objected to Westmoreland's appointment, as did McNamara. The thought of giving a wide range of political responsibilities to a field commander who was already occupied with leading a vast and complicated military force troubled Rusk and McNamara.[15] Bunker, convinced that such an arrangement was not "workable," was unwilling to serve under a hybrid general-ambassador.[16] Westmoreland had no interest in the position, realizing that an ambassador should be someone experienced in political and diplomatic matters.[17]

Faced with the understandably strong opposition of Rusk, McNamara, Westmoreland, and Bunker, the president backed off. Probably, the designation of Westmoreland as ambassador was a presidential ploy to get civilian acquiescence for the imminent military takeover of pacification support and to demonstrate how serious LBJ was about military control. Appointing a serving general officer as ambassador was so obviously inappropriate that civilian agencies vehemently and rightly resisted, but it showed them that Johnson was willing to consider extreme methods to realize his goal. The alternative of giving the military responsibility just for pacification would seem by contrast more reasonable and would be harder for the civilians to withstand. Whatever the president's motives, in mid-March he appointed Ellsworth Bunker as ambassador and Eugene Locke, then ambassador to Pakistan, as deputy ambassador. Komer, the president wrote, "will be specifically charged with pacification" and serve as Westmoreland's civilian deputy.[18] By this action, pacification support was put under the military. Komer had advanced that outcome in his seminal memo on pacification back in August 1966.

Komer, however, was somewhat discomfited at the new arrangements. From the end of January to early March, he fully expected a high-level presidential appointment in Saigon. After Johnson had made his decision, Komer felt slighted, confiding to the president he was "somewhat disconcerted and confused about the changed role you now have in mind for me. I had thought you intended to send me as No. 2 to run the whole civil side. The change in plans ... seems to downgrade me to No. 3 (or No. 4 coming after Westy), and dealing only with 'pacification'—a lesser role than Porter himself had."[19]

In addition to naming a new team to serve in Saigon (Bunker, Locke, and Komer), the president selected General Creighton W. Abrams to become Westmoreland's deputy and specifically charged him to improve South Vietnam's forces. Rostow expected Abrams to spend as much time as possible remolding ARVN into a first-class counterguerrilla force, a job he called the "guts of the pacification problem."[20] Abrams's appointment, which would give a strong boost to pacification, was significant in another way. In April, Johnson could not accede to Westmoreland's request for an additional eighty to two hundred thousand U.S. soldiers without, as Komer put it, "first making a crash effort to get more for our money out of the 650,000 Vietnamese Forces." The charge to Abrams represented a clear signal that the president wanted South Vietnam's forces to do more on their own behalf.[21] To drive the point home, Johnson also told Westmoreland that revamping and remotivating ARVN was "top priority business."[22] As in August 1966, when Johnson had resisted the notion of having Americans take a direct role in pacification operations, he feared that the South Vietnamese would allow the Americans to assume an even larger share of the war.

The March appointments presaged further organizational changes. Following the president's announcement, General Westmoreland and Komer met in Saigon and agreed on a series of guidelines that defined Komer's role and set the pattern for subsequent American organization. Not just a coordinator or an adviser, Komer was to function in effect as the component commander in charge of the American contribution to pacification. Westmoreland delegated to Komer alone the authority to manage the effort. This arrangement gave Komer access to the commander and gave Westmoreland the right to relieve his manager should he fail. More important, the arrangement invested in one person authority for both military and civilian pacification support. At Westmoreland's insistence, Komer was to be deputy for just one function: pacification. He was deliberately not to be called a deputy commander because the general wanted to be certain that no civilian would command U.S. forces should both Abrams and he be absent. Abrams would assume command in Westmoreland's absence.[23] Westmoreland made only a few changes in Komer's draft of the NSAM to assure his own control over Komer in pacification affairs.

Westmoreland and Komer decided the new organization would be a mixture of civilians and military from headquarters in Saigon to the districts, the lowest advisory echelon. Each level would have a single manager to establish a single chain of command as well as designate one official voice at each level for dealing with the South Vietnamese government. That manager would integrate civilian and military planning, programming, operations, evaluations, logistics, and communications. To achieve a smooth transition, Komer and Westmoreland agreed to meld existing civil and military organizations. The entire OCO would be incorporated into the new organization, which Westmoreland named Civil Operations and Revolutionary Development Support.[24]

President Johnson still had not signed the NSAM officially reorganizing American support of pacification when Komer, along with General Abrams, arrived in Saigon on May 4. The president wanted the support of Bunker, who had taken up his new post as ambassador in mid-April, for the transfer of pacification responsibilities to Westmoreland and the assignment of Komer as Westmoreland's deputy. Johnson did not want to impose changes without first enlisting the support of the officials who would have to carry them out. Nor did Johnson want to create the impression that he was weakening the civilian leadership in Saigon or compromising its right to be heard.[25] Bunker agreed that Komer would serve as Westmoreland's deputy for pacification, with the personal rank of ambassador, to supervise the civil and military aspects of pacification. Bunker also endorsed the idea of a single advisory chain of command and the principle of appointing the best qualified man, civilian or military, as senior pacification adviser for each region and province. On May 9, the president signed NSAM 362, which formally authorized the new arrangements.[26]

To allay the fears of the civilian agencies that the military would dominate the entire American effort, the new leadership in Saigon emphasized the roles that civilians would play under the new setup. Bunker sought to allay the civilians' fears of military domination under the new arrangement. He stressed that the military would now have a formal obligation to support pacification so that civil and military resources could be pooled under civilian control. He was emphatic that he would retain full authority for resolving interagency disputes arising from the change and would strive to see that neither the civilians nor the military dominated the new office. When he met with the press on May 11 to make an official announcement of the reorganization, the ambassador announced that he intended to keep fully informed about pacification and to involve himself in policy formulation. Komer also sought to ease the anxieties of civilians as well as still critics who interpreted the reorganization as a step toward further militarization of the American effort.

American military domination of pacification could not be discounted as a possibility. Pacification would now be run from within a large military headquarters that had little appreciation of the managerial style of civilian agencies. The assumption of military responsibility could be read as implying failure on the part of the civilians. The military services prided themselves on their ability to carry out difficult missions under duress, a self-ascribed "can-do" attitude, and to act and organize quickly and decisively. One astute observer in MACV headquarters, Brig. Gen. John R. Chaisson, USMC, who served as director of the Combat Operations Center for Westmoreland, believed at the time CORDS was set up that Komer's organization would have difficulty getting along with Westmoreland and the MACV staff. He later modified this view.[27]

After all, Komer had justly earned a reputation as a strong-minded individual and a skilled master of the Washington bureaucracy, the Blowtorch who relentlessly pursued his objectives. Komer had a trump card, which was unavailable to Porter, that he did not hesitate to play. His close association with the president gave him an intangible but invaluable advantage in dealing with MACV and the embassy.[28] Moreover, his new organization had already absorbed in toto MACV's Revolutionary Development Support Directorate. After arriving in South Vietnam, Komer actively participated in MACV commanders' conferences and hardly ever missed an opportunity to boost his programs or send proposals directly to Bunker or Westmoreland on issues that even remotely touched on pacification. Although Komer's assertion of an activist role for himself and his organization within MACV at times aggravated his military and civilian peers, it was a tactic employed to make CORDS's position in MACV visible and viable. For Westmoreland's part, he wanted to stress the civilian role. In naming the new office Civil Operations and Revolutionary Development Support, he deliberately gave the greatest prominence to the word *civil.*

An early indication of Komer's ability to function in MACV came in regard to his relationship with his co-deputy, General Abrams. The president intended that Abrams enhance ARVN's ability to support pacification. Abrams's charter and Komer's seemed to make them rivals. According to Komer, Westmoreland defused that potential conflict. As the U.S. commander, he continued to deal directly with the ARVN high command, building on the personal ties he had established over several years. Komer would focus on making the RF/PF into a competent local security force for the villages and pacification cadres.[29] Abrams would concentrate on improving ARVN logistics and erasing the shortages of supplies and equipment that afflicted RF/PF units. He would also launch a review of the RF/PF training program in order to improve the training regimen.[30]

A New Start

By MACV directive, Komer was responsible for "supervising the formulation and execution of all plans, policies, and programs, military and civilian, which support the government's Revolutionary Development program and related programs." His official title was deputy to the commander, United States Military Assistance Command, Vietnam (COMUSMACV) for CORDS, or DepCORDS. CORDS's unique feature was to incorporate civilians into a military chain of command. In building the new organization, Komer devised a single chain of command that consolidated control of pacification support. He exercised command of all pacification personnel from Saigon to the provinces. At each level, pacification advice and support were placed under one man. CORDS interleaved civilian and military personnel throughout its hierarchy. Of the province senior advisers, roughly half were civilian, and half were military, although the less secure provinces and districts tended to have a military head. The integration even extended to job ratings. Civilians wrote the performance reports of their military subordinates, and army officers evaluated the Foreign Service officers under them. In general, civilian advisers had military deputies and vice versa. Komer became the first ambassador to serve under an American military commander and exercise command responsibility for military personnel and resources. Without that authority, Komer feared that his organization would be absorbed into the military structure.

Komer worked to establish CORDS's independence. He won Westmoreland's approval to replace province advisers. Komer, in consultation with the Field Force commanders, the corps DepCORDS, and the chief of the CORDS staff, selected his nominees and then sent their names to Westmoreland for concurrence. By taking the leading role in the selection and assignment of province advisers, Komer sought to foster organizational loyalty.

In a move that significantly strengthened CORDS's autonomy, Komer won Westmoreland's approval to put pacification advisers and U.S. Army advisers to ARVN divisions into separate chains of command. John Vann, on whom Komer was to rely heavily for advice, had pushed the idea. He did not want the military interfering with or directing pacification support in the field, as had happened in CEDAR FALLS. Division advisers were excluded from CORDS to ensure that the province senior advisers actually functioned as the single managers for pacification support in the provinces and were responsive to CORDS alone.[31]

Komer pushed the idea of a separate chain of command for pacification further in order to stake out CORDS's area of competence. He pressed Westmoreland on the necessity of commanders observing the pacification "chain of command." Pacification issues requiring command attention, Komer insisted, should be brought up with the deputy for CORDS rather than with COMUSMACV or his deputy. Komer wanted corps senior advisers and U.S. division commanders to deal directly with him first on these matters since he was Westmoreland's deputy for pacification. This chain of command usually proved workable. The generals who also served as the corps senior advisers were occupied with the large-unit war and readily delegated routine pacification business to their DepCORDS.[32]

The CORDS staff, called Military Assistance Command, Civil Operations and Revolutionary Development Support (MACCORDS), resulted from the merger of OCO and MACV's Revolutionary Support Directorate and functioned as a regular staff section under the MACV chief of staff.[33] Lathram, formerly OCO staff director, became assistant chief of staff (ACS) for MACCORDS, and Brig. Gen. Knowlton became his deputy (see Figure 6.2). Although Komer usually observed the formality of working through the chief of staff, whom he outranked, in practice he often dealt directly with the CORDS's staff. Most of CORDS's business went through an unwritten channel: Komer (or Lathram) to regional DepCORDS to province adviser. The exceptions to that rule concerned questions of money and manpower and involved the corps senior advisers.

Apart from the CORDS staff, Komer relied on a small group of close advisers that served as an informal brain trust and independent channel of information. He picked Maj. Gen. George I. Forsythe of the army as deputy. In addition to backing up Komer and establishing good working relations with the other sections of the MACV staff, Forsythe often consulted with Thieu, whom he had known during an earlier posting. Komer's executive officer, Robert Montague, gathered information, frequently proposed new ideas, and analyzed staff reports for Komer's personal use.

Unifying support for the pacification program under the military did not alter South Vietnam's responsibility to carry out the program. The American role remained advisory. In managing pacification support, Komer developed close contacts with many ministers of the South Vietnamese government, making visits and exchanging memoranda and personal correspondence. CORDS sought to develop professional working relationships with other levels of the South Vietnamese government. Many CORDS advisers had offices alongside their South Vietnamese counterparts. These relationships formed an essential part of the institutional practices by which CORDS sought to influence South Vietnamese officials.

Komer had long held that local security was paramount to pacification. If sustained local security was to be improved under CORDS, then Komer and his advisers wanted the RF/PF under their tutelage, and they pushed for this. Komer had come to the conclusion that the territorial forces represented the single most important underutilized South Vietnamese manpower resource, demonstrably less well paid, equipped, and trained than ARVN. Involving those units directly in pacification would be a quicker and easier way to expand the scope of pacification operations than to augment the number of RD Cadre teams. Because of the scarcity of trained teams and limited facilities for preparing additional teams, the RD Cadre could cover only a small fraction of the hamlets of South Vietnam.[34] General Westmoreland agreed. He transferred responsibility for advising and supporting the RF/PF from the J-3 section (Operations) in MACV to a directorate within CORDS. No single organizational change was more important to the eventual course of pacification. It allowed CORDS to increase substantially the number of advisers and at last gave the pacification program access to forces that could provide sustained local security.

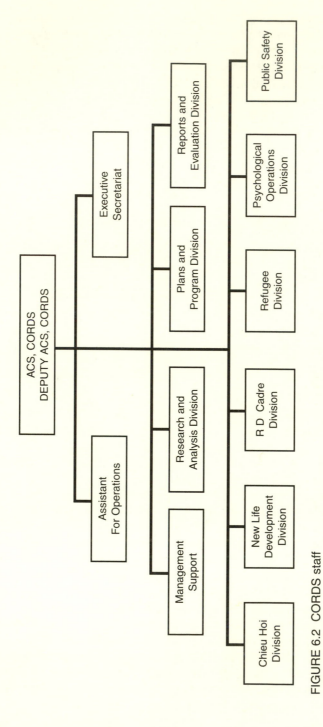

FIGURE 6.2 CORDS staff

Source: Thomas Scoville, *Reorganizing for Pacification Support* (Washington, D.C.: GPO, 1981), p. 59.

To get a better picture of the condition and location of the RF and PF, Col. Irwin Brigham of the CORDS staff chaired a task force that in mid-1967 devised a monthly measurement system to keep tabs on the strength and operational readiness of the several thousand PF platoons and several hundred RF companies spread throughout South Vietnam. Called the Territorial Forces Evaluation System (TFES), it required the American officials closest to the territorial units, the district senior advisers, to gather information periodically on unit strength, training, and equipment and forward the data to CORDS headquarters. This information would alert the staff to problems so it could take corrective action. The system, which emphasized the collection of such easily quantifiable data as number of radios or rifles per unit, had limitations. Important intangibles affecting a unit's combat proficiency, such as morale and the quality of leadership and training, eluded statistical measures.[35]

Almost all programs eventually came under CORDS: new life development, refugees, National Police, and *Chieu Hoi* from AID; RD Cadre and census grievance from the CIA; civic action and civil affairs from MACV; field psyops from the Joint U.S. Public Affairs Office; and responsibility for reports, evaluations, and field inspections from all agencies. AID continued to run its nation-building programs in such fields as public administration, economic stabilization (anti-inflation efforts and currency control), education, and public health.[36] The CIA agreed to yield overall direction and funding of the RD Cadre program to CORDS. CIA personnel in South Vietnam would assist CORDS in planning and budgeting for RD as well as for training programs under its overall direction. The transfer of responsibility occurred on April 1, 1968.[37]

As part of the consolidation of American support of pacification, CORDS assumed staff responsibility in August for U.S. Army civil affairs companies and oversight of army civic action. General Forsythe proposed to use the three companies (the 2d, 29th, and 41st) that were already attached to U.S. Army units in South Vietnam for a provincial-level civic action program. The companies' new role would be to help coordinate the civic action activities of American units with CORDS programs. A separate civic actions branch was established within the New Life Directorate of MACCORDS. The branch forwarded specific projects through the province adviser to the province chief for approval.[38] Employed as platoons and squads, the companies helped distribute food and clothing to refugees and worked with U.S. Army engineer units on local construction and repair projects.

Civic action represented only one aspect of CORDS's efforts to help improve rural living conditions; another was the program to open roads and waterways. In the first months of the new organization's existence, Komer negotiated with AID the transfer of that agency's roads and waterways program to MACV. Responsibility for the whole highway rehabilitation program and for liaison with the Ministry of Public Works was brought under the MACV Directorate of Construction (MACDC). Funds came from the DOD military construction budget. As a deputy to General Westmoreland, Komer regularly met with the head of the directorate,

Brig. Gen. Mahlon E. Gates, and Colonel Robert Clark, the chief of the MACDC highway division, to obtain U.S. Army engineer support to reopen roads so civilians could more easily transport their goods to markets. Eight U.S. Navy Seabee (Construction Battalion) teams of thirteen men were also assigned to rural roads projects. Usable roads were also needed to move soldiers and military supplies. Opening roads represented a clear example of a program that mutually benefited army operations and pacification.[39]

The CORDS organization for each corps was modeled on that of CORDS in MACV headquarters. The corps DepCORDS, usually a civilian, was a full deputy to the U.S. military senior adviser, a three-star general officer who also served as commander of U.S. forces in the region. The corps DepCORDS was placed above the corps commander's chief of staff and had authority to supervise the formulation and execution of military and civilian plans, including all aspects of South Vietnamese military involvement in pacification.[40] CORDS organization in IV Corps was different because fewer American combat forces served in the delta than in the other regions of South Vietnam. Elements of the U.S. 9th Infantry Division were the only American ground combat forces there. The delta had the greatest number of civilian advisers and was the only corps where Komer proposed that Westmoreland consider naming a civilian senior adviser. Also in contrast to the other corps, command channels there devolved along two broad lines: one for ARVN and one for the pacification advisory effort.

The province advisory team, unified under the province senior adviser, reported directly to the regional DepCORDS. The province senior adviser had operational control of all American advisers assigned to South Vietnamese units when they were attached to the province chief for direct support of pacification.[41] The district senior adviser headed the district advisory team and was subordinate to the province adviser.

Generally speaking, province and district advisers helped coordinate local military operations and combat support, provided advice to ARVN and South Vietnamese territorial forces, and assisted and advised representatives of the ministries of the central government on the entire range of pacification programs.[42] However, advisory roles were not fixed or uniform and varied from place to place. Advisers in relatively secure provinces, such as An Giang or Chau Doc, could concentrate on programs of economic development and be bothered only by occasional outbursts of terrorism. Army officers serving as advisers in heavily contested I Corps provinces, such as Quang Nam, had to deal with a serious armed struggle between NVA regiments and friendly conventional forces in addition to an active Viet Cong insurgency. Security concerns and the need to care for refugees of necessity preoccupied advisers in this region.

The demands on advisers were considerable. John Paul Vann, who would during the course of the war run the CORDS program in III and IV Corps, expected an adviser to become within thirty days of his arrival "the world's leading expert" on the functional and geographical areas of his assignment. At a minimum, Vann expected a district adviser to know in detail the district's political, social, educational, and demographic structure; the local economy; the strengths and effectiveness of all components of friendly and enemy forces; the strengths and weaknesses of local political and military leaders; the training and equipment of South Vietnamese forces (ARVN to police); the steps being taken to improve those forces; and the location of all friendly, contested, and enemy-controlled hamlets. Vann's list went even further, but he regarded it as representing "only a fraction of the knowledge" an effective district adviser would need to have at his fingertips.[43]

Although the size of district teams averaged around four persons, the provincial advisory units varied in number from province to province. There was no single standard organization for the province teams. The large province team in Binh Dinh, for example, had 37 civilians, 159 military personnel, 41 South Vietnamese, and 5 third-country nationals. In some provinces, the team was split into two main elements: one for civil operations and the other for security. In other provinces, the senior adviser divided his organization into functional subteams. Specialists within each subteam advised their counterparts. The operations subteam, for example, might consist of a senior operations adviser, an S-3 adviser, an RF/PF adviser, a psyops adviser, a civil affairs adviser, and a *Chieu Hoi* adviser.[44]

District advisers were also responsible for compiling the controversial Hamlet Evaluation System (HES) reports. Based on the U.S. Marine Corps practice of using a standard questionnaire, HES was approved by the Mission Council in December 1966. The system was an attempt to devise uniform quantitative data on the status of pacification in every South Vietnamese district. Each month, district advisers evaluated the military, political, economic, and social situation in each hamlet in their area. Regulations prohibited anyone, including superior officers, from tampering with the adviser's rating. HES ranked hamlets into one of six categories: Hamlets rated A, B, or C were considered under varying degrees of government control; hamlets labeled D or E were viewed as contested; and those listed as V were recognized as belonging to the communists. CORDS inherited the HES from Porter's organization. By July 1967, the system was operational, and by the following month the White House was using the data.[45]

HES evaluated each hamlet in six areas: Viet Cong military activity; subversion and political activities; defensive and security capabilities of friendly forces; administrative and political activities of the government; health, education, and welfare activities; and economic development. Three indicators or questions measured each area, for a total of eighteen indicators per hamlet. Each indicator had a range of six possible ratings (A, B, C, D, E, V), from strong government influence to VC control. The eighteen indicators were averaged to obtain the overall hamlet evaluation. Built into the system were criteria that higher headquarters had set in advance as a means of differentiating secure from insecure hamlets. For each indicator, the adviser selected the rating that he felt best described circumstances in the hamlet. The adviser thus had to interpret local conditions in the light of arbitrarily set standards.[46]

Although systems analysts in the Defense Department stressed that HES was designed as a management information tool to keep track of forces, weapons, and equipment as well as uncover trouble spots, almost from the system's inception officials tended to use it as a public measurement of progress. In the fall of 1967, the State and Defense Departments counseled MACV to delay the release of HES data to the press until other reinforcing statistics were available. The purpose was to "hinge evidence of progress not on one statistical series but the totality of evidence."[47] Unfortunately for CORDS, HES statistics came close to being identified as nearly synonymous with the course of pacification.

The leaders of CORDS tried to nurture close contact between different levels of the organization. To get firsthand knowledge of the situation in the countryside, Komer, Forsythe, Montague, and MACCORDS staff members routinely visited province and district advisers. In turn, province senior advisers would call on Komer and his assistants when they visited MACV to discuss local issues and obtain help in resolving problems.

Komer set up the Pacification Studies Group, a staff section of U.S. and South Vietnamese evaluators, to conduct field investigations. These evaluators were encouraged to dig for problems and make recommendations directly to Komer's office, a practice that sometimes irked U.S. officials in the field who resented the "snooping" of visitors from higher headquarters. Since the evaluators worked for the CORDS staff, they had immunity from pressure to hew to the local orthodoxy, and it was hoped they would offer a more detached perspective on the local situation than local officials. Like the visits to headquarters by field advisers, the evaluators' reports gave CORDS headquarters an independent source of information on the countryside. Their assessments supplemented the regular monthly reports of district and province advisers, which reached MACV through regular command channels.

In launching CORDS, Komer realized that building a strong relationship with General Westmoreland would be crucial. But by mid-August, Komer was feeling unsure of whether he had Westmoreland's "full trust and confidence." In a letter to the general, Komer said his ability to contribute was hampered because he was bypassed by the MACV staff, the corps senior advisers, and sometimes even the general himself.[48] The separate pacification chain of command that Komer had tried to institute was not working as well as he would have liked. Although Komer was bothered, he felt confident enough about his relationship with his boss to raise the issue directly with him. Komer believed Westmoreland grew to rely on him. General Westmoreland, so long as it was always understood that he was in command, over time delegated to Komer broad freedom of action.[49] The developing rapport between the military commander and the pacification chief gave Komer the chance to run an innovative program within the normally confining bounds of a military staff.

Unifying pacification support under CORDS had not resolved all jurisdictional disputes. The new pacification organization was barely functioning when AID attempted to retrieve some of its programs. In June, AID administrator William

Gaud proposed that Undersecretary of State Katzenbach support a narrowing of CORDS's scope and relieve AID from congressional accountability for the activities that CORDS assumed. Gaud wanted to provide the funds only to programs that AID fully controlled.

Komer viewed that move as an attempt to subvert the president's decision and return to the status quo ante CORDS. He tartly reminded Gaud that carving pacification programs to fit the peacetime jurisdictions of agencies in Washington had hampered past efforts and that was why the president set up CORDS. McNamara and Bunker as well as Komer successfully resisted Gaud's move, and AID remained accountable for the programs now managed by CORDS. By settling the issue before it reached the presidential level, the State and Defense Departments indicated their desire to give CORDS the chance to get started.[50]

After the formation of CORDS, Ambassador William Leonhart, who had served in South Vietnam in the 1950s, succeeded Komer in the White House and served as a Washington backstop for pacification support. Komer had hoped that Leonhart would be his alter ego and that the president would grant him the same title and broad authority that Komer had enjoyed, but this did not happen. After several months, Leonhart felt ambivalence. He never established a close personal relationship with Johnson and suggested that the president eliminate the special White House office overseeing the other war. Arguing that the major agencies— State, AID, DOD, JCS, and CIA—were supporting pacification adequately, Leonhart suggested that Komer's old post was no longer necessary and that oversight of the other war be returned to Rostow's staff. The president disagreed, directing Leonhart to continue overseeing pacification support from the White House. Johnson had no wish to reinstitute management of pacification by interagency committee.[51]

While running Washington support of the other war in the White House from March 1966 to May 1967, Komer advocated better and unified management of American support of pacification. During that time, he concluded that MACV should manage the advisory and support effort because of all American agencies or departments in South Vietnam, it could best provide the security necessary for lasting pacification. MACV also had the largest budget, the most people and facilities, and great influence on what was, after all, primarily a South Vietnamese military regime. Making Westmoreland responsible for supporting pacification would, or so Komer hoped, help reorient the U.S. Army toward providing population security and bolstering ARVN so it could better protect pacified areas.

To President Johnson and Komer, a military takeover of pacification support had seemed almost inevitable even as OCO was being established. Komer believed that taking the next step would end the confusion inherent in dual civil-military responsibility, provide significantly greater resources for pacification, and get Westmoreland to pay more attention to supporting the South Vietnamese pacification program. The president and Komer were interested not in having Americans take over another facet of the war but in using military funds and personnel to help improve South Vietnam's effort to gain control of the countryside.

OCO's short life, during which civil support for pacification was consolidated, proved to be the period in which the military takeover of pacification support was arranged.

In contrast to past pacification efforts, even to OCO, CORDS was a large organization. It derived power from the strong backing of the president. With expanded resources, the support of Westmoreland, and high visibility within the American headquarters, CORDS established a secure foundation. Most important, it had a single purpose: support of pacification.

With the establishment of CORDS, the president contemplated no additional reorganizations. With the unprecedented decision to place civil programs under the military, the public and press, not to mention the White House and civilian agencies in Washington, would expect tangible results. The new organization faced a jury that was at least as demanding as McNamara, Komer, and Rostow had been on OCO. After months of applying pressure on others, Komer now had to produce. Shortly before he left for Saigon, Komer wrote Johnson, "I believe that by this time next year we can break the back of the VC in South Vietnam—even if the war continues."[52] Could CORDS help stop the insurgency and help build strong, respected local governments where other organizations had failed? Would growing American involvement in pacification as represented by CORDS nourish or starve South Vietnamese self-reliance? Was it possible for the Americans, with their money, technical know-how, pride, and self-confidence, to restrict themselves to advising an ally that was inferior in financial resources and technical skills? Could they resist the temptation to become surrogates for their weaker partner? If pacification became Americanized, as the main force war had, it would represent a clear failure of the administration's policy to build a sovereign government capable of sustaining itself. The stakes for CORDS and Johnson's policy were high.

7

The Early Days of CORDS, May–December 1967

Establishing CORDS within the military headquarters in Saigon was no guarantee that it would escape OCO's fate. Placing a former White House official in charge of American support of pacification could not assure success. As the head of the new organization, Komer faced serious challenges. Getting military and civilian American officers working as a team was an obvious one. Institutional loyalties and long-standing bureaucratic practices had to be subordinated so that the new organization could develop a cohesive pacification program that countered all aspects of the Viet Cong insurgency.

Improved local security and strengthened anti-infrastructure efforts, two areas of weakness that had doomed earlier attempts at pacification, would receive special attention. The relative scarcity and low quality of local security forces restricted the possible expansion of pacification. The undiminished vigor of the VCI and the continuing potency of the guerrillas made problematic the shrinking of areas under communist influence. To deal with these challenges, Komer sought to consolidate management of programs and resources, enhance the influence of American advisers on South Vietnamese officials, invigorate efforts to combat the Viet Cong infrastructure, and improve the RF/PF. Shortly after arriving in Saigon, he prepared a plan to achieve these ends.

Project Takeoff

Komer took charge of CORDS with characteristic enthusiasm and confidence. He did not intend to become bogged down as OCO's leaders had in the process of getting organized and staffed. "I have come out from Washington," he told Ambassador Bunker early in May, "with an 8–10 point crash program to show better results in pacification. My intention is to start pushing it as soon as I am anointed."[1] True to his word, he directed the nascent organization to undertake a comprehensive review of all programs and set forth a series of eight "action programs," to use his phrase, that would help unify the management of pacification support. Komer dubbed this effort Project Takeoff, hoping it would elicit a more vigorous South Vietnamese commitment to pacification and induce local officials to conduct government programs more efficiently.[2]

Project Takeoff bore the unmistakable imprint of the man who had proclaimed himself "general manager of the subsidiary corporation called pacification." Takeoff stressed themes that he had long sounded: the debilitating effects of poor management and planning, underfunding, and poor coordination on past efforts. He sought to transplant in Saigon the ideas he had practiced in Washington. He wanted improved management oversight that analyzed progress and a stronger commitment from all levels of the Saigon government to pacification's goals. In Komer's view, the project would establish priorities and unify guidance from Saigon to the districts. As he expressed it, Takeoff was "the bible for what we pressed on the South Vietnamese all up and down the line."[3] Project Takeoff represented a way for CORDS to influence the South Vietnamese.

Although Komer had Bunker's and Westmoreland's support, obtaining Saigon's endorsement proved difficult. In June and July, Komer sought Ambassador Bunker's help in getting the South Vietnamese leadership to adopt Takeoff's principles and issue guidance about the project's priorities to provincial and district officials.[4] Concerned with the forthcoming September presidential elections, Thieu and Ky, who were running for office, had little time to launch a new pacification project or to ensure that cabinet ministers gave it priority. In the absence of an express top-level South Vietnamese direction, CORDS was forced to act on its own, bidding advisers and program managers in August to coordinate Takeoff programs with their counterparts. In other words, CORDS issued guidance to the South Vietnamese through its advisory network, hoping its advisers would be able to get local officials committed to Takeoff.[5] As an exercise in leverage, Takeoff was inauspicious since CORDS failed to convince the government to issue orders to its own officials. Without obvious, high-level South Vietnamese endorsement, Takeoff could be viewed only as an American effort.

Takeoff's eight action programs, which came under the overall direction of CORDS chief of staff L. Wade Lathram, were as follows:

> Improve 1968 pacification planning
> Accelerate *Chieu Hoi*
> Mount attack on VC infrastructure
> Expand and improve ARVN support to pacification
> Expand and supplement RD team effort
> Increase capability to handle refugees
> Revamp police forces
> Press land reform

These programs represented an effort to enhance ongoing activities. Aside from the new program to attack the VC infrastructure, the rest were already part of the

1967 annual pacification plan, which laid out South Vietnamese and American responsibilities. Of the eight Takeoff programs, the effort against the infrastructure assumed the greatest importance. CORDS actions in this area were largely directed toward the creation of a new, coordinated anti-infrastructure effort, the Phoenix program.

The first action program, to improve pacification planning for the coming year, represented an effort to codify the special initiatives of Takeoff and focus government ministries on carrying out a series of interrelated efforts that Komer hoped would bring greater coherence to pacification in the future. The government had not planned the 1967 pacification campaign as a unified effort; individual planning documents and plans—the RD guidelines, the province RD plans, and the combined campaign—had focused primarily on the RD program and not on pacification as a whole. While in the White House, Komer had criticized the 1967 plan as short on details. Combined U.S.–South Vietnamese planning was lacking. American influence on planning at the national level was negligible.[6]

Under Takeoff, planning for the 1968 annual campaign improved. The CORDS organization, through liaison with high-level ministerial officials in Saigon, played a critical role in sustaining a coordinated planning effort and keeping pressure on the government to clarify how it should organize and carry out the pacification process. CORDS also established a joint planning group composed of representatives of CORDS, AID, and the Joint United States Public Affairs Office (JUSPAO) to review pacification plans from all involved agencies and develop guidelines for 1968 that promoted more effective coordination of all related pacification programs. CORDS's position within the MACV staff made it easier to integrate military plans and those concerned with pacification, which was a failing of the 1967 plan. The combined campaign plan for 1968, AB 143, represented the fruition of the allied planning effort, integrating civil and military aspects of pacification. The plan represented the most comprehensive treatment of pacification to date, setting forth in some detail the responsibilities of South Vietnam's civil ministries and military forces.[7]

Pushed by the Americans, the Saigon government established in November a central RD council and subordinate councils at corps and province. The councils were to provide a focal point for monitoring the pacification plan, but few were functioning satisfactorily by the end of 1967. Although planning had improved, the ministries exhibited a chronic inability to make decisions quickly or effect minimal coordination with each other, factors that weakened the execution of plans.[8]

Chieu Hoi, another action program, showed some improvement. The government increased its spending on the program to 85 percent of obligated funds in 1967 from only 31 percent for the previous year. The capacity of *Chieu Hoi* reception centers doubled in 1967. CORDS also increased the number of advisers assigned to the program. During 1967, over 27,000 persons defected from Viet Cong or North Vietnamese forces. About 65 percent (17,671) were from military components of the Viet Cong, roughly about 20 percent of all enemy killed or captured.

The other 35 percent of the returnees had held political or administrative posts in the VC. The number of armed propaganda teams, defectors who encouraged other Viet Cong to desert, increased. During Project Takeoff, about half of the approximately twenty-six hundred armed propaganda teams received arms (pistols, machine guns, and carbines) by November. With more teams, a growing percentage of ralliers were actively engaged in fighting their former colleagues.[9]

Despite the program's potential, CORDS had trouble convincing the government that the rallier could be an asset. In 1967, only about fifty-four hundred ralliers received vocational training, and of that total over four thousand were trained by an American consulting firm or the U.S. Navy Seabees. The *Chieu Hoi* Ministry trained slightly more than one thousand.[10] Just as the government showed little trust toward them and did little to ease their reentry into South Vietnamese society, ARVN had difficulty viewing ex-members of the Viet Cong as new allies. In Hau Nghia, the province chief jailed defectors instead of rehabilitating them. He had the support of Major General Le Nguyen Khang, the commander of South Vietnamese forces in III Corps. In Phuoc Tuy, soldiers of the 18th ARVN Division were known to take defectors out of the *Chieu Hoi* centers and beat them.[11]

Improvement of ARVN's support of pacification had two overriding goals. One was to upgrade the effectiveness of units supporting pacification, defined narrowly as military forces providing security in and around areas where government cadre teams worked. During Takeoff, CORDS obtained authorization to add advisers, improved the communications and logistics capabilities of those forces, and established special motivation and training programs. The other goal was to increase the number of ARVN units actually supporting pacification. Between January and June, that number climbed from thirty-eight to fifty-three, and CORDS pushed a reluctant ARVN to provide even more.

ARVN's support of the cadre teams remained spotty. Although 90 percent of all ARVN battalions had received orientation in the RD program, ARVN commanders expressed little enthusiasm for providing security for the cadre teams. Operational results also aroused concern. From August to November, ARVN's nighttime operations, those most clearly linked to population security, were unsatisfactory. Slightly over 1 percent of them resulted in contact with the enemy. The rate for RF/PF operations engaging the VC after dark was about the same. This showing was especially disappointing in light of friendly forces' familiarity with local areas and knowledge of the Viet Cong's nocturnal activity. The obvious inference was that South Vietnamese forces were not trying very hard to find their foe.[12]

The effort to improve the RD teams showed mixed results. Inheriting oversight of this program from MACV and CIA, CORDS initiated and funded a new training program to improve the leadership of the cadre teams, got the government to accede to joint monitorship, and convinced the Ministry of RD to have local people, not cadres from Saigon, run the program.[13] In addition to the more than seven thousand persons who received regular RD training at Vung Tau between

July and December, over seven hundred graduated from the new course. Although recruiting of cadre members had increased during the latter half of 1967, reaching 555 teams and twenty-eight thousand cadre members by December, attrition from desertions, expiration of service, and casualties continued to be worrisome. At CORDS's urging, the government provided a number of incentives to stem the attrition. Saigon increased the rice allowance, opened the ARVN post exchange system to cadres, increased pay slightly, granted more leave, and improved the quality of the RD cadres' clothing. In addition, the government placed the cadres under the military justice system to deter desertions and unexcused absences. As of December 1967, however, these reforms had failed to reduce the number of cadres leaving the RD program.[14]

American officials gave village development, one of the tasks of the RD Cadre, high priority. But the Ministry of RD, showing less enthusiasm for developing local political and economic autonomy, did not. It neglected to assign a full-time official to manage village programs. General Thang placed the director of RD programs, Phan Van Quang, in charge of the village program in addition to other duties. Aware that the effort would suffer from inattention, Donald MacDonald, the AID administrator in South Vietnam, and Komer interceded, persuading Thang to allow Quang to devote more time to village programs.[15]

Another Takeoff program, refugee care, which CORDS inherited from AID, also faced serious problems. At the end of June, the strength of the refugee field staff stood at less than half the authorized level, new construction lagged, and temporary resettlement centers were overcrowded. Some civilian staff members resented what they saw as the militarization of a humanitarian program, although they acknowledged that CORDS's aegis brought substantial military resources to the refugee effort.[16] The root problem was the low priority Saigon gave to refugee matters. The neglect of refugee care was manifested in weak administration and a reluctance of province chiefs to make land available for resettling refugees.

Senator Edward Kennedy brought these long-standing problems before the American public. In May, August, September, and October 1967, the Senate Subcommittee on Refugees, which he chaired, held hearings on the plight of the refugees. (Congressional hearings in 1965 had also addressed refugee concerns.) Kennedy was convinced that official South Vietnamese actions reflected callousness toward the refugees and created resentment against the government that was trying to gain their support.[17] A powerful indictment of the current refugee program, the hearings had the effect of stimulating additional U.S. government action. CORDS felt the heat. To cope with these problems, CORDS doubled the number of refugee advisers in the field and pressured the government to give more attention to refugee affairs in the 1968 national plan and to remove three of the five refugee chiefs in I Corps.[18]

Other refugee issues demanded CORDS attention. No clear policy goals existed on the purpose of the program: whether to resettle refugees in secure areas or return them to their native hamlets. Nor was there consensus on the wisdom of deliberately generating refugees through military operations. The arrival of U.S.

Army troops in April 1967 as part of Task Force OREGON (composed of brigades from the 25th Infantry Division, the 101st Airborne Division, and the 196th Infantry Brigade [Light] under the command of Maj. Gen. William Rosson) in Quang Ngai and southern Quang Tin provinces highlighted the issue of intentionally displacing villagers. To spare them from the ravages of battle, the task force frequently moved peasants from their homes. Although responsibility for the care of refugees remained with local South Vietnamese government officials, many of them indifferently provided barely minimal care.

In response to Komer's prodding and criticism in the U.S. press and Congress, MACV modified its policy in the fall of 1967 and agreed that American forces, on an emergency basis, would initially care for persons displaced by military operations within their areas and assist government agencies. The command also stated that its units would not deliberately generate refugees, except in those few cases where the civil populace would be endangered if allowed to remain in areas where intensive military operations were planned. The MACV position essentially represented a compromise: It involved the U.S. military officially in providing some refugee care, yet permitted the relocation of people in special cases.[19]

The effort to revamp the police forces made headway. During Project Takeoff, recruiting rose, and police strength exceeded seventy-three thousand by the end of the year. The National Police Field Force grew to sixty-seven operational companies and drafted new operating procedures more oriented toward an anti-infrastructure role, but some province chiefs disregarded police directives about deploying units in villages and hamlets. During the latter half of 1967, the government replaced thirteen provincial police chiefs for inefficiency or corruption, but with no assurance that replacements would represent a significant improvement. Other actions to upgrade the police fell short. The South Vietnamese budget office withheld money for constructing additional detention facilities, stalling efforts to build prisons. Salaries remained low, encouraging venality. CORDS evaluators concluded that Project Takeoff had not significantly improved the level of police training.[20]

Further expansion of the police forces was difficult. Government manpower policies placed on South Vietnamese males aged eighteen to twenty-eight an obligation to serve in the military and prohibited the police from recruiting men from that group. The police could recruit veterans between the ages of twenty-four and thirty-eight, but those men could be recalled to military service. Low pay and keen competition with other government agencies for the best nonmilitary manpower meant that the police was often forced to accept into its ranks unsophisticated men unappreciative of the political threat or economically constrained people who might be induced to let security suspects bribe their way out of jail.[21] Police authorities had trouble attracting and keeping well-trained and experienced men.

The final action program, land reform, proved to be extremely nettlesome. The issue divided the Americans and the South Vietnamese and put AID and CORDS at odds. One of President Johnson's major concerns, land reform, had a comparatively low priority with the Saigon government, which feared it might alienate politically powerful, large landowners. If carried out on a large scale, land reform had the potential to shift the balance of social and economic power in the countryside. The government showed little enthusiasm in 1967 for such a change. In addition, despite President Johnson's support of land reform, U.S. officials in South Vietnam were not of one mind on the subject. AID objected to expropriating land in Viet Cong areas, which CORDS advocated, and opposed any land tenure changes in areas recaptured from the communists.[22]

Unable to forge a mutually satisfactory land reform policy with AID, Komer withdrew CORDS from further involvement. With Bunker's approval, Komer, in his own words, "waspishly" informed the White House and AID headquarters in Washington that "If, as, and when [a] new land reform program emerges, CORDS will support its execution in the field."[23] Until 1969, land reform would remain a relatively dormant issue as far as CORDS was concerned.

After several month's experience with Project Takeoff, Komer felt that it had served its purpose of pulling together the diverse American agencies and offices involved in pacification support. Although Takeoff had not uniformly improved the pacification program, it had channeled American efforts to obtain a stronger commitment to pacification from the South Vietnamese, an area where more obviously needed to be done. Never officially terminated, Takeoff became less important as the CORDS organization began to operate routinely. Several months of seasoning in Saigon had also convinced Komer that Project Takeoff was not sufficiently focused to serve as the prototype for future pacification plans. During its life, additional programs and reporting requirements were layered onto the original plan, obscuring its initial priorities. Rather than focusing CORDS's energies, Takeoff threatened to diffuse them. To concentrate CORDS's efforts in the coming year, Komer decided to reduce the number of action programs. Having brought a measure of organizational coherence to CORDS and established a footing for the pacification program, Komer was hopeful that 1968 would yield genuine progress in establishing Saigon's governance of the countryside.[24]

Takeoff provided a valuable service for CORDS, uncovering serious problems in the design and execution of programs. With problems sharply defined, CORDS was in a better position to find solutions. More money for the *Chieu Hoi* program only highlighted the persistence of the government's hands-off attitude toward the defectors. ARVN units showed little enthusiasm for supporting the work of the cadre teams. Desertions and low-quality recruits weakened the RD program, limiting its expansion. The government's interest in carrying out village development seemed perfunctory relative to the high hopes of American planners. On the question of refugee care, Saigon's official attitude of neglect persisted. Land reform proved to be a lost cause during 1967.

Project Takeoff showcased Komer's style of management. His approach was to develop a program and then try to persuade the government to carry it out. His organization would monitor the program and allocate resources, attempting thereby to improve the performance of the pacification program. CORDS was a bureaucracy dedicated to finding ways, usually standardized programs or plans, to get the South Vietnamese to perform better in pacification. Yet it proved difficult to obtain a formal commitment to Project Takeoff from the highest levels of the South Vietnamese government. The critical issue was to develop competence within the government and get it to perform—a problem Komer recognized. But how much could CORDS realistically expect the South Vietnamese to do? Project Takeoff surfaced underlying problems that American managerial skills and enthusiasm could ameliorate but not solve.

Stronger Local Forces, Stronger Local Defense

Westmoreland's decision in May 1967 to give CORDS responsibility for territorial security forces was critical to its mission of helping the South Vietnamese deal with the insurgency. His decision made CORDS responsible for dealing with the threat to local security, a critical deficiency of previous pacification efforts. To counter this threat, Komer sought more advisers to help improve the underutilized RF/PF. He envisioned a more active military role for the RF/PF, with greater reliance on tactics of mobility. The additional advisers would enhance CORDS's ability to assist South Vietnamese efforts at bolstering local security and help improve RF/PF performance.

Mainly U.S. Army personnel, the advisers had several functions. They monitored American assistance programs, aided the South Vietnamese in planning and carrying out operations, and provided higher commands with evaluations of the local security situation and South Vietnamese performance. In recognition of their importance, Komer labeled them CORDS's "eyes and ears in the countryside"[25] and believed that additional advisers would help obviate the need for a major new U.S. troop commitment.

The need for more advisers for the RF/PF was undeniable. In May 1967, the American advisory effort to the territorial forces consisted of 109 soldiers in PF training centers, 32 in RF camps, and subsector advisory teams, comprising 2 officers and 2 enlisted men who offered part-time assistance. Those numbers translated into a ratio of 1 adviser for every 929 RF/PF soldiers. Moreover, the army assigned advisers on an area basis regardless of how many RF/PF soldiers were stationed there, whereas it posted the same number of advisers to each ARVN infantry battalion. The ratio of advisers to ARVN soldiers was 1 to 23. Thus, the RF/PF advisory effort was seriously understaffed.[26]

With good reason, Komer wanted more advisers and not just for the territorial forces. In July 1967, he asked Secretary McNamara for additional advisers for province, district, RD, and RF/PF assignments. The secretary granted tentative approval in early August, but the expected arrival date in South Vietnam was unknown.[27] This was too indefinite for Komer, who wanted the extra advisers as soon as possible. In August, he pleaded to McNamara, "You said you would help me get all the people and resources needed for pacification. I need help. ... In every category—district, province, corps, Saigon—we [CORDS] have shortages. ... And this is exclusive of the 3,000 odd additional advisers which I see as the best investment we could make in greater pacification and RVNAF effectiveness."[28] McNamara was responsive, approving 3,151 additional field advisory spaces for fiscal year 1968, roughly the number of people Komer wanted.[29]

Komer had McNamara's approval and Westmoreland's authorization to add RF/PF advisers but ran into an unexpected roadblock. The MACV chief of staff, Maj. Gen. Walter Kerwin, who had reservations about Komer's militarily unorthodox methods and the high priority for the RF/PF, proposed deleting over half the spaces designated for RF/PF advisers, believing the request to be too high. In an unequal test of influence between Komer (who already had the support of the MACV commander and the secretary of defense) and the chief of staff, Westmoreland, as expected, supported CORDS. He authorized 2,981 more advisers for CORDS by the end of June 1968—an increase of 128 percent over the 2,314 advisers then authorized. The most significant increase was in the number of RF/PF advisers, highlighting the dramatic growth of CORDS's involvement in local security (see Table 7.1).

Komer also lobbied for quality. In response, the Department of the Army, which supplied most of the advisers, sought to upgrade advisory assignments and attract officers with higher qualifications. With the arrival of U.S. Army units in South Vietnam in 1965, advisory assignments had become a less desirable means of career advancement than service with combat units. It was harder for officers serving as advisers to win awards and decorations than for officers serving with line units. Serving far from normal supply channels, advisers often had to live on the local economy and needed a higher living allowance. They were not rated by a general officer but by a colonel. General Johnson, the army chief of staff, conceded that advisers were in a comparatively unfavorable position when being considered for promotion.[30]

Undersecretary of the Army David E. McGiffert concluded that the army had failed to interest its best people in advising. He recommended that the army provide incentives for advisers, liberalized pay and allowances, and credit for command duty and joint combined staff duty in order to make "advising more competitive with other assignments."[31] Although General Johnson agreed with the idea of raising the status of advisory assignments, he cautioned that advising could not be elevated in importance above leading troops. Commanding troops to close with the enemy remained the army's core mission. The incentive program, which was implemented in December, included all McGiffert's proposals save granting credit for joint combined staff duty, to which Westmoreland had objected. In line with Westmoreland's and Komer's views, however, province and district advisers would in the future receive credit for command time.[32]

Nevertheless, CORDS would not receive the advisers as quickly as it wanted. Wheeler warned Westmoreland that filling advisory positions with personnel of the desired branch and grade qualification by the June 1968 deadline would be

TABLE 7.1   Increases in Advisers for CORDS

Advisory Level	FY 1967 Authorization	Increase for FY 1968	Percent Change
Province	1,088	266	24
District	1,118	472	42
RF/PF	108	2,243	2,076
Total	2,314	2,981	

Source: Fact sheet, MAC J-314, sub: MACV Advisor Authorization, 11 November 1967, CMH.

difficult.[33] The reasons were complicated. The Defense Department had established a ceiling on the number of military personnel in South Vietnam. Thus, an increase in advisers would require cuts elsewhere. Adviser training programs at Fort Bragg would need to be expanded. Also, by 1967 competing demands for manpower had become a serious problem. In 1965, the president had decided not to call up the reserves. His decision forced the army to rely on draftees, soldiers stationed in Europe, and units from the strategic reserve to meet personnel requirements for South Vietnam. The resulting personnel turbulence and shortages would add to the difficulty of finding the caliber of people that Komer wanted by June 1968.

Faced with unavoidable delays in obtaining advisers, CORDS experimented with the concept of deploying roving teams of advisers to assist the RF/PF. According to Maj. Gen. George Forsythe, who advocated the concept, mobile advisory teams (MATs), moving from unit to unit, would be the quickest way to improve the RF/PF, provide material support, and train the paramilitary on the spot.[34] They instructed the RF/PF in small-unit tactics and weapons training, emphasizing night operations, ambushes, and patrols. The MATs also covered the construction of field fortifications and indirect fire support.[35] To build on the experiment, Komer and Forsythe proposed that Westmoreland assign MATs to each district and have them upgrade the RF/PF forces there.

General Thang, who had moved from the RD Ministry to become vice chief of staff for the Joint General Staff, where he dealt with territorial security, was receptive. He viewed the mobile team concept as an improvement on the U.S. Marine Corps Combined Action Platoon (CAP) program, which operated in I Corps. He opposed the CAP concept because the South Vietnamese were "inclined to sit back and let the Marines" do the work. Since the MATs were mobile and small, local security forces would not become dependent on their presence. For essentially the same reasons, Komer also was not enamored of the combined platoons.[36]

With the approval of Westmoreland and Thang, mobile advisory teams were assigned at first to each province in the delta and later to all RF/PF headquarters and districts in South Vietnam—a total of 354 teams. Each consisted of five U.S. Army personnel (two officers and three NCOs) and two South Vietnamese. The teams moved from one RF/PF unit to another, returning to a home base only to refit and rest. Mobility also permitted better use of manpower because individual teams could cover more than one village or unit. They would provide more than local security; Komer wanted the mobile teams to train the RF/PF in anti-infra-structure operations as well.[37]

The activities of the teams were wide ranging. They participated in operations to clear settlements of the Viet Cong; consulted with RF/PF unit leaders; provided minor medical help to civilians; taught classes on weapons, tactics, and night pa-trolling for paramilitary forces; helped plan joint operations of American units and territorial forces; and accompanied RF/PF units providing convoy security. The MATs also helped defend settlements from guerrilla attacks.[38]

Westmoreland also set up mobile advisory logistics teams (MALTs), closely re-sembling the MATs, to improve the logistics capabilities of the territorial forces logistics companies in each province. One team was assigned to each area logisti-cal command, with one additional team each to III and IV Corps. A total of seven MALTs provided assistance and training in supply and maintenance problems and supervision of maintenance work. By year's end, several hundred MATs and MALTs had been deployed.[39]

To prepare army officers and NCOs to handle the unique work of the MATs, CORDS set up a special training school for them at Di An, a village in Bien Hoa province. Lieutenant Colonel Vernon Staum, of the U.S. Army, served as the first head of the school. A former district adviser, Staum was well aware of the special problems that faced army officers working with South Vietnamese military forces. Staum got the training program off to a promising start.

By December 1967, five months after CORDS had started operations, Komer had obtained the adviser incentive package, authorization for the desired adviser staffing level, and a broad operational scope for CORDS. CORDS believed it had the tools to develop the RF/PF into a viable security force.

Battling the Communist Underground

No single aspect of pacification was more crucial than the effort to dismantle the Viet Cong infrastructure—the clandestine communist command-and-control organization within South Vietnam that provided political and military direction to the guerrilla war. The infrastructure recruited manpower for the Viet Cong; engaged in subversion, terrorism, propaganda, and intelligence gathering; and collected taxes and supplies. A highly structured bureaucracy, the infrastructure sustained the communists in their long struggle against the government of South Vietnam. The infrastructure was also a direct political rival of the government. Defeating the infrastructure would give the Saigon regime the chance to build a political community without interference from its deadly adversary. Under Komer's direction, CORDS developed a new approach for confronting this covert organization.

Organizationally, the Viet Cong consisted of the People's Revolutionary Party, the National Liberation Front, and all allied associations and groups. The People's Revolutionary Party (PRP) of South Vietnam was established in 1962 to act as the organization for the southern element of the Dang Lao Dong. An arm of the PRP, the infrastructure operated at six levels—COSVN, region, province, district, village, and hamlet—and performed all governmental functions. Members of the infrastructure frequently served as heads of province guerrilla companies, district platoons, and hamlet squads (see Figure 7.1).

The infrastructure, like the Viet Cong movement as a whole, came under North Vietnamese control. Hanoi issued party directives that determined communist strategy and policy in South Vietnam, placed high-ranking North Vietnamese Dang Lao Dong members in command positions in communist organs in South Vietnam, and sent "regroupees" (natives of the South who were trained in the North) to assume leadership positions in the districts and provinces. Throughout the war, Hanoi infiltrated cadres into South Vietnam to join the infrastructure. The North Vietnamese also established a reunification department to administer all supplies and personnel Hanoi sent south to aid the VCI.[40]

American intelligence analysts divided the VC infrastructure into two types of personnel. They termed an unarmed member secretly affiliated with the party but openly living among the people a "legal" operative since outwardly he or she was indistinguishable from other law-abiding citizens. The other type, the "illegal" cadre, was an armed member, openly affiliated with the communists, who lived in heavily fortified villages or secret bases in the jungles. This category encompassed the top-level leadership up to and including COSVN.

The infrastructure had a well-defined hierarchy. The top-level executive leadership consisted of longtime communists who, because of loyalty and ability, had attained important positions and provided continuity and firm control. Midlevel communist officials at the villages mobilized the local populace and carried out the plans of higher headquarters. Below the village level the infrastructure was organized less formally, but part-time cadres could be found. Despite the somewhat less intense commitment from part-time cadres, the infrastructure remained tightly knit. The leadership exercised tight control of the rank and file and, depending on the local political situation, drew or exacted material and political support from dominated villages. To official American observers, the infrastructure's strong leadership; centralized, hierarchical organization; and iron discipline explained much of its success.[41] To them, the VCI was essentially a coercive organization. In contrast, some critics of American policy considered the VCI as part of a national revolutionary political movement that enjoyed popular support.

The VCI consisted of a number of agencies differentiated by function. At the province level, they were known as sections or committees. The Current Affairs Committee directed day-to-day activities. The Administrative Committee handled correspondence, and the Organization Section attended to personnel matters. The Finance and Economy Section collected taxes, prepared budgets, and allocated funds. Efforts to raise money ranged from formal taxation of Viet Cong–governed villages to armed cadres collecting money through intimidation. The communists collected taxes in crops or in cash and goods transported along VC-controlled roads and waterways. Other sections of the infrastructure dealt with

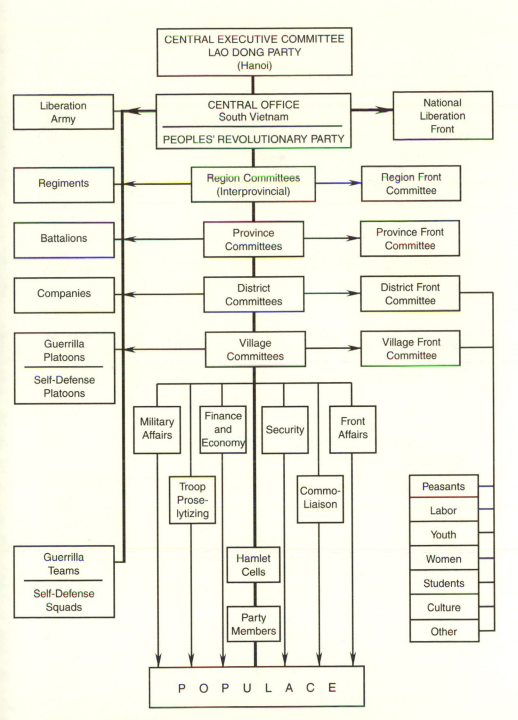

FIGURE 7.1 Communist structure of South Vietnam

Source: Memo, sub: Hanoi, the Lao Dong Party and the Insurgency in South Vietnam, May 1967, LBJ Library, NSF, VN, vol. 71.

logistics, propaganda, and proselytizing among South Vietnamese military and civilians. The Political Struggle Section tried to foment disorder in South Vietnamese–controlled territory. The Security Section ran the VC counterintelligence espionage network that operated within South Vietnamese security and intelligence offices. It was also responsible for the kinds of action that allied officials labeled *terrorism*—the abduction, assassination, or wounding of South Vietnamese officials or people.[42]

More than half the infrastructure's estimated strength was concentrated in thirteen provinces, which were grouped in three clusters. The first consisted of the five contiguous, coastal provinces from Quang Nam in the north to Phu Yen in the south; the second consisted of Kien Hoa, Vinh Long, Vinh Binh, and Dinh Tuong in the Mekong Delta; and the third, also in the delta, comprised Chuong Thien and An Xuyen. The remaining two provinces, Binh Thuan and Tay Ninh, were located outside the clusters. The provinces of great VCI strength were, not surprisingly, the same provinces with the highest friendly casualties.[43]

The South Vietnamese were responsible for the anti-infrastructure effort. From the early days of the struggle, the South Vietnamese police and security services had achieved little success in attacking the infrastructure. Although Diem had won some victories against the underground in the late 1950s, his successors had not. The NPFF, created in the mid-1960s, was intended to mount a strong effort against the infrastructure but had made little headway.

Although Saigon's anti-infrastructure campaign was unsuccessful, the communist cadres found themselves in trouble in 1966 and 1967. Under pressure from allied military operations, which were carried out in areas long considered Viet Cong preserves, a number of the best cadres, in the judgment of the CIA, had been killed or wounded or had defected. Their replacements were judged less able. This qualitative loss was most noticeable at the lowest level of the organization. Hanoi's decision in 1964 to shift some members of the infrastructure into military units deprived the VCI of some experienced personnel. Nevertheless, the infrastructure still remained a potent threat.[44] The allies could not ignore it or expect to destroy a highly organized, deeply rooted political movement through military operations alone.

Timely information on the infrastructure, essential for identifying and apprehending suspects, was seldom available to police officials. Duplication of intelligence collection and scant cooperation among South Vietnamese agencies hampered the work of collating and analyzing current information. The many producers of intelligence—the ARVN G-2, the Military Security Service, the Special Branch of the National Police, the Central Intelligence Office, the Provincial Reconnaissance Units, the census grievance workers—were usually separated from one another.[45] An array of interrogation facilities scattered in the districts and provinces added to the difficulty of sharing information that had been obtained from disparate sources. Province operations and interrogation centers, consisting of representatives of South Vietnamese intelligence organizations and their American advisers, were established in the mid-1960s. Jointly staffed combined intelligence coordinating centers were located in and around Saigon. Province interrogation centers supported by the CIA and operated by the National Police tried to synthesize information obtained from informers, prisoners, and defectors. But the absence of a strong central South Vietnamese intelligence authority that could direct the fight against the infrastructure at the working level allowed the wasteful duplication of effort to continue. South Vietnam's CIO did not effectively fill that coordinating role.[46]

The American side experienced similar problems. The CIA, by nature a covert agency, was reluctant to share information with the military. MACV's intelligence office, the J-2, was by training and organization more interested in the enemy order of battle and the military use of intelligence than in the collection and exploitation of data on Viet Cong subversion. By mid-1967, the South Vietnamese and Americans had begun to establish intelligence coordination centers in the districts. The idea was to integrate the efforts of the numerous South Vietnamese intelligence centers and agencies, but absent strong local authority, interagency disputes hampered the timely sharing of intelligence.

A unified anti-infrastructure campaign was needed. In view of the multitude of agencies involved, it was perhaps inevitable for the man who merged civil and military programs under CORDS to propose a similar solution to the fragmented battle against the VCI. When still in Washington, Komer had sought the CIA's recommendations for a new South Vietnamese program to strike at the infrastructure and asked for a study. William Colby, a high-ranking CIA official who had served as CIA station chief during Diem's rule and later would play a key role in CORDS, worked on the study in Washington. Although it contained useful material, Komer found it too generalized to serve as the basis of a program. He had concluded that police techniques were the way to attack the infrastructure and that the South Vietnamese needed an operating field agency resembling an American police station. Its primary role would be to coordinate the work of existing intelligence agencies and the police. New facilities established in the country's districts would gather and analyze information on the infrastructure from all intelligence sources and issue orders to field elements.[47]

The CIA-CORDS concept, developed during Project Takeoff, was first called infrastructure coordination and exploitation (ICEX). Under ICEX, South Vietnam's police would have primary operational responsibility for the anti-infrastructure program. An officer detailed from the CIA and working for CORDS under Komer's aegis would administer American advice and support. The Americans were to play an "energizing and advisory role," and South Vietnamese police units, particularly the NPFF, the Special Branch, and the PRUs, would both collect and act on intelligence against the communist underground.[48]

To carry out ICEX, Komer needed the backing of the American military, but he ran into opposition. Generals Walter Kerwin, the MACV chief of staff, and Philip Davidson, the new MACV intelligence chief, balked at the CIA-CORDS proposal, fearing it would establish two separate, competing intelligence systems and diminish the authority of the military intelligence staff. The two generals wanted the MACV J-2 (General Davidson) to assume responsibility for collecting and analyzing information on the underground and supervising the efforts of the CIA and CORDS, while also continuing to produce order-of-battle and regular military intelligence.[49] Komer argued that the J-2, having so many functions to carry out, would shortchange the anti-infrastructure program. Kerwin's and Davidson's opposition threatened to scuttle ICEX. The issue went to Westmoreland for resolution.

In a major victory for the new organization, Westmoreland supported Komer over the opposition of his staff. In doing so, the general concurred with Komer's position that the South Vietnamese police was better suited to attack the communist underground than conventional military forces and that CORDS, rather than the MACV J-2, ought to handle the advisory aspect of the intelligence effort.[50] The U.S. commander was willing to try a militarily unorthodox approach that delimited the role of his intelligence officer. His decision marked a significant point in CORDS's history. Komer later remarked that Westmoreland's decision did more than give the new organization an important role in the war; it put CORDS "in business."[51] Westmoreland's determination was as critical to CORDS's mission of supporting the counterinsurgency program as the one giving it responsibility for the RF/PF.

CORDS determined that the new anti-infrastructure program should concentrate on capturing full-time cadres and key leaders. Komer, Vann, and Montague were not enamored of county fair operations as practiced by U.S. Army units because they picked up almost everyone in a village from farmers to bakers. In July, MACV headquarters issued a directive for the ICEX program that targeted the communist elite. It established a hierarchy of ICEX committees consisting of American military and civilian advisers at each corps, province, and (eventually) district under the direction of a central ICEX committee. The committees were designed to focus South Vietnamese attention on collecting information on the leadership. Operationally, ICEX committees were to advise the province and district intelligence organizations in evaluating information so that the police could capture key members of the local infrastructure. The police, according to ICEX guidelines, would on the basis of fresh, accurate information seek out specific individuals or groups.[52]

ICEX was designed to conform to existing South Vietnamese laws and procedures on national security. Saigon's officials arrested civilian suspects and brought them to centers where interrogators would seek information of military value and determine the status of each individual. A security committee was established in each province, consisting of the province chief, the provincial deputy for security, the provincial prosecutor, the ARVN S-2, and representatives from the National Police, the Military Police, the Military Security Service, and the RF/PF. These committees were authorized to release suspects if there were insufficient grounds for trial. They could also send cases to court for trial or recommend detention or house arrest for up to two years. If the government had sufficient evidence, it could try suspected members of the infrastructure in accordance with

South Vietnamese law in either regular military courts or, more frequently, military field courts that traveled through each corps.

Within CORDS, CIA and AID public safety officials shared advisory responsibility for the police attacks on the infrastructure. AID advisers working under the direction of the chief of the Public Safety Directorate of CORDS were frequently retired Federal Bureau of Investigation (FBI) agents or former chiefs of American police forces.[53] The Public Safety Directorate advised the NPFF. A special branch of CORDS provided advisers, supplies, equipment, and funds to the Special Police. They also helped with technical advice on espionage and clandestine counterintelligence.[54]

JUSPAO agreed to provide psyops support for ICEX. Psyops techniques were designed to discredit individuals in the infrastructure by publicity that either exposed them or cast doubt on their reliability. Public identification of or even suspicion that an individual was a communist would, the Americans believed, render him or her less valuable to the Viet Cong or make it more dangerous for the South Vietnamese to cooperate with him or her. In either event, the person would lose influence in the village. Themes of the psyops campaign were coordinated through the local ICEX committees.[55]

American advisers in the district centers needed special training for what was essentially a counterintelligence, police-type assignment. Few U.S. Army officers had such training. In September, CORDS set up the first training courses for ICEX. A one-week intelligence adviser/agent/ICEX coordinator course trained military and civilian personnel for assignment to coordinator, staff, or field positions. CORDS wanted all ICEX personnel to complete the instruction by the end of 1967.[56] The South Vietnamese Combined Intelligence Staff also conducted a four-week course of instruction in intelligence gathering and analysis for members of the police.

In addition to the new training programs, CORDS wanted to establish an accurate and uniform field reporting system. Uniformity was critical since data came from a variety of South Vietnamese and American sources and passed through numerous channels. Evan Parker, a CIA official whom Komer recruited to manage the anti-infrastructure project, needed information on the Viet Cong to develop a full picture of the enemy's constantly changing *political* order of battle. CORDS required each province ICEX committee to list by name, position, rank, function, and party status (whether PRP, NLF, etc.) all Viet Cong cadres who were captured, killed, or had defected. The command wanted to base the report on all available information—South Vietnamese or American—and expected all members of the province team, regardless of their agency affiliation, to contribute each month. CORDS also expected advisers to provide copies of the report in South Vietnamese to their counterparts. CORDS intended the reporting system to facilitate the sharing of information.[57]

Despite these administrative efforts and constant liaison with Government of (South) Vietnam (GVN) ministers, by the fall of 1967 CORDS had not yet elicited South Vietnamese endorsement of ICEX. In a series of meetings in the summer and fall of 1967 with the minister of the interior and security, Linh Quang Vien, and the director general of the National Police, Nguyen Ngoc Loan, Komer urged greater police involvement in collecting evidence on specific important individuals. Vien was receptive; Loan agreed in principle but wanted to move slowly— much to Komer's chagrin.[58] Without a national-level commitment, district and province officials demonstrated little support for American initiatives.

Only after President Thieu's and Vice President Ky's election in September did the South Vietnamese government seriously consider the ICEX concept, and only in December, after six months of lobbying by the Americans, did the government take action. On December 20, Prime Minister Nguyen Van Loc instructed the ministers of interior, defense, revolutionary development, and *Chieu Hoi* to establish joint intelligence committees from the central to the district level "to carry out the mission of annihilating VC infrastructures." The instructions rather vaguely spelled out specific operational responsibilities. Provincial and district committees, for example, were responsible for conducting "intelligence activities" and "implementing the mission." The decree stipulated that the National Police still had the "main task" but went no further in saying how coordination would be effected or how police operations would relate to the committees.[59] The government called the ICEX program *Phung Hoang*, or "All-seeing Bird." The closest English term was *Phoenix*. After the December 1967 signing of the directive, the Americans called the South Vietnamese anti-infrastructure program Phoenix, not ICEX. The term *ICEX* passed into obscurity, while Phoenix was destined to achieve notoriety.

Thieu's decree enlarged the Special Branch's responsibilities for anti-infrastructure operations. It was expected to remain in a village, making arrests, recruiting informants, seeking to penetrate the infrastructure, and helping screen civilians detained for questioning. The Special Branch also maintained dossiers, prepared blacklists of known communists, and developed information on operations and enemy activities, which it was to forward to the provincial and district centers. The Special Branch became the main contributor of intelligence to Phoenix committees as well as the largest intelligence service in South Vietnam. Special Police officers also gathered information at *Chieu Hoi* centers from VC defectors. Loan and Komer hoped the Special Branch strength could reach fifteen or sixteen thousand nationwide.[60]

The initial euphoria that Komer and other officials felt when the Saigon government finally signed a formal decree soon yielded to more sober thoughts in early 1968. They realized that the decree would have little operational effect without the enactment of additional implementing directives that assigned specific responsibilities. In meetings with top police officials, Komer endeavored to have them disseminate guidance to the field, set up committees, establish specific procedures at the working level to smooth the sharing of information among government agencies, and develop an official reporting system to monitor performance and problems. In conferences with General Vien, Westmoreland and Komer urged the chief of JGS to encourage active ARVN participation in the district intelligence operations coordinating centers. They also urged President Thieu to do more personally to get the Phoenix program rolling. In one meeting with General Loan, Komer threatened to withdraw support if Loan failed to get Phoenix operations started quickly.[61] American officials at the staff level sought as well to end the government's inertia. Parker and his assistant, Colonel William Greenwalt of the U.S. Army, met frequently with police and Interior Ministry officials, getting them to write draft directives and instructions. The goal of the liaison effort was to get the South Vietnamese to accord Phoenix the priority the Americans felt it warranted.

But as of April 1968, the government's Phoenix effort still had a long way to go. The government had formed committees in 29 of 44 provinces but only in 31 of 240-odd districts. Meanwhile, CORDS had established committees in all provinces and throughout 100 districts. The government's slowness in forming district committees disturbed American intelligence advisers, for at that echelon the Phoenix program would succeed or fail.[62]

To make Phoenix work, the government had to be able to identify individuals in the infrastructure. To facilitate this, the CORDS Public Safety Division wanted the government to establish a national identification (ID) card and fingerprinting system whereby the police would issue "tamperproof" ID cards to all South Vietnamese over the age of fifteen. AID had initiated such a program in 1966 but had had difficulty in getting the Saigon authorities to act with dispatch. Following the establishment of CORDS, Komer personally advocated the system and made it part of Phoenix because he viewed it as invaluable in helping identify members of the infrastructure. The goal was a nationwide system to trace the movement of individuals in the infrastructure—for example, of someone arrested in Binh Dinh province who might later be recaptured in Lam Dong.[63] Although such a system would have been vehemently rejected in the United States, it was not out of place in war-ridden South Vietnam. It sought to remove the cover that covert communist operatives enjoyed.

Komer's idea proved difficult to carry out. For one thing, the government had too few people in the countryside filling out forms and taking fingerprints. It also took time to set up a national center in Saigon and train enough South Vietnamese to file and collate fingerprints. The government's inexperience also manifested itself in an inability in the first months of the program to keep track of captured members of the communist underground. After a suspect was taken out of a district or province for trial, further questioning, or detention, local officials could no longer account for him. As a consequence, local authorities often targeted or even processed the same person more than once because they were unaware of a prior record. Members of the VC infrastructure used numerous aliases, which complicated the work of intelligence agencies. They might unknowingly have information about the same individual under different names in different repositories without uncovering his identity.[64] Bribery of officials created another loophole.

Other South Vietnamese practices were not uniform throughout the nation, militating against the enforcement of personal safeguards and undermining the anti-infrastructure program. Authorities used the broadly phrased national security laws as grounds for incarcerating political opponents and noncommunist dissidents, while releasing known members of the Communist Party after they had served short sentences. For example, between January 1967 and the end of May 1968, province officials in Tuyen Duc arrested more than twelve hundred persons, released over one thousand, and sent no cases to the military courts. The province security committee tried sixty-three persons, passing the rest of those arrested to other agencies. Of those sentenced, a Dalat city communist official received a mere three-month term, a bogus *hoi chanh* who had seized a police weapon and given it to the communists was put in jail for six months, and guerrilla squad and platoon leaders earned the maximum two years behind bars. An outraged William Colby, who then served as head of the CORDS staff, reacted, "If this kind of activity can only result in a maximum of two years punishment, there is very little deterrence to the VC effort here."[65]

Unknown numbers of Viet Cong insurgents eluded the police. Enemy documents instructed VC youths and women how to pass through police checkpoints, noting that the "majority of the policeman accept bribes." "You can give them [the police] the excuse of visiting relatives, [or] running away from the battlefield, then hand them several hundred piasters, that will do for the escape during search and checks."[66] Even confirmed infrastructure members bribed their release. After gaining freedom, they could retaliate against those who had identified them or the families of the officials who had captured them.

Existing courts and detention centers were unable to handle the number of suspects. Accordingly, CORDS planned the construction of new detention centers to relieve overcrowding, and the government authorized four additional military field courts (one for each corps) to expedite trials. The South Vietnamese also expanded jurisdiction of the field courts to cover most civilian security offenses.[67]

The Thieu government's problems in implementing Phoenix stemmed from several causes. The inexperience and seemingly inherent inefficiency of the government itself precluded the new Thieu administration's being well enough organized by January 1968 to run a coordinated anti-infrastructure program. But unfortunately, the government was not even of one mind. General Loan still preferred to move slowly, and distrust and rivalry among South Vietnamese police and military elements continually hampered the cross-flow of information at the working level. General Le Nguyen Khang, the III Corps commander, supported the joint intelligence concept—as long as the military ran it. In his view, the Special Branch police at the district level were incompetent. John Paul Vann, now deputy for CORDS in III Corps, feared that because of Khang's attitude, Phoenix would receive little attention. The ARVN intelligence chief for II Corps, Lieutenant Colonel Nguyen Ton Nghia, received an official reprimand because he had helped establish a working Phoenix program before obtaining formal directives and guidelines. His superiors ordered him to stop, obviously reducing support for Phoenix in II Corps. Only at the end of May 1968 was Nghia allowed to resume work.[68]

Establishing a comprehensive anti-infrastructure program raised anew the issue of measuring progress. The number of communists captured, killed, or rallying or the number of district intelligence centers operating could demonstrate movement toward an objective but not disclose "how badly" the infrastructure was hurt. A smaller, cohesive, underground organization could still fuel an insurgency, albeit on a reduced scale. The elite of the infrastructure was the cornerstone of its strength and would serve as the source of its regeneration.

U.S. government agencies and the American military disagreed over the size and structure of the VC underground, making it difficult to measure. The Defense Intelligence Agency (DIA) and MACV intelligence disagreed with the CIA on the question of whether an estimated 10,000 to 30,000 nonprofessional support personnel at district and above should be counted as part of the infrastructure. Accordingly, the CIA estimated the size of the VCI between 90,000 and 120,000; MACV and DIA calculated a probable range of 75,000–85,000. Without an agreed estimate of the infrastructure's strength, there could be no universally accepted baseline from which to measure results. Disagreements over the infrastructure's size meant that claims of progress in weakening the underground could meet a skeptical audience in the CIA.[69]

Although CORDS successfully laid the framework for a stronger and more unified effort against the infrastructure, it faced continuing and considerable obstacles in getting a serious commitment from South Vietnam's officials to carry that effort out. Despite Westmoreland's and the CIA's support, Komer's efforts as of January 1968 had achieved no breakthroughs against the underground or even gotten the South Vietnamese to clarify the administrative details of the Phoenix program. To get the Thieu government to flesh out the basic directive with detailed guidance to local officials would require the continued application of leverage by the CORDS leadership.

In many ways, CORDS had laid a solid managerial and organizational foundation for supporting the South Vietnamese pacification program. Project Takeoff helped the new organization coalesce. Komer had obtained the mission of supporting the territorial forces and increased the number of Americans advising them. He had also won responsibility for combating the infrastructure and devised a new program, Phoenix. By these steps, he sought to rectify two serious deficiencies that had vitiated earlier pacification efforts—the inability of the Saigon government to protect the rural population from Viet Cong guerrillas and the government's incapacity to loosen the infrastructure's political and military grip on the countryside. With the Phoenix program and the responsibility for the RF/PF, CORDS moved closer to developing an integrated and comprehensive pacification program. By virtue of its ability to call on U.S. Army units and logistics support as well as its increased budget, CORDS was better equipped than its predecessors to support South Vietnamese–run programs.

These accomplishments begged the larger question, could CORDS use its advantages to get better performance from government pacification officials and ultimately realize the genuine progress that had eluded Saigon's earlier efforts to quell the Viet Cong movement? Project Takeoff and the struggle to establish Phoenix showed the government's failure to execute programs, underscoring that CORDS could do little without the government's support. In American eyes, the question of better performance on the part of South Vietnamese officials and forces raised the sensitive issue of leverage.

8

Leverage: CORDS's Quest for Better Performance

The exercise of leverage proved troublesome. Despite massive amounts of material and financial aid and the presence of over half a million men and women in uniform and a small army of officials in mufti, Washington frequently found it difficult to get the Saigon government to carry out U.S. plans or reforms. Nowhere was this more true than in pacification. Komer's attempt to use Project Takeoff as a way of influencing the government was an exercise in frustration. Coordinating American efforts and devising an integrated pacification effort were only the start of CORDS's work. CORDS's raison d'être was to get the South Vietnamese to improve the pacification program.

In the latter half of 1967, CORDS tried in various ways to enhance its ability to leverage South Vietnamese authorities at the ministerial and provincial levels. As used during the war, the term *leverage* encompassed a range of actions from seeking to influence the South Vietnamese by example, persuasion, and continual liaison at all echelons of government, to threats to withhold assistance, to direct requests to replace government officials. CORDS faced the monumental task of persuading the South Vietnamese, who had been at war with the communists for over a decade, to reform long-standing attitudes and practices. Getting the South Vietnamese government to put into office able leaders and middle managers, persons always in short supply, was an especially formidable problem because political and military leaders often rewarded loyalty above ability and integrity.

From the early days of American involvement, the issue of leverage had proved extremely vexing. To what extent and on what issues should American advisers seek to influence the South Vietnamese? At one extreme were direct management of South Vietnamese programs and control of their forces. In 1967, Brigadier General Leonard Shea, director of international and civil affairs for the army's deputy chief of staff for operations, argued that the policy of nonintervention in South Vietnamese internal affairs had "blunted the effectiveness" of the advisory effort. Americans would "have to override our extreme sensitivity to the stigma associated with intervention in the affairs of the GVN." The role of advising ought to be transformed "into one of directing on key issues" to prevent South Vietnam's failure.[1] Washington ruled out this policy because it would infringe on South Vietnam's sovereignty. At the other extreme lay the equally unacceptable alternative of granting aid and military assistance without oversight. Since American funds and materials were involved, U.S. advisers were accountable and had to be more than passive tutors.

Throughout the war, Washington sought a middle ground that encouraged the initiative of the South Vietnamese while holding them to some reasonable standard. As a support organization, CORDS walked a tightrope. It did not want to direct the South Vietnamese, nor was it equipped to do so, yet it took actions that directly involved it in South Vietnam's affairs. As Sterling Cottrell, senior CORDS adviser in the delta, remarked, although the South Vietnamese government desired to plan its own RD campaign, "without the hairy American hand, we *must* have our hand in it."[2] The growing numbers of American advisers working for CORDS brought fresh opportunities for reviving some leverage tools that had fallen into disuse and devising new ones.

The Waning of Leverage

Before 1965, American advisers could influence their counterparts through the troika signoff. Before releasing monies for South Vietnamese projects, the AID provincial representative and the U.S. Army sector adviser reviewed them with the province chief. The procedure embodied de facto veto power. AID abandoned the signoff in 1965, believing the procedure inhibited the development of indigenous management. With this decision, American advisers relinquished a means of influencing the planning and funding of South Vietnamese programs at the critical province level. The government implemented most programs here. Moreover, title to commodities passed to the South Vietnamese on receipt of the items,[3] making it more difficult for province representatives to see that the goods were used properly.

During 1966, the United States sought to revive a modified version of the troika signoff. The Mission Council set up a piaster imprest fund (with AID financing) for all district advisers. This fund provided a revolving cash account of 50,000 piasters, or $625, to finance projects that the subsector adviser (military officer at the district level), AID district representative (civilian), and the district chief jointly approved. The directive set forth general principles for using the fund: emergency construction or repair, employment of temporary workers for specific jobs, emergency interim assistance of South Vietnamese dependents, and rewards for captured weapons and personnel.[4]

The South Vietnamese cabinet objected. It feared the imprest fund might subvert the government's normal budget process and the work of General Thang's RD Ministry. But, like Diem in the early 1960s, the cabinet worried even more about dependence on U.S. assistance and too much American influence at the local level.[5] Thang in particular resented this fund because it openly circumvented the South Vietnamese administrative system by handling requests for funds through American channels, which in American eyes were more efficient. Thang felt American advocacy of the imprest fund directly negated the American policy of encouraging the development of competent South Vietnamese administration. In his view, the Americans espoused self-development but advocated policies that undermined it.[6]

Perhaps the most notorious example of how the South Vietnamese could deflect American pressures was the Chinh-Hunnicutt affair, a cause célèbre that erupted in December 1966. This contretemps revealed the difficulties advisers faced in eliciting satisfactory performance from their counterparts. Colonel Cecil Hunnicutt's actions as senior adviser to the ARVN 25th Division had angered the commander, Brigadier General Pham Truong Chinh. Chinh publicly accused Hunnicutt "of trying to have him removed, of attempting to dismiss other division officers, of bypassing the chain of command, and of destroying the 'spirit of cooperation between Americans and South Vietnamese.'" Chinh also complained that dependence on U.S. material assistance was destroying South Vietnamese independence.[7] The American command, which held Chinh in low esteem, wanted the government to replace him, but the division commander, an ally of III Corps commander General Le Nguyen Khang and Prime Minister Ky, continued in his post.[8] The South Vietnamese high command refused to reassign one of its generals at American bidding. The U.S. Army replaced Colonel Hunnicutt with another adviser, and the uproar eventually subsided.[9]

The affair, which revealed the sensitivity of the issue of leverage, prompted General Westmoreland to review American–South Vietnamese relationships. In December, he reminded advisers to avoid violating South Vietnamese pride and "to temper counterpart relations with patience and restraint."[10] In March 1967, Westmoreland urged advisers to develop close, harmonious relationships with their South Vietnamese counterparts, stressing that the key to the achievements of common objectives was "the complete cooperation of South Vietnamese officials."[11]

In the aftermath of the Chinh-Hunnicutt affair, MACV had set down a standard of behavior for advisers that reaffirmed South Vietnamese officials' authority and restrained U.S. leverage. MACV believed that too much pressure on the South Vietnamese would be counterproductive to American and South Vietnamese goals, which were inextricably entwined. MACV policy placed a premium on winning the cooperation of South Vietnamese officials, but that made it more difficult for advisers to persuade or force their counterparts to tackle serious problems, such as pervasive corruption, that negated efforts to improve public administration. The adviser faced a dilemma. If he was insensitive or too critical, he might alienate his counterpart, the individual responsible for carrying out pacification. If the adviser tolerated some degree of corruption and inefficiency, he risked condoning the status quo, which he was supposed to improve. The effective use of leverage required advisers with cultural and political sophistication. MACV policy was not really helpful in drawing a clear line between cooperating with the GVN and holding officials to reasonable standards of accountability.

Over the years, American officials in Saigon spurned many of Washington's proposals to improve adviser effectiveness through increased leverage (such as the encadrement of American and South Vietnamese forces in the same unit under American command) and tighter control of resources. Both the embassy and MACV were worried (as was Washington) about possibly infringing on South Vietnamese sovereignty and frustrated because that sovereignty permitted Saigon to resist or deflect American proposals. A State Department message laid out the issue and made a strong case for the limited use of leverage:

> It is axiomatic that we [the United States] are dependent on GVN mechanisms to carry out meaningful RD and nation building programs. U.S. does not have independent system through which it can independently accomplish significant programs. We cannot force Vietnamese to do anything they do not want to do, especially when we try to lever a local official to do what his superiors have not agreed to. The history on this is too clear to be ignored.
>
> We must accept reality of overall GVN manpower, piaster and administrative limitations. ... [The United States] must harmonize what the GVN wants to do and is capable of doing with modified ambitions on U.S. side relative to essential nation building activities.[12]

Who should exercise leverage and in what form were issues the State Department message left unresolved.

The Revival of Leverage

Leverage remained an inescapable issue, especially in view of the Johnson administration's desire to show that the war was not stalemated. Undersecretary of State Nicholas Katzenbach saw the period following Thieu's and Ky's electoral victory as an opportunity to increase leverage on the South Vietnamese at a time when more Americans were questioning Washington's support of Saigon. Katzenbach believed that the effects of increased behind-the-scenes leverage, if visible to the American people, could quell some of the criticism heard in the United States that the South Vietnamese government was corrupt and inept.[13]

Washington's interest in seeking better performance did not escape Komer's notice. He saw regular liaison with General Thang, the RD minister and most influential South Vietnamese pacification official, as a high priority. Shortly after arriving in Saigon, Komer sought to establish a close working relationship with Thang. "I hope," he wrote,

> we can communicate with each other with great informality and utter candor, avoiding formal letters except where officially needed.
>
> In this spirit may I address to you frequent informal memoranda like this one, asking questions or suggesting possibilities.

I would expect to do so in full recognition that the MORD [Ministry of Revolutionary Development] program is *your* program, and that I am merely an interested advisor.[14]

Komer hoped to reinforce the idea that he would not try to run pacification because his job was to support the South Vietnamese. But obviously, despite his coy disclaimer about being "merely an interested advisor," he anticipated an active role for himself. Considering the extensive American resources invested in pacification and his mandate from President Johnson, he expected the South Vietnamese to at least weigh his counsel carefully before they made decisions.

Following this, Komer took other steps "to exert more influence" with government officials in Thang's ministry. To inform Thang about CORDS's policies on a systematic basis, Komer directed Assistant Chief of Staff Lathram to assign an army officer to liaison duty with Thang's office and give Mark Huss (who had dealt with the general for months) the additional duties of monitoring the RD budget and keeping track of who saw Thang and on what business. Komer also initiated the general policy that CORDS officials meet with their counterparts in the ministry as often as possible.[15]

In addition to beefing up liaison at the ministerial level, Komer sought other ways to enhance the influence of CORDS officials. In May 1967, he asked the CORDS staff for an "action proposal" on the use of leverage that could possibly lead to a formal CORDS policy on the issue. The initial proposal was drafted by Lieutenant Colonel Volney Warner, who worked on Komer's White House staff and was temporarily assigned to South Vietnam. Warner sought to integrate leverage into nearly all procedures by which the Americans supported South Vietnamese pacification activities. He wanted the allocation of U.S. commodities and funds to be contingent on effective South Vietnamese use of resources and the execution at all levels of jointly agreed on plans and directives. To that end, Warner proposed that all advisers in the chain of command exercise control of program funds and have "the veto power of selective withdrawal of resources." Advisers would have broad discretion in deciding whether their counterparts were effective and deserved American support.[16]

Komer found Warner's proposal too diffuse and too sweeping to oversee effectively.[17] He desired focused and practical ways to exercise leverage. His reaction indicated a fresh sensitivity to the limits of American influence after several weeks of dealing with the South Vietnamese on a daily basis.[18] He wanted to use American influence to root out corrupt or incompetent province and district chiefs, proposing that the embassy develop a "blacklist" of government officials the Americans regarded as corrupt.[19] He chose this level because in his view it was where the exercise of South Vietnamese leadership was most critically related to performance.[20]

Komer's proposal evoked opposition within the embassy. John Calhoun, minister for political affairs, and General Lansdale, head of SLO, had strong misgivings. They were chary of compiling lists, which, if they fell into South Vietnamese hands, could embarrass the U.S. mission and hamper the work of advisers. In their view, the Americans should work through the institutions of the nascent government, encouraging South Vietnamese control and initiative. Direct American involvement in South Vietnam's administrative machinery, they believed, would stifle the development of these new institutions. Having autonomous South Vietnamese inspectorates uncover and remove dishonest officials was preferable to the rude intervention of the "hairy American hand."[21] They wanted the South Vietnamese government to learn how to handle corruption. However, South Vietnamese history since 1954 offered little hope that the government would take the necessary draconian steps.

There was a compelling practical need, Komer successfully argued, to act in the near term because months would pass before the South Vietnamese inspectorates were staffed and operational. The embassy agreed that advisers could compile lists of ineffective officials but reiterated that only South Vietnamese authorities could replace these officials. MACV directive 381-9 embodied the policy,[22] authorizing a quasi-intelligence role for advisers, who were encouraged to file reports on the actions of their counterparts.

The CORDS staff used information gleaned from advisers at corps, province, and district to prepare the first of numerous lists. The first list of officials whom CORDS wanted removed included 11 of 44 province chiefs and 33 of 200 district chiefs. Komer suggested that Ambassador Bunker discuss the names with President Thieu.[23] Occurring shortly after Thieu's election as president in September, Komer's initiative came at a propitious time because the new government was attempting to build a power base and fill government positions at all levels with Thieu supporters. Komer hoped to exploit the new regime's desire to install loyalists by pressuring it to replace the worst officials.

Unfortunately, political ties protected many corrupt or incompetent officials, who held their posts thanks to a powerful patron or group. General Chinh was held up as such an example. In another, the American advisory teams in Chau Doc, An Giang, and Kien Phong urged CORDS to ask the government to replace the chiefs of the *Chieu Hoi* program in those provinces, whom the Americans deemed incapable of performing their jobs. Yet the government hesitated, fearing the Hoa Hao sect might protest the removal of the chiefs, who were sect members, as an attempt to weaken the sect's influence. It was not uncommon in other instances for the government to transfer individuals to other positions in other provinces instead of dismissing them outright.[24] The government continued to deflect American pressure for reform and involvement in South Vietnamese political affairs.

Komer tried other approaches to make the high levels of the Saigon government function more efficiently. In September 1967, he advocated to Ambassador Bunker periodic joint review of the entire South Vietnamese budget. Since American dollars supported the pacification efforts of several South Vietnamese ministries, joint budget review would provide the Americans with a means to monitor the gamut of the government's pacification activities and a stronger voice in how personnel and funds were allocated. Komer realized that formal joint budget review might foster South Vietnamese dependence on U.S. budgetary and planning expertise but believed the process would on balance be beneficial by speeding the flow of funds to the working level. If provincial officials received sufficient funds when needed, the adviser could then concentrate on getting his counterpart to work on specific projects. Progress on those projects would serve as yardsticks for the adviser to evaluate his counterpart's effectiveness. This approach, like many other leverage efforts, was mechanical, but even getting officials to undertake projects was seen as helping overcome government inertia.

The attempt to review the entire South Vietnamese budget would have greatly augmented CORDS's authority. The review, which obviously impinged on South Vietnam's sovereignty, was not enacted. Lu Van Tinh, the minister of finance and director general of the budget and foreign aid, refused to go along. With a reputation for honesty and recognized technical competence owing to long experience in budgetary matters (he had held this key post continuously from the time of Diem), Tinh possessed considerable political strength and was instrumental in killing the proposal.[25]

Thwarted on the issue of formal review of the entire budget, Komer then tried using review of one key aspect of the budget, the American aid chapter (funds from U.S. government sources), as a lever to move South Vietnamese officials. This step would not require Saigon's ratification. Through budget review, the head of CORDS hoped to speed implementation of pacification plans and establish a precedent for direct U.S. monitoring and technical assistance in the area of planning and fund allocation. Komer justified such a review because the government's record was poor. Saigon was not even spending the funds it had on hand. The regime allocated U.S. funds budgeted for the refugee programs so slowly that only 13 percent of the aid appropriated for refugee programs in 1967 had actually been spent by the end of August. Moreover, the Ministry of Revolutionary Development by September had spent only 33 percent of the funds allocated for the calendar year. The amount of unspent money was a rough measure of government inaction and inefficiency. Fearing a "failure of implementation ... at the province level,"[26] Komer offered to assign American program and budget analysts to the RD Ministry and suggested that the government allow U.S. Army engineers to review U.S.-funded construction projects.[27] Realizing that the ministry needed American expertise to carry out the 1967 plan, General Thang agreed to this proposal, which largely restricted the American role to technical assistance in programming and engineering. Komer's plan was palatable because it did not directly infringe on South Vietnamese control.[28]

At the province and district level, Komer advocated that advisers use assistance in kind (AIK) as leverage. AIK was a fund of U.S.-purchased piasters that the Ministry of Defense allocated to cover U.S.-incurred expenses, such as local labor and local building costs.[29] Komer obtained AIK funds for CORDS advisers in September. Of the total of 3.5 billion piasters ($2,966,100) of AIK money, 1.5 billion ($1,271,100) were allocated to CORDS. With more money came increased influence. CORDS gave each province adviser AIK funds to cover emergencies or projects delayed by red tape. The adviser had discretion over the use of the piasters; CORDS supplied only general guidelines. AIK funds gave the adviser leverage because he could make their availability contingent on the performance of his counterpart. The audits of adviser accounts in turn became a lever on U.S. advisory teams. As Komer put it, "This was one indicator of which province teams were on the ball and which weren't. If you weren't spending you weren't doing."[30]

CORDS made other attempts to boost its leverage. In November 1967, General Forsythe wanted an American official to participate in joint field reviews of provincial pacification plans and cosign the plans. His recommendation would have given the Americans enormous influence and near-veto power over South Vietnamese planning and conduct of pacification. Nguyen Bao Tri, who succeeded Thang as minister of revolutionary development, refused to go along. He allowed that General Forsythe, General Knowlton, Lathram, or other representatives of CORDS would be welcome to accompany the official South Vietnamese entourage as it toured the provinces, but only as observers. "All final decisions," he bluntly told General Forsythe, "rested solely with his Ministry."[31] Forced to concede the point, Forsythe reminded Tri that he still needed to consult with the Americans if he expected them "to support his decisions." Despite Forsythe's effort, the attempt to require *formal* joint approval of province planning was stymied.

Although the American notion of joint approval of budget and program planning documents never became formal policy, in practice American advisers retained a powerful voice in planning. Behind the scenes, CORDS officials helped write the 1968 province plans and the annual combined campaign plan, AB 143. These documents required joint approval at MACV and the JGS. Moreover, the province adviser and the corps senior adviser assisted in the development of both the RD plan and province pacification plans. Despite the rebuff to Forsythe, Americans were thoroughly enmeshed in pacification planning and allocation of resources, giving them a strong voice in shaping the content of the pacification program.

American leverage schemes tended to follow a pattern. U.S. officials would assert a broad claim to monitor some South Vietnamese function. If the South Vietnamese resisted, then the Americans would settle for less sweeping authority. The South Vietnamese, sensitive to any perceived infringement on their sovereignty, would take a firm stand whenever they felt their autonomy was endangered. The record was mixed. The Americans established procedures for oversight, but the South Vietnamese could veto, evade, or thwart them.

In the first months of existence, CORDS had set in place a variety of techniques for improving South Vietnamese performance, such as regular liaison with officials in Saigon, review of plans and budgets, blacklists of ineffective officials, and use of AIK funds. Komer wanted to fortify the leverage role of the province adviser, a key pacification operative, because province advisers worked without general guidelines for applying pressure on the South Vietnamese to help ensure the execution of plans. Pacification would succeed or fail in the provinces.

In September, Komer circulated to his province advisers the leverage concept that III Corps DepCORDS John Paul Vann had devised. Vann directed each province adviser to write a monthly letter to his South Vietnamese counterpart reviewing past accomplishments and suggesting remedies for problems his counterpart could solve. Vann hoped this procedure would force South Vietnamese officials to resolve problems through South Vietnamese channels. The adviser's role was to see that his counterpart effectively carried out the directives and instructions of the adviser's superior.[32] If there was no improvement, the adviser would seek his superior's help. He in turn would try to persuade higher-level government officials to correct the problem. Komer adopted Vann's procedure as an interim policy and continued to search for standardized leverage procedures for advisers.[33]

In October 1967, Komer asked Sterling Cottrell, the DepCORDS for IV Corps, to prepare a pilot leverage proposal for Go Cong province. Drawing on MACV's policy of compiling dossiers and Vann's plan, Cottrell called for the application of increasing pressure to improve the performance of government officials or secure the removal of the corrupt or errant. The adviser would build a dossier on the district or province chief and try first through personal intercession to correct deficiencies. If that failed, the province adviser would send a formal complaint to the corps adviser, who in turn would make an inspection and bring the deficiencies to the South Vietnamese corps commander's attention. If South Vietnamese authorities still did not rectify the problem, it would reach Komer's desk. The U.S. adviser at each level would encourage his counterparts to take remedial action. The adviser would accumulate evidence to present to his counterpart. If all else failed, Cottrell suggested, the Americans should then suspend program support for the province or district. That decision would be made in Saigon and not in the field. It is noteworthy that Cottrell's procedure was to work within the South Vietnamese and the American chains of command and was designed to get the South Vietnamese to take action. Only if they refused would the Americans consider the unilateral step of suspending assistance. The procedure neatly balanced a respect for Saigon's sovereignty with the American desire to be involved in the government's affairs in an effort to improve performance.

Cottrell's proposal formed the basis of a leverage policy that CORDS issued in January 1968. Komer adopted Cottrell's procedures but not his proposal for suspending support. Komer decreed that CORDS would curtail assistance but would not "desert the GVN."[34] Komer feared that if he cut off essential support to a province chief, the Viet Cong would quickly increase its efforts against that province. Although Komer granted trusted deputies such as Vann some latitude in the exercise of leverage, he refused to give carte blanche to all advisers. The leverage policy of January 30 limited the adviser to collecting evidence. The decision to seek the removal of officials or cut off nonessential aid remained in Komer's hands because he was convinced that only at his level did the Americans possess enough "clout."[35] The leadership of CORDS would use its influence to have government officials removed only after province and district advisers had tried and failed to elicit improvements from the South Vietnamese.[36]

Komer tried to devise a policy that was workable, believing that some applications of leverage were administratively or politically unfeasible. After rebuffs over the issue of budget reviews and the directives for Project Takeoff, he concentrated on attainable, practical goals, such as replacing corrupt or ineffective officials. The scale of American financial and material support to the South Vietnamese, combined with the numerous U.S. civilians and Army officers in daily contact with the South Vietnamese at all levels, would do more, in Komer's view, to generate South Vietnamese responsiveness than the clumsy and arbitrary application of leverage.[37] The way to make the government more honest and skillful, Komer felt, "lies in better management which we must provide behind the scenes."[38] In effect, the leverage policy codified the procedures Komer and his civilian military staff had employed since the formation of CORDS. Better management "behind the scenes" sounded suspiciously like surrogate control. The tension expressed in Komer's letter to Thang between "helping" the South Vietnamese and compelling them to accept American ideas was left unresolved.

Leverage was central to CORDS's mission. Driving Komer's efforts to beef up his advisory corps, unify American support, and influence the South Vietnamese was the desire to achieve visible results in pacification. The reasons for wanting to demonstrate progress had political overtones. Having recently departed from the inner circle of the White House, Komer was fully cognizant of the need to convince critics that pacification was contributing effectively to the prosecution of the war and that the Johnson administration's policies would eventually lead to a satisfactory outcome.

The Balance Sheet at Six Months

As 1967 ended, CORDS could attribute some changes in the South Vietnamese pacification program to the exercise of leverage and months of liaison meetings. The Ministry of Revolutionary Development agreed to tighten joint controls over commodities for the RD program and prepare provincial plans on a three-year basis so officials would gain a long-term perspective on what needed to be done.[39] CORDS also obtained the government's acceptance of a system of geographic priorities for carrying out pacification. This important step would, it was hoped, ensure more efficient allocation of funds and cadres. Another positive step was the formation of the Central Revolutionary Development Council, composed of the cabinet ministers involved in pacification, to oversee government efforts at the national level and the establishment of similar councils in the corps and provinces. Unfortunately, few of the local councils were actually functioning at the end of 1967.

The government paid more attention to pacification in other ways. General Thang was transferred to the Joint General Staff as vice chief of staff for territorial security, where he gained control of the RF/PF and RD Cadre programs. In his new position, Thang was expected to improve coordination of the RD Cadre, the territorial forces, and the ARVN battalions supporting the cadres. Thang's appointment was part of Thieu's plan to develop two forces in South Vietnam: a regular army to fight large enemy units and a "pacification" army of RF/PF and RD Cadre teams.[40]

In the area of development, over ten thousand self-help projects, double the previous year's total, were carried out, and the amount of cash, labor, and construction materials that villagers contributed increased by 150 percent over the 1966 figure. CORDS set up a system of provincial warehouses, which the South Vietnamese initially ran, to provide logistical support for the self-help program. To help reduce corruption and increase American control at the warehouses, CORDS persuaded the U.S. Army to assign supply sergeants as warehouse managers.[41]

Arguably, the greatest shortcoming of pacification was a paucity of strong leadership at the district and provincial levels. The many programs that had to be implemented and the myriad problems facing pacification made it crucial for the government to assign experienced officials that were capable of pushing development programs and engaging citizens' participation. Such officials were at a premium. The ongoing Viet Cong terror campaign, which singled out the able, may have considerably thinned the talent pool, but the government's tendency to appoint to local office cronies with dubious reputations or little experience undermined the nation's long-term interests. Too often local officials improperly executed programs. Some province chiefs, for example, used funds intended for local, volunteer self-help projects to hire outside contractors to do the work.

Early in January 1968, after working with the South Vietnamese for over six months, Komer became more aware of the flawed nature of the government and privately expressed his misgivings that the South Vietnamese might not be able to overcome the seemingly ingrained handicaps. The new South Vietnamese ministries set up after Thieu's inauguration were neither well organized nor adequately functioning, clearly a necessary step, despite Thieu's repeated assurances that the new government would solve its problems in the coming post-Tet period. Komer and General Forsythe feared the pacification programs and changes Thieu had advocated remained hollow pronouncements. Ambassador Bunker shared Komer's and Forsythe's anxieties, believing that South Vietnamese bureaucratic inefficiency and inadequate leadership were the "critical variables" in the equation of victory.[42]

General Thang likewise voiced growing frustration with the inaction of the administration. He detected a "frightening reluctance" on the part of the Thieu government to exploit what Thang felt were good prospects for success. Too many of his countrymen, Thang alleged, were willing to sit back and let the Americans "bear the brunt of the war."[43] He saw three major problems: corruption in the provinces and districts, inefficiency at corps, and incompetence in Saigon. These were problems that only the South Vietnamese could solve. In January 1968, a frustrated Thang resigned from the Joint General Staff. Regarded by U.S. officials as one of the most able men in the South Vietnamese pacification program, Thang left office in protest over the entrenched power of the corps commanders and the disorganization and slow pace of the new government. To Thang's dismay, Thieu had postponed a reorganization of the armed forces that would have reduced the power of the corps and division commanders over the provinces and the territorial forces. To Komer, Thang's departure would be a major pacification setback unless a replacement of equal caliber was found.[44]

Thieu sought to reassure the Americans. He promised to show them by March 1968 the results of careful planning that, he said, had been proceeding since he took office. At frequent meetings with General Forsythe, Thieu took pains to bring attention to his methodical, unflamboyant nature. Thieu refused to act precipitously against corrupt commanders lest he endanger the national unity his government sought to foster. As for pacification, he advocated caution, desiring to expand control slightly in insecure areas while consolidating his government's hold over already secure areas. If Thieu's guarded approach did little to assuage Americans who were impatient and dissatisfied with pacification, his intransigence pointed out the limits of American influence.[45]

The Americans found themselves in a bind. Aware of the South Vietnamese difficulty in executing plans, the Americans could not compel Saigon to change. Given the fundamental problems facing the regime—a shortage of skilled technicians and efficient managers, the political influence of the corps and division commanders, a fragile base weakened by deep political and social divisions, the spotty military performance of the armed forces in prosecuting the war and helping run the country—the Americans chose to provide more resources and offered to help improve the way the South Vietnamese carried out programs. To the Americans, better management represented an essential step toward strengthening the operations of South Vietnam's government and a precondition for ultimate self-sufficiency. But the danger remained that the South Vietnamese would become habituated, if they were not already, to American largesse and resist reforms that would enable them to compete better with the communists.

American concern about South Vietnamese performance extended beyond the confines of South Vietnam. Officials also feared the effect of adverse publicity when the American press, which had refrained from criticizing the new government in its first months of existence, took up the issue of Saigon's inaction.[46] Komer, like the Johnson administration, believed that the longer the war dragged on without indisputable progress, the harder it would be to retain public support. The question that would loom large in 1968 was this: When would tangible and incontrovertible progress be made in pacification?

9

The Tet Offensive
and Pacification

1968 may not be just another year of grinding down the enemy. The indications that Hanoi is planning some kind of political initiative, plus its unusual surge effort suggest that Hanoi is shifting strategy too, which could make 1968 a year of surprises. Maybe the enemy can't stand attrition as well as we thought, maybe he's just seeking a respite to rebuild his forces. Maybe he wants a compromise. No one knows yet, but something is in the wind.

—Memo, Komer to Bunker, January 24, 1968

On the Eve of the Offensive

During 1967, American leaders in Saigon felt the tide was against the communists' forces. Allied military power had reached formidable levels. Available for combat were 278 maneuver battalions, 28 tactical fighter squadrons, 3,000 helicopters, and 1,200 monthly B-52 sorties. American military strength reached 486,000 troops during the year. American ground forces were well armed, well supplied, well trained, and mobile. By the end of the year, the total strength of South Vietnam's military had reached 643,000—an increase of 129,000 (about 25 percent) since the end of 1964.[1]

Thanks to firepower and mobility, allied forces could mount large operations inside formerly inviolate enemy sanctuaries within South Vietnam and keep steady pressure on enemy units. Even when inflated body counts were taken into account, statistical trends made clear the growing casualty toll. Estimated enemy combat deaths went from seventeen thousand in 1964 to eighty-eight thousand in 1967.[2] The Viet Cong also had to contend with understrength units and recruiting difficulties in the delta. The VC suffered losses not merely from battlefield casualties but also from desertions, disease, and defections—over twenty-seven thousand soldiers and political cadres in 1967—to the government.[3] Insubordination was reported among the Viet Cong in An Xuyen, a province where it had great strength. With the percentage of North Vietnamese fillers in Viet Cong units growing, Westmoreland estimated that by the end of 1967 half the enemy combat battalions had come from the NVA.[4] Friction arose between the North Vietnamese and the guerrillas and between the native southern cadres and the northern regroupees.

Under steady military pressure, the enemy resorted to unpopular measures. With the drop in recruiting and tax revenues, the communists increased levies in the areas they controlled. VC revenues were also lower because military operations had opened more roads to commerce, making it more difficult to tax goods in transit. In parts of the country, the VC taxed goods at their source, imposing a direct and onerous burden on the farmer. Most important, captured enemy documents indicated a decline since 1965 in Viet Cong–controlled population. An enemy cadre's notebook seized in January 1967 during Operation CEDAR FALLS estimated that the number of people living in areas under the Viet Cong's authority had fallen by more than 1 million between mid-1965 and mid-1966. A loss of anything near that magnitude represented a significant reduction of the tax and recruiting base.[5]

In addition, the long-term prospects for pacification looked promising. CORDS possessed more funds, personnel, and equipment and by sheer mass of resources seemed to be better equipped than its predecessor to wear down the insurgents. The South Vietnamese presidential and legislative elections of 1967 promised an end to political instability and, Washington hoped, represented the first step toward a broad-based popular government. Looking ahead to 1968, Komer focused pacification planning on four areas: improving further the RF/PF, pressing the attack on the infrastructure, helping provide better refugee care, and fostering the economic revival of South Vietnam.

Dismayed that little sense of American and South Vietnamese progress in the war had come across in press and television accounts, President Johnson asked Bunker, Westmoreland, and Komer in the fall of 1967 to "search urgently for occasions to present sound evidence of progress in Vietnam." To Johnson, persuasively demonstrating progress at that time was a "critically important dimension of fighting the war."[6] His reasons were largely political.

During the coming year, the president was expected to seek reelection, which increased the likelihood that the presidential campaign would become a referendum on American policy in Vietnam. An antiwar wing developed in the Democratic Party, and Senator Eugene McCarthy of Minnesota, a fellow Democrat, decided in November to challenge the president for his party's nomination. Johnson's immediate goal was to convince the American public and press that the war was being won, and he launched a public relations campaign to counteract what Rostow called the "stalemate doctrine"—the erroneous view expressed in the media that the war was deadlocked.[7] As part of that effort, both Bunker and Westmoreland returned to Washington in November and spoke before the U.S.

Congress, reassuring the public and the legislature that the allies were winning the war. Westmoreland promised success and declared that the "enemy's hopes are bankrupt." Meanwhile, Komer returned to Washington to rebut the stalemate doctrine in background sessions with the press.[8] American officials expressed confidence that the enemy was being worn down.

Despite the losses, the communists' will to continue remained unshaken. Vo Nguyen Giap, North Vietnam's minister of defense and architect of the victory at Dien Bien Phu, was convinced the war was deadlocked, a situation that favored Hanoi. He believed that growing hostility to the war in the United States threatened the American military commitment. In his analysis, American forces in South Vietnam, only 20 percent of which were in combat units, were stretched thin, creating an opportunity for a successful military blow.

A military offensive appealed to the party for two reasons. First, the high command realized that the trends of 1967, if allowed to continue unchecked, would jeopardize North Vietnam's objective of unifying Vietnam. Second, by imposing severe losses on the Americans, the communists could make the war even more unpopular in the United States and increase domestic pressure for withdrawal.[9] In mid-1967, Hanoi devised a new strategy for the winter and spring of 1967 and 1968 whereby NVA units would lure U.S. Army forces away from populated areas. This would allow local guerrilla forces to operate in populated areas and Viet Cong main forces to attack urban centers. The new strategy called for "continual attack," culminating in a "general attack and general uprising." The general uprising would occur wherever the opportunity arose: rural areas, small towns, or large cities. The ultimate goal was to "deal a decisive blow to the enemy."[10]

On the basis of numerous intelligence reports of unusual enemy preparations, General Westmoreland and his staff in late 1967 and early 1968 became apprehensive about the enemy's intentions. MACV expected some form of enemy attack or offensive in early 1968, most likely in the northern provinces,[11] but the American command doubted that the communists could carry out an all-out offensive and provoke a general uprising simultaneously. The CIA station in Saigon termed those goals "unattainable" within the "specific and short period of time"— namely, the Tet holidays—that the plans described.[12]

In contrast to the Johnson administration's public optimism, Komer in early January could find little solace in what the pacification program had achieved since May 1967. During the first six months of CORDS's existence, the number of hamlets rated secure had increased by only 268, far short of the annual goal of 1,103.[13] "Our side," he lamented, "is not very significantly expanding territorial security via clear and hold operations, despite our success against enemy units, heavy enemy losses, and our generally improved military and pacification posture." He felt that South Vietnamese forces supporting pacification had failed to exploit the military successes achieved by American units.[14]

The stage was set for the most dramatic event of the war. The communists had decided to change strategy. The Americans generally believed the communists would be incapable of carrying it out. The Johnson administration, convinced that the military and political position of the allies had grown stronger in 1967, heavily invested its political capital in seeking to prove that it was winning the war. Would coming events confirm the optimism of the Americans or fulfill the expectations of the North Vietnamese? What impact would the anticipated enemy offensive have on a struggling pacification program that had not yet made significant inroads in weakening the Viet Cong's hold on the countryside?

The Tet Offensive

To allow South Vietnamese and North Vietnamese forces to celebrate the most important Vietnamese holiday, the lunar new year, or Tet, the two sides agreed to the kind of cease-fire they had observed in prior years.[15] But there was one crucial difference in 1968: To take advantage of the cease-fire and gain surprise, the North Vietnamese and Viet Cong planned their nationwide offensive to begin on the last day of Tet, January 31. For maximum military and psychological effect, they intended to hit all objectives at the same time.

Luckily for the allies, the Viet Cong prematurely attacked a number of cities in I and II Corps in the early hours of January 30. Nevertheless, the scale and timing of the attacks caught the Americans and South Vietnamese off guard. The full weight of the enemy's thrust was felt the following day. From the delta to northern I Corps, the VC infiltrated forces into more than one hundred cities and towns, including Saigon, thirty-nine of forty-four provincial capitals, and seventy-one district capitals. Most Viet Cong units reached their targets unnoticed.[16]

Even with the advantage of surprise, the offensive achieved few military gains. The Viet Cong's efforts in Saigon were piecemeal, uncoordinated operations undertaken by forces too small to hold any objectives against counterattack. The raiding force that breached the wall of the U.S. Embassy compound was wiped out in a few hours, never entering the embassy building itself. Except in Hue, where the communists held out for three weeks, allied units repulsed the Tet attacks within several days.

The prolonged fighting in Hue left that city a shambles. CORDS field evaluators estimated that 60–80 percent of the city had been damaged; over twenty-four thousand homes had been destroyed or damaged, and 80,000 people out of a population of 150,000 had been made homeless. Rather than promoting a general uprising in Hue, the communists had systematically killed during their occupation some 2,800 people—South Vietnamese and foreigners. After the battle, local officials found the victims buried in mass graves on the outskirts of the city.[17]

The attacks in the cities had a severe impact on urban residents. As of February 7, CORDS had received reports, based on incomplete information, of 280,000 people made refugees, over ten thousand homes destroyed, 769 civilians killed, and over 8,000 wounded.[18] A week later, the estimates, based on additional reports, rose: 13,000 civilians dead and 27,000 wounded, over 600,000 refugees, and property damage estimated at $173.5 million. The fighting closed countless schools and businesses and shut down public utilities. By the end of March, after the first wave of attacks had run their course, some eighty-one thousand private homes had been damaged.[19]

Although the attacks caused extensive physical damage in many cities, the economic effect on urban areas—with the exception of Hue, Ben Tre, Vinh Long, and a few other cities—was not long lasting. The VC had not tried to destroy businesses and utilities since it had expected to occupy the cities. Farm crops were ample, but urban markets were generally empty for a short period after the attacks because shippers did not want to transport produce over insecure roads and canals. In Saigon, the government set up rice distribution points and released stocks of frozen pork, thereby easing the likelihood of food shortages and price increases. Route 4, the main artery from Saigon to the food-growing regions of the delta, reopened in February. The petroleum depot at Nhe Be, which supplied Saigon, was also untouched.

Urban residents displaced temporarily because of the fighting or made homeless because of destruction suffered the most. For the first time in the war, refugees moved out of the towns. Prior to Tet, the cities generally had offered haven. The new homeless came from the areas of the most severe fighting. Over 60 percent came from the Saigon–Gia Dinh area and the delta. Most refugees in the delta came from the cities of Ben Tre, My Tho, and Chau Phu, where the destruction of housing was also the heaviest. Over half of I Corp's total was found in Hue.[20] Reasonably accurate estimates of persons forced to evacuate their homes during the offensive proved difficult to make for several months. Of the more than eight hundred thousand government-registered evacuees, over five hundred thousand had not been resettled or been able to return home by the end of April.[21]

The offensive weakened the government's standing in the countryside. Nearly five hundred of the five thousand RF/PF outposts were abandoned or overrun, and the government moved RF/PF units out of rural villages into besieged towns and cities to provide additional defensive forces. Over sixty-five hundred territorial forces soldiers were killed, were missing, or had deserted. The Viet Cong attacked a number of RD Cadre teams, and the government reassigned roughly half the RD teams, half the ARVN battalions supporting them, and National Police and NPFF units to help defend the cities.[22] Most ARVN battalions resumed pacification duties only at the end of February. The pacifiers also suffered losses of records, vehicles, and supplies.[23]

The withdrawal of soldiers, cadres, and police contributed to a drop in territorial security. As measured by the Hamlet Evaluation System, the population under Saigon's control dropped over 7 percent in February; contested and enemy-controlled population increased by the same percentage.[24] The departure of Saigon's agents made rural villages undergoing pacification vulnerable to terrorism, taxation, and conscription. Moving government forces out of the countryside, where most of the South Vietnamese lived, might have a negative psychological effect, American officials feared, making the people wary of the staying power of the kind of a government that failed to protect them during a crisis.[25]

Equally serious was the malfeasance of some National Police and ARVN units. General Loan, chief of the National Police, defended his force against complaints of pilfering, brazenly asserting such acts should be expected because his men were poorly paid.[26] Perhaps the most egregious example was the 43d Ranger Battalion defending Vinh Long city. According to Craig Johnstone, a CORDS evaluator in the delta, the battalion commander ordered his men to stop fighting, after which the "VC and Rangers proceeded to sack the city. The testimony to this is unanimous." The enemy occupied the unprotected city, while the rangers returned to their compound and sorted their loot.[27]

The Tet Offensive disrupted the Phoenix program, which was barely under way. At the time of the offensive, the central government had not yet promulgated operating instructions to the military and police units and interrogation centers involved in the new anti-infrastructure effort.[28] Many interrogation centers ceased to operate during the offensive, although the fighting caused little physical damage to facilities. The centers that remained in operation had to turn their attention from analyzing the infrastructure to interpreting current intelligence on enemy troop movements. The Viet Cong attacked sixteen detention centers, overran five, and freed over twenty-two hundred prisoners. About fifteen hundred were released in Hue during the communist's occupation. To increase security, CORDS got ARVN to accept responsibility for protecting the jails.[29]

Despite setbacks to Phoenix, Tet offered an unexpected opportunity: a chance to capture those leaders of the underground who in the expectation of victory had shed their cover. In Khanh Hoa, the infrastructure openly assisted in the assault on Nha Trang city. The National Police Special Branch arrested thirty identified VC cadres and over fifty suspects. As a result, the Nha Trang Viet Cong committee was reported to be virtually eliminated. The police had similar success, if not quite on the same scale, in Quang Tri and Pleiku provinces.[30]

The offensive proved costly to the Viet Cong. Guerrillas, local force battalions, and sapper units led the attacks and suffered heavy losses. On February 6, the embassy reported that more than twenty-one thousand enemy soldiers had already perished in action. Over the course of the January–February offensive, communist losses, according to official U.S. estimates, reached at least thirty-two thousand killed and fifty-eight hundred captured. Allied casualties were one thousand Americans and about two thousand South Vietnamese. The Politburo in Hanoi had apparently decided to let the erstwhile jungle fighters, the Viet Cong insurgents, carry the fight to the cities, and so they bore the brunt of the casualties. Main force units were held in reserve or given supporting roles. One journalist estimated that 40 percent of the infrastructure were killed or immobilized by Saigon's counterattacks. Many of those lost were experienced mid- and low-level leaders, who helped provide cohesion for the movement at the local level and intimately knew the local political and military environment. Given their organizational skill and stature within the VC, these leaders could not be easily replaced.

The inability of the insurgents to hold the cities also undermined the Viet Cong's reputation of invincibility.[31]

Although the situation varied from province to province, certain difficulties— inactive RD cadres, urban-bound RF/PF, and defensive-minded ARVN support forces—were nearly universal. In I Corps, the cadres were reluctant to work in unprotected settlements, but most RD teams were able to return by the end of February to hamlets that were scheduled for pacification in 1968 or to hamlets, narrowly concentrated around the provincial capitals and along Route 1, in which pacification had not been fully carried out in 1967. Government efforts at restoring security were limited and cautious. The province chief of Quang Tin stationed three ARVN battalions around the province capital instead of using them to push communist forces away from villages that had been undergoing pacification.[32]

Only four provinces in II Corps—Tuyen Duc, Darlac, Pleiku, and Kontum— suffered seriously from the offensive. In others—Lam Dong, Quang Duc, Phu Bon, Ninh Thuan, and Cam Ranh city—it only slightly affected ongoing programs. The deployment of RD teams at the end of February gave an overall impression of normality. One hundred twenty of the 166 cadre teams and 64 of the 75 RD Cadre teams assigned to Montagnard villages resumed their work in the countryside. The other teams were stationed in provincial or district capitals or performed security duty inside hamlets.[33]

The situation in Binh Dinh and Phu Yen, two large, important coastal provinces in II Corps, remained serious. In Binh Dinh, only the environs of the province and district capitals and the areas along the major roads, Highways 1 and 19, stayed secure. Provincial advisers were aware of a decline in security since late 1967. To help prepare for the offensive and enhance political control, the North Vietnamese increased their infiltration into the lowlands. The absence of strong anticommunist organizations, such as the Hoa Hao, Cao Dai, or the Catholic church, and the weakness of the government in Binh Dinh in late 1967 and early 1968 allowed the Viet Cong to make gains. Paramilitary forces were guarding installations and bridges rather than protecting pacification cadre teams or villagers. Yet even in troublesome Binh Dinh, CORDS evaluator Jerry Dodson, who visited there in March, saw an opportunity. He believed the communists had not taken control of the areas that the government did not control. Parts of the province, in other words, were up for grabs.[34]

In neighboring Phu Yen province, poor security and continued Viet Cong activity prevented many RD teams from entering hamlets scheduled to undergo pacification in 1968. But the Viet Cong was unable to hold Tuy Hoa city and probably could not have. Captured members of the VC said they were to hold the city for five to seven days, but their basic ammunition load (a skimpy 30–100 rounds per person) and their food ration (one ball of rice) would have hardly sufficed to hold the city against counterattack. Inadequate food and ammunition allowances suggested that the VC's ability to wage war in Phu Yen had diminished.[35]

In Gia Dinh, one of the hardest-hit III Corps provinces, the Viet Cong at the end of February were still conducting operations and distributing propaganda.

The government was forced to remain on the defensive, protecting towns and caring for new refugees. Elsewhere in the corps, officials focused attention on girding government forces for an expected second wave of attacks and deferred work on the 1968 pacification plans.

In the IV Corps provinces of Go Cong, Kien Hoa, Vinh Long, Kien Phong, Dinh Tuong, An Xuyen, Bac Lieu, Chuong Thien, and Kien Giang, work on the pacification program stopped in February, and ARVN and paramilitary forces remained in urban centers. In early March, a CORDS evaluator visited Kien Hoa and described security there as critical. Enemy forces were not the only reason. ARVN units defending the provincial capital were undisciplined. The deputy province chief for administration was absent at Tet and had failed to return to duty. Other administrative officials performed poorly, and government services in Kien Hoa broke down exactly when people most needed them. The evaluator reported that the situation in Go Cong was nearly as bad. He concluded that the government only controlled enclaves around Go Cong's district and provincial capitals. The province chief, fearful and indecisive before Tet, was no less so afterward. During February, he made no attempt to restore control over the villages that the RD teams were scheduled to enter.[36]

By the end of March, the situation in the delta had noticeably improved, according to CORDS evaluators after a visit there. Most advisers agreed, believing that the government was no longer on the defensive. One reason for the change was a military campaign that the new corps commander, General Nguyen Duc Thang, started on March 9 against known VC bases. Thang ordered every ARVN division and regiment to conduct at least two operations a week, each lasting a minimum of two days. He directed the RF/PF in each district to conduct at least four operations and ten ambushes over the same period. He sought to enhance pacification by protecting roads and bridges, retaking abandoned RF/PF outposts, and protecting RD Cadre teams that returned to the countryside. Thang's offensive compelled South Vietnamese forces to act more aggressively. Noting that military contact with the enemy had been infrequent during the offensive, division commanders and advisers concluded that the VC wanted to avoid combat and in some areas had returned to its bases.[37]

In March, province and district advisers and CORDS evaluators touring the countryside saw glimmers of hope breaking through the Post-Tet gloom and could cite a number of hopeful developments. In addition to Thang's operations in the delta, there was evidence in Binh Dinh that the Viet Cong had not taken over the rural areas abandoned by the government. Most RD Cadre teams had returned to work in II Corps. Unable to hold any cities, the VC had suffered significant losses. No general uprising had occurred. Westmoreland and Komer concluded that pacification was not hurt as badly as they had feared in early February and that Tet was not as calamitous a setback as many observers had believed it was.

Disenchantment and Reappraisal

By the end of February, the worst of the enemy's offensive had passed, but the prevalent view in the United States that pacification was in trouble lasted well into the summer. Immediately after the attacks, the American press singled out pacification as being virtually hopeless. Ward Just in the *Washington Post* of February 4 intoned that the Tet attacks had "killed dead the pacification program." On February 13, the *Christian Science Monitor* averred that "pacification has been blown sky high," and a day later the *New York Times* concluded that South Vietnam had abandoned the countryside in many provinces. The February 19 issue of *Newsweek* offered scant solace when it opined that the program had been "dealt a blow from which it would recover slowly—if ever."

Washington officials seemed to absorb the media's pessimism about pacification in the aftermath of the attacks. Returning to Washington in early March for a brief visit, Komer quickly became aware of the widely held government belief that pacification had sustained a serious wound. The head of the East Asia Bureau at the State Department, William Bundy, felt that the Tet attacks had been "shattering," especially in the area of pacification. For a time, Bundy believed that South Vietnamese society was too fragile to survive the blows.[38] CIA analysts expected both sides in the struggle to continue suffering high losses and making no decisive gains. They saw no evidence that Saigon could seize the initiative and estimated that "the overall situation ten months hence will be no better than a standoff."[39] A special CIA report concluded that Tet's effect on pacification was "severe" in most of South Vietnam and expected losses of personnel and matériel to mount as gaps in information were filled.[40]

Secretary of Defense Clark Clifford (who had succeeded McNamara on March 1) concluded that the present U.S. course was not only "endless, but [also] hopeless" and urged gradual disengagement.[41] Clifford's advisers were especially critical of pacification. In a memorandum to Clifford, Assistant Secretary of Defense for System Analysis Alain Enthoven stated that the Tet Offensive revealed not only that the United States had failed to provide a security shield but also that the South Vietnamese government and armed forces had made no real headway in pacification prior to the Tet attacks. As he interpreted the data provided by HES, "most (60 percent) of the 1967 gain results from accounting type changes to the HES system, not from pacification programs." Believing that the Viet Cong at that time largely dominated the countryside, Enthoven determined that the enemy offensive had killed pacification "once and for all."[42] An article in the February *Southeast Asia Analysis Report* prepared by Enthoven's staff was equally negative. According to the article, the offensive taught the people of South Vietnam that "no one can protect you, not even in the cities."[43]

These gloomy assessments seemed to be confirmed by Westmoreland's request late in February for an estimated 205,000 additional U.S. troops for South Vietnam by the end of 1968. General Wheeler apparently had cajoled Westmoreland into making the request because Wheeler viewed the added troops, which were linked to a reserve call-up, as a way to beef up U.S. reserve forces. The need to supply soldiers to fight in South Vietnam had over the years strained army forces around the world, and the president's refusal to mobilize the reserves put an added burden on active duty soldiers. Many of those who enlisted were forced to serve multiple tours in Vietnam.

At the February 28 cabinet meeting, Wheeler reported on his visit to Vietnam. In seeking to bolster his argument for more troops, he concluded that U.S. forces "will be required to assist and encourage the Vietnamese army to leave the cities and towns in order to wrench control of large areas of the countryside from the VC."[44] But Westmoreland had told Wheeler he wanted additional forces so that they could attack the enemy's sanctuaries in Laos and Cambodia, not act as reinforcements to stave off defeat. Wheeler sowed confusion by not clearly representing Westmoreland's intentions. Rostow, the president's national security adviser, expressed his uncertainty to the president: "We don't know whether we are being asked to send forces to prevent a radical deterioration in our side's position, or to permit him [Westmoreland] to conduct in the second half of the year a vigorous offensive."[45] The incoming secretary, Clark Clifford, a man of well-honed political instincts, was disturbed. He bluntly asked the president how his administration would explain the need to send large numbers of reinforcements after it had tried with great fanfare to convince the public and press, as part of the public relations campaign against the stalemate doctrine, that the enemy was losing the war.[46]

Westmoreland's request caused the administration to begin a reappraisal of its strategy in Vietnam. Instead of sending Westmoreland the requested soldiers, Clifford, during a critical March 4 meeting of the president's senior foreign policy advisers, advocated a change in strategy from, in his words, "protecting real estate to protecting people," a strategy emphasizing pacification and population security. Clifford envisioned American troops merely as a shield behind which the South Vietnamese military and government could grow stronger and assume a larger role in the war. Several times Clifford advised Johnson that the strategic guidance to Westmoreland should be changed, that there was uncertainty about the present strategy (search and destroy). "We are not convinced that this is the right way. ... We are not sure under the circumstances which exist that a conventional military victory, as commonly defined, can be had." Sweeping aside Westmoreland's arguments and rebutting the optimism of the fall's public relations campaign, Clifford concluded that additional American troops would make no difference between victory and what he viewed as an indefinite stalemate.[47]

In March, when the president had to respond to Westmoreland's request, he confronted not only growing administration dissent against current strategy but also increasing public, media, and congressional clamor against the war. He also had to consider the economic ramifications of providing more troops to Westmoreland. A reserve call-up, in addition to being unpopular, would mean, Secretary of the Treasury Henry Fowler warned, bigger federal budgets, tax increases, federal wage and price controls, credit restrictions, and eventual devaluation of the dollar. Such costs proved too high for a president who previously had spurned new taxes to finance the war and decided not to mobilize the reserves. Johnson rejected the request for more troops and effectively vetoed once again a military strategy of invading enemy sanctuaries in Laos and Cambodia. The U.S. command in Saigon would have to operate essentially with the manpower already on hand. The March announcement reaffirmed the president's earlier decisions of November and December 1967 to limit the size of U.S. forces, prohibit cross-border operations, and strengthen South Vietnam's regular and territorial forces so they could carry a heavier burden of the war.

What choice of strategy was left—continue to emphasize search and destroy and the attrition of enemy forces, or concentrate on improving the ability of the South Vietnamese to defend and govern their nation? The big-unit war, with which Westmoreland was identified, had become a political liability. As Clifford argued, greater attention had to be paid to protecting people. The importance of pacification to the war effort was thus reconfirmed even as Washington entertained serious doubts about the program's health.

The Tet Offensive of 1968, the pivotal event of the long Vietnam War, undermined the Johnson administration's Vietnam policy and increased disenchantment in the United States with the war. Erupting shortly after repeated official, public pronouncements in 1967 of steady progress, the offensive shattered the credibility of U.S. policy and achievements. During 1968, it became obvious that Tet had opened a wide psychological chasm between those in the field and those in Washington and had intensified public and media criticism of the war.

At the same time, however, the offensive seriously weakened Viet Cong forces, and the communists failed to achieve any militarily significant gains inside South Vietnam. By the end of March, it had become clear that pacification's demise had been greatly exaggerated in the reports that were filed in the immediate aftermath of Tet. Komer's contention that the March provincial reports indicated that pacification was alive and that the communists were not in control of the countryside, a contention that was essentially correct, did little to sway critics. It seemed to Komer, as he pungently remarked later, that Washington "had turned off its hearing aid."[48] Pacification had survived, but at a high cost.

Something had to be done in the coming months, Komer realized, to restore confidence in the administration's policy and the South Vietnam's ability to carry out pacification successfully. He recognized that in the post-Tet period Saigon had an opportunity to return in force to the countryside and extend its authority to areas previously beyond its rule because Viet Cong forces were weaker. In Komer's view, Saigon had to act quickly and decisively. Could the South Vietnamese themselves sustain a long-term recovery to make up the Tet losses? Would it be necessary for CORDS and the rest of the U.S. mission to galvanize the government to assume the offensive? Did CORDS as an organization have enough leverage to spur the Thieu administration into taking effective action? The Tet Offensive had raised these questions, but as of March the answers remained unclear, and the American leadership in South Vietnam understood that time was running out.

10
What Next?

In the aftermath of the Tet Offensive, CORDS faced a twofold challenge. First, it had to support the government's recovery program. The Tet Offensive forced pacification officials to use funds and supplies originally allocated for development projects in the countryside to rebuild damaged urban neighborhoods and care for the homeless. This need was so apparent that it occasioned little debate. Second, Tet forced the Americans and South Vietnamese to reconsider what kind of program to carry out in the months ahead. Those months witnessed fundamental disagreement between the two over when and how to resume the pacification program.

Project Recovery

The effort to aid victims of the Tet Offensive, dubbed Project Recovery by the Americans, could begin within days of the first attacks because the enemy failed to hold the cities. Vice President Ky urged Thieu to act quickly to strengthen national unity by declaring martial law, mobilizing South Vietnam's people, and launching an austerity program. Ky believed only dramatic steps would underline the seriousness of the situation and make plain the government's earnest intent to act. The more conservative Thieu preferred not to take any bold steps until he better understood the extent of the damage.[1]

On February 2, hoping to stimulate the South Vietnamese, General Westmoreland suggested to Ambassador Bunker that a joint South Vietnamese–American recovery committee be established to oversee a rebuilding and resettlement program. Bunker wasted no time, raising the issue with the Mission Council and President Thieu the same day. Bunker believed a speedy recovery would help offset the psychological and physical losses of the attacks. He pledged American funds and material in helping the nation return to normal as quickly as possible.[2]

The following day at a meeting attended by principals of the South Vietnamese government and the American country team, President Thieu approved the establishment of a joint task force, known as the Central Recovery Committee, which would operate through existing ministries and field organizations. Thieu assigned Ky to head the recovery committee, despite their long-standing political rivalry and the fears of some of Thieu's advisers that Ky would gain politically. Thieu had little choice. No high-ranking South Vietnamese minister or general wanted the job. Thieu also agreed to let General Thang, a protégé of Ky's, serve as chief of staff of the Central Recovery Committee.

Komer served as Ky's counterpart on the committee. Bunker designated Komer, as the head of CORDS, to coordinate American support for the recovery program, because CORDS as a civil-military undertaking had access to AID assets as well as to the vast personnel and material resources of MACV, specifically U.S. Army engineer units. Komer had full authority to direct the activities of U.S. civilian agencies during the recovery and even sat in on South Vietnamese cabinet meetings. Komer's deputy, General Forsythe, oversaw the daily operation of the committee, served as principal liaison officer with the South Vietnamese, and worked closely with General Thang. This small group of Americans operated almost as part of the South Vietnamese government and did most of the planning and programming for the recovery effort.[3] Represented at both the executive and staff levels of the Central Recovery Committee were the Ministries of Interior, Refugees, Defense, Revolutionary Development, Health, Economics, Prisoners of War (pows), and Information and the Directorate of the National Police.[4]

On the American side, Komer and Forsythe met regularly with the cabinet and established a number of American task forces to deal with specific problems, such as logistical and engineering support, refugee relief, and social welfare.[5] They assigned to the task forces military officers from MACV, Foreign Service officers from the embassy and AID, and regular members of the CORDS staff. Daily face-to-face meetings at the executive, planning, and working levels between the South Vietnamese and the Americans gave the Americans an important source of leverage in the days following the first Tet attacks, and Komer hoped Project Recovery would offer a way to institutionalize American influence within government ministries. He and his staff used the Tet Offensive as a litmus test to rate government officials. Komer passed several carefully documented lists of officials who performed well or poorly to Thieu and encouraged the president to weed out the nonperformers.[6]

To help speed rebuilding, CORDS granted corps and province advisers authority to shift programmed funds and materials to the restoration of public utilities, roads, and markets or to the reequipping of police or paramilitary forces. Advisers could approve shifts of commodities and use emergency piaster funds from the MACV budget and the government special fund. In all, MACV made available to field advisers over 600 million piasters ($5 million) from various accounts as a supplement to regularly budgeted government funds.[7] Unfortunately, some funds went unused because the central government failed to inform province officials that additional monies were available and was slow in disbursing them to the provinces.[8]

To get commodities and funds to those in need as quickly as possible, Project Recovery relied on ad hoc solutions and field expedients rather than formal reconstruction schemes. Deficiencies in paperwork, Komer decided, could be corrected later. Getting funds and supplies to the victims quickly would stimulate the local economy and restore confidence in the government's ability to act rapidly in time of crisis. The so-called ten/ten/five program successfully tested by CORDS and the Ministry of Social Welfare in III Corps typified what CORDS wanted. Every refugee head of family received ten bags of cement, ten double sheets of tin roofing, and a resettlement allowance of 5,000 piasters (about $42). Refugees could use these supplies for themselves, sell them, or trade tin roofing for cement, for example. In addition, all war victims would receive the government's standard six-month rice allowance based on the rate of five hundred grams per person per day, pending the reconstruction of destroyed areas.[9]

U.S. Army support for Project Recovery encompassed a wide scope of activities. In addition to efforts carried out through the CORDS organization, army logistics units furnished supplies and labor, while medical personnel gave immunizations and provided hospital and clinical care to South Vietnamese civilians. Signal units assisted in repairing damaged telephone lines and poles. U.S. Army and ARVN engineer outfits worked together in clearing rubble from the badly damaged sections of Saigon and Cholon and helped construct housing units.[10]

Restoring normal economic activity took priority under Project Recovery. After the attacks, curfews and travel restriction kept merchants, farmers, and businesses from carrying on normal trade, created a scarcity of goods, and contributed to inflation. A severe backlog of unloaded vessels threatened to shut down the port of Saigon. Although petroleum and oil products were in good supply and storage facilities were intact, fuel shortages occurred in Saigon and III and IV Corps because the same government restrictions hindered the movement of stocks to the capital from the nearby storage facility at Nha Be. On lifting curfews and travel restrictions in the cities, especially Saigon, Thieu remained more cautious than Komer.[11] Only at the end of February did Thieu consent to shorten the curfew period in some secure Saigon neighborhoods.[12] On this matter and others, the American sense of urgency and Thieu's desire to proceed deliberately conflicted throughout most of 1968, just as they had in the fall of 1967 over the pace of activity of the new government.

Project Recovery, which had gotten off to a promising start in early February, sputtered at the end of the month. Some province officials, nurtured on bureaucratic routine, refused to release funds and commodities until recipients met all formal requirements. Other province officials with grand ideas pushed for elaborate multistory housing projects that would take months to complete. Such plans generally went no further than the drafting stage.[13] The movers and shakers of the committee, Ky and Thang, left for political reasons. Ky in particular was stung by charges that he was deliberately building his own power base and bypassing President Thieu. Ky's replacement, Prime Minister Nguyen Van Loc, who was a Ky supporter, proved less active. Saigon ministries, in the view of the Americans, worked on the recovery effort only halfheartedly in spite of exhortations from Komer, Forsythe, Clayton McManaway, and others at the almost daily meetings of the Central Recovery Committee. Without strong energetic direction from the top, recovery work at the district and province levels suffered. Local government officials tended to act better when prodded from above. In less than a month, the recovery effort exhausted the special 600 million piaster fund, although the United States made additional piasters available for relief.[14]

The South Vietnamese pacification program as a whole suffered from the absence of a top-level, oversight body similar to CORDS, despite Bunker's and Komer's hope that the Tet emergency would prompt Thieu to overhaul his administration. The Central Revolutionary Development Council, the closest South Vietnamese organizational counterpart to CORDS, met irregularly and lacked a working staff.[15] The absence of an effective indigenous executive body impeded CORDS's efforts to get the government to act with greater unity and urgency. Bunker, Komer, and others pushed the South Vietnamese but failed to convince the Thieu government after Tet to take such an obvious step as instituting a strong executive council to direct the multifaceted pacification effort. This proposal was not realized until 1969.

On May 5, a second wave of enemy attacks, concentrated on Saigon and suburban Gia Dinh, Kontum province, and the Quang Tri–Dong Ha area in I Corps, set back the recovery effort. The May attacks, although better coordinated, were less effective than the first set since widespread dissemination of plans had compromised security. Outside the Saigon and Gia Dinh neighborhoods where the fighting occurred, "mini-Tet," the name the Americans gave to the May offensive, had little effect. In II and IV Corps, the offensive was largely limited to attacks by fire and to harassment. The offensive was so limited in its scope and effects that it failed to prevent those corps from making modest security gains in May. In III Corps, CORDS deputy John Vann concluded that the offensive had not disrupted pacification. Even in hard-hit I Corps, CORDS deputy Charles T. Cross was concerned less with the attacks than with returning Regional and Popular Forces to rural areas, resettling refugees, and fulfilling the revised 1968 RD plans.[16] The government shifted far fewer RD Cadre teams and ARVN battalions supporting pacification than it had in February. Only sixteen RF/PF outposts were lost or abandoned throughout South Vietnam.

The May offensive compelled CORDS and the government to revive the recovery effort. The use of helicopter gunships to root the VC from densely populated neighborhoods exacerbated civilian casualties and property losses and caused resentment and anger.[17] The fighting resulted in over 116,000 evacuees and destroyed large numbers of homes.[18] Two districts of the city and parts of suburban Gia Dinh required extensive rebuilding: 11,800 homes in Saigon and 6,000 in Gia Dinh. As in the beginning of Operation Recovery, pacification officials diverted resources and attention from tasks in rural areas to the dual burdens of resettling the homeless and rebuilding ravaged neighborhoods. The government was more responsive than it had been earlier. Police-escorted convoys kept the city supplied, and the government distributed rice in poorer neighborhoods.[19] The Central Recovery Committee, still in existence, again served as the catalyst and focal point for the government's rebuilding and resettlement efforts.[20]

With support from U.S. Army engineers, the government launched Operation *Dong Tam* ("Hearts United") to replace the housing damaged or destroyed in the May fighting. It was General Westmoreland's idea to set up a task force of representatives from the MACV Directorate of Construction to work with the CORDS staff and the Central Recovery Committee to assist ARVN engineers in clearing rubble, building and repairing roads and bridges, developing sites, and constructing houses. Brigadier General Andrew P. Rollins, director of construction for MACV, supervised the American planning and engineering work. The task force also worked closely with the Ministry of Public Works, the mayor of Saigon, and officials from Gia Dinh. The U.S. 46th Engineer Battalion, under Lieutenant Colonel Pendelton A. Jordan, bivouacked at Pho Tho racetrack, where, with the help of hired civilian laborers, it built prefabricated housing components. Material, labor, and funds came from a variety of sources. The AID supplied concrete pipe and cement and obtained $1 million in funds. An American civilian contractor in Vietnam, Pacific Architects and Engineers, provided laterite and rock; the U.S. Army, lumber; the government, roofing sheet metal; and the Saigon Power Company, electrical transformers. The 46th Engineer Battalion and a U.S. Navy Construction Battalion completed over three hundred housing units in Gia Dinh and Saigon by the end of June.[21]

On balance, the achievements of Project Recovery outweighed any shortcomings. Government agencies allocated over 1.7 billion piasters ($14.5 million) for the homeless. Strong executive action by South Vietnamese authorities in the aftermath of the January and May attacks helped minimize the economic disruption of the fighting. The number of persons made homeless by the Tet battles sharply and quickly declined, indicating how the rebuilding effort helped resettle large numbers of people. The number of evacuees in Saigon rose to 116,000 at the end of June but a month later dropped to 30,000. In Gia Dinh province, the number of evacuees peaked at 65,000 in early June and then fell to 7,000 by the end of July.

The daily meetings of the Central Recovery Committee provided officials from Komer on down with an opportunity to push the government, which had been jolted by Tet, to make better use of its resources. Project Recovery also forced the new Thieu government—in office five months when the enemy struck—to get organized perhaps more quickly than it would have otherwise. Even if Project Recovery diverted funds, staff attention, and material from rural pacification projects, it nevertheless helped ease the suffering and devastation in the cities. And this occurred at a time when some American officials and correspondents, mesmerized by the drama of the Tet Offensive, had written off pacification.[22]

Taking the Offensive

After Tet, CORDS had to do more than coordinate the recovery effort and resume normal pacification operations. At high levels CORDS was considering what strategy to pursue the remainder of the year. Komer, among others, repeatedly expressed Washington's displeasure with the Saigon government's inaction. In March, he warned President Thieu that continued backing for the American position in Vietnam was "critically dependent" on what the South Vietnamese did over the next few months to demonstrate that they merited continued support.[23] In the face of admonitions from Westmoreland and Komer in February and early March to move South Vietnamese forces back into the countryside, Thieu refused. He worried about new attacks against the cities; reasserting control over the villages remained a distant second in his priorities.[24] With criticism of the war growing in the United States, could pacification officials afford to carry out the regular 1968 campaign as if the offensive had not happened? Did the South Vietnamese government have the time to slowly make up lost ground, or, as Komer believed, was a more ambitious program imperative? How could CORDS motivate the South Vietnamese to undertake a more intensive strategy aimed at quickly erasing the losses of the recent attacks?

In March, CORDS directed its advisers to try convincing their counterparts that improving rural security ought to be their first goal. In response, ARVN conducted several company-sized "show the flag" operations to reinsert territorial security forces temporarily into hamlets abandoned during the enemy offensive. The effort was essentially psychological: to demonstrate that the government had the ability and will to return to the villages. But CORDS was unable to persuade the government to restation on a long-term basis the forces it had withdrawn in February.[25]

The Americans made other efforts to galvanize the South Vietnamese. Westmoreland hosted a joint commanders' conference, attended by American and South Vietnamese military leaders on March 31 in the city of Nha Trang. Here he proposed that General Vien, chief of the Joint General Staff, and the commanders of the allied forces jointly undertake a general counteroffensive. Westmoreland sought to get South Vietnamese forces back into the countryside before the enemy had a chance to recover strength. Domestic political concerns convinced the Americans at the end of March of the need for an offensive. General Abrams, who had just returned from meeting with the president, also addressed the assembly of American and South Vietnamese leaders. He averred that even though the communists had not scored a military victory in the Tet Offensive in South Vietnam, they had gained a psychological victory in the United States. As a result, President Johnson was losing support. The president's political position, Abrams concluded, rested largely on the performance of the South Vietnamese.[26] Abrams hoped "dramatic evidence" of their ability to defend their country would alter the attitude of the American people.[27] Abrams's words by and large accurately reflected the American political climate.

The South Vietnamese rallied to Westmoreland's call for a counteroffensive. This effort emphasized three themes: destroying the enemy's infrastructure and main force units, mobilizing South Vietnamese armed forces, and reemphasizing delayed pacification programs. Each had a direct bearing on pacification; none broke new ground. Westmoreland's summons to the offensive required neither new strategy nor new techniques but a redoubling of effort. It represented an American attempt to motivate the South Vietnamese—boost morale and counter the psychological effect of the Tet Offensive—and take advantage of what he saw as the enemy's weakness. Unfortunately for pacification, the conference failed to produce a plan with specific goals and deadlines.

An added incentive to carry out an offensive was the communists' political moves. First, they agreed in the spring to participate in formal talks on settling the war, raising the possibility of a cease-fire. Second, their decision in 1968 to increase the numbers of "liberation committees"—locally organized communist political units that could press for representation at the national level—reinforced the notion of a possible cease-fire. The committees, first established in 1967, were situated almost exclusively in Viet Cong–controlled areas. Third, the communists established in June 1968 the Vietnamese Alliance of National, Democratic, and Peace Forces, a front organization to serve ostensibly as a legitimate political alternative to the Saigon government or the communists.[28] The underlying purpose of these committees and the alliance was, the Americans believed, to establish the foundation for a coalition government or territorial partition.

Komer believed the enemy's political moves confirmed its military weakness. In his view, the communists had been unable to defeat the Americans and the South Vietnamese on the battlefield and had suffered enormous casualties. They had therefore little choice at the time save shoring up their political position. If the South Vietnamese government, he reasoned, gained control of the countryside, that would limit the communists' access to the rural population, promote the expansion of pacification programs into new areas, and strengthen Saigon's position at the bargaining table.[29] The communists were vulnerable, and Komer urged an attack. During the spring, he urged this course of action repeatedly to Thieu.

However weak the enemy, Thieu remained wary of risking a pacification offensive. Rather than expand pacification into new areas, as Komer had urged, Thieu instead preferred to clear lines of communications and establish security zones around the cities. Well into July, Thieu remained cautious, fearing another enemy onslaught against urban areas. When he met that month with Secretary of Defense Clifford, who was visiting South Vietnam as President Johnson's representative, he told the secretary that only after the government consolidated its grip on the cities and their environs and on the areas where South Vietnamese forces were already stationed would he propose moving into contested zones. As a sop to Clifford, Thieu did not completely rule out the possibility of altering his strategy in the future.[30]

Upset with Thieu's caution, Komer continued to push during the summer for a "political-pacification" offensive to overcome the government's passivity.[31] At a commanders' conference on July 20, he advocated a pacification offensive featuring a series of spoiling attacks to get the South Vietnamese forces that he deemed still to be in static positions (about 50 percent) on the offensive, helping provide population security. According to Komer, a major attack on the infrastructure and an offensive by territorial security forces and ARVN battalions supporting revolutionary development would provide an effective countermeasure to the enemy's liberation committees in the villages. The combination of Phoenix operations to root out these committees and Saigon's armed forces to provide village security would effectively undercut the enemy's claims to the countryside. Komer wanted particularly to ensure that the RF/PF actively patrolled, that the NPFF was positioned to defend the towns, and that the RD Cadre moved back into the hamlets.

This was the first commanders' conference that General Abrams held after he became the MACV commander, and he was not ready to embark on a new offensive.[32] He had just replaced Westmoreland, who had assumed duties as army chief of staff, and used the conference as a sounding board. (Although Westmoreland's reassignment had been planned for months, the events of Tet and Clifford's call for a new strategy may have hastened the general's departure.)[33] The change of commanders affected Komer's role. Although in private Komer continued to push the offensive, he did not get along with Abrams as well as with Westmoreland. Abrams was less tolerant of Komer's freewheeling style and heeded the complaints of some generals who disliked Komer's pressure and felt he strayed too often into purely military affairs. Until Abrams had time to set his own course, he could hardly endorse Komer's initiative. Moreover, Abrams had a more pressing concern: preparing for the enemy's anticipated third wave of attacks.

Lasting from August 18 to 24, the third wave was feeble compared with the January–February and May offensives, never reaching countrywide proportions. Local force Viet Cong units did most of the fighting, launching 81 ground assaults and 103 attacks by fire. Communist forces achieved no significant victories and lost fifty-four hundred men, many from air strikes and B-52 attacks. The Americans and South Vietnamese had anticipated this wave, were aware of enemy plans, and deprived their foe of the advantage of surprise.[34] So insubstantial was the enemy's effort that II Corps DepCORDS Robert Matteson even reported modest pacification gains in August. IV Corps DepCORDS Wilbur Wilson noted no significant changes in local security and no Viet Cong successes. III Corps even reported a significant decrease in enemy activity. In Quang Nam and Quang Tri provinces in I Corps, the VC had some success in small guerrilla operations.[35] Especially encouraging was the performance of ARVN, which did most of the defending.

The enemy's feeble third wave failed to interrupt the allies' continued progress over the summer in restoring security. The relatively secure population (HES categories A, B, or C) had fallen from a January high of 67.2 percent to 59.8 percent in February. By September, CORDS held that the population living in relatively secure hamlets had rebounded to 66.8 percent, continuing an upward trend that had begun in March.[36] To Komer, this steady improvement confirmed the military weakness of the communists and the wisdom of moving government forces into contested or enemy-controlled areas.

A Stronger Base

Although the Thieu government remained reluctant to take the offensive, it took measures, particularly the significant step of mobilizing, to prepare itself better. In February, Thieu augmented an existing mobilization decree (the partial mobilization law of October 1967) by suspending discharges, recalling reservists eighteen to thirty-three years old who had prior service of less than five years, and drafting youths aged sixteen to nineteen. In June, the South Vietnamese National Assembly enacted a general mobilization bill requiring all males sixteen to fifty years of age to perform military service in either the regular or paramilitary forces and extending their tours of duty to the end of the war. Although General Westmoreland in particular had long pressed for general mobilization, Thieu and his predecessors had resisted, fearing adverse political consequences. The Tet Offensive and related events—American insistence on Saigon improving its performance, the ceiling on the number of U.S. troops, and requests from South Vietnamese civilians for arms to defend themselves—had changed Saigon's thinking.[37]

Unfortunately, mobilization was not carried out efficiently. Inexperienced South Vietnamese administrators indiscriminately selected males for military service regardless of their skills as civilians or as civil servants. Civil engineers or the few trained members of the RD Cadre, for example, could wind up in the infantry. Extensive lobbying by Komer and other American officials finally convinced the South Vietnamese to establish a limited deferment system to lessen the misuse of skilled manpower.

To involve inhabitants of villages and hamlets, many of whom had requested arms in their own defense, the government established a local militia, the People's Self-Defense Force (PSDF), for men sixteen and seventeen and thirty-nine to fifty years of age, who served part time. CORDS had long advocated such a force but without success. Its creation helped people provide for their own security and further expanded the paramilitary forces in the pacification program. The PSDF unrealistically planned to have four hundred thousand persons trained by the end of the year.

Perhaps the most encouraging development for pacification in the months after the offensive was the government's promulgation of the Phoenix program. On

July 1, 1968, after extensive lobbying on the part of CORDS officials, especially Komer and his new assistant chief of staff for CORDS, William Colby,[38] President Thieu signed a decree (which Colby had drafted) establishing the national Phoenix, or *Phung Hoang*, program. The decree established a procedure for implementing the decree of December 1967 and applied to all South Vietnamese military and civilian agencies involved in attacking the infrastructure. Thieu's law made Prime Minister Tran Thien Khiem responsible for the program. South Vietnamese funds came from the Ministry of the Interior's budget. The decree authorized a series of *Phung Hoang* committees at Saigon, corps, province, and district to coordinate plans, programs, and operations and gave the Special Branch and the NPFF the principal operational role.[39] The passage of Phoenix into law signified that at least on paper the government was ready to attack the infrastructure.

The Thieu government's slowness in implementing the December decree had several causes. Foremost was the Tet Offensive. But even without the disruption of Tet, the government was hardly well organized enough to run a coordinated anti-infrastructure program, nor was the government of one mind on this issue. Chief of the National Police Loan, a key player and an ally of Ky, had delayed implementation of the program. Thieu approved Phoenix while Loan was recovering from wounds suffered in the May 1968 offensive. In addition, rivalry between police and military intelligence officials remained a source of contention. General Khang, the IV Corps commander, supported the concept of joint intelligence as long as the military was in charge.[40]

Along with the July 1968 decree, the government published standard operating procedures and enabling directives that listed specific tasks for each committee at every level of government. The district level was critical. The District Intelligence Operations Coordinating Centers (DIOCCs) were to mount operations against communist armed units and the infrastructure based on information gathered by American and South Vietnamese intelligence agencies, police, and military units. The centers' purpose was to facilitate the timely exchange and exploitation of intelligence. The district chief controlled operations at the DIOCC and directed the work of other agencies engaged in anti-infrastructure activities.[41]

Thieu's decree also officially codified the composition of the infrastructure, providing district officials with guidelines on how to classify members of communist political groups. It considered as part of the VCI all political and administrative organizations established by the Communist Party as well as cadres who controlled other parties and organizations. VC military units, members of mass organizations set up by the communists, and citizens forced to perform as laborers were not defined as infrastructure.[42] The guidelines helped ensure that important members were indeed detained and hangers-on were not given unduly harsh sentences. The government divided the infrastructure into three categories and established maximum and minimum sentences for each group. The guidelines also eased legal requirements for the production of evidence against infrastructure and Communist Party members, allowing detention even if they were not caught in the act of breaking a law.[43]

The July 1968 decree and its enabling directives marked the beginning of Phoenix as an operating program. The small Phoenix office in CORDS, composed of CIA and U.S. Army personnel, drew on the resources of the CIA station and MACV headquarters and functioned as a central coordinating, management, and administrative staff. At the MACV-Saigon level, the staff worked with and advised the government's Secretariat General of the Central *Phung Hoang* Committee. The staff provided guidance for Americans in the field and established reporting and training requirements.[44]

Another reason for hope was the growth of South Vietnamese pacification forces since the inception of CORDS. In mid-1966, the RF/PF totaled 300,000, but by September 1968 that number had increased to over 385,000. During the same period, the RD Cadre expanded from 35,000 to well over 50,000, and the National Police increased by one-third, from 60,000 to 80,000. Total American and South Vietnamese pacification funds had almost doubled between 1966 and 1968, jumping from $582 million to over $1 billion, of which the Saigon government supplied (depending on accounting procedures) 40–50 percent.[45]

The Americans also progressively upgraded the equipment of South Vietnamese forces, giving all RF/PF units and even the NPFF in Gia Dinh M-16 rifles.[46] Giving the territorial forces M-16s also released their old weapons, such as M-1 carbines, for the PSDF, which represented a distinct improvement for that force. The RF/PF had not received better weapons earlier in the war because they had a lower priority in the eyes of army planners. U.S. Army units naturally received M-16s first; the ARVN were next in line as production of the weapon grew. The RF/PF began to receive the rifle in 1967 after the Johnson administration made clear that it expected Westmoreland to get better performance from South Vietnamese forces. Beefing up the territorials' firepower signified American recognition of their importance in providing local security for the South Vietnamese people.[47]

These developments—improved security, better-armed security forces, the start of Phoenix, mobilization, the coming of age of CORDS during Project Recovery, and the enemy's political moves—encouraged Thieu. By late August, he was beginning to talk also of improving the Popular Forces and even possibly of expanding the number of relatively secure areas.[48] To counteract the liberation committees, he also considered establishing clandestine pro-Saigon councils in Viet Cong areas.[49]

Moving Toward Expansion

The favorable trends of the summer and the possibility that Thieu might change his position only added to Komer's eagerness to go on the offensive. Butting heads with Thieu over pacification policy had led nowhere. Impatient with the meager results of exhorting the South Vietnamese to exploit a favorable moment, Komer again sought Abrams's support for a major expansion of the pacification effort, seeing an opportunity to move into the power vacuum in the countryside. In mid-September, Komer set before Abrams the differences in approach between the Americans and Thieu and pointedly asked, "Should we concentrate on improving our hold over what we have or on expanding our presently relatively unsatisfactory hold?"[50] Abrams, aware of the enemy's problems and of the desirability of expansion, chose the commanders' conference of September 20 as a forum for discussing the idea of rapidly expanding pacification. At that meeting, Colby presented a proposal for an accelerated pacification effort.[51]

He believed that the enemy would concentrate on getting a better political grasp on the countryside and seek a cease-fire at the Tet holiday of 1969. Colby proposed to counter the enemy's moves with a coordinated four-part campaign undertaken by all allied military and civil forces and lasting until February 1969 or until the start of a cease-fire, should that come first. His concept called for expanding the government's control of areas where over three-fourths of the population lived. Success in those areas in conjunction with the population already under Saigon's relative control (estimated at about 66 percent) could enable the government, in Colby's judgment, to claim control of over 90 percent of the people of South Vietnam, "enough to meet any VC political challenge to its sovereignty."[52] Colby set targets for South Vietnamese and American forces and envisaged joint military and pacification operations. The plan would allow the government's pacification programs to resume normal operations after Tet 1969.

Colby's proposal evoked skepticism among some of Abrams's generals. Major General George Eckhardt, senior military adviser in IV Corps, feared that there was too little time to motivate the South Vietnamese to launch an offensive before the Tet holiday, stressing in particular the shortage of weapons for territorial forces in IV Corps. General Kerwin, now senior military adviser of III Corps, wondered what could reasonably be expected from the Saigon government in such a short time. Believing that the concept summed up what "we've already been doing," General Peers, senior military adviser in II Corps, claimed he needed more territorial forces in order to expand operations in the countryside. Even John Vann expressed doubt. "If cessation of war is imminent" he warned, "this proposal is good. However, if such cessation is not imminent, this effort will have to be redone."[53]

Despite the cool reception, Abrams endorsed the proposal. As far back as the March 31 commanders' conference, he had recognized the necessity of getting the South Vietnamese to take bold action after the Tet attacks. He became even more convinced after Secretary Clifford's visit in July underlined Washington's skepticism about the Thieu government's commitment to the war. With the defeat of the third wave of the enemy's offensive and the start of negotiations, there were no compelling arguments for postponing the effort to enlarge the government's position in the countryside. To get the proposal off the ground, Abrams wanted a workable plan promulgated jointly by the Americans and South Vietnamese.

The proposal that Komer submitted to Abrams at the end of September incorporated specific goals and firm, short-term deadlines that would assist the Americans in assessing the campaign and prodding South Vietnamese commanders into action. Komer advocated six interrelated campaigns: a military spoiling campaign under the JGS to keep large enemy units off balance; a Phoenix campaign under the Ministry of the Interior; a preemptive military and pacification campaign under the RD Ministry to expand political control in the countryside; a *Chieu Hoi* campaign under the *Chieu Hoi* Ministry; a PSDF campaign to beef up the militia; and, in the most pointed reference to the stalemate doctrine, a political-psychological campaign to stress Saigon's achievements.[54] Since only Thieu could commit the South Vietnamese, Komer sought Abrams's help in personally persuading the South Vietnamese leader. Within the next five days, Komer wanted to convince Thieu and Tran Van Huong, who had replaced Loc as prime minister in May, to accept the American concept and have the South Vietnamese ministries issue directives no later than October 7. He also wanted the South Vietnamese leadership to postpone the beginning of next year's combined campaign plan (AB 144) until the end of the accelerated campaign, which Komer believed deserved higher priority. How could Komer's timetable be met when for months the government had procrastinated about embarking on an offensive? Where would it find the will to expand pacification?

Getting the South Vietnamese on Board

Abrams and Komer had yet to take the hardest step: to convince the South Vietnamese to abandon the strategy of slow consolidation in favor of the special pacification campaign. Based on past experience, both men knew that mere exhortations were unlikely to modify South Vietnamese policy; getting a commitment to carry out a specific plan was the only possible way. At a meeting of top American and South Vietnamese officials on October 1, roughly four days after Komer had first showed the revised plan to Abrams, the Americans set out to change Thieu's mind. Led by Ambassador Bunker, the American contingent included Abrams, Colby, and Komer. After listening to Komer's arguments, Thieu was unconvinced. He still preferred to proceed slowly. In December, he wanted to begin consolidating control of the relatively secure areas. Only in 1969 would he aim at establishing a measure of security in contested hamlets, those rated D and E. Any new pacification effort, Thieu seemed to imply, would be considered only for the following year. To the discomfort of the Americans, Thieu was still unwilling to expand pacification into contested hamlets.[55]

The Americans strongly objected to Thieu's tentative and vague initiatives. Bunker championed a pacification offensive before December. Komer feared that Thieu's program would falter because it lacked military support and did not target the infrastructure. Agreeing with Bunker that December was too far away, Komer advocated, as a compromise, a *three-month* intensive effort, preceding Thieu's 1969 campaign, to expand pacification quickly and build momentum for the coming year. Instead of measured consolidation, Komer broached an arbitrary goal of raising the security rating of one thousand contested hamlets (rated

D or E) to relatively secure status (rated A, B, or C) by the end of January, about one hamlet per district per month.

Thieu reacted warily. He was unsure whether his government possessed enough RF/PF units and RD Cadre teams to improve security in such a large number of contested hamlets in a relatively short time while retaining those already rated A, B, or C. To Komer, the issue was not the number of forces but the redeployment of existing forces to make rapid expansion feasible. Under pressure, Thieu agreed to consider Komer's approach and asked Vien to consult with the corps commanders and determine by October 10 whether South Vietnam had adequate manpower for an accelerated campaign.

Vien's consultations provided Abrams and Komer with a crucial opportunity to influence the South Vietnamese. By acting quickly, they hoped to win South Vietnamese support for the plan even before Vien undertook his own study. On October 2, Komer sent a personal message to American field force commanders and the four CORDS deputies asking them to persuade their counterparts at once of the feasibility of an accelerated pacification campaign (APC). General Abrams asked his senior commanders to encourage South Vietnamese corps commanders to view the thousand hamlet goal affirmatively.[56] On the following day, Komer sent CORDS's own feasibility study to Lieutenant General Nguyen Van La, vice chief of staff of JGS. The study, which had been prepared in advance, concluded that the South Vietnamese could upgrade more than one thousand hamlets by reassigning half the territorial forces and district and province cadre teams from secure to contested hamlets. Additional territorial units could be freed if ARVN assumed the reserve and reaction missions of the RF/PF.[57]

Not surprisingly, General Vien told Thieu on October 10 that the corps commanders had "sufficient capability to reoccupy more than the number of hamlets designated."[58] Given Vien's endorsement, Thieu agreed to launch the campaign, which he named *Le Loi* in honor of a former Vietnamese emperor. The campaign would begin, Thieu decreed, on November 1. Endorsing its other components— the *Phung Hoang, Chieu Hoi*, political, psychological, and self-defense campaigns—Thieu wanted to establish "effective administration in contested hamlets" so that 80 percent of the population would come under his government's control. He directed Prime Minister Huong to publish by October 20 a "Special Pacification Plan" and assigned Huong overall supervision.[59] The Americans called it the Accelerated Pacification Campaign.

The Americans had left Thieu no real choice, particularly after his generals certified that the offensive was feasible. After the political and military events of 1968, the South Vietnamese leader, whose country was dependent on the United States, could ill-afford to appear uncooperative. Washington had built up Thieu politically and stood by him in the face of mounting domestic political pressure and the upcoming American elections. Washington had also built up the regime militarily, providing modern arms and underwriting the training of South Vietnam's forces. How could he refrain from using them? The offensive also met Thieu's domestic political needs; he had to strengthen his grip on the countryside, especially if the communists tried to negotiate a cease-fire in place. The implied offer of American military support to carry out the campaign probably clinched the matter. All these factors made the notion of rapid expansion palatable. Bunker, Abrams, Colby, and Komer could take satisfaction in having convinced Thieu to forsake a policy of consolidation for one of rapid expansion. But the Americans had persuaded Thieu in a manner that left South Vietnamese self-respect intact. The South Vietnamese could still employ Thieu's consolidation strategy at the end of the special campaign.

The Special Pacification Plan called for maintaining security in secure hamlets and restoring it to contested ones. The government wanted 1 million persons enrolled in the PSDF and two hundred thousand weapons distributed, with one self-defense group of fifty members in each target hamlet. RF companies would conduct mobile operations on the perimeters of relatively secure (A, B, and C) hamlets, while the militia (supported by PF platoons) operated inside the hamlets. The PF would operate inside contested and enemy-controlled (D, E, and V rated) hamlets, while regular ARVN forces and the RF would provide security. In enemy-controlled areas, ARVN and RF were expected to conduct search-and-destroy operations to disrupt enemy logistics and troop movements.[60]

The *Phung Hoang* part of the APC called on each corps, province, and district to attack the infrastructure in concert with pacification and tactical operations. The government's goal was to "neutralize" three thousand members of the communist apparatus per month nationwide, although the Americans had advocated a more realistic figure of two thousand. Members of the liberation committees and the Vietnamese Alliance of National, Democratic, and Peace Forces; finance and economic cadres of the People's Revolutionary Party; chiefs and deputies of party committees; and communications liaison cadres received the highest priority.[61]

Although planning proceeded relatively smoothly at the national level, CORDS officials uncovered problems with GVN directives at lower echelons that threatened to weaken the campaign. The III Corps plan failed to delineate the respective roles of the RF/PF and RD Cadre. Province plans contained contradictory instructions from province chiefs and the provincial heads of the RD Cadre.[62] In addition, within the space of a week the government had issued conflicting guidance regarding the RD Cadre's role. It took Komer's intervention to resolve the issue.[63] Inconsistent instructions for the APC stemmed from the absence of centralized South Vietnamese management to coordinate the efforts of the various government ministries. CORDS had long felt that the government needed a functioning high-level body chaired by a deputy prime minister for pacification to coordinate programs and oversee the accelerated campaign. The central RD committee was too feeble and its head, General Hoang Van Lac, too preoccupied with RD affairs to manage the gamut of pacification programs.[64]

CORDS's persistence in monitoring the government's planning paid off in an especially important aspect. President Thieu agreed to Komer's suggestion to use the HES both for selecting target hamlets and measuring progress toward the campaign's goals. As a result, only hamlets with an HES rating of contested (D or E) could be designated as targets. That decision gave the Americans enormous influence because U.S. advisers gathered the hamlet data. Employing the same measurement standard before, during, and after the campaign would help assess results fairly and consistently. But such reliance on statistical measures concerned some senior officials in Washington. William Bundy concurred with the focus and direction of Komer's thinking—the need to convince the American people of progress in South Vietnam—yet hoped to "avoid publicity that tends to focus on a numerical set of targets. I think we all know the pitfalls of this in the past." He was also concerned that the plan might overextend the South Vietnamese.[65] Contending that the goals of the campaign were "not half as ambitious as they sound," Komer insisted that specific quantitative targets and firm deadlines were essential.[66] Komer's ultimate goal for the offensive went well beyond numbers: "We can and must achieve victory. By Tet 69, we can make it clear that the enemy has been defeated."[67] Colby, soon to succeed Komer, stood equally firm. The accelerated campaign, he averred, was not a "numbers game."[68]

Despite Komer's and Colby's disclaimers, Bundy had touched on an intractable problem. In relying on numerical targets, the APC was at a disadvantage even before it began. Especially after the surprise of the Tet Offensive, official statistics lacked credibility. If the numbers were suspect, how could CORDS convincingly document any gains in pacification? How could CORDS demonstrate that the enemy had been defeated? The APC solved the problem of how to recover from Tet but raised anew the larger issue of how to demonstrate success and shore up political support for the war.

In reflecting on the origin of the campaign, Komer wanted to give the South Vietnamese credit for it: "It is they who took the decisions and it is their forces who will play the primary role in everything but pre-emptive/spoiling operations."[69] Yet the record showed clearly that the Americans, notably Komer, conceived the idea for the offensive, took the initiative in ceaselessly promoting it, and convinced the South Vietnamese to do it. More than any other individual, military or civilian, Komer was responsible for the genesis of the APC. He understood that the post-Tet period was an opportunity not only to recover the ground lost during the offensive but also to expand Saigon's influence into areas where it was by and large unknown.

Winning hearts and minds—a U.S. Navy corpsman carrying a South Vietnamese child to a county fair operation near Danang in September 1966. Photograph from National Archives 306-PSC-66-3366.

A member of the Viet Cong defecting to an American GI and a South Vietnamese soldier under the *Chieu Hoi* program. Photograph from U.S. Army Military History Institute.

A member of a Popular Forces platoon, liberated in 1967 by the 101st Airborne Division, who had spent two years in a Viet Cong prison. Photograph from National Archives 306-PSC-67-2783.

Top: General William Westmoreland, MACV commander from 1964 to 1968. Photograph from U.S. Army Military History Institute.

Bottom: Prime Minister Nguyen Cao Ky and General Nguyen Van Thieu listening warily to President Lyndon Johnson (back to camera) at the Honolulu conference of February 1966. Photograph by Yoichi Okamoto, LBJ Library.

William Porter, Ambassador Henry Cabot Lodge's deputy, receiving his marching orders in January 1966 from President Lyndon Johnson and his national security adviser, McGeorge Bundy. Photograph by Yoichi Okamoto, LBJ Library.

Robert Komer (with pipe), appointed by President Lyndon Johnson (foreground), as special White House assistant for pacification in March 1966 (presidential adviser Robert Nathan in background). Photograph by Yoichi Okamoto, LBJ Library.

Robert Komer (foreground) and Ambassador Henry Cabot Lodge at a White House meeting in May 1966. Photograph by Yoichi Okamoto, LBJ Library.

Ambassador Ellsworth Bunker (left) conferring with President Lyndon Johnson and his national security adviser, Walt W. Rostow, who replaced McGeorge Bundy in 1966. Photograph by Yoichi Okamoto, LBJ Library.

President Lyndon Johnson with Robert Komer on May 1, 1967, shortly before Komer left the White House to manage American support of pacification in Saigon. Photograph by Yoichi Okamoto, LBJ Library.

President Lyndon Johnson meeting on February 9, 1968, with his advisers Secretary of State Dean Rusk (right of LBJ) and Secretary of Defense Robert McNamara (left) to assess the Tet Offensive. Photograph by Yoichi Okamoto, LBJ Library.

A confident General Creighton Abrams, MACV commander, briefing the president and his cabinet on March 27, 1968, about the post-Tet situation. Photograph by Yoichi Okamoto, LBJ Library.

Principals of the MACV staff at the start of the Accelerated Pacification Campaign in November 1968: General Creighton Abrams (seated front row center); Robert Komer, head of CORDS (to left of Abrams); William Colby, deputy to Komer (seated behind him); and General Andrew Goodpaster, Abram's deputy (to right of Abrams). Photograph from U.S. Army Military History Institute.

Ambassador William Colby, wearing traditional Vietnamese peasant garb, with members of a Revolutionary Development Cadre team about to set up a night ambush in Ba Tri district, Kien Hoa province. Photograph courtesy of William Colby.

Communist defectors under the *Chieu Hoi* program listening to a lecture at an "Open Arms Center" in 1966. Photograph from National Archives 306-PSC-66-1750.

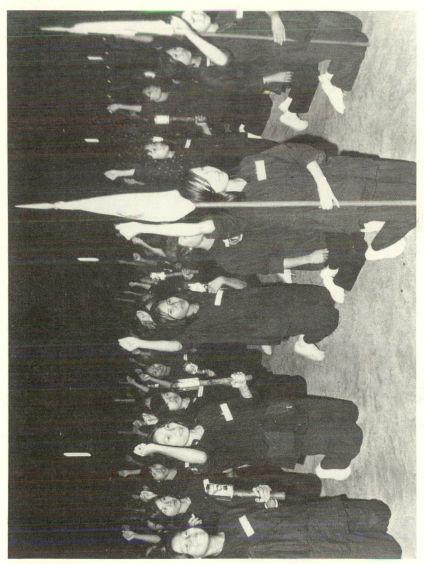

Youthful graduates of a Revolutionary Development Cadre training course taking the oath of service in an evening ceremony. Photograph from National Archives 306-PSC-67-195.

Civilian members of a People's Self-Defense Forces unit showing off their recent weapons training in November 1970. Photograph from U.S. Army Military History Institute.

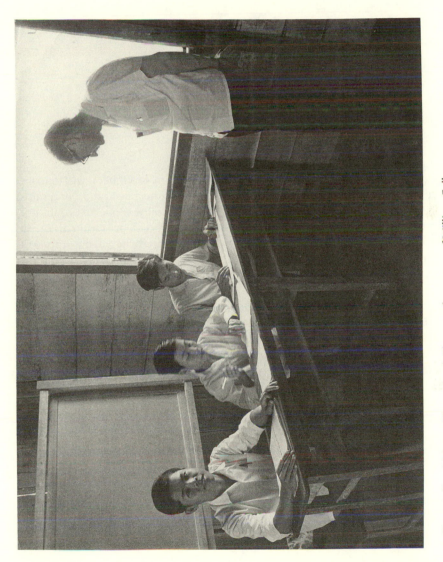

William Colby visiting a village school. Photograph courtesy of William Colby.

11

Abrams in Command: Military Support of the APC

The primary goal of the APC, which began officially on November 1, was to make secure over one thousand contested hamlets. The various pacification programs that CORDS, now headed by Ambassador William Colby, supported could not take root in areas where the communists intimidated, taxed, or recruited. After a modicum of security was established, then, the Americans believed, the process of development could begin—electing local officials, stimulating rural economic growth, and opening roads. Government forces—the police, RF/PF, and militia—all had important roles in providing local security, but their efforts were contingent on ARVN and U.S. Army operations to clear Viet Cong main forces from contested areas.

To Abrams, the APC represented an opportunity to go after the infrastructure and enemy local forces. He had determined that the enemy's heavy casualty toll in the three major offensives of 1968—240,000 men killed or wounded, thousands of tons of supplies captured, heavy losses in the ranks of leadership cadre, and erosion of the guerrilla structure—probably precluded further large-scale attacks. Moreover, the communists had largely avoided contact with the Americans since Tet. Abrams expected the communists to strike isolated outposts, fire support bases, and provincial and district capitals, anticipating that ARVN would bear the brunt of any enemy effort. To compensate for lack of success on the battlefield, the communists, he believed, would apply political and psychological pressure on villages not fully under government control. On the basis of this analysis, Abrams concluded that his commanders needed only to use some forces to form a reconnaissance screen against possible large-scale attacks, freeing additional American troops to go after the Viet Cong and support the APC.[1]

I Corps

In the first half of 1968, allied forces in Quang Tri and Thua Thien provinces had succeeded in driving Viet Cong and NVA main force units from the populated lowlands, opening more areas for pacification. American forces used several types of operations: spoiling operations to preempt the enemy's reaction to the government's presence in contested or target hamlets, large sweeps to clear the Viet Cong from villages and hamlets so government cadres could return, and reconnaissance-in-force operations in coordination with district chiefs to screen VC main and local forces from a particular district.

Army, marine corps, and ARVN forces in the corps supported the APC. The U.S. XXIV Corps, commanded by Lieut. Gen. Richard Stilwell, consisted of the 3d Marine Division, the 101st Airborne Division, the 1st Cavalry Division (now commanded by General Forsythe), and the 1st Brigade of the 5th Mechanized Division. The XXIV Corps, along with the ARVN 1st Division, was responsible for Quang Tri and Thua Thien provinces, conducting screening operations in Quang Tri as far west as the Khe Sanh plateau as well as into the demilitarized zone to detect North Vietnamese or VC main forces returning from out-of-country sanctuaries. In Quang Nam, Quang Tin, and Quang Ngai provinces, the III Marine Amphibious Force (MAF) under Lieut. Gen. Robert E. Cushman Jr., consisting of the Marine 1st Division and the Army's 23d Division (Americal), had responsibility, along with the ARVN 2d Division and the South Korean Marine Brigade, for supporting the campaign.[2] Cushman and Lieut. Gen. Hoang Xuan Lam, the corps commander, issued complementary directives for deploying forces for the APC.

In I Corps, repeatedly the scene of the heaviest fighting in Vietnam, the campaign started well. South Vietnamese forces and cadres met little opposition when they entered 140 target hamlets, which were occupied in a little over a month, prompting Colonel Montague to argue that the government should add new ones. General Stilwell and Maj. Gen. Ngo Quang Truong, commander of the ARVN 1st Division, agreed. Perceiving an opportunity to make additional gains at the expense of a weakened enemy, the government raised the goal to 198 hamlets.[3] As Abrams expected, the communists increased terrorism against local government officials, while the number of direct attacks declined. ARVN's support of the APC was uneven. The ARVN 1st Division earned an enviable reputation, but CORDS officials in I Corps held that the ARVN 2d Division under Maj. Gen. Nguyen Van Toan required prodding.[4] Among many operations in I Corps, two illustrated the virtues and limits of American military support of the accelerated campaign: VINH LOC in Thua Thien and MEADE RIVER in Quang Nam.

Operation VINH LOC

Operation VINH LOC took place in Vinh Loc district, Thua Thien, South Vietnam's fourth most populous province. Hue, the former imperial capital of Vietnam and a focal point of Vietnamese culture and politics, was located here. Control of Hue and its environs was second only to control of Saigon in psychological importance for the government. Saigon's hold over the province had steadily slipped since 1963. After Tet, it was estimated that the communists controlled over half the population.

Vinh Loc district, a coastal island separated by a shallow channel from mainland Thua Thien province, was fifteen miles southeast of Hue. Rich in truck gardens, fruit orchards, and rice paddies, Vinh Loc was a slender, almost completely flat strip of land edged on the east by sandy beaches and on the west by a levee. A lone road traversed the length of the island. During the Tet Offensive, nearly the entire district came under Viet Cong control after local RF/PF units withdrew to fight at Hue. Roughly half the district's people left the island for refugee camps. The communists quickly established a sanctuary, situating supply and munitions caches and firmly entrenching their infrastructure. Only the area around the district headquarters remained under government control. CORDS sent its first district advisory team to Vinh Loc in August 1968. An abortive sweep of the district by three RF companies in early September met fierce resistance.[5]

Maj. Gen. Melvin Zais, commander of the 101st; General Truong; and Colonel Le Van Than, the province chief, approved the concept of a joint land-sea cordon and search of Vinh Loc district. A task force comprising elements of the 101st Airborne Division, U.S. Navy patrol craft, and South Vietnamese forces conducted the operation, which lasted from September 10 to 20.

As the operation began, elements of the ARVN 54th Regiment moved into blocking positions along the opposite shore of the inland waterway bordering Vinh Loc. One company of the 1st Battalion, 501st Airborne Infantry (U.S.) and the 3d Troop of the ARVN 7th Cavalry sealed road and land access into Vinh Loc. On the first day of the operation, three companies of the ARVN regiment came ashore at six landing zones on the seaward side of the island and moved westward. They conducted intensive patrolling, reconnaisance-in-force operations, and night ambushes.

The district was cordoned without alerting the enemy. Reconnaissance prior to the operation was limited. Neither artillery nor air strikes were employed beforehand. The sparing use of preparatory fires not only added to the surprise of the operation but also helped minimize property destruction and the number of civilian casualties and refugees.[6] Caught unaware by the scale, speed, and suddenness of the operation, many Viet Cong forces were unable to take cover and were detained along with civilian bystanders. Those identified as Viet Cong insurgents or North Vietnamese soldiers were moved to a pow compound, interrogated, and evacuated through U.S. channels. Of significance to the pacification program were the capture of 116 members of the infrastructure and the rallying of 56 members of the Viet Cong to the government by the end of the operation. In General Stilwell's assessment, the operation helped destroy the VC C-33 Local Force Company. The enemy lost 154 killed, 370 captured.

VINH LOC marked a turning point in the district. At the end of the operation, paramilitary forces were permanently deployed to villages within the district, making it more difficult for the VC to return. The results of the operation were incorporated into the accelerated campaign, even though none of Vinh Loc's hamlets was on the initial APC list and the operation preceded the formal start of the campaign. After touring the district in December 1968, a CORDS evaluator

concluded that the operation had helped lay a foundation for government control. A year later, the Vietnam Special Studies Group (VSSG), an interdepartmental body in Washington established by the Nixon administration, confirmed these
findings. In December 1969, it held that Vinh Loc district no longer contained any
Viet Cong–controlled hamlets.[7]

CORDS believed that operation VINH LOC warranted emulation as a model
of joint military operations in support of pacification. U.S. Army commanders
were enthusiastic. General Stilwell called the operation a "spectacular success,"
and Lieut. Gen. John Tolson, who commanded the 1st Cavalry Division from
April 1967 to July 1968, was even more unstinting in his praise. "VINH LOC," he
later wrote, "was not a mere demonstration of modern technology and sheer
power; it was a microcosm of the problems facing all our forces in Vietnam—the
shadow Viet Cong 'government' and how to deal with it."[8] American officials
praised the South Vietnamese Special Police, the RF/PF, and the province chief for
successfully executing the plan and believed the operation showed to good advantage the capabilities of South Vietnamese forces.[9] U.S. military and pacification
officials praised VINH LOC as a model joint cordon-and-search operation.

Despite the hyperbole, the operation had limited utility as a prototype. The terrain made VINH LOC unique. Unlike most areas in South Vietnam, the terrain
offered no chance for guerrillas to flee undetected to protected sanctuaries. Surprise and the ability to seal the boundaries of the district made the operation a
notable success. Atypical conditions diminished VINH LOC's value as a model.

Operation MEADE RIVER

Immediately south of Thua Thien lies Quang Nam province, site of the autonomous city of Danang and the location of a major American air base and the headquarters of III MAF. The rural areas outside of the city were continually contested,
the scene of some of the fiercest fighting in the populated areas of South Vietnam.
Twenty percent of all U.S. combat fatalities occurred in this area. Saigon's authority was tenuous because local political parties, rather than national loyalties, had
long played a significant role in determining who held office in the provincial bureaucracy. As a result of enemy strength and government weakness, one analyst
characterized the "GVN as the invading force in villages where segments of the
population loyal to the GVN and all vestiges of GVN officialdom had long since
fled the area."[10] Until August 1968, government control had been limited to less
than one-quarter of the population; the enemy threatened district towns and kept
the RF/PF and RD Cadre on the defensive. The APC dramatically helped reverse
the situation.

Operation MEADE RIVER was conducted in Dien Ban, the most populous district in Quang Nam. The district, which encompassed a longtime Viet Cong haven, had a heavy concentration of North Vietnamese forces and served as a
staging area for attacks against Danang and Hoi An, the provincial capital. In
mid-November, after the start of the APC, two NVA battalions briefly occupied

the district town of Vinh Dien and the headquarters of the ARVN 2d Battalion, 51st Regiment. Such events prompted Colby to label Dien Ban as perhaps the most contested of all I Corps areas. American officials had little esteem for the newly appointed district chief, Major Hoang Ngoc Du, who was a nervous, inexperienced administrator concerned primarily with defending the district headquarters. The communists had assassinated his highly regarded predecessor.[11]

Because of strong enemy pressure and problems coordinating U.S., South Vietnamese, and South Korean forces, the APC began shakily here. Maj. Gen. Roderick Wetherill, who had replaced Forsythe as Komer's and then Colby's military deputy, visited Quang Nam during the early stages of the campaign and found the situation disquieting. The South Vietnamese, hampered by what he called the "miasma of fear" hanging over the province, were timid in executing the special offensive. He believed the APC would continue to lag in Dien Ban without more friendly forces and more pressure on local officials.[12]

In late November, allied forces planned to loosen the grasp of the Viet Cong. MEADE RIVER, a joint cordon-and-search operation larger than the effort in Vinh Loc, became the chosen vehicle. The action involved six U.S. Marine Corps battalions, three battalions of the ARVN 51st Regiment, and one battalion of South Korean Marines. Those forces were to sweep the target area, and the National Police and elements of the Special Branch would interrogate civilians in an effort to identify guerrillas. The operation was planned and fully coordinated by corps and province officials: General Cushman; Maj. Gen. Carl A. Youngdale, commander of the Marine 1st Division; General Lam; Lieut. Col. Truong Tan Thuc, commanding officer of the 51st Regiment, Lieut. Col. Le Tri Tin, Quang Nam province chief; Warren Parker, province senior adviser; National Police officials; and their CORDS advisers.[13] Abrams and Colby saw MEADE RIVER, like VINH LOC, as an example of the benefits of close coordination among tactical units and elements of the National Police in counterguerrilla activity.

Launched in an area roughly three by six miles and bounded by natural barriers, MEADE RIVER began on November 20 with a U.S. Marine heliborne assault from ships of the U.S. Navy's Amphibious Task Force 76 stationed in the South China Sea. After U.S., South Vietnamese, and South Korean forces cordoned the area, they moved residents to a relocation center set up by CORDS and the National Police. Here the police screened and interrogated civilians. Of the three thousand people interrogated during the operation, seventy-one were identified as members of the infrastructure. Villagers returned to their homes after regular forces cleared the settlement.[14] The operation ended December 9.

Unlike Vinh Loc district, the situation in Dien Ban required continued allied efforts to maintain security. General Cushman established a joint force of ARVN and U.S. Marines to operate in the district.[15] Continual U.S. Marine patrolling, free-fire zones, sensors, and scanners were all needed to prevent the enemy from massing forces to attack isolated PF outposts. Nor did the APC eradicate the infrastructure of Quang Nam. Viet Cong agents still circulated freely among the people and carried out assassinations.[16] Colby feared that local officials had devoted insufficient resources and attention to the area, citing General Lam's sketchy future plans for wresting control of the western portions of the district from the Viet Cong.[17] Dien Ban could not be considered pacified at the close of the APC. The campaign left unaltered the dependence of pacification in the district on active military operations.

Security in I Corps improved at the end of the accelerated campaign (January 1969), but observers were unwilling to predict how long the newly extended government control would endure. Improved security gave government cadres their best chance so far to help the villagers. After the APC, the ability of the government and its security forces to protect the people and build a political community would be tested.

II Corps

II Corps, the largest of the four, contained South Korean Army (the Capital and 9th Infantry Divisions) and marine units (2d Brigade) in addition to American and South Vietnamese forces, which complicated coordination of military support. (The South Koreans resisted attempts to put their forces under the operational control of the Americans or South Vietnamese.) To achieve an integrated effort, Lieut. Gen. William Peers (I Field Force commander), Maj. Gen. Lu Mong Lan (II Corps commander), and Maj. Gen. Myung Shin Chae (commander of the South Korean forces in South Vietnam) issued a trinational directive. According to the concept of operations, ARVN and South Korean units along the coast of II Corps would conduct operations to deny the Viet Cong access to rice harvests. Peers ordered U.S. Army units to protect the population centers and the South Vietnamese territorial forces engaged in the special campaign.[18] To help ensure that American commanders supported pacification, Peers required them and all advisers to attend monthly meetings held by the province chiefs and the South Vietnamese corps commander.[19]

After the Tet attacks, the enemy emphasized insurgent activity and eschewed regimental-sized attacks except in Kontum and Pleiku. NVA battalions withdrew to sanctuaries in Laos and Cambodia and to areas of III Corps, and Division and regimental headquarters left. Overall enemy strength, including administrative and support elements, dropped by twelve thousand during 1968 and early 1969, a significant reduction. To rebuild guerrilla forces, Hanoi added North Vietnamese soldiers to VC local force companies and increased the number of main force Viet Cong battalions from fourteen to twenty-two. With the departure of some North Vietnamese forces, Peers saw a chance to probe established enemy bases, destroy enemy supplies, and make it more difficult for the communists to return in force later.[20]

As in the northern provinces, American forces contributed significantly to the APC. The largest U.S. force in the corps, the 4th Division, stationed its brigades near the highland cities of Kontum and Pleiku and near Dak To in order to function as a security shield and to detect the return of enemy units across the Laotian-Cambodian border from Kontum to the northern part of Quang Duc province. The division devoted 30–50 percent of its efforts to pacification from the start of the campaign. Maj. Gen. Charles Stone, its commander, concluded that abating enemy resistance allowed him to use more of his forces to support pacification, and he targeted operations against communist villages southwest of Kontum city and in the vicinity of the Plei Mrong Civilian Irregular Defense Group (CIDG) camp. He kept his forces screening the border as light as possible so that he could assign more division elements to fight Viet Cong main and local forces and guerrillas. The 4th Division also aided pacification by conducting numerous cordon-and-search operations with the NPFF and ARVN and by working with police and provincial officials against the infrastructure.[21] The division established a leadership school for RF/PF officers and NCOs as well as a training program for Kit Carson scouts—enemy soldiers who had defected under the *Chieu Hoi* program and were used on patrols and other missions.[22]

General Stone's concept of operations was sympathetic to the security needs of pacification. Stone deliberately decided to defend the strategic points in his area of operations—the cities, the CIDG camps, the critical terrain, and the population—by blocking the enemy's avenues of approach. He chose this course rather than scouring the remote and sparsely populated jungles of the central highlands for an enemy that seldom massed its forces for a large-scale fight. Stone's comment "I have everything the enemy wants and he has nothing I want" pithily summed up his philosophy.[23] He refused to fight the communists on their terms or chase them through outlying areas. To make any headway in II Corps, the enemy was almost compelled to attack the 4th Division's strong points. Close cooperation between American and ARVN units made it more difficult for the enemy to single out South Vietnamese installations for attack without exposing its forces to the risk of heavy losses from counterattacking American firepower. Joint operations and a concern with defending population centers severely curtailed enemy access to the people.[24]

The involvement of South Korean forces in pacification was not as close, and they were slow to support the APC unless South Vietnamese authorities specifically requested their help. Province and district chiefs, who found South Korean tactics and methods in populated areas somewhat harsh, were reluctant to request assistance from the South Koreans. Villagers often avoided South Korean soldiers. Concerned about the gulf between the South Koreans and their allies, Peers directed each adviser whose province had South Korean forces to try persuading the province chiefs "to lay additional requirements" on those forces and to foster better understanding between the South Koreans and the South Vietnamese.[25]

Peers's efforts bore some fruit. In Phu Yen the province chief included the South Koreans in his military planning conferences, and South Korean forces were often employed in conjunction with security forces in target hamlets. In the western portion of Tuy Hoa valley, the South Koreans provided a screen against Viet Cong infiltration south of the Song Ba River.

Although numerous American generals praised the thoroughness and professionalism of South Korean Army operations,[26] American commanders and advisers had reservations. As General Wetherill put it, the forces had to be closely monitored to be effectively used. Even though they could be aggressive and provide security, South Korean commanders used their forces methodically and conservatively in order to minimize their casualties. The Americans criticized these forces for operating independently, overplanning, and then slavishly adhering to plans.

South Korean pacification efforts also drew critical scrutiny. William Colby directed the evaluation branch of the CORDS staff to study the South Korean Army's influence on the pacification programs that CORDS supported in II Corps. The report, which took two months to prepare, was based on extensive fieldwork—interviews with district chiefs, district senior advisers, and the civic action staff officers (G-5s) of American and South Korean divisions—and personal observations of South Korean operations. The project had the consent of the South Korean command on condition that it not criticize their techniques. The report ignored that injunction and censured the South Koreans for the antipathy they aroused among the South Vietnamese people and for insufficient coordination with South Vietnamese authorities. The charges in the report angered General Peers, one of the few officials authorized to see it. He castigated the report as unbalanced and misinformed, protesting that the evaluators had exceeded their authority, specifically the mandate against criticism.[27] Peers's complaints called into question CORDS's role within MACV and its relationship with field commanders.

For one thing, Peers was upset because the report circumvented established reporting channels.[28] For the Field Force commander, this issue was a long-standing irritant. Prior to the APC, he had remonstrated with Komer about CORDS inspectors who came to II Corps without informing local officials or having the requisite background information. Peers vigorously objected to evaluations conducted "outside the concept of single managership within the Corps area."[29] On another occasion, he bluntly told Komer that he had no "business going to any tactical commander and telling him anything without first checking with me."[30]

In December after Komer had left South Vietnam, Peers again sharply expressed his distress about the existence of separate reporting channels. As the II Corps senior adviser, he felt he was the official spokesman to higher headquarters, and the occasional disparity between the perceptions of visiting Saigon staff and his own understanding of the situation aggravated him.[31] Peers urged Abrams to establish a single operational system that would function along recognized command and staff channels and eliminate many of the technical or special reporting networks, such as those CORDS used.

Peers's plea threatened the autonomy of the pacification reporting system, which Westmoreland and Komer had built into the MACV directive that established CORDS. That directive gave CORDS authority to evaluate *all* civil-military pacification activities, including "provision of security for RD" by friendly military forces, and report on the progress, status, and problems of RD support. Under that directive, the corps DepCORDS was charged with executing *all* military and civilian plans and programs supporting pacification in the corps. Military commanders could comment on CORDS's reports but by regulation could *not* change them to conform to the conclusions of military command reports. Peers's proposal would have weakened CORDS and involved U.S. Army commanders directly in the CORDS chain of command, something that Komer and Westmoreland had resisted when setting up the organization.[32] Peers suggested that CORDS was out of control and that its independent reporting undermined allied unity, but his solution could suppress dissenting views or unwelcome news.

Abrams shared Peers's anguish over the quasi-sovereignty of CORDS, having long resented CORDS's and Komer's autonomy. There was tension between Komer and Abrams dating from their arrival in South Vietnam.[33] Although Abrams did not shut down the separate CORDS reporting system, he circumscribed it, insisting that CORDS strictly observe MACV command channels and cut the flow of information that CORDS had routinely provided directly to the White House. In a May 1969 letter to Komer, Colonel Montague called the status of CORDS under Abrams "a long, sad story of general loss of power and influence since your departure."[34]

More was in dispute than the role of the South Koreans. CORDS also took issue with the conduct of the APC in II Corps, and General Peers took exception to CORDS's analysis. Responding to the criticism, he denied that planning for the campaign had fallen behind schedule and disputed CORDS's contention that the APC was less successful in II Corps than elsewhere. Peers believed that evaluations of the corps' performance were too abstract and failed to take into account the differences among provinces. He objected to the use of planning schedules and statistical quotas as performance measures.[35]

At issue for Peers was more than the success or failure of the APC. An underlying concern was the implicit assessment of the performance of the leadership in II Corps, military and civilian, American and South Vietnamese. Peers bluntly acknowledged to Colby that the criticism "does not reflect particularly well on Mr. [James] Magellas [the II Corps DepCORDS] or myself" and worried that the career of General Lu Lan might also be jeopardized.[36]

The situation in II Corps was far from satisfactory at the end of the APC. Although the enemy limited its reaction against the special campaign to terrorism, and Viet Cong and North Vietnamese forces generally avoided decisive engagements, territorial security had improved only slightly by December 1968. Over seventy hamlets on the initial government list should have been disqualified because they were already secure. The Phoenix and *Chieu Hoi* programs fell below CORDS's expectations. The PSDF lacked sufficient arms and received inadequate command attention from ARVN officers; the RF/PF were not yet fully deployed. Government forces in certain areas undertook few operations and infrequently made contact with the enemy. The situation seemed worst in Tuyen Duc province, which, according to Colonel Montague's estimates, purportedly enjoyed a 20 to 1 force advantage over the enemy. In spite of this, South Vietnamese units stayed in their outposts, apparently awaiting the enemy's moves.[37]

President Thieu was dissatisfied because government forces and cadres had failed to occupy all target hamlets quickly enough, forfeiting the advantage of surprise the campaign envisioned. Thieu ascribed the halting start of the APC to faulty planning and execution by corps and province officials. By December, friendly forces still had not entered 57 of 285 target hamlets.

As disturbing as the defensiveness of South Vietnamese pacification forces and poor results in II Corps was the practice of relocating people. Local officials moved peasants from insecure and contested villages to areas under government control rather than bringing security to where peasants lived. Relocations occurred in parts of Binh Thuan, Lam Dong, Quang Duc, and Tuyen Duc provinces in contravention of the intent of the special campaign. Colby had the new ACS of CORDS, George Jacobson, his successor in that post, redraft the 1969 pacification plan to prevent the recurrence of this practice. Yet new guidance seemed superfluous since the campaign's directives had already prohibited relocating people to improve security scores and in 1967 Komer had gotten MACV to change its policy on relocation. The root problem was the inability of the Saigon government to have its political officials and generals faithfully carry out its avowed policy.[38]

In December, Thieu addressed his concerns at a special conference of province officials held at the coastal city of Nha Trang. To halt the relocations, he affirmed that the APC was intended to expand Saigon's control to new areas and not uproot the rural population. He would allow some relocation of the Montagnards to consolidate, and thus make it easier to protect, their far-flung settlements.[39] Acknowledging that II Corps fell below expectations, Thieu goaded local officials to do a better job on the APC. He criticized province chiefs by name and wanted them to take responsibility for all company-sized operations in the province and reduce the number of fruitless ones. Thieu also stressed that government officials should be more active in consolidating control of newly occupied areas. Having elected village officials involve citizens in the PSDF was one measure that Thieu emphasized.[40] All in all, Thieu's efforts at Nha Trang demonstrated his strong interest in pacification and his desire that local officials work harder to establish the government's presence in the countryside.

Thieu was not the only official dissatisfied with the APC in II Corps. James Magellas worried about the dependence of the pacification program on military security and the length of time it took to transform basic military protection for the populace into a psychological feeling of safety. The communists made no systematic reaction against the APC, granting the government a chance to solidify its presence in target hamlets. But the slow pace in doing so disquieted Magellas. He found scant evidence that the PSDF was ready to, or was being groomed to, assume the security role of the RF/PF so they could deploy to less secure areas. Government plans for resettling refugees and using police, militia, territorial forces, and regular soldiers in support of pacification seemed too modest and poorly focused to take advantage of a favorable situation.[41] Although Magellas viewed the frequent visits of high political figures such as President Thieu as helpful, he feared their personal intervention might stifle and intimidate local officials. The coming year would signal whether the government would begin to translate the gains of the APC into enduring political support and whether army commanders could resolve their differences over pacification support and reporting.

III Corps

It was natural that U.S. and ARVN commanders would emphasize the APC in III Corps. Bordering the enemy's sanctuaries in Cambodia, this generally flat area contained the seat of national government and a large proportion of the people and arable land. Abrams chose to focus on the Viet Cong threat to Saigon's control of the countryside rather than on the enemy's main forces and to use American forces to protect critical populated areas, especially the capital. In the summer and fall of 1968, he redeployed three powerful units—the 1st Cavalry Division, the 101st Airborne, and the 3d Brigade of the 82d Airborne—from the northern provinces to the Saigon area. This corps was critical for both the government and the communists.

Lieut. Gen. Walter Kerwin, the II Field Force commander, and Lieut. Gen. Do Cao Tri, the corps commander, gave priority to a band of provinces circling Saigon and extending from the South China Sea to the Cambodian border. In this section of the corps were located 239 of the 250 target hamlets: 80 in Gia Dinh, 40 in Bien Hoa, 36 in Long An, 30 in Phuoc Tuy, 22 in Hau Nghia, 20 in Binh Duong, and 11 in Tay Ninh. Three other provinces (Binh Long, Long Khanh, and Binh Tuy) shared 11 hamlets, and Phuoc Long had no target hamlets.

The enemy had moved most of its main force units to the remote areas of the corps and resorted to increased terrorism. In December 1968, the VC attempted to counter the campaign by infiltrating target hamlets and by harassing and intimidating the PSDF, whose progress in arming, training, and recruiting South Vietnamese citizens was already slow enough without the extra enemy interference.[42] The enemy avoided a frontal attack against the expansion of pacification, allowing the RF/PF to deploy to target hamlets ahead of schedule. In certain areas the police replaced the deploying RF/PF units. By the end of December, South Vietnamese forces had been assigned to every target hamlet in III Corps.[43] In fact, the quota was even increased to 279 hamlets. American and South Vietnamese combat forces tried to engage Viet Cong units and cordoned off areas where target hamlets were located. But not all operations could focus on pacification: The American and South Vietnamese division commanders still had to prepare for possible North Vietnamese attacks from Cambodian sanctuaries.[44]

Because of the intrinsic importance or severity of the problems, certain provinces received extra attention from CORDS. What happened in these provinces dramatically illustrated the difficulty of carrying out the APC. None could be considered typical owing to geographical differences and variations in the enemy's strength, but to make a real difference in South Vietnam, the APC would have to make headway in these troubled areas.

Gia Dinh

The Thieu government was determined to make the Saigon region secure, and so Gia Dinh province, which encircled the capital, received extra attention. Twenty-eight percent of the target hamlets for III Corps were in Gia Dinh, and the government had by far deployed more RF companies and PF platoons in support of the special campaign here than in any other province in the corps.[45] In the 1964 *Hop Tac* campaign, the government had also tried to gain control of the population living on the outskirts of the capital.

Within Gia Dinh, Binh Chanh district was critical. Forming a cup around the south and southwest borders of Saigon, the district had long proved difficult to bring under control. Back in the 1950s, the French had been unable to dislodge the Viet Minh from the district, and in 1954 Ho Chi Minh had given the Viet Minh forces here special recognition. South Vietnamese forces were even reluctant in 1965 and 1966 to operate in Binh Chanh. In 1966, the VC virtually controlled the district, overran a police station at the edge of Saigon, and cut off bridges and roads to Long An province.[46] Operation FAIRFAX in 1966–1967 only slightly loosened the enemy's grip on the district. The presence of American troops forced some of the enemy to depart and the guerrillas to shift underground, but in 1967 the VC still collected taxes and recruited.[47]

At the end of the APC, Saigon's position in Binh Chanh remained essentially unchanged. Although the government might control the APC hamlets in the district by day, night still brought the danger of infiltration and assassination. According to field surveys conducted in January 1969, government officials slept outside their homes, and people feared death and destruction from large attacks.[48] The three-month-long campaign was too short to displace the Viet Cong and transform an enemy-controlled district into a government-controlled one.

Hau Nghia

As befitting a troublesome province, Hau Nghia offered perhaps the most trying case of U.S. military support of pacification. The enemy's strength and tenacity in Hau Nghia forced the allies to depend heavily on military units to provide security for cadres and local officials. The U.S. 25th Division significantly contributed to the APC, but with its support came disagreements between pacification officials and military officers over the role of pacification and the measurement of progress. American advisers and the commanders of American and South Vietnamese units long coexisted uneasily in Hau Nghia. The 1966 Chinh-Hunnicut imbroglio occurred here, and in June 1967 the province adviser was replaced after a dispute with the American brigade commander.

Hau Nghia was unusually difficult. Diem had pieced together the province in October 1963 from enemy-dominated parts of Long An, Binh Duong, and Tay Ninh provinces. It was his attempt to focus government attention on trouble spots. An analyst with Rand Corporation remarked in 1965 that if "progress in pacification can be made in Hau Nghia, then progress may be possible anywhere in Vietnam."[49] This was no exaggeration. In Cu Chi district, security dropped in the post-Tet period as American formations were unable to prevent large enemy units from infiltrating into populated areas. ARVN units had been absent from Cu Chi since October 1967. Viet Cong base areas were located on the borders of Duc Hue district. In one village in the district, ARVN took no action against a withdrawing enemy force and did not protect the inhabitants. With five NVA battalions in the province, the government could exert little control beyond the provincial and district capital and the main roads.[50] After the May attacks disrupted ongoing programs, the province senior adviser in Hau Nghia, Colonel Carl Bernard, had to devote all his attention to security.[51]

Lack of security was not the only problem hampering pacification. Some American and South Vietnamese officials resented the province chief, the strong-willed Lieut. Col. Ma San Nhon, and sought his removal even though he was acknowledged as one of the few movers and shakers in Hau Nghia. Nhon clashed with the III Corps commander, General Tri, and was at odds with U.S. Army commanders. To Nhon's dismay, army units often acted unilaterally and initiated civic action projects without consulting him or the province advisory team.[52]

Prior to the APC, the 2d Brigade, 25th Division, was poorly deployed to provide local security. Rather than assigning a battalion to a district permanently, the brigade frequently changed the battalions' operating areas before staffs could become familiar with them or develop intelligence on local conditions. Moreover, the firepower of the brigade, although often used in response to enemy-initiated incidents, frequently destroyed civilian property, leading some South Vietnamese to conclude that American troops cared little for the welfare of the South Vietnamese people.[53]

With the start of the APC, the U.S. 25th Division directly focused on pacification and local security. In late October, the division, under Maj. Gen. Ellis Williamson, who had assumed command in August, began a series of operations called COLORS UP. Communist main force units had withdrawn to their Cambodian sanctuaries, so Williamson deployed elements of his division along roads, waterways, and other likely avenues of approach to await the enemy's return. He also directed his brigades to intensify their spoiling and preemptive operations and assigned a battalion to each district. He assigned the 2d Battalion, 14th Infantry (2d Brigade), to Duc Hoa district and gave it the mission of eliminating enemy support elements that provided guides and logistical assistance to main force units.[54] Colonel Bernard credited the brigade's operations with helping establish an unprecedented degree of government control.

But consolidating that control was problematic for several reasons. During the APC, tenuous security throughout the province prevented the government from reassigning many RF/PF units to contested areas. Only six of sixteen RF companies and ten of fifty PF platoons participated. The RF/PF and armed PSDF enjoyed only an estimated 2.5 to 1 strength ratio over Viet Cong forces and the infrastructure, the second lowest ratio in III Corps.[55] The police performed so poorly that Komer threatened to withdraw American advisory and commodity support from the province. The less-than-full pursuit of the enemy by South Vietnamese forces distressed American commanders. The government was slow to dispatch political and administrative cadres to hamlets that American troops had cleared of enemy forces and only gradually established hamlet and village councils, many of which were hesitant to begin work.[56] The questionable performance of local government officials and forces caused Bernard to fear that the continued presence of American soldiers was required to maintain security and preserve the gains of the APC.[57] It was hard to avoid the conclusion that South Vietnam's civil and military resources proved inadequate to the task of consolidating the tactical gains made by American units.

As in II Corps, evaluating the campaign divided the military and CORDS. General Williamson set a campaign objective of raising *every* contested or enemy-controlled hamlet within the division's area to a C rating before the campaign ended. What both frustrated and motivated Williamson was the apparent deterioration of security since his previous tour in Hau Nghia. When he had commanded the 173d Airborne Brigade in 1965, he had believed the area secure, but by 1968 Hau Nghia had become, in his words, "the thorn in our side." To him, lack of enemy resistance to U.S. Army firepower was a measure of security. Cultivating support for the government and diminishing the political vitality of its adversary were issues of less concern to him.

General Williamson's stance led to strong disagreements with John Vann, the senior pacification official in III Corps, about the relationship of pacification and military operations. Vann strenuously argued that the military's excessive dependence on firepower was detrimental to winning the political struggle. Williamson in turn resented Vann's attempts to interfere with or restrict military operations and was critical of an insufficient initiative on Vann's part. Unconvinced of the organizational benefits of CORDS's stewardship of pacification support, Williamson felt pacification could be handled equally well by his division G-5, which normally handled civil affairs. He saw no functional difference between civil affairs and the pacification programs supported by CORDS. The central feature of both, he argued, was American support of civic projects.

Williamson's requirement to upgrade every contested hamlet led to disputes with CORDS officials over the measurement of hamlet security.[58] He found it difficult to understand why HES should list a hamlet as enemy controlled when he could move large units through it. In his eyes, the presence of American forces was evidence of friendly control. Pacification advisers, however, were convinced that the enemy's wily shadow government would scarcely surface in the presence of an overwhelming American force that was essentially passing by. HES, of course, measured hamlet security and enemy strength in more ways than the presence of armed resistance.[59]

While CORDS officials piously reiterated the official line that HES was designed to be nothing more than a management tool, field commanders like General Williamson properly objected to the unwarranted inferences drawn from it. Rather than merely being a means to identify trends and collect uniform data on the countryside, HES became, in the absence of any other clear and universally accepted standard, one of the principal yardsticks of progress and inferentially a measure of individual performance. If the number of enemy-controlled hamlets in an operational area did not decline, this could be interpreted as a sign of poor performance and used as a means to compare advisers and unit commanders. In January 1969, Colonel Montague warned Colby that General Kerwin, the II Field Force Vietnam commander, gave subordinate commanders an ultimatum to meet their APC goals, which were rooted in the HES. This requirement moved inexorably down the chain of command to the 2d Brigade of the 25th Division, whose commander, Col. (later Brig. Gen.) Eugene (Mike) Lynch, warned battalion commanders that they would lose their jobs if any enemy-controlled hamlets remained in their areas of operation at the end of the APC. He did not regard his statement as a threat, Lynch later said. He was simply making clear the situation facing him, and he felt in as much jeopardy as they were.[60] CORDS condemned the use of HES to evaluate performance and told Williamson to ease up on "record keeping,"[61] but the system's universality and air of objectivity made it a nearly irresistible gauge of success to commanders bent on reaching objectives.

Pressure to meet statistical goals did more than weaken the integrity of HES; it apparently encouraged deceit. In Tay Ninh, U.S. Army platoons would walk through an enemy-controlled hamlet along with two or three RF/PF units and then depart to certify for the HES evaluation that government officials had been there. Press reports claimed that local officials gerrymandered hamlet boundaries to eliminate enemy-controlled hamlets and that brigade commanders pressured district advisers (whom the commanders outranked) to upgrade low scores.[62] Such practices boosted HES scores without improving real security.

An incident at An Thinh village in Trang Bang district, the most populous district in Hau Nghia, graphically demonstrated how pacification and military operations could work at cross-purposes. The incident occurred during an operation by the 1st Battalion, 5th Infantry (Mechanized), which was part of the 2d Brigade, 25th Division, early in December 1968. The operation received press and congressional scrutiny.

Under the sway of the Viet Cong, Trang Bang was located along an enemy supply route that ran from Cambodia to War Zones C and D. In 1966, American advisers estimated that only eighteen thousand of the district's seventy-three thousand people lived under Saigon's influence. The government's military and civil presence was almost entirely restricted to the district capital and the Roman Catholic community to the west. By night and day, the Viet Cong retained almost complete freedom of movement.[63] The Viet Cong–controlled village of An Thinh was about one mile south of the district capital. From 1960 to 1968, neither the South Vietnamese nor the Americans stationed forces in An Thinh, which served as a staging area for two NVA regiments during Tet.[64] The communists also used the village as a training base and command-and-control center and inflicted numerous casualties on South Vietnamese and American forces in ambushes and firefights in the vicinity.[65]

In December 1968, American forces hoped to rid An Thinh of the Viet Cong. Unfortunately, the operation was inadequately coordinated with pacification advisers and local South Vietnamese officials. South Vietnamese units and government cadres were not fully involved because they were working on pacification projects elsewhere. The absence of South Vietnamese forces made it difficult for the villagers to understand why the operation was being carried out. It was equally hard for CORDS advisers and government officials to explain the operation because advisers and the district and province chiefs were not privy to plans or involved at the beginning of the operation.

Unfortunately, unnecessary destruction and excessive use of firepower characterized the operation. The Americans used Rome Plows, bulldozers fitted with cutting blades powerful enough to shear trees at ground level, to clear away vegetation from areas the soldiers considered to be possible enemy hiding places. Viet Cong forces inside the village shot at American troops, which returned fire. The ensuing firefight destroyed some forty homes, and the operators of the Rome plows deliberately uprooted numerous fruit trees in the village, although they had been instructed to spare the trees, which were a source of food for the villagers. While loading and unloading supplies, the bulldozers also dug up the marketplace. The village was cleared for artillery fire, making it temporarily uninhabitable for its several thousand residents. District adviser Ollie Davidson, surveying the village afterward, said that "the area appears as if a tornado had passed through it."[66] Operations in the area were extended for over two months, producing a continuing cycle of small VC-initiated incidents and massive U.S. retaliation. Eventually, at least two hundred homes were destroyed, and three thousand refugees fled to Trang Bang.[67] The destruction in An Thinh did nothing to boost popular support for the government or to achieve security. Lamenting the use of such shortsighted tactics, Bernard saw little hope for gaining the commitment of local people to the Thieu government.[68]

The long-run prospects of ARVN and South Vietnamese government in Hau Nghia were not reassuring. Skilled indigenous officials were in short supply. High RF/PF casualties and the inefficiency of South Vietnamese forces created serious doubts about the government's ability to protect people after the Americans withdrew. Low popular regard for ARVN and government officials was evidence of how difficult it would be to transform Saigon's official presence in Hau Nghia into a functioning political system that enjoyed the people's loyalty. In the view of the province adviser, American military accomplishments were irrelevant if the local populace tolerated the ARVN and Saigon's officials as temporary intruders.[69]

At the end of the pacification campaign, CORDS viewed the overall trends in III Corps as favorable. With good support from allied military forces in all but two provinces (Binh Duong and Long Khanh), the campaign more than met its initial goal of raising 260 contested hamlets to relatively secure, or C status. By the end of January 1969, security had improved in all save 10 of these hamlets. This represented about six hundred thousand more people living in hamlets the government claimed to be under its control.[70] In Hau Nghia and the rest of South Vietnam, the communists had been shaken, losing personnel and confidence. Eric Bergerud, author of a perceptive study of the province, concluded that the NLF "badly required a respite" to prevent its collapse, though he saw no evidence that Saigon had converted the communists' weakness into government strength.[71]

IV Corps

By a number of measures, the delta's importance was disproportionate to its size, and Colby decided that nearly half the APC hamlets scheduled for upgrading should come from this area. Constituting 22 percent of the land of South Vietnam, the delta contained 34 percent of its people and produced 80 percent of its rice, poultry, swine, cattle, and vegetables. The VC controlled parts of the delta, exacting heavy taxes in rice. At the time of the APC, the South Vietnamese primarily faced guerrilla forces; the NVA had no units in the delta. The South Vietnamese provided strong backing under General Nguyen Viet Thanh, the corps commander.

Besides army and navy advisory teams, only one major U.S. ground unit, the 9th Division, was assigned to the delta. The division helped secure population centers and assisted ARVN and the RF/PF. The division's civic action projects contributed to the welfare of the civilian population. Its tactical area of interest covered Gia Dinh, Long An, Go Cong, Dinh Tuong, Kien Tuong, Kien Hoa, and Kien Phong provinces.[72]

The division tailored some of its operations to the unique conditions of the delta, instituting an innovative campaign with the U.S. Navy reminiscent of the river operations of Union ground and naval forces in the Civil War's western theater. The Viet Cong used the thousands of miles of interconnecting inland waterways as its chief routes for transporting personnel and equipment in the delta. The riverine force of combined U.S. Army and Navy forces sought to dislodge Viet Cong forces, protect food-producing areas, and stem the movement of the enemy's supplies. The 2d Brigade of the 9th Division lived on navy barracks ships, which transported infantry and artillery units to battle and provided fire support from heavily armed and armored river craft called monitors. Thanks to the blending of ground and sea forces, the Mobile Riverine Force, as it was known, kept pressure on the Viet Cong and attacked hitherto inviolate enemy bases. Navy craft also provided minesweeping and protective escort.

Led by Maj. Gen. Julian Ewell, the 9th Division incorporated pacification into its basic mission, but his conception of the term differed from that of CORDS officials. Feeling that civic action (as he was wont to describe pacification) could be overdone, Ewell contended that maximum pressure on the enemy boosted pacification more than anything else, that "the only way to overcome VC control and terror is by brute force." Using American units in static defensive positions or on population security missions was to him a waste of time that could be better spent in small-unit operations seeking out the VC.[73] In measuring results and evaluating subordinates, he emphasized the favorable ratio of friendly to enemy casualties and analyzed those ratios over time.[74] Because his approach was to wear down enemy forces by unrelenting military pressure, a favorable body count was proof of success. At this point in the war, however, statistics such as the body count had earned a growing measure of public and media scorn.

The division launched a major operation in conjunction with the APC—SPEEDY EXPRESS—that aimed to enhance security in the upper delta. Relying on air strikes, artillery, and helicopter gunships in the densely populated provinces, the 9th Division asserted that it killed 10,883 enemy troops while suffering only 267 combat deaths. In accomplishing those gains, the division listed 244 combat operations; 372 intelligence–civil affairs projects, which integrated intelligence-gathering, civic action, and psychological operations; 138 medical assistance operations; and 63 separate psychological operations.[75] By applying unrelenting pressure, Ewell's division claimed to have "reached" the favorable casualty ratios he expected, but the results of SPEEDY EXPRESS were hard to take at face value, especially when the division captured less than eight hundred enemy weapons. According to some accounts, many noncombatants—Viet Cong supporters and innocent bystanders—were probably eliminated in addition to enemy personnel bearing arms. The division's operational statistics were probably stretched to satisfy the quest for high kill ratios.

To CORDS advisers, the division's obsession with numbers masked a fundamental problem: The division had little understanding of the pacification program, overemphasizing civic action and equating it with pacification.[76] In the advisers' view, the division did not recognize that lasting pacification was more than digging wells or providing health care. The painstaking process of consolidating political loyalty was easily derailed by the careless or callous use of American firepower.[77] CORDS received reports of incidents in which civilians were killed, wounded, or poorly treated by American soldiers. The Saigon press talked darkly of "massacres" of South Vietnamese civilians and ridiculed the division's statistics, which, if accurate, meant, according to the press, that the division had killed more VC forces in its area of operation than were believed to exist in the entire delta. The 9th Division had provided a security umbrella and thus aided pacification, but any positive effect was counterbalanced by incidents in which the division's firepower had needlessly caused civilian casualties. Some CORDS advisers even looked forward to the division's departure, feeling it had hampered pacification and in its zeal usurped too many of the responsibilities belonging to the less aggressive and less effective ARVN 7th Division.[78]

During the APC, the division helped improve security even in enemy strongholds such as Kien Hoa.[79] The most densely populated province in South Vietnam, Kien Hoa had historically fostered peasant revolts and been an early stronghold of the insurgency. Prior to the APC, the government only controlled an estimated 10 percent of Kien Hoa's population.[80] HES scores improved in seventy-one hamlets by January 1969, prompting province adviser Albert Kotzebue to declare that "the VC have been dealt a blow from which they may well never recover."[81] Kotzebue's enthusiasm proved ill-founded. The government could only claim "influence" over 23 percent of the rural population at the end of the campaign, and ARVN's performance in Kien Hoa was disappointing. The 10th Regiment (7th Division), the principal ARVN unit in the province, was unaggressive, even though it outnumbered the local VC forces, which had suffered heavy losses during Tet and had withdrawn four battalions from the province. The 10th operated mainly in daylight and rarely encountered enemy forces; its few forays at night followed a well-worn routine and were unproductive. The infrastructure remained strong, dominating the rural population. The people reportedly still feared the communists even in Ba Tri, the most pacified district in the province. There the Viet Cong still recruited, taxed, and operated military proselytizing camps. The APC achieved only modest gains in Kien Hoa, and the VC remained a potent political and military adversary.[82]

The 9th Division helped improve security in Dinh Tuong, one of the richest delta provinces and one heavily under the enemy's sway. Communist control grew between 1960 and 1964, reaching approximately 65 percent of the people before Tet 1968, and elements of the enemy's infrastructure could be found in every village in the province.[83] In the aftermath of the enemy's offensive, Dinh Tuong's territorial forces proved marginally effective and did little to restore the central government's ability to protect its citizens. Only 2.4 percent of RF/PF operations made contact with the enemy, and an almost negligible 1.4 percent resulted in an enemy death.[84] As in Kien Hoa, the 9th Division contributed greatly to the pacification campaign. The 1st Brigade, which was assigned to Dinh Tuong, weakened four of the seven Viet Cong battalions in the province and caused the enemy to disperse its forces into smaller units away from populated areas. South Vietnamese control of Dinh Tuong's population jumped from 10 to 45 percent during the APC.[85]

With only elements of the U.S. 9th Division in the delta, the South Vietnamese military largely bore the main burden of pacification support, and CORDS evaluators voiced criticism of the way that role was carried out. ARVN units, limited to providing security, had little involvement with the political or civil aspects of pacification. None of the American advisers to ARVN battalions received formal briefings on the accelerated campaign. The province chief barely exercised nominal control over ARVN units within his province; the division commander had the final word. Often provincial officials were unaware of plans initiated at the battalion or regimental level and approved at division headquarters.[86] American advisers complained that ARVN's operations were deliberately cautious. Few lasted more than a day, and all too frequently the South Vietnamese willfully worked where there were few known Viet Cong.

The Saigon government's ability to preserve the gains of the APC remained moot with the departure of the U.S. 9th Division in July 1969. That departure ended the innovative riverine operations with the U.S. Navy and made the ARVN 7th Division responsible for securing the southern approaches to Saigon. Thus, the responsibility for military support of pacification fell fully on the 7th Division. Its desertion rate rose rapidly, becoming in September 1969 the highest of any ARVN division. The number of defectors also dropped after the 9th Division left, a sign that the ARVN unit was putting less pressure on the enemy. The 7th made such feeble efforts that Dinh Tuong province adviser Colonel Harry Amos referred to the division as being "adamant in refusing to act against the infrastructure."[87] The continued activity of the infrastructure and the psychological and military threat of the Viet Cong vitiated popular support for the Saigon government. During the accelerated campaign, the government had been unable to convince the citizens of Dinh Tuong that it could protect them.[88]

The Saigon bureaucracy interfered with the development of local government, attempting instead to strengthen the central government's role. The taxes the central government collected in villages under its control were transferred to the director general of the budget and financial affairs in Saigon for redistribution to the villages, a slow and unwieldy process. It proved particularly debilitating to those villages that had already drafted their own budgets. They had to wait until Saigon in effect returned local tax revenues needed to undertake local projects. In the villagers' eyes, this cumbersome process belied Saigon's claim that it was trying to strengthen local government.[89]

Despite difficulties in very troublesome provinces, such as Kien Hoa and Dinh Tuong, the overall results of the APC in IV Corps pleased the Americans. CORDS officials counted 770 contested hamlets raised at least to a C rating in the HES, exceeding the goal of 400. Several important roads were opened. Route 29 from Moc Hoa to Cai Be, largely freed from enemy harassment, reopened to traffic for the first time in three years, allowing Kien Tuong province to participate more freely in the delta's economy. Secondary routes to district towns and areas slated for pacification were also opened. From November to January, the number of enemy-initiated incidents decreased according to American statistics, as the Viet Cong generally avoided contact with large friendly units and concentrated on sapper activity and terrorism. Intelligence reports at the end of the campaign concluded that the enemy was engaged in retraining, recruiting, and resupplying in apparent preparation for another offensive. Looking at the overall results of the APC, Maj. Gen. George Eckhardt, the senior adviser in IV Corps, pronounced the campaign an "unqualified success."[90] However, the pervasive problems confronting the government in tough-to-pacify provinces, such as Kien Hoa and Dinh Tuong, raised questions about the permanence of recent gains. Many South Vietnamese officials remained fearful of Viet Cong retaliation, believing that recently secured hamlets might slide back to enemy control.[91]

Of critical importance to the conduct of the APC was the extensive support rendered by American units. Their operations provided a shield for government pacification cadres and territorial forces striving to improve the well-being and security of the targeted hamlets. American units participated in a significant number of joint operations with South Vietnamese army, police, and territorial forces to clear enemy forces and secure populated areas. According to data compiled by Pentagon analysts, only 0.5 percent of American military operations and 5 percent of U.S. expenditures in South Vietnam supported pacification before the accelerated campaign. During the campaign, it was estimated that half of all American ground operations supported pacification, for the first time focusing the U.S. Army's efforts on the struggle for control of the people.[92] Even those pacification advisers who criticized the tactics of some U.S. units acknowledged that American forces had provided essential protection for many areas undergoing pacification.[93]

Unfortunately, U.S. Army support for pacification still exhibited some of the unfortunate traits that had characterized some pre-CORDS operations. The operations of the 9th Division seemed closer to attrition than to a pacification-oriented strategy. The tactics of a commander like General Ewell were, in the view of CORDS evaluators, inimical to the program. The operation in An Thinh in Hau Nghia province, among others, indicated that the army was still mounting operations in populated areas without consultation with CORDS personnel and local South Vietnamese officials. Many of the problems evidenced in the pre-CORDS period—the transitory presence of U.S. Army forces in rural settlements during county fairs and the 1966 operation at Long Huu village and the abysmal coordination between army unit commanders and pacification officials during CEDAR FALLS—remained shortcomings. Improving the army's support of pacification would require continuing proselytizing by General Abrams.

12

The Impact of the APC

Early in January 1969, near the end of the accelerated pacification campaign, Abrams proclaimed at a conference of his assembled commanders that the APC was "really the most important thing we are doing" and vividly said why:

> If we are successful in bashing down the VC and the government can raise its head up, the villages and hamlets can maintain their RF/PF units and keep a few policemen around and people are not being assassinated all the time, then the government will mean something. The government will be where it belongs—out in the villages. Pacification is the "gut" issue for the Vietnamese. That is why I think we cannot let the momentum die down.[1]

Abrams and Colby, who replaced Komer as head of CORDS in November, pushed to achieve two major goals during the special pacification effort. First, they wanted the South Vietnamese government to take the initiative and expand its control of the rural population. Expansion would strengthen the government's position internally as well as enhance its negotiating claim to sovereignty over South Vietnam's territory and people. Control of the villages had become especially important with the advent of the Paris peace talks in November.[2] President Thieu refused to concede to the Viet Cong de facto control of any part of South Vietnam and agreed to participate in the talks only after the Americans assured him they would not recognize the National Liberation Front as a separate political entity.[3] An in-place cease-fire based on competing claims to control of the rural population was an outcome that concerned both Thieu and Colby. The need to provide substantial evidence for Thieu's claims of sovereignty made the achievement of the campaign's first goal especially urgent. Evidence of control would derive from HES statistics and the ability, as Abrams put it, to bash down the VC, maintain the RF/PF and police, and stop assassinations.

Second, Abrams, Komer, and Colby hoped the campaign would help convince critics in the United States that the war was winnable and pacification succeeding. Such an outcome would, they hoped, also impress the new administration in Washington. The campaign was scheduled to conclude just as President Richard M. Nixon entered office. This goal would be more difficult to realize than the first one, especially as CORDS would be relying on statistical data to make its case. As in the past, pacification statistics would spark controversy.

Whose Standards?

According to the campaign plan, the Americans and South Vietnamese were supposed to list as targets only those hamlets the HES rated as "contested." This step was meant to prevent the inclusion of already secure hamlets in the campaign and provide a standard for measuring results, but compiling hamlet lists turned out to be more difficult than perhaps CORDS had anticipated. One difficulty was the absence of accurate, up-to-date information. In contested and enemy-controlled areas, some hamlets had been destroyed or abandoned unbeknown to government officials, who had not recently visited these sites. U.S. advisers had to undertake new village surveys, occasionally with the help of army engineers, to determine the current location of the rural population in these areas. The Dinh Tuong provincial administration pulled out of its files a list of hamlets originally drawn up for the strategic hamlet program. Hearing of this, Colby remarked wryly that he would not be surprised to find some Saigon agency "using a list developed by the Emperor Le Loi," the fifteenth-century ruler who had led the movement to expel the Chinese from Vietnam.[4] As late as the beginning of January 1969, CORDS was still unsure how many unpopulated hamlets remained on the government's lists. Colby feared the Viet Cong could claim control of deserted real estate for propaganda purposes, enhancing its position at the Paris talks.[5]

South Vietnamese planners did not strictly follow APC guidelines for selecting hamlets. In October, army advisers and CORDS officials at MACV had discovered that of the 1,000 hamlets on the government's initial list, HES rated 216 as already secure.[6] CORDS insisted that the government observe the prime minister's decree to use HES as the criteria for selecting only contested hamlets.[7] After a joint review by the CORDS staff and the South Vietnamese, the government agreed on January 10 that HES criteria would govern the selection of hamlets for the special campaign as well as those to be included in the 1969 pacification program. After months of discussion and near the end of the APC, the Saigon government agreed to adhere to one of the key elements of the plan; using the HES as the sole standard for choosing targets before the campaign and measuring change at its conclusion.[8]

CORDS had to fend off other South Vietnamese efforts to misuse the HES. In mid-November 1968, without consulting U.S. officials, General Hoang Van Lac, the deputy minister of revolutionary development, had ordered South Vietnamese provincial authorities to establish, with the help of the American province advisers, the "true situation of each hamlet," a way of bypassing HES or opening the scores to possible tampering. Fearing an upward revision of pacification ratings, Colby resisted Lac's move and directed province and district advisers to ignore Lac's order.[9] The situation was resolved at the end of November. In a new directive, Lac affirmed that South Vietnamese and U.S. Army officers and civilians assigned to CORDS could not change any hamlet rating. Disagreements between American and South Vietnamese officials over the rating of a hamlet would be forwarded to Saigon, where the government and CORDS would attempt to settle the issue.[10]

Saigon's acceptance of HES as the standard measure of hamlet security proved short-lived, illustrating the government's inclination to act independently of its stronger partner. On January 16, Thieu, in quasi-Orwellian fashion, directed his officials not to use HES categories and descriptive terms, such as *contested*, in official documents. He rejected the notion of a contested area "because such an area is lying in the area under our control, but its degree of pacification and development is not so high as the areas ... known as secure." He ordered the phrase *area or hamlet controlled by the government* used in place of categories A, B, C, D, and E. The phrase *VC control* was likewise excised from the South Vietnamese lexicon in favor of *area or hamlet not yet fully controlled by the government.*[11] This blatantly political step, designed to help Thieu's negotiators at Paris, indicated the ever-present temptation to tamper with the HES for political reasons. Obviously, contested areas and Viet Cong controlled–hamlets remained in the countryside, if not in the official South Vietnamese vocabulary. Continual meddling could only undermine HES's integrity.

The perversion of HES dismayed American advisers, especially the head of CORDS. Conscious of the politics involved in Thieu's directive, Colby directly raised with him the fundamental point of achieving real, not propaganda, gains. Colby stressed the absolute need that pacification be credible both to the American government and the people of South Vietnam. He warned Thieu that the main vulnerability of his government was internal, that it might delude itself about its standing with its people, who would judge the government by its ability to improve their lot. Fearing a repetition of the inaccurate reporting on strategic hamlets that had misled Diem's administration, Colby warned Thieu that in 1969 "there was no room for optimists or pessimists, only for realists."[12] Colby instructed CORDS to ignore Thieu's directive. Although the Americans could censure the South Vietnamese for misusing the HES, they had no authority to prevent the South Vietnamese government from using its own measurement standards for evaluating security. The Paris talks and the APC induced the government and CORDS to rely on statistical measures, but the Americans involved in pacification were more concerned about the integrity of the HES than the South Vietnamese were.

Mixed Results in South Vietnam

South Vietnam's conduct of the campaign loomed as a critical issue. From the beginning, General Abrams realized that although U.S. Army units would support the campaign, indigenous forces had to bear the brunt of the burden in securing the countryside against VC forces and infrastructure. Based on his experience, he was openly worried about the Thieu regime. "They've [the Vietnamese] got to shape up to impress the new administration," he warned his commanders in late November. "They are letting days slide by—very important days—while they fool around with secondary matters."[13] Although he applauded Thieu's decision to pacify contested areas, Abrams realized that the government had yet to prove it could act effectively. This was the acid test of pacification, not the statistics that spewed from CORDS computers.

That the South Vietnamese often let procedural questions impede their execution of the APC offered little solace to the Americans. Owing to imprecisely drawn directives, the Thieu government failed to define clearly official relations between the pacification program and the ARVN division commander.[14] In the absence of clear-cut guidance, the precise role of ARVN units in the pacification program, which was critical, continued to be debated among CORDS, South Vietnamese officials, and the Joint General Staff. This debate diverted attention from the conduct of the APC. The result was predictable. Out of confusion or lack of interest, ARVN division commanders as a rule provided minimal support for pacification.

The Americans in Saigon tried to view the regime's shortcomings in carrying out the APC in the context of the serious handicaps the relatively new government had had to overcome. It had had to battle the Viet Cong while trying to surmount the crippling political inheritance of the colonial past and the 1963 coup. On top of that, the Tet Offensive, occurring five months after Thieu's inauguration under a newly written constitution, had delivered a traumatic blow to South Vietnam, requiring the fledgling republic to defeat a full-scale military attack and then carry out a large rebuilding effort in the nation's cities.

Thieu made special efforts to facilitate the APC, especially now that the South Vietnamese had come to accept the need for a central pacification authority. He set up the Central Pacification and Development Council (CPDC), with a staff that reported to the prime minister and kept close ties with CORDS. The new council sought to unite the efforts of all South Vietnamese ministries, agencies, military forces, and civilian cadres working on different aspects of pacification. Meeting for the first time on November 20, the CPDC gradually assumed control of the conduct of the APC. This central council at the ministerial level, which built on the example of the Central Recovery Committee, was a logical first step in developing a national network of central pacification councils in the corps, provinces, districts, and municipalities that sought to put in place "a single manager" for pacification at each echelon of government. Thieu made frequent trips to the provinces to impress on local officials his commitment to the APC and subordinated regular ongoing programs to the requirements of the special campaign, which assumed precedence.

To Colby, the real importance of the special campaign was that the government had preempted the Viet Cong threat in the countryside. The South Vietnamese had overcome their fear of renewed VC attacks and begun to exercise control in contested areas. The campaign thus served as an antidote to the Tet Offensive and the defensive attitude that stifled the government throughout most of 1968.[15] That the government's decision to carry out the APC elevated pacification to a higher priority seemed obvious. What was far less certain at the end of the campaign was how well the South Vietnamese had actually carried out the program. On that point the evidence was not fully reassuring.

The Numbers

By the end of January 1969, the government had attained the most prominent goal of the campaign: raising over 1,000 contested hamlets to relatively secure status (HES scores of A, B, or C; see Table 12.1). Of the 1,317 contested hamlets on the target list, 195, or less than 15 percent, remained in the HES categories of contested or enemy controlled. Significantly, nearly 50 percent of the upgraded hamlets were located in the delta, the most populous region in South Vietnam. This emphasis on the delta was intentional, according to Colby. He argued that the delta provinces should be accorded top priority, even though relatively few ARVN units and one American division were assigned there. To Colby, this was a means of declaring that pacification was not a "military chore but one of local security and development."[16] The delta received preference on the allocation of self-defense weapons, newly authorized RF/PF units, and cadre teams. To reinforce the importance attached to the delta, Komer had transferred John Vann to run the CORDS effort in IV Corps prior to the APC.

The numbers were unprecedented. In the last quarter of 1968, the population living in relatively secure areas, as measured by HES, rose by 1.7 million people. This gain was appreciably greater than what the government had achieved in all of 1967, when the relatively secure population increased by 1.3 million. The APC data were more significant than the 1967 results because over half the improvements of that year were attributable to changes in accounting procedures and population movements, not to the pacification program.[17]

The APC data were even more significant when compared to previous plans. Prior to the Tet Offensive, CORDS and the South Vietnamese government had set a goal of increasing the population under South Vietnamese control to 73 percent, while reducing communist control to 13 percent by the end of 1968. In the bleak days after the offensive, those targets seemed almost ludicrous. In February, most CORDS and government officials believed that Tet had rendered the 1968 plans obsolete, but they were wrong. By the end of December, the pacification program had reached both goals. The HES reported 76.3 percent of the people lived in relatively secure areas, while the Viet Cong's control had slipped to 12.3 percent. The APC helped the Saigon government overcome the Tet setback and put the program about where Abrams and Colby had hoped it would be at the end of 1968.

The campaign was not a snap. A significant number of target hamlets accommodated, willingly or unwillingly, the presence of the Viet Cong. When the cam-

TABLE 12.1   HES Rating for the End of the APC

Corps	Hamlets in Categories A, B, or C	Hamlet in Categories D or E	Hamlets in Category VC (V)
I (198)[a]	155	41	2
II (272)	214	56	2
III (281)	279	2	0
IV (566)	474	87	5
Total (1,317)	1,122	186	9

[a]The number of target hamlets is in parentheses.
Source: Rpt., sub: Accelerated Pacification Campaign, 1 October 1968–31 January 1969, A Statistical Summary of APC Results as Reported in the Hamlet Evaluation System, 31 March 1969, CMH.

paign began, the enemy had liberation committees in 29 percent of the APC hamlets, collected taxes in 45 percent, and stationed infrastructure elements in 36 percent.[18] In view of the enemy's presence in a not-insignificant number of APC hamlets, improved local security took on added significance. But the gains in the countryside would prove fragile if the government did not establish its own political roots. Thus, an element of ambiguity attached itself to the APC results.

The prevalence of communist influence in so many target hamlets meant that the programs designed to weaken the infrastructure—*Chieu Hoi* and Phoenix— assumed near-critical importance in the campaign. *Chieu Hoi* was the most successful aspect of the accelerated campaign. Over eighty-six hundred members of the VC defected, exceeding the campaign's goal of five thousand by a comfortable margin. A disproportionate share (75 percent) of Viet Cong ralliers came from the delta, a development that CORDS evaluators attributed to improved security there.[19] Coming after the Viet Cong's losses at Tet, the *Chieu Hoi* program further eroded communist ranks. A weakened Viet Cong gave the government breathing room to consolidate its security gains.

The government surpassed its *Chieu Hoi* goal but missed meeting the campaign's equally ambitious objective for the Phoenix program. CORDS military and civilian analysts estimated that the campaign "eliminated" some seven thousand members of the communist infrastructure, a shortfall of about two thousand from the campaign's mark. Many of those seven thousand losses resulted from the tendency to credit the Phoenix program with any member of the communist apparatus taken out of action by surrendering, defecting, or being killed by military or police action. Thus, the numbers were no measure of the Phoenix program's effectiveness. Nevertheless, the number of killed or captured infrastructure members was higher than any previously amassed, and CORDS felt the government had laid the groundwork for a more effective future attack against the infrastructure.[20] The results were not decisive, however, leaving room for disagreement.

CORDS may have underestimated the impact of the Phoenix program on the VCI. One historian and war critic, Gabriel Kolko, argued that the revolution knew that its political infrastructure was "badly hurt in the rural regions and decimated in the cities," even if the Americans, "hypnotized by their own data," thought the program had not reduced the size of the VCI and registered scant success against high-level cadres. "The CIA disdained to regard rank and file NLF members, sympathizers, occasional workers, or tax collectors as real infrastructure." In Kolko's view, CORDS's attention to statistical data created a myopia that obscured its understanding of the full extent of the serious damage done to the infrastructure, which "was incapable of persevering without its grass-roots workers."[21] In retrospect, the much-maligned statistics may have diverted attention from the reality behind the numbers, rendering observers unable to appreciate the enemy's losses.

The campaign helped weaken the infrastructure, but local communist organizations still constituted a potent threat to the government. In contrast to Kolko, many army advisers in the field felt that Phoenix operations did not root out the infrastructure or even seriously harass it in many target hamlets.[22] Saigon's arbitrarily high quotas complicated the program for local officials, who often attained the quotas with difficulty or on the basis of dubious figures. Quotas also encouraged officials to apprehend large numbers of low-ranking VCI members. Few key leaders were captured or eliminated. A resilient infrastructure stood in the way of Saigon's efforts to consolidate its control of the hamlets entered during the APC and had the potential to unravel the security gains made to that point.

The South Vietnamese claimed gains in other aspects of the accelerated campaign. They exceeded their goals for organizing and training PSDF personnel, even though fewer weapons reached the self-defenders than planned because of the shortage of arms, essentially discards from the RF/PF, and the reluctance of government officials to distribute them.

	National Goal	*APC Results*
Organized	1,000,000	1,106,853
Trained	400,000	659,701
Armed	200,000	170,373

CORDS viewed the existence of organized and trained self-defense forces as an indication of a rudimentary political commitment to the government and an important aspect of local self-defense. This was a controversial position. The PSDF was more a symbolic, than a true, military force. PSDF trained to a lower standard than the RF/PF, which many considered inadequate. The critical variable over time again would be South Vietnamese performance. Would the PSDF be able to stand up to VC raids? Would its presence help deter the proselytizing of the VCI?

The APC sought to establish a permanent government presence in the targeted hamlets, many of which had been without government representation since the Tet Offensive or longer. If local qualified persons were unavailable to serve, the government appointed someone from the RF or PF to serve in local office until elections could be held. By the end of the campaign, the government had installed locally elected officials in 544 hamlets and appointed officials in 730 others. Only 61 of the target hamlets lacked government officials. Put another way, Saigon believed it had organized a political foothold in over 95 percent of the APC hamlets, a necessary step toward consolidating political control. Loyal local officials at the hamlet level would, the Thieu regime hoped, allow the government to consolidate its position in the countryside.[23] But how effective would they be? Would they be able to build support for the central government?

Nationally, the enemy's reaction to the APC was muted. Enemy military operations declined dramatically from the Tet high point to the last quarter of 1968. Battalion-sized enemy attacks dropped drastically from 64 in the first quarter of 1968 (Tet) to 2 in the last quarter (APC), while ground assaults of all sizes fell from 635 to 162 over the same period. Attacks by fire (rockets, mortars, snipers, etc.) likewise steadily declined, falling in the last quarter to about 50 percent of the total of the first three months of the year. Enemy-initiated attacks were limited to a few hamlets in remote areas, consisting mostly of attacks by local force Viet Cong units.[24] Communist-initiated incidents (terrorism, sabotage, propaganda, etc.) also dropped over the same period from 12,567 to 6,945.[25] MACV concluded that the enemy's reduced capability, stemming from serious losses at Tet, had dictated the comparatively low level of activity.[26] U.S. sources listed thirty-two thousand enemy killed and over five thousand captured during the attacks. The infrastructure, expecting to lead the anticipated popular uprising, surfaced during the offensive and suffered serious losses during Saigon's counterattacks. With depleted force levels, the communists were in no position to respond effectively to Saigon's challenge.[27]

To rebuild and control losses after Tet, the Viet Cong tended to disperse its military units, especially in IV Corps.[28] A policy aimed at conserving strength prevented the Viet Cong from effectively challenging the APC. Enemy forces may have been well positioned to resist the APC in hamlets close to base areas but were poorly situated to stop the government from reestablishing control of settlements vacated at Tet. This was especially true in the delta, where nearly one-half of the upgraded hamlets were located. In early 1969, the Viet Cong, operating without the aid of NVA units, could not prevent government gains, particularly in the region of South Vietnam most critical to the insurgency. After the war, an official North Vietnamese account candidly acknowledged that the communists were unable to stop the "very fierce and sweeping pacification operations" owing to their limited capabilities.[29] The absence of a sustained enemy counterthrust vindicated Komer's view that the aftermath of the offensive had left a vacuum in the countryside, an opportunity for government forces and cadre teams to resume pacification in abandoned areas and establish control in contested ones.

If the Viet Cong did relatively little to counteract pacification militarily, it remained active politically. The infrastructure strove to establish liberation committees.[30] In the fall, American intelligence officials noted a substantial increase in the number of these committees since the spring and summer of 1968, a growing percentage of which were located in areas outside enemy control. CORDS became aware of the latest facet of the enemy's organization when government cadres and forces moved into contested hamlets during the APC.

Between September 1968 and mid-January 1969, the number of hamlets with liberation committees leapt from 397 to 3,367. The communists increased the number of liberation committees in government-controlled areas. In November, about one-third of the hamlets with liberation committees fell into the contested or relatively secure categories. By mid-January, that figure had reached 59 percent. The percentage of committees in enemy-controlled areas fell over the same period. Using the HES, the Americans identified about 70 percent of the hamlets with liberation committees in January. The remainder (if they actually existed, which was difficult to verify) were hard to locate. At the end of the campaign, CORDS was unsure how many committees actually existed or to what extent they could carry out their intended functions.

The committees offered advantages for the communists. Like the Saigon government, the Viet Cong sought to improve its bargaining position at the Paris negotiations. The network of liberation committees provided the VC with an aura of political legitimacy. In the event of a cease-fire, the communists would represent these committees as a quasi-legal basis for political control. They could serve as administrative units as the Viet Cong sought to strengthen its political control over the population, while preventing the government from extending its rule into communist-held areas.[31]

The growth of these committees, coupled with the decline in military activity, signified a noticeable change in the enemy's operations. Weakened militarily, it attempted to weaken the government's hold in the countryside, increasingly resorting to terrorism. The number of persons assassinated inside APC hamlets rose 86 percent over precampaign figures. And if the enemy continued to scale down its military operations by mounting fewer battalion-sized attacks and relying more on terrorism and raids by local force units, this had implications for the army's attrition strategy. If large communist units in remote areas were less active, U.S. units would need to pay more attention to those parts of South Vietnam where enemy guerrilla forces threatened the rural population.

American officials in Saigon judged the APC a watershed event in the other war. The APC enjoyed greater military support from U.S. Army units than any previous pacification effort. Because the APC brought together to an unprecedented degree the disparate facets of the pacification program in pursuit of an integrated campaign plan, it allowed the South Vietnamese to take advantage of the Viet Cong's military losses to make unparalleled security gains. By the end of the campaign, the government controlled more people and had deployed its territorial security forces and cadre teams in more hamlets than ever before. It had also begun to train and organize PSDF and conduct elections of local officials. These were essential first steps in helping the central government consolidate its political ties with the countryside.[32]

CORDS believed the results of the campaign would help the American negotiators in Paris demolish the enemy's claim of controlling 80 percent of the population. In January, Colby sent Ambassador Averill Harriman, the U.S. representative at the Paris talks, HES reports and maps of Vietnam with overlays depicting the location of RF/PF units, RD Cadre teams, National Police, and villages and hamlets with elected or appointed government officials. The information, Colby believed, clearly demonstrated that the densely populated areas fell under Saigon's authority, that the government's presence extended to every part of the country.[33] The security gains that HES measured constituted an integral part of the evidence, as Colby put it, with which to "knock down the silly NLF claims in Paris."[34] The White House agreed. Continuing progress in pacification was, according to national security adviser Walt Rostow, the "best bargaining lever" the allies had in the negotiations.[35]

Pleased with the campaign's achievements, the American civilian and military leadership realized that the government's performance had not eased doubts about Saigon's future. There was a strong degree of ambivalence on the part of the Americans in South Vietnam, a sense of progress coupled with suspicion that Saigon still had not measured up. Ambassador Bunker, speaking for General Abrams and Ambassador Colby, was not fully reassured. In Bunker's view, the Thieu government, the "best and most effective" in many years, was "still plagued by inefficiency and corruption. It is still not strong enough." He felt that the campaign could have had an even greater impact. "By mid November the enemy was in such a state of disarray that he could have been knocked out of the war completely had he been pursued in the manner that U.S. forces pursued the German and Japanese armies in World War II."[36] Even boosters of the accelerated campaign conceded that the government's performance needed further improvement to defeat the communists. According to CORDS estimates, in 21 percent of the target hamlets pacification programs were ineffectively managed. Ambiguous numbers and nagging questions were indications of a continuing stalemate.

The View from Washington and Saigon

At the end of the APC, Washington civilian agencies were less ambivalent and more skeptical than their Saigon colleagues. They assessed the campaign and the pacification program at the request of the incoming Nixon administration. The president's national security adviser, Henry Kissinger, compiled a list of questions and requested the views of all government agencies involved in Vietnam. OSD, the CIA, and the State Department judged the gains of the APC as "inflated and fragile" and questioned the reliability of the data on which this "progress" was based. Another setback like Tet, they feared, would easily erase the campaign's gains, if they were not gradually eroded beforehand.[37]

A common thread ran through the critics' arguments. Although they agreed that the Thieu regime had indeed extended its presence into contested areas in the form of officials and programs, they insisted that the government had not established permanent security. OSD, the CIA, and the State Department further contended that the APC's achievements were based on unique circumstances: heavy dependence on U.S. Army operations to keep enemy forces at bay and the absence of a strong challenge from the enemy.[38] The CIA, more critical of the South Vietnamese government than Ambassador Bunker, found the regime lacking the skills and resources needed to improve its conduct of pacification and particularly laggard in coping with the political threat of the infrastructure. The critics concluded the enemy, if it so chose, could undo the gains of the APC.

General Abrams put a different twist on the arguments of critics. He believed that "the enemy must generate some type of strong reaction against the successes of the pacification program. I don't see how he could do otherwise."[39] In Abrams's mind, a failure to react would further harm enemy morale, already shaken by the military defeats of 1968. Communist documents reflected considerable disillusionment, concluding that some in the movement had "become doubtful of victory, pessimistic, and display a shirking attitude."

Abrams was correct. In February 1969, communist forces mounted another Tet Offensive, which targeted pacification and U.S. installations. The Viet Cong proved unable to regain the settlements it had lost in 1968. Enemy forces were able to occupy only 138 of the approximately 7,000 hamlets rated A, B, or C. The number of refugees created, homes destroyed, outposts given up, cadre teams withdrawn, and civilian casualties sustained was a fraction of the total for Tet 1968.[40] Based on HES data, 8 percent of the APC hamlets regressed from relatively secure to a lower ranking, while 11 percent actually improved from the end of January to the end of April 1969. During this period, U.S. Army ground forces provided territorial security, and according to HES data, the government's presence in the countryside continued to grow.[41] Did communist forces retain the capability to roll back the APC? In 1969, the answer was clearly "no." The CIA and other Washington agencies gave greater weight to the enemy's capabilities than was warranted.

To an extent, the differences in assessment between Washington and Saigon, which had persisted throughout 1968, were differences in perspective. The Americans in Saigon worked daily with the South Vietnamese and were intimately aware of the political, administrative, and military difficulties the regime faced and gave these factors extra weight in evaluations. What seemed important to American officials in Saigon was that the regime had overcome its Tet losses and, by making up for its past disappointing performance, offered hope for the future. Reflecting impatience, Washington was not as interested in Saigon's potential as in knowing how close the allies were to ending the insurgency.

MACV and the JCS argued that the campaign's achievements could not be summarily reversed. MACV judged South Vietnam's forces as stronger and more improved and the enemy as weaker than did the State Department or the CIA. The South Vietnamese had sufficient territorial forces to enter one thousand contested hamlets and attempt to make them secure, something the doubters had believed impossible immediately after the Tet Offensive. MACV and the JCS regarded the 227 RF companies and the 710 PF platoons (15 percent of the total) stationed in contested or enemy-controlled hamlets during the campaign as evidence that the government had begun to establish permanent security in those settlements. The distribution of one hundred thousand M-16 rifles to the territorial forces provided them with additional firepower and boosted their confidence. The presence of 353 MATs in the countryside helped stiffen the resolve of the RF/PF, improved their training, and increased the availability of air and artillery support. To CORDS and MACV, the territorials were becoming a capable local security force. The military regarded the recent pacification offensive as only a first step toward the establishment of lasting security. The military also believed that the communists, weakened after Tet, were less able to reverse the APC gains. The government had indeed established a sizable presence in the countryside, but how would those government officials, cadres, territorial forces, and soldiers perform over time? The question of the permanence of the APC could be answered only in the future.

Much of the disagreement between the civilians and the military over the gains of the APC stemmed from the interpretation of HES data. After the Tet attacks, Washington put less faith in HES findings than did MACV and the JCS, viewing the numbers as an inflated and unreliable index of rural security.[42] (Ironically, critics frequently and freely cited HES to demonstrate declines in population security.)[43] Yet none of the analysts in CORDS claimed that HES could demonstrate with certainty and precision how many South Vietnamese enjoyed security at any given moment.[44] It was the need to demonstrate progress to a skeptical press and public that had driven the Johnson administration and the MACV late in 1967 to latch onto HES scores and other statistics and publicize them in an effort to prove that the war was not stalemated.

But pacification officials used HES as more than a barometer of progress. They utilized the system, which had been operational since January 1967, to track long-term trends, assess progress, and highlight problems. To them, HES had proven its sensitivity to changing conditions after the Tet Offensive. During the APC, it helped locate newly established liberation committees, allowed CORDS to monitor the selection of target hamlets, and helped identify areas that would benefit most from U.S. Army support. National trends over a period of several months could be used with a degree of confidence, especially if they could be correlated with other statistical trends, such as the number of enemy-initiated attacks. No one in CORDS relied solely on HES figures for information on conditions in the countryside. CORDS analyzed HES data on population security in conjunction with *Chieu Hoi* rates, incidents of terrorism, reports from CORDS evaluators and province advisers, and intelligence information. The HES was only the most visible and notorious indicator; it was by no means the only one.

When viewed in the longer perspective, the APC marked the start of a period, roughly 1969 to early 1972, of uninterrupted gains in population security throughout South Vietnam and further erosion of the Viet Cong. The government mounted a more intensive and better-coordinated effort than in the past. At the end of January, government forces and cadre teams were located in many previously contested areas, and they were stationed there primarily because the government had decided to embark on a special offensive. This new presence represented an opportunity for Saigon authorities to challenge the Viet Cong in other settlements.

The special offensive integrated all pacification programs and the activities of the South Vietnamese ministries into a cohesive campaign. It did not devise new programs or experiment with major innovations. It simply obtained a commitment from the South Vietnamese to intensify work on existing programs and reallocate military and paramilitary forces and cadre teams to concentrate on upgrading contested areas. In that regard, the APC constituted a distinct improvement over the disappointing pacification plans of the past. By focusing pacification efforts on unambiguous, short-term goals, and taking advantage of the enemy's weakness in the countryside, the program attained the results inside South Vietnam that Komer had had in mind when originally advocating a special counteroffensive.

The APC illustrated America's ability to influence its ally. Komer could advocate a special campaign because he functioned as the single manager of pacification support and could help ensure that a special effort did not founder as a result of insufficient technical or logistical assistance or conflicting advice from American military and civilian officials. As the deputy to the American military commander and as a part of the military chain of command, he was in a position to obtain U.S. Army support for the campaign. Komer obtained the support of Bunker and Abrams. The three Americans acting together persuaded President Thieu to expand pacification when his conservative instincts inclined him to the less risky course of consolidating his grip on what was already in his hands. A united front of American advisers, the continued erosion of support for the war in the United States, and the need to gain a political advantage over the communists forced the hand of the South Vietnamese leader. For political and military reasons, Thieu could not ignore American pleas for action.

Unfortunately for CORDS, the campaign had little impact outside South Vietnam. Komer hoped that visible progress in pacification would help resolve the conflicting perceptions that Washington and Saigon held about the situation in Vietnam and help make a convincing case to the administration, the press, and the American public that the war was winnable. Yet despite the success of the accelerated campaign in extending Saigon's presence into the countryside, which even State Department and CIA critics acknowledged, the two capitals continued to view the war from different perspectives, deadlocked, conceding the enemy could not defeat the United States but maintaining it could push the government out of the newly gained villages. To critics, the APC had failed to prevent the communists from future political and military offensives.

The statistical results of the campaign itself were ambiguous, reflecting the crudity of the measurements and the still-unresolved situation in the countryside. Observers could find grounds for optimism or pessimism. A basic question remained unanswered at the end of the APC: Would the Viet Cong be able to rebuild its military strength and transform the liberation committees into a serious political movement before the Saigon government could consolidate its recent gains?

How should the APC be judged? On the basis of CORDS statistics, the results are inconclusive. The arguments of Colby and authors such as Kolko suggest that pacification succeeded despite the dearth of adequate and convincing statistical evidence. Perhaps the use of such data, flawed and viewed with disbelief following the Tet attacks, fatally compromised the APC. The campaign employed data that too many people considered unreliable to make the case that the countryside was more secure at the end of 1968. Therefore, the gains were not persuasive. Colby's position is instructive. He ran CORDS, helped design the APC, endorsed the notion of using statistics to set goals, and thus bears a degree of responsibility for the system that produced the numbers. He wanted the numbers sent to Paris because they demonstrated the success of pacification. Yet after the war, he downplayed them, writing, "Some of the statistics, though, we thought were fairly soft, to put it mildly."[45]

If Abrams's criteria—establishing police and RF/PF units in the villages, bashing down the VC, and protecting people against terrorism—are used, then the APC has to be judged again as inconclusive. After all, the enemy stepped up assassinations during the APC, and the police and RF/PF, which had entered the contested settlements, had yet to prove convincingly that they were up to the task of providing long-term security. Pacification, as Abrams recognized, was the "gut issue" for the South Vietnamese, and at the end of the APC it was still up to them to make their government "mean something."

Writing after the war, Colby argued that the APC's basic accomplishment was in getting the South Vietnamese to carry it out. In the past, many programs to turn the war around "had foundered on a Vietnamese inability or unwillingness to execute the programs according to the American formula. Komer and I ... realized that the key to making the APC work lay with President Thieu and the Vietnamese chain of command down to the provinces and districts."[46] If they believed in the program, they would support it. The APC launched pacification as a major strategy, in Colby's estimation.

The end of the APC coincided with the end of President Johnson's term in office. His administration's attempt to counteract the so-called stalemate doctrine and Komer's hope of convincing the skeptics had ended in failure. Their efforts had not halted the decline of domestic political support for American policy. Colby, who did not feel as keenly as Komer the need to convince the doubters in Washington, intended to concentrate on pressing pacification to win the people's war in the countryside, a position that Colby believed Nixon endorsed.[47]

Toward that same end, General Abrams was already working in early 1969 on plans to increase the involvement of army ground forces in pacification and to reduce tensions between pacification and military operations. In his mind, the accelerated campaign had reinforced the overall benefits of army operations in support of pacification. One of his goals would be to persuade his commanders to transform that support from a peripheral concern to a "gut issue," to borrow the term he used in addressing them at a January conference. His comments (quoted at the beginning of this chapter) formed part of an ongoing educational effort to convince his subordinates of pacification's paramount importance. The inauguration of Richard Nixon as president of the United States in January 1969 would have direct consequences for Abrams's and Colby's nascent plans.

13

New Directions

The pivotal events of 1968—the Tet Offensive, President Johnson's decision not to run for reelection, the start of peace talks, and dwindling popular support at home for the war—forced the major players to seek new approaches. Incoming president Richard M. Nixon could not continue the seemingly open-ended military commitment of the previous administration, in part owing to growing public and congressional dissatisfaction with the war. Nor could North Vietnamese and Viet Cong forces, badly hurt by losses sustained in their 1968 offensives, afford to pursue doggedly the same costly military strategy of the past year. With the start of serious bargaining at Paris in the fall of 1968, President Thieu needed to prepare for a fresh challenge to his regime's legitimacy: a political settlement that might lead to de facto recognition of the communists.

In this new environment, pacification would have great significance. For Nixon, the program's progress would serve as one benchmark of his administration's policy of "Vietnamizing" the war—that is, building up South Vietnamese capability to prosecute the war while gradually withdrawing American forces.[1] For Abrams, pacification would become a major purpose of American military operations. For Colby and Thieu, it was the most direct avenue to an independent and sovereign South Vietnam. For the communists, pacification was a direct threat to their hopes in the countryside.

Looking for an Exit

The war was a major issue in the 1968 election campaign. The turmoil of 1968—violent protests against the war, the assassinations of black civil rights leader Martin Luther King Jr. and Senator Robert F. Kennedy, and urban race riots born of poverty and racism—put pressure on both candidates, Nixon and Vice President Hubert Humphrey, to find a way out of an increasingly unpopular war and devote more attention to domestic problems. Richard Nixon took advantage of his position as the challenger to advocate a new strategy. Speaking before the Republican Party's platform committee on August 1, 1968, he called for a greater emphasis on mounting small-unit actions, rooting out the VCI, and training and equipping South Vietnamese forces so they could gradually replace American combatants. To an extent, Nixon's speech foreshadowed the direction of his policy as president.

Shortly after taking office, the new administration sought to determine South Vietnam's capacity to fight and govern on its own. The administration solicited the entire spectrum of official views from U.S. agencies in Washington and Saigon. The responses revealed little reason for optimism. Washington agencies conceded the Viet Cong and North Vietnamese could not win militarily against American combat units, but they concluded that allied military operations were unlikely to force Hanoi to capitulate.[2] They agreed that attrition had little chance of succeeding because the enemy could recruit and infiltrate sufficient replacements, although of lower quality. The Joint Chiefs of Staff concluded the North Vietnamese and Viet Cong could replenish their ranks for several years even at the high loss rates of the 1968 Tet Offensive. The Viet Cong infrastructure and order of battle also remained essentially intact. Another point in the enemy's favor was its ability to control the casualty rates of both sides. The enemy chose the time, place, type, and duration of most battles. Only a relatively low percentage of allied-initiated small-unit operations resulted in contact with the enemy.[3] There was agreement that Hanoi based its strategy on the premise that the American will to persist would steadily weaken and consequently would protract the war.

A drawn-out, costly war had grave implications for the administration. Public opinion polls showed that more people came to believe the war was a mistake the longer it continued.[4] Additional American casualties from continued fighting would intensify public pressure for withdrawal. The administration well understood this correlation. Foremost among Nixon's advisers advocating an American pullout was Secretary of Defense Melvin Laird. In mid-March, he related to Nixon the results of a visit to South Vietnam, arguing the case for phased, *unilateral* American troop withdrawals, a policy MACV and JCS vigorously opposed.[5] Nixon faced a dilemma: To hastily disengage American forces risked abandoning the South Vietnamese; not withdrawing U.S. forces quickly enough courted serious political risks in the United States.

In April, Nixon issued National Security Study Memorandum (NSSM) 36, a classified document directing Laird to develop a timetable for pulling American armed forces out of South Vietnam without a reciprocal reduction by the North.[6] In June, the withdrawal policy became public at a Midway conference when Nixon met with Thieu and announced that twenty-five thousand American soldiers would leave South Vietnam before the end of August without precondition.[7] Hanoi had not pulled any of its forces from South Vietnam, nor had it agreed to do so, although mutual withdrawals had been a key proviso of Nixon's speech in mid-May, his first presidential address on Vietnam.

Nixon's announcement signaled a policy of gradual withdrawal that he hoped would moderate antiwar criticism in the United States while prolonging the time South Vietnam had to strengthen its hold over the countryside. The administration linked the *rate* of disengagement of American forces to continued progress in three areas: the Paris negotiations, improvement of South Vietnam's armed forces and the pacification program, and the level of enemy activity, that is, the number of American casualties. With this position, the administration could argue that it was carrying out regular and orderly troop withdrawals under favorable conditions. Although the official rationale implied that the withdrawals would be slowed or halted if Nixon's conditions were not met, the announcement at Midway marked the start of an irreversible process. The administration's willingness to withdraw unilaterally was an expression of growing political pressure to end U.S. involvement in the war. The administration's position, withdrawing according to a timetable, established a context for Nixon's conduct of the war but yielded to Hanoi an inestimable advantage. The communists had the opportunity to rebuild their guerrilla forces and local political organizations during the period that American forces were departing from South Vietnam. Hanoi was not compelled to withdraw forces from South Vietnam, nor had it any good reason to settle the war quickly. The burden would be on the South Vietnamese government to take up the slack from the Americans.

Kissinger advanced two broad criteria for successful pacification. First, Saigon's pacification cadres and territorial forces had to demonstrate a capacity to protect the South Vietnamese people and their villages from guerrilla incursions and terrorism.[8] Second, the Saigon government had to "establish a political and institutional link between the villages and Saigon" to broaden its political base so that it was stronger for the political contest with the communists.[9]

The White House wanted an objective, credible system to assess progress in attaining these goals. The Nixon White House believed that HES produced vague, ambiguous findings and realized that government claims based on HES scores provoked skepticism. The responses to NSSM 1 disclosed that government agencies sharply disagreed over the interpretation of HES. Was a C hamlet adequately protected from guerrilla incursions and terrorism? Should the large segment of the population rated C—then some 2–3 million persons—be regarded as living in contested hamlets, as some Washington agencies contended, or in relatively secure ones, as CORDS claimed? The administration desired a measurement of the balance of power in the countryside that would prove more persuasive than HES, an index that would offer more realistic numbers to help pace the withdrawals and support the negotiators at Paris.

To help meet that requirement, President Nixon established in September 1969 an interagency body composed of officials from the military services, the State Department, and the CIA. Called the Vietnam Special Studies Group, it undertook systematic analyses focusing on the situation in the countryside and in specific provinces and sought to develop a clearer picture of the course of the war.[10] Under Kissinger's direction, the group combined available data into a composite index of governmental or enemy control. The ongoing presence in a hamlet of a government official or a political administration plus adequate protection by local security forces indicated governmental control. VC control was indicated if the VCI ran a settlement, if the VCI inhibited the work of government officials in a settlement, or if effective guerrilla combat units were defending a settlement or could launch at least a platoon-sized attack from bases one to two hours away. The administration considered control a more useful indicator than relative security. Despite civilian skepticism in the Defense and State Departments and the CIA about HES, the VSSG's numbers and its concept of control were based by default on HES data. HES was more reliable and systematic than anything else available. The VSSG in essence refined HES numbers, equating the two highest HES categories (A and B) with government control.

CORDS and MACV ignored the VSSG index, continuing to define A, B, and C hamlets as relatively secure. According to HES, relatively secure meant that local defense forces were adequate to deal with *local* enemy forces, the local party apparatus was largely neutralized, citizens participated in self-defense, local government and self-improvement efforts were proceeding, and the population was generally progovernment. The qualifying words—*adequate, largely,* and *generally*—allowed these criteria to cover a wide range of conditions. Relative security, like beauty, was in the eye of the beholder.

Nixon's Vietnamization policy set the context within which Abrams and Colby would operate. Pacification, as Komer liked to remind people, was already a "Vietnamized" program since South Vietnamese officials and forces carried it out. Pacification was intended to allow South Vietnam to stand on its own and represented a way to pursue the war at a lower cost to the United States. Yet Vietnamization meant fewer and fewer American forces would be available to provide security for cadre teams, government officials, and territorial forces implementing pacification. There would also be fewer advisers overseeing South Vietnamese planning and program administration. Would fewer advisers mean less American leverage on Saigon during the hoped-for transition to an autonomous South Vietnam? Would the smaller numbers of forces and advisers be able to facilitate this transition? How should General Abrams and Ambassador Colby pursue the war within the policy of Vietnamization?

A New Commander

In mid-1968, when Abrams became MACV commander, political and military circumstances demanded a fresh approach. In the aftermath of Tet, Defense Secretary Clifford urged the president to adopt a new strategy, and Abrams knew from his visits to the United States that political support for the war was waning and that time to achieve results was running out. Abrams had the opportunity to exploit the communist's Tet 1968 military defeat, which led them to shift many main force units into sanctuaries where they could avoid contact. In Abrams's view, the enemy, weakened by heavy losses, would be unable to operate as freely as before because U.S. ground and air operations had disrupted its logistics system.[11] The Politburo in Hanoi returned to scaled-down guerrilla operations, and Abrams reacted to the change with increased small-unit patrols, although to cope with the entire spectrum of the communist threat, he tried to keep maximum pressure on the VC and NVA.[12]

With the start of the APC, Abrams repeatedly exhorted his commanders to orient military operations in support of pacification and eschew large sweeps of unpopulated areas. Embellishing the theme enunciated by Ambassador Bunker at the birth of CORDS in 1967, Abrams asserted in October 1968 that the big-unit war and pacification were "one war,"[13] that the "order of the day is to intensify your offensive against infrastructure, guerrillas, and local force units."[14] In January 1969, he told his senior advisers (the top American military leadership in each corps) that the objectives of the current pacification and development plan were paramount.[15] He wanted his commanders to give precedence to attacking the Viet Cong political apparatus because "the VCI are the ones who support the main force units."[16] "It is," he insisted, "the duty of every friendly armed formation to see that necessary security is provided."[17]

The thrust of Abrams's thinking on pacification and military operations can be traced to 1968, but Nixon's Vietnamization policy forced the general to push his ideas of population security and one war more vigorously and to rely on the South Vietnamese government and military to an even greater degree. The withdrawal of American forces formed the framework of Abrams's military operations in the Nixon years.

Since the time he became commander, historians have debated whether Abrams initiated a new strategy. Two key members of Abrams's staff, Komer and Gen. Davidson, MACV J-2, categorically asserted that Abrams did not do so in 1968.[18] But Abrams did set up planning groups that year to examine new ways to prosecute a changing war, desiring to link army operations more directly to the ultimate goal of building a viable government and political community in South Vietnam. Under the attrition strategy, large American units had used their superior mobility to thwart the enemy's main forces, but all too often such engagements had little influence on the local balance of power. Some American commanders erroneously equated their operations, or the mere presence of their forces, with rural security. To help reorient army operations, Abrams created the Long-Range Planning Task Group (LORAPL) in July 1968, selecting as its head Lieutenant Colonel Donald Marshall, who had worked on the army's PROVN study in 1966 when Abrams had served as army vice chief of staff.[19] PROVN had advocated more pacification and less attrition. Abrams's selection of Marshall as a long-range planner indicated the direction of his thinking. The LORAPL report, which Abrams received in November 1968 after Komer's departure, concluded that security was critical to victory. The APC was seen as a turning point, redirecting American military strength in support of rural security efforts. According to the report, U.S. resources should be devoted to three main functions: population security, CORDS support of pacification, and national development.

The report was the basis of the MACV strategic objectives plan, Abrams's strategy for achieving U.S. objectives in South Vietnam. Approved in March 1969, the plan defined the ultimate American objective as a "free, independent and viable nation of South Vietnam that is not hostile to the United States, functioning in a secure environment both internally and regionally,"[20] a formulation not far removed from the Johnson administration's policy in NSAM 288. The prime role of American and South Vietnamese forces was to provide population security and thus support pacification. Abrams wanted to expand the secure areas within which the government carried out its development programs and assist it in developing meaningful institutions and an environment for economic growth and social change. Viewing the political and military components of the war in Vietnam as inseparable, Abrams sought, especially after the APC, to change the mindset of his commanders from a focus on body counts and attrition to a greater concern with population security. The strategic objectives plan showed that Abrams looked at the war differently from Westmoreland. Regardless of whether Abrams's view was the result of changed military circumstances or the new political climate, he tried to modify the way the U.S. Army fought.

Not all army generals were enthusiastic about Abrams's approach. General Ewell, the II Field Force commander, allegedly exclaimed after being briefed on the strategic objectives plan, "I've made my entire career and reputation by going 180 degrees counter to such orders as this."[21] Nevertheless, Ewell instructed his subordinates to operate in small units until they made contact with the foe and then to pile on in strength. Lieut. Gen. Melvin Zais, commanding general of XXIV Corps, supported Abrams's approach, telling Colby in 1970 that "we need to integrate the efforts of the tactical units and CORDS to a greater extent." Tacitly acknowledging that not all tactical commanders had comprehended Abrams's strictures about providing security, Zais lamented that "many tactical units ... are thrashing around spending untold thousands of man-hours looking for an elusive enemy."[22] He also noted a failure on the part of division commanders to make their unit leaders "understand our pacification goals and develop proper attitudes with Vietnamese officials and other personnel in the populated areas."[23] Although commanders observed the letter of Abrams's order, not all of them internalized the underlying message and changed their mode of operations.

With Ambassador Bunker's support, Abrams sought Washington's endorsement of his strategic objectives but failed. His objectives did not comport with Washington's. As Defense Secretary Laird explained, the administration viewed the goal of a noncommunist government in South Vietnam as possibly conflicting with Nixon's offer to abide by the results of a free election in South Vietnam.[24] Nor did the administration seek a military victory in South Vietnam, an implicit goal of Abrams's plan. The administration wanted him to press the enemy hard, forcing it to negotiate. In July, the White House sent Abrams a new mission statement giving priority to Vietnamization, pacification, and choking of the enemy's supply lines. Absent was any reference to a military victory or attrition.[25] Abrams was placed in a bind: He wanted to use pacification to help win the war; the White House wanted to use pacification to help America withdraw.

Change in CORDS

On Komer's departure in November 1968, William Colby took control of a fully operational organization. Heading CORDS in the first year and one-half of its existence, Komer had institutionalized a single manager system for American support of pacification from the district level to MACV headquarters. He had also guided the buildup of U.S. Army advisers for pacification, the growth of the RF/PF, and the development of an integrated government pacification program during the APC. Staffed mainly by U.S. Army personnel, CORDS had become a fixture within MACV headquarters, and its advisers were stationed throughout the countryside. The organization had benefited from increased budgets and greater access to U.S. military support. Although some civilian advisers who had worked for OCO grumbled that the new organization was too bureaucratic and "militarized," CORDS's establishment had greatly unified pacification support.

Colby also operated differently from Komer. The new head of CORDS, while sharing Komer's determination to advance pacification, was more inclined to operate within regular channels. In contrast to Komer, who rarely missed an opportunity to remind others of his own, and his organization's, prerogatives, Colby tended to be conciliatory—for instance, letting Abrams's deputy, General Andrew Goodpaster, handle an issue within CORDS jurisdiction. "We are all one outfit," Colby remarked, "and I don't feel anything is 'mine.'"[26] His desire to administer CORDS with a less confrontational profile may have stemmed in part from his personality, but he also had to contend with Abrams's determination to rein in CORDS. Some generals, including Abrams, had become irritated with Komer's tendency to disregard normal procedures and intrude into areas outside his charter.[27] From their first days in South Vietnam, Komer and Abrams, both assertive personalities, had viewed each other warily.[28]

Colonel Montague played a key role in the transition. As Komer's executive officer, he had filled a number of important roles, supervising the day-to-day functioning of the staff. Colby insisted he remain, especially after General Forsythe, Komer's deputy, left to command the 1st Cavalry Division. Montague assumed an important liaison role with government officials. Under Colby, he dealt frequently with Lieutenant General Dong Van Quang, Thieu's chief aide.

Colby stressed the continuity of pacification, encouraging the redeployment of cadre teams and territorial forces to allow the expansion of pacification into contested areas, just as Komer had. Colby also carried on Komer's policy of upgrading territorial forces' weaponry and expanding their numbers, helping ensure that local security forces would be able to support the expansion of pacification. By early 1969, CORDS estimated that 84 percent of the RF companies and 79 percent of the PF platoons possessed firepower equal to or better than that of nearby Viet Cong units. All RF/PF units would receive M-16 rifles, M-60 machine guns, and M-79 grenade launchers. Total RF/PF strength at the end of 1969, 475,000, was 20 percent higher than the 1968 figure, 392,000.[29]

Colby could take advantage of an existing base of security. Expecting the government to consolidate its control of the countryside in 1970 and 1971 as the enemy military threat was reduced to levels manageable by government forces, he brought his own approach to pacification. Hoping to broaden the government's political base, he advocated bringing together the responsible political forces in South Vietnam and increasing political involvement by citizens at the village level.[30] His goal was to convince them that a better life was "coming down the road as the result of their own efforts in support of government programs."[31] The development of provincial and village councils with authority to draft laws and raise taxes for local projects, Colby believed, would promote greater popular involvement in local government, and he urged Prime Minister Khiem's support.[32] Colby's chief concern was preparing the Saigon government for competition with the communists. In his view, South Vietnam needed to develop the political and social resources needed to sustain itself over the long term, a position in full accord with Nixon's Vietnamization policy. "Three selfs" summed up Colby's goals for pacification: self-defense, self-government, and self-development.

But based on South Vietnam's dismal record of carrying out programs, how could anyone be certain that the government would indeed make the requisite effort on its own? Would it be necessary, as Colonel Warner, senior military aide to the chief of staff of the army, put it, to force the South Vietnamese government to reform and deliver the goods to its people?[33] With the departure of advisers and soldiers, American influence would likely wane.

According to the reports of the province senior advisers in September 1968, the performance of local officials was rated good in only one province and poor in eighteen.[34] Many of the government cadres stationed in the provinces were weak and unresponsive to the direction of the province chiefs. Village councils showed little initiative in collecting taxes, depending instead on government subsidies for operating funds. The government drafted many local leaders and administrators into the armed forces, replacing them with less talented and experienced persons. In contested provinces such as Phu Yen, village chiefs were marginally effective, closing their offices early in the afternoon so that they could return to more secure areas by nightfall. This record was hardly encouraging for the long-term pacification of South Vietnam.

President Thieu's Pacification Plans

In 1969, President Thieu gave increased attention to the political side of the war. The Vietnamese leader assumed that the communists could not win a military victory in the short term but would resort to guerrilla warfare and political activity to shore up their position in the countryside. He envisioned a period of decisive political struggle against the communists and was determined to prevent the Paris peace negotiations from frustrating his government's preparations for that struggle. His unyielding stance was summed up in the "Four Noes": no coalition government with the Viet Cong; no compromises on South Vietnam's territorial integrity, which meant he would not concede any areas to the Viet Cong or agree to the presence of Hanoi's army inside South Vietnam; no acceptance of the Communist Party as a legal political entity; and no neutralism.[35] In contrast to Nixon and Colby, Thieu's rigid position allowed little room for compromise. He defined his position entirely in negative terms, closing the door on political accommodation.

To strengthen his government politically, Thieu gave priority to village development, rural elections, and land reform. He hoped to engage villagers in their own defense and in local public works projects, believing such involvement would help establish unity among the people and between the people and the government. In addition, the president bolstered the government's organization for pacification, creating a high-level position, deputy prime minister for pacification, to coordinate the work of the ministries involved in pacification and help run CPDC. He appointed Tran Thien Khiem, a political ally and minister of the interior, to the new post.

Representing the combined efforts of the newly formed CPDC, various ministries, and CORDS, the 1969 pacification plan required corps commanders to preserve the security of areas already pacified and extend security to cover more of the population.[36] Like Abrams, Thieu focused on military support of pacification. To be able to secure more villages, the 1969 plan reshaped the RD Cadre. The government divided the fifty-nine-person RD Cadre teams into two teams of thirty, thereby doubling the number of villages that could have teams. Although the government eliminated the small security force from the cadre teams, it felt confident that the growth of local forces would compensate for the absence of a security element. RD teams were assigned more or less permanently, along with a PF platoon and a PSDF unit, to particular villages, where they would help identify the VCI, organize and train the PSDF, institute local elections, and initiate self-help programs.[37]

Under the plan, the government intended to bring security to the population and return people to their home villages. At least on paper, this provision repudiated the past practice of relocating people from their homes in contested or enemy-controlled areas to camps or settlements, where the government could "protect" them from communist recruiters and tax collectors. In theory, the 1969 plan limited population relocation primarily to situations where authorities deemed it otherwise impossible to extend government protection. In practice, exceptions would severely strain this policy.[38]

Other government steps taken in 1969 and 1970 as part of pacification constituted what one observer aptly called a "comprehensive political strategy" composed of village elections, administrative decentralization, and sweeping land reform.[39] The Thieu government held elections for village councils throughout 1969. By the end of the year, twenty-one hundred locally elected bodies governed 94 percent of South Vietnam's villages. The government passed legislation increasing the authority of local elected officials, placing the local PF platoon and

local cadre teams under the operational control of the village chief. It also authorized the village council to spend up to 100,000 piasters ($850) on local projects
without approval from higher echelons. Saigon also raised the salaries of village
officials and no longer required village bodies to submit their budgets to the capital for approval. The government also changed its procedures for village subsidies
to encourage village authorities to develop local revenue sources and achieve
greater self-sufficiency.[40]

Completing the political program was the long-awaited enactment of land reform. Many observers had long been convinced that genuine land reform was the
key to defeating the insurgency and that the grant of land and titles to poor landless farmers would go far in undermining the Viet Cong's appeal. The NLF's
grants of land in the villages it controlled were a powerful weapon in mobilizing
support. The Land to the Tiller Law, which was enacted in March 1970, sought "to
eliminate tenancy, expropriating and distributing all land not directly cultivated
by the owner."[41]

The Thieu government's improved planning and emphasis on local political
development generally pleased the Americans. They also found encouraging his
concern with control of the rural population and his political efforts to counter
the Viet Cong. Thieu had learned what would satisfy the Americans, and his program reflected American concerns. To be sure, he did not advocate elections and
land reform just to placate his powerful and wealthy benefactor, but the depth of
Thieu's commitment to greater democracy and stronger local government was
hard to gauge. How well Thieu's regime translated theory into practice would be
the acid test.

The Communists Adjust

After the APC ended in January 1969, communist forces mounted another Tet Offensive. In addition to targeting pacification, the enemy called for attacks by fire
on U.S. installations, hoping to inflict heavy American casualties. The attacks
were more intense than the May and August 1968 efforts but were easily repulsed,
and the enemy failed to gain the dramatic psychological advantage of the 1968 attacks.[42]

The 1969 offensive began on February 23, but, alerted by good intelligence, allied forces thwarted the enemy's plans. Fearing a major enemy assault against the
capital by the estimated four NVA divisions then in Cambodia, Abrams, like
Weyand before him, had moved American units to protect Saigon. In October
1968, Abrams pulled the U.S. 1st and 25th Infantry Divisions from the Cambodian
border to support South Vietnamese units and the pacification program in the
heavily populated districts nearer to the capital. Also in October, Abrams ordered
the 1st Cavalry Division to redeploy from northern I Corps to a forty-eight-hun-
dred-square-mile area of operations in War Zones C and D in III Corps. Abrams
wanted to use the air mobile unit, able to move its battalions by air quickly over

large expanses of territory, to provide a screen along the border to break up thrusts by North Vietnamese divisions.[43] With these units protecting the capital, the attacking NVA 1st and the VC 5th Divisions failed even to enter the city. The enemy's effort achieved no military gains.[44]

The effort was costly, however. Between February 23 and March 29, enemy combat fatalities soared to 5,000 each week, and the weekly number of defectors rose to a record 1,000. These losses came on top of the serious casualties of previous months. From October 1968 to February 22, 1969, enemy battle deaths, according to MACV data, averaged 2,500 per week. Between November and January, defections averaged around 650 and infrastructure losses about 500 a week.[45] The period from January 1968 to February 1969 was a costly one. Tet 1969 was the enemy's last major military effort until 1972.

The 1969 offensive had a slight effect on pacification. Compared with the previous year, the 1969 attacks produced no real harm, leading MACV to doubt the Viet Cong's ability to reverse the gains of the APC.[46] Less than 1 percent of the RF/ PF units redeployed to defend the cities, compared to 33 percent in 1968. The figures show a decline in the VC's military potency, suggesting it was a spent force incapable of checking the advance of pacification.

	Government Losses	
	Tet 1968	*Tet 1969*
Outposts lost or abandoned	477	8
RD Cadre teams withdrawn	296	11
Civilians killed or wounded	34,500	7,811
Refugees created	750,000	27,600
Homes damaged over 50 percent	158,000	6,673

In the aftermath of the 1969 offensive, the communists had little choice but try checking the erosion of their holdings in South Vietnam that had begun with the APC. Seeking to project an image of a still-vigorous political force,[47] the party abandoned the quest for a dramatic victory through large-scale battles and resorted to a low-cost/high-impact political military campaign of protracted warfare,[48] hoping to maximize American casualties and quicken the growth of antiwar sentiment in the United States. In July, the party issued COSVN Resolutions 9 and 14, its revised basic guidance. (Resolution 14 contained the instructions for carrying out the new policy.) Under the resolutions, the party called for a return to small-unit tactics and decided to break big units into small self-sufficient guerrilla groups to preserve its forces. The RF/PF and PSDF, to a lesser extent, became the enemy's main military targets since they embodied the government's attempt to mobilize the people. The party also called on its cadres to intensify terrorism and proselytizing in order to undermine Saigon's efforts to broaden its political base in the countryside. The underlying objective was to put the party in the strongest possible position for a post–cease-fire political struggle with Saigon.[49]

The resolution envisioned a critical role for Viet Cong guerrillas and infra-structure. They would provide the essential political structure in the countryside, establish a logistical base for future military operations, and prevent the South Vietnamese and Americans from concentrating their attacks on main forces. The communists took steps to protect their infrastructure from the Phoenix program, relying to a greater degree on legal cadres, persons living as ostensibly normal citizens in government areas who were secretly serving the Viet Cong. The communists also "compartmentalized" the lower echelons of the infrastructure. The less they knew about the organization and its leaders, the less information they could reveal to government authorities if arrested and interrogated.

The focus of activity shifted to the delta. To rebuild forces in IV Corps, Hanoi, beginning in the spring of 1969, sent five NVA regiments from III Corps to the delta to try halting the pacification program there and compensate for personnel losses. A fresh infusion of personnel, the communists hoped, would help revital-ize local guerrilla operations and rebuild the network of cadres. The new regi-ments were also expected to build up enemy base areas.[50] In spite of the infusion of NVA troops, and the enemy's efforts to control losses by resorting to economy-of-force tactics and careful selection of apparently vulnerable targets for military operations, communist forces continued to decline in numbers in 1969 and 1970. Communist losses came at the hands of South Vietnam's regular and territorial forces. The last elements of the U.S. 9th Division departed from the delta in the summer of 1969.[51]

After the allied incursion into the communists' Cambodian sanctuaries in May 1970, they continued to conserve forces, shifting roughly half their units in III Corps to Cambodia, an advantage for the Americans and South Vietnamese. With fewer forces available, enemy attacks in this corps fell below 1969 levels.[52] These deployments left remaining communist forces in the region vulnerable to further government inroads. In Tay Ninh province, continued allied military pressure deprived the Viet Cong of its customary freedom of movement and ac-cess to the population, and tax collections and recruiting declined.[53]

As part of the antipacification campaign, the party used terrorism, especially at the village and hamlet level, to eliminate local officials and RD cadres, disrupt programs, and intimidate the population into disavowing the Thieu regime. The Americans classified terrorist actions into three categories: coercion (recruitment, taxation, and conscription), destruction of civilian and government facilities and vehicles, and violence (assassinations, abductions, and woundings). Civilian ca-sualties resulting from terrorism averaged twenty-six thousand in 1969 and 1970. Only in 1971 did the number fall below twenty thousand.[54] The impact of terror-ism in a country the size of South Vietnam was hard to measure psychologically, but the numbers represented substantial losses. According to the Defense Depart-ment, these losses would be the equivalent of eliminating fifty thousand U.S. citi-zens annually.[55]

Hanoi shifted away from big-unit fighting and concentrated on political sub-version as the U.S. Army began to withdraw. The communists obviously had to deal with the ARVN but regarded it as a less potent force that was susceptible to guerrilla warfare and subversion. Hanoi believed that it could always return to a big-unit conflict to strike a final blow after the Saigon government had been undermined politically and the American divisions had departed.

For different reasons and with different goals, the communists, like Abrams, Colby, and Thieu, sought to change the tenor of the war from the major clashes of big units so prominent in 1968 and prior years to scaled-down fights for control of the population. Not expecting to defeat the United States militarily, the communists hoped to hold pacification in check and strengthen themselves politically.

In August 1969, Nixon pulled the first American soldiers out of South Vietnam. The imperatives of Nixon's policy dictated that withdrawal continue and that the best face be put on the situation, despite the strong reservations of the American commander. Abrams, who sought to improve the integration of military strategy and pacification goals, was uncertain whether American efforts to support pacification and strengthen South Vietnam's forces would produce the kind of success that could justify on purely military grounds the reduction of U.S. combat forces. He did not believe the South Vietnamese would be militarily ready in the near future to stand in for departing U.S. units and cope with the full range of the enemy threat.[56]

During the period that Nixon devised Vietnamization, the Viet Cong retrenched, and the Thieu government readied itself to expand pacification. The stage was set for the next phase of the war. Would the government's pacification program have enough time to take effect, or would the inexorable American withdrawal leave it in a vulnerable position?

14

One War or Business as Usual?

To what extent did General Abrams change strategy? Aside from the broadly conceived joint strategic objectives plan and a rather abstract area security concept, Abrams issued no formal order or directive mandating his new approach to the war. Yet his pronouncements seemed to indicate that he viewed the war differently from Westmoreland, desiring to link ground operations more directly to the goal of building a viable government and political community. But in what ways did U.S. forces operate differently from how they had under Westmoreland? Given that the body count was not Abrams's criterion of success, how were his concepts carried out at the operational level? Were they understood and accepted by subordinate commanders?

Davidson's discussion of whether Abrams changed strategy fails to clear up the matter. According to Davidson, Abrams did not change strategy in 1968, but his subordinates carried out a new approach to the war. "It has become conventional wisdom to claim that the new concept [embodied in the joint strategic objectives plan] suffered severely because Abrams's senior commanders refused to support it. This is nonsense. In many cases the general officers in Vietnam agreed with Abrams's strategy and carried it out with dedication. Even those who disagreed with the concept dutifully, if unenthusiastically, gave it their full support."[1]

Lewis Sorley, a biographer of Abrams, contended that Abrams did change strategy, but Sorley's treatment likewise does not settle the issue. In Sorley's account, when Abrams assigned General Kerwin as commander of II Field Force, he provided the general with no written instructions. "Abrams communicated what he wanted by his own example. ... Abrams was sure that Kerwin knew exactly what to do—they had been talking about it for a year."[2] If Sorley is correct and Abrams communicated by example, then how can a directed change in the conduct of the war be documented? Abrams's lack of a specific charge to Kerwin also implies that he allowed his commanders a wide degree of latitude in prosecuting the war, giving them at most a general operational framework.

A look at combat actions during Abrams's tenure suggests that the picture is not as clear-cut as Sorley insisted. Not all commanders adhered to Abrams's approach to pacification support. Not all commanders eschewed Westmoreland's attrition strategy. Nor were all operations animated primarily by a concern for the welfare of the populace. According to Davidson, Abrams in 1968 never voiced his dissatisfaction with large-unit search-and-destroy operations. So was there a change?

American military support of pacification during General Abrams's tenure varied from region to region. The DepCORDS for III Corps, Charles S. Whitehouse, was convinced that the U.S. Army played a signal role in pacification. In 1969 and 1970, the operations of the U.S. 1st Infantry Division in Binh Duong and Binh Long provinces helped pressure the enemy into breaking up its forces into small groups. The movement in 1969 of several NVA regiments from III Corps to the delta left mostly small units remaining in the region. They interdicted roads, mounted small-unit attacks, and engaged in terrorism. The diminished enemy threat allowed the 1st Division to saturate its operations area with companies and platoons, directly attack Viet Cong guerrilla bands, and help provide security in populated areas. In Whitehouse's view, the army helped reduce the Viet Cong to manageable size, and the pacification program was a success.[3]

Operations elsewhere exemplified the contrasting approaches to population security, some more commendable than others, that coexisted under Abrams's strategy. In the strongly contested provinces of I Corps, the enemy's pervasive influence and entrenched strength enormously complicated the task of pacification, and some American campaigns seemed to contradict Abrams's strategy. In Quang Ngai province, American forces conducted Operation RUSSELL BEACH to eliminate an especially vigorous enemy threat, but the operation conflicted with the ends of the pacification program. By contrast, in the critical II Corps province of Binh Dinh, where the communists were strong and entrenched, the U.S. 173d Brigade conducted Operation WASHINGTON GREEN, providing exemplary support to pacification. WASHINGTON GREEN and RUSSELL BEACH, perhaps two extremes, illustrated the very dissimilar ways U.S. ground commanders conducted operations under Abrams, making it hard to assert conclusively that the MACV commander had successfully changed strategy.

Within the context of Vietnamization and Abrams's one-war philosophy, the criteria for evaluating military operations were twofold. How effective were they in supporting pacification? How effective were they in weakening communist forces?

A Step Forward:
Operation WASHINGTON GREEN

In March 1969, Lieut. Gen. Charles A. Corcoran assumed command of First Field Force and endeavored to carry out Abrams's one-war concept. Corcoran directed that future operational planning in the region "focus at the district level in support of pacification."[4] Brigadier General John Barnes, commander of the 173d Airborne Brigade, in turn launched WASHINGTON GREEN, a campaign for the pacification of Binh Dinh province that adhered to Corcoran's criteria. Barnes viewed WASHINGTON GREEN as a sharp break from previous operations. After the war, he wrote that when he assumed command in December 1968, he inherited from his predecessor the "mission of searching out and destroying the enemy throughout our area of responsibility." The enormous losses suffered during Tet 1968 had caused the VC and NVA to change their mode of operations, forcing them to go into hiding while rebuilding forces and resupplying bases. The enemy

> fragmented his forces to avoid detection and, in turn, we have gone after him saturating the areas he once could call his own, ... ferreting him out and destroying him. This was our mission until the 15th of April [the start of WASHINGTON GREEN] when we became the test unit of a new program, which, if successful, would be instituted by all U.S. divisions and separate brigades in Vietnam. The new program was pacification. Overnight, our combat mission of finding, fixing, fighting, and destroying the enemy changed to a pacification mission of assisting the South Vietnamese people in establishing or restoring their political institutions, economic infrastructure and social fabric. We became a Brigade of advisers.[5]

Barnes told his commanders that they would no longer chase the Viet Cong and NVA and that the body count would no longer be the criterion of success. He banned harassment and interdiction firing (random artillery barrages at suspected enemy positions) and required U.S. and South Vietnamese artillery to get clearance to strike at a specific target. His aim was to secure the people and their homes, "to deny the VC their support from their hamlets, without which they cannot survive."[6] To attain that end, Barnes broke down American forces into small units and placed them in hamlets long dominated by the Viet Cong. Such formations would also allow the Americans to cover more hamlets and still be able to handle local guerrilla bands. By remaining in one location, Barnes believed, the smaller units would contribute to lasting security. WASHINGTON GREEN began in April 1969.

WASHINGTON GREEN's descent from Abrams's one-war concept seems clear, but what really changed? Barnes noted that the losses at Tet forced the enemy to change, which implied that American operations changed in response to the enemy's new tactics. His discovery of pacification in April is curious. Pacification was not a new mission. He took over the brigade in the midst of the APC, which required unprecedented support of pacification from American units. The goals and procedures of WASHINGTON GREEN were less a break with past operations than a continuation of the APC.

An extraordinarily large and strategically important province, Binh Dinh was an inevitable battleground. The communists had long used the province as a major command-and-control center. They had controlled parts of the province for years, some since the 1950s, and consequently the party had built up a considerably stronger, more entrenched organization than in most other provinces in South Vietnam.[7] The North Vietnamese and Viet Cong committed sizable forces to the province, at times up to four main force regiments, nearly ten thousand local force troops, and over fifteen thousand guerrillas.[8]

To meet a threat of this magnitude, the allies had deployed sizable forces in Binh Dinh. In addition to the 173d, American forces included the 4th Infantry Division, which operated in the western and northwestern sections of the province. Two regiments of the ARVN 22d Division covered the central portion of Binh Dinh. Numerous RF companies and PF platoons were scattered throughout the province. The Republic of Korea's Capital Division operated in the southern part of the province and the area around the city of Qui Nhon.

For WASHINGTON GREEN, General Barnes, in coordination with province officials and the commander of the 22d Division, Maj. Gen. Nguyen Van Hieu, divided the strongly contested, heavily populated districts of Tam Quan, Hoai An, Hoai Nhon, and Phu My into six operational areas, assigning a maneuver battalion from the 173d or a regiment from the 22d to each. Barnes co-located his battalions' headquarters alongside the district staff and combined the command posts of the American and South Vietnamese units that would work together. Each battalion was to assist the territorial forces in providing local security and to help bring the four districts, some 350,000 people, under Saigon's control.[9]

The emphasis on district-level operations made the district senior adviser the focal point for liaison between the battalion staff and government officials. Especially in the initial stages of the operation, battalion headquarters relied on the pacification expertise of the CORDS staff, which was more familiar with local conditions.[10]

The district chiefs likewise assumed a prominent role. In cooperation and coordination with the battalion staffs, these chiefs planned the employment of troops and exercised some control over day-to-day operations. The chiefs were also in charge of carrying out district pacification plans, which listed the hamlets and villages to be pacified.[11] The local leadership seemed up to the task since the government had replaced several ineffective district chiefs with stronger leaders at the start of WASHINGTON GREEN.[12]

WASHINGTON GREEN sought first to upgrade contested hamlets to relatively secure status (HES A, B, or C). At the start of the operation, less than one-third of the 260 hamlets in these districts were considered relatively secure.[13] To achieve an HES rating of C, each target hamlet had to recruit and organize a PF platoon from its own population to provide local security. In the final phase of the operation, September to December 1970, dismantling the infrastructure had top priority. The goal was to remove all vestiges of communist political control.[14]

WASHINGTON GREEN began at an opportune time. The enemy's main forces had pulled back from the coastal plains to the Que Son Mountains to rest and refit, generally avoiding contact with allied forces. Viet Cong sappers and small guerrilla forces (local force companies, platoons, and hamlet squads) constituted the main thrust of the enemy's resistance.[15] With the reduced main force threat, Barnes felt he faced little risk in focusing entirely on pacification, although he did leave some units in reserve to respond to any buildup of enemy main forces.

During the operation, which consisted of numerous small-unit engagements, U.S. Army and ARVN units provided screening forces around target hamlets so RF/PF and National Police could search for Viet Cong. Combined forces manned checkpoints, constantly patrolled the hamlets, and laid ambushes at night. Strong fire discipline characterized most engagements, minimizing the destruction of property and civilian casualties. Barnes reported that after remaining in the hamlets for a while, American troops came to recognize outsiders and developed rapport with residents, who volunteered information and pointed out booby traps.[16]

American soldiers, besides offering security, also trained the RF/PF. In many cases, Barnes assigned U.S. platoons to work with PF platoons so that operations and training were all conducted together. Hundreds of U.S. Army soldiers, supplementing the efforts of the twelve MATs stationed in the four districts, helped train the RF/PF in marksmanship and small-unit tactics. The 3d Battalion, 319th Artillery established an artillery training program for the RF/PF in Tam Quan and Hoai Nhon districts. Consisting of fifteen to thirty hours of instruction, the course sought to ensure that each RF/PF unit had trained forward observers and would know how to obtain timely support from ARVN artillery units.[17] Other elements of the 173d conducted integrated operations with their co-located RF or PF elements and also provided formal instruction in leadership for RF/PF noncommissioned officers and junior commissioned officers. The Americans also instructed the PSDF in weapons care, marksmanship, and patrolling to prepare Saigon's local forces to defend hamlets by themselves.

Friendly forces provided the sustained local security that denied the enemy access to food, money, and personnel. The communists also ceded a psychological advantage to the government. No longer subject to communist terror and extortion, the people had the opportunity to live in peace and the government a chance to gain popular confidence. But these benefits depended heavily on the government's ability to root out the clandestine infrastructure and to improve the territorial and police forces enough so that they could continue to provide security without help from the U.S. Army.

During WASHINGTON GREEN, the 173d disrupted the enemy's organization and denied it access to hamlets in the area of operations and kept its forces from hamlets. The Americans counted 1,961 enemy combat deaths, and the South Vietnamese detained over 5,000 suspected members of the VCI. Allied forces also captured significant amounts of enemy supplies: four tons of wheat, sixty-seven tons of rice, and over two tons of salt. American firepower, matériel, and training were instrumental in improving security in part of the province. The presence of South Vietnamese officers among the American soldiers entering hamlets demonstrated to residents that their government was involved. Combined U.S. and South Vietnamese operations and American deference to South Vietnamese authority (despite the temptation to take charge) also boosted South Vietnamese confidence.[18]

Of all American actions carried out in accordance with Abrams's one-war concept, WASHINGTON GREEN was perhaps the most acclaimed. General Barnes prepared a special briefing and presented it to the Army Policy Council, composed of the top army leadership in the Pentagon, the State Department's Vietnam Training Center, and the assistant secretary of defense for international security affairs. A group of lawmakers brought the operation to President Nixon's attention, expressing the hope that Barnes's approach would be replicated in other areas of South Vietnam. Members of the House of Representatives praised General Barnes for discontinuing the body count, restricting the use of firepower, deemphasizing large-unit actions in favor of night patrols and ambushes, and working closely with the territorial defense forces and local government.[19]

Before WASHINGTON GREEN actually ended, the 173d redeployed some forces in the autumn of 1970 to help cover the operational area vacated by withdrawing elements of the U.S. 4th Division. The three-part pacification mission of upgrading hamlets, training territorial forces, and uprooting the communist underground continued in Phu My, but on a reduced scale. In the spring of 1971, the 173d Brigade received orders to withdraw from South Vietnam, leaving ARVN and territorial forces to take over. The last elements of the brigade left in August 1971.

The army earned well-deserved plaudits for its approach in WASHINGTON GREEN, but the long-term accomplishments of the operation failed to live up to the lavish praise the operation initially received. Over time, the performance of South Vietnamese officials and military forces disappointed the Americans. In northern Binh Dinh, local government officials and forces were reported in 1971 to maintain a token presence for a few hours each day, and the Americans regarded South Vietnamese units as only marginally successful in keeping the Viet Cong away from hamlets.[20] Soldiers of the 173d who worked with the South Vietnamese were frustrated with their counterparts. As an evaluator from the CORDS Pacification Studies Group observed in 1969, "After a few weeks of close associations without any improvement the U.S. soldier is prone to be intolerant of Vietnamese ineptitude and particularly of indications of irresponsibility."[21]

Unfortunately for the South Vietnamese, early in 1970 the Viet Cong began to step up recruiting and proselytizing, rebuilding for the day when American troops would be gone. The communists worked to rejuvenate their district-level political base, strengthen their cadres, and increase the percentage of the population under their control. The infrastructure in this area had bounced back after losses suffered during the Tet Offensive of 1968, and it did so again after WASHINGTON GREEN. In 1971, the VCI began to grow, jumping from nine thousand in September to about fifteen thousand in October. The Phoenix program in Binh Dinh was weak and seemed unable to stem this expansion. Colonel Billy Mendheim, who became province senior adviser in November 1969, remarked in December 1970 (the last month of WASHINGTON GREEN) that "as U.S. forces pull out of areas where they alone were responsible for security, the place reverts to communist control."[22] Daniel L. Leaty, who succeeded Mendheim in May 1971, agreed. The enemy's resurgence was also reflected in HES security scores, which dropped in 1971 after the departure of U.S. Army combat elements.[23]

Examined over the long term, WASHINGTON GREEN offered little reason for optimism. This finding is significant, for WASHINGTON GREEN was a model operation, lasting far longer than most and using conventional forces in a sophisticated counterinsurgency role. The Viet Cong, however, was as determined and resourceful as ever and was able to rebuild. The performance of government forces and officials during the operation raised doubts in the minds of advisers about whether the regime by itself could cope with a resurgent Viet Cong movement. To achieve broad and lasting control of a province like Binh Dinh would require an even greater effort than WASHINGTON GREEN.

A Step Backward: Operation RUSSELL BEACH/BOLD MARINER

If WASHINGTON GREEN adhered to Abrams's views on the use of ground forces to support pacification, then RUSSELL BEACH/BOLD MARINER apparently did not. A U.S. Army and Marine Corps operation that employed two battalions of the 23d Division (Americal) and two U.S. Marine Corps battalion landing teams, RUSSELL BEACH involved the deliberate relocation of people and destruction of property.[24] Unfortunately, the operation marked a return to practices that had characterized earlier sweeps, such as CEDAR FALLS, through enemy-controlled populated areas.

RUSSELL BEACH took place early in 1969 in the Batangan Peninsula, a dangerous area in Quang Ngai, one of the most hostile provinces in South Vietnam. Between 1967 and 1972, Quang Ngai alone accounted for 6 percent of American combat deaths.[25] Operations by American, South Vietnamese, and South Korean forces in 1967 and 1968 had failed to clear the Viet Cong from the peninsula, site of the infamous My Lai massacre of South Vietnamese civilians in March 1968. A year after My Lai, allied forces still had made little headway against the Viet Cong. Enemy forces attacked American units and fired rockets on the province capital, Quang Ngai city.[26] RUSSELL BEACH involved the relocation of civilians from their homes, a tactic that was discouraged.

In mid-1968, Abrams had reiterated Westmoreland's policy that military operations be conducted to minimize property destruction and the generation of refugees. This policy was in accord with pacification's long-standing goal of expanding security to populated areas rather than forcing residents into "secure" zones.[27] The combined campaign plan (AB 144) and guidance from CPDC also aimed to curtail the practice of relocating people in order to mount military operations, requiring the submission and prior approval of plans.[28] CORDS refugee officers and officials from the Ministry of Refugees insisted on having a voice in making the decisions to relocate.[29]

Despite Abrams's guidance and the CPDC's policy, the issue of relocation was not clear-cut. In some cases, relocations made sense. The displaced people were anxious to flee communist terror, operations were mounted to extract them from areas dominated by the party, and new land was available to them for cultivation. In other cases, relocations were handled poorly. The ministry and CORDS were not informed of military operations that included evacuation until they were in progress and it was too late to prepare for the relocation. Food, land, or jobs were unavailable, causing resentment among people hastily shunted into such settlements. In some cases, people were relocated from areas that were scheduled to be pacified later. The lack of thought and advanced planning, Louis Wiesner concluded, "botched what might have been successful resettlements, or caused relocations which did not need to take place at all."[30] Unfortunately, RUSSELL BEACH did not turn out as planned.

The object of RUSSELL BEACH/BOLD MARINER was to further the goals of the APC. Billed as a county fair operation, RUSSELL BEACH/BOLD MARINER was intended to cordon the peninsula and clear out enemy forces.[31] The inhabitants were to be moved to a tent encampment inaptly called Resurrection City, screened for VC cadres, and then returned home. Because the operation envisioned the return of the refugees to their native villages in about a month, CORDS and the government approved the population relocation. The Batangan Peninsula was targeted for pacification in the 1969 plan, and pacification officials hoped the operation would convert a Viet Cong stronghold into an area of government control.[32]

The operation began on January 13 when two U.S. Marine Corps battalion landing teams stationed with the Seventh Fleet disembarked on the peninsula, one by helicopter and the other from the sea about twelve miles south of Chu Lai. One NPFF platoon, one RF platoon, and three armed propaganda teams were attached to each marine battalion. On the same day, Task Force Cooksey, composed of units from the U.S. 23d Division, the 5th Battalion, 46th Infantry regiment, and the 4th Battalion, 3d Infantry regiment, sealed off the southern boundary. The U.S. battalions and two battalions of ARVN infantry pushed the enemy toward the sea. Although the marine units pulled out at the end of January, the cordon lasted until February 6, and army units continued the operation until it officially ended in July.

The landings met little resistance; most casualties resulted from concealed mines and booby traps. The peninsula was laced with tunnels and caves. Two platoons from Company B of the 26th Engineer Battalion destroyed close to 13,125 yards of tunnels in the early part of the operation. All houses in the area of operation were destroyed to preclude the enemy from continuing to use them and to facilitate the location of tunnel entrances. By the time the operation officially ended, American forces suffered 56 combat deaths; the Viet Cong, 158.

Government officials, with U.S. civilian assistance, designated approximately 1,000 persons for further screening. According to the operational report of the 23d Division, 256 members of this group were identified as belonging to the VCI.

Other reports more accurately placed the number of confirmed members of the infrastructure captured during the operation at less than 50.[33]

The allied sweep displaced close to twelve thousand people, over 40 percent of the population of the peninsula. Villagers were evacuated by helicopter to a holding area and interrogation center. After screening, roughly eleven thousand of those relocated were crowded into a camp of 125 tents at Thien An. To make the camp habitable, the Ministry of Social Welfare and Relief dug wells and latrines and provided food, water, firewood, and cooking utensils. Red Cross workers, the 29th Civil Affairs Company, and MILPHAP teams provided meals and medical care and helped run schools. The operation was conducted in the middle of the cold rainy season. The government supplied some blankets but did not have enough for everyone. A large undertaking, RUSSELL BEACH drained resources from other aspects of the provincial refugee program.

In RUSSELL BEACH, complications hampered the work of caring for the newly homeless. Persons displaced during these operations were not registered as refugees with South Vietnamese authorities and were therefore ineligible for government refugee assistance. Three-man teams from the U.S. Army's 29th Civil Affairs Company working in Quang Ngai could make little headway in improving the plight of a refugee population estimated at 213,000 in mid-1969 in the Americal's area of operations. The teams concentrated on helping district officials, some of whom were poorly trained, make the system work. The teams helped officials, some of whom were poorly trained and obsessed with bureaucratic procedure, prepare official paperwork, formulate plans to upgrade the facilities at the camps, and submit requests for supplies and materials.[34]

By late February, province officials were beginning to resettle refugees in new hamlets. U.S. Army engineer units cleared land and constructed roads to provide access to the new resettlement sites located south of the peninsula. The government provided material to build new homes but refused to allow people to rebuild on their original homesites. RD Cadre teams and marine corps CAPs were stationed in the new hamlets. In addition to the CAPs, two RF companies, 400 men of the Americal Division, and 400 ARVN soldiers were located nearby. Despite the presence of allied forces, security remained poor, delaying the completion of road work until late March.[35]

The refugee problem remained grave. The new camps were inaccessible by land and difficult to expand because of mines and booby traps in the surrounding area. In January 1970, some refugees were still unable to return to their original hamlets, mainly because security remained poor and communist-planted minefields were a continuing hazard. Farmers were unable to work their farms. In Phu Chi hamlet of Binh Duc village, one of the interim settlements, 275 families dwelled in encampments surrounded by barbed wire. They were living on manioc because they had exhausted their six-month government rice allowance. The provincial office of the Ministry of Social Welfare and Relief, the province's distribution point, had also run out of rice. To feed persons displaced from the Batangan Peninsula, General Hoang Xuan Lam, I Corps commander, ordered the ARVN 2d

Infantry Division to provide them with the thirty-six tons of rice it had confis-
cated from the Viet Cong.[36] Not until 1971 did security in the Batangan Peninsula
improve enough to permit all refugees generated during RUSSELL BEACH to return to the areas where their homes had once stood.[37]

The usual justifications for moving people were to deny manpower and resources to the enemy, to regroup villagers into more defensible locations, and to
open up free-fire zones. There was a tacit justification as well. Moving villagers
from enemy- to government-controlled areas may have been proscribed, but it
was done. It was a way to meet goals for the number of people living under government control. In the case of RUSSELL BEACH, the government violated the
spirit, if not the letter, of its own policy. CORDS officials in I Corps and in Saigon
approved the operation, but before acceding to RUSSELL BEACH, they should
have taken a harder look at the proposed relocations and their probable effect on
the population and tried to attach more stringent requirements for taking care of
those to be made homeless. The promise of returning refugees to their homes in
about one month was unrealistic in an area like the Batangan Peninsula.

In any event, CORDS did not have final authority; others did. If the South Vietnamese insisted on relocating people despite advice to the contrary, the most
CORDS could do was to push the South Vietnamese to develop adequate plans
for taking care of the displaced. If U.S. Army or Marine Corps commanders decided to displace people from populated areas during military sweeps in order to
minimize civilian casualties and facilitate the operation, then CORDS had to defer to their professional military judgment.

RUSSELL BEACH bestowed little political advantage because the government
poorly handled the relocations and was unable to bring security to the area for
about two years. In fact, the operation likely increased the degree of political
alienation. As CORDS refugee adviser Louis Wiesner concluded, "Bringing in
people against their will causes them to resent the government."[38] As carried out,
the operation caused unnecessary suffering. The relocation added to the already
heavy woes of officials in Quang Ngai, the province with the worst record in handling refugees. Additional numbers of displaced persons forced the diversion of
relief personnel and rapidly depleted funds and supplies.[39] The actions of provincial officials aggravated the problem of persons displaced by military operations.
On the one hand, the officials approved the evacuation of villages, and on the
other, they cited government policy as authority for denying the evacuees the status of refugees and access to government benefits. Wiesner angrily summed up
the situation, "When the relocated people are then left without adequate assistance by the GVN, their enmity is further increased. ... The GVN is bringing
groups of the enemy into its midst and hardening their hostility by the callous
treatment it accords them. This is a good recipe for losing the war."[40]

Although the U.S. Marines considered RUSSELL BEACH/BOLD MARINER a
"successful invasion of an enemy sanctuary" and the province adviser called it a
symbol of the successful expansion of government control,[41] these "gains" proved
ephemeral. Allied forces had entered a communist stronghold but had failed to

eliminate it. Viet Cong forces in the area continued to levy taxes and abduct local officials. Over eleven thousand people had been uprooted and their homes destroyed. Judged as an operation, RUSSELL BEACH was inconclusive. It was followed in February 1970 by another 23d Division operation, NANTUCKET BEACH, to support pacification in the same area. NANTUCKET BEACH seemed to repeat its predecessor. The soldiers of the 23d Division encountered little organized enemy resistance, but numerous GIs were injured or killed by booby traps and mines. Engineer battalions continued to destroy tunnels and bunkers and clear minefields in nearly the same sites as the prior operation.[42] By January 1971, elements of the VC 48th Battalion were again active in the peninsula.[43]

The Americans and South Vietnamese paid little heed to the sad lessons of RUSSELL BEACH. Involuntary relocations continued. Several other operations of the Americal Division and decisions of South Vietnamese officials produced over twenty-two thousand new refugees during 1969. Between October 1970 and May 1971, province officials relocated large numbers of people without adequate preparation. The problem grew to such proportions that the CPDC was compelled in the spring of 1971 to reissue policy guidance that security be brought to the people. It ordered halted any relocation that did not have explicit CPDC approval and required provinces to submit comprehensive plans for the movement and care of those uprooted, obtain approval by regional pacification authorities, and pass an on-site inspection by a CPDC delegation.[44] The relocation of people for their own security or for removal from enemy control was to be kept to an absolute minimum.

Although the government reissued stringent requirements, relocations continued. CORDS was unable to prevent South Vietnamese officials from deliberately uprooting people in order to carry out military operations. In March 1971, General Lam, the Corps commander, and Maj. Gen. Nguyen Van Toan, commander of the ARVN 2d Division, wanted to clear ten thousand people out of the western part of Son Tinh district of Quang Ngai province, an area plagued by poor security, into a resettlement camp near Phuoc Loc protected by territorial forces. Lam and Toan intended to make the western part of the district into a free-fire zone. Province senior adviser Henry B. Cushing objected, arguing that such relocations could be carried out only with the CPDC's permission. In his judgment, such resettlements of people were inconsistent with national and provincial plans and would divert resources from other geographical areas and refugee programs. He pointed out that the return to village program (returning refugees to their native settlements), upgrading of resettlement sites, and assistance to war victims would likely suffer if the relocation occurred. The relocation would also require redeployment of territorial forces from the southern part of the province. Cushing raised the issue with Colby. Both Colby and the CPDC objected to the plan, and the government ruled it out. Unfortunately, the story did not end there.

In August, ARVN engineers began to open up a road through western Son Tinh, which Cushing expected would enable the government to return displaced persons to their homes. The ARVN generals apparently viewed the road differently. To them, it was a way to open the area for military operations. They raised anew the issue of relocating people and creating a free-fire zone. This time they prevailed. After the province chief assured the CPDC that the province had made adequate plans for this movement, Major General Cao Hao Hon, head of the CPDC, approved the relocation and authorized funds to pay for it. Corps DepCORDS David Lazar objected to the relocation, as did Cushing. An angry Lam complained to Lieut. Gen. Welborn Dolvin, commander of XXIV Corps, that American province and district advisers were disrupting an ARVN operation. According to Cushing, General Dolvin had little choice save to defer to the South Vietnamese. He had no authority to block General Lam's plan. Resentful of American interference, General Lam called for Cushing's relief.[45] There was little Colby or other American officials could do to protect Cushing. The highest South Vietnamese authority in the corps had objected to Cushing's performance, effectively ending his ability to proffer advice. He left his post in October. It was not the only time South Vietnamese officials had forced the reassignment of an American adviser. In 1966, it had happened to the adviser of the ARVN 25th Division, Colonel Hunnicutt.[46]

An Abrams Strategy?

Despite the prevalence of small operations and military support of pacification during Abrams's command, the occurrence of large-scale conventional fighting, such as the bloody battle for Hamburger Hill, even if anomalous, challenged the notion that U.S. ground forces were operating differently under Abrams. Unwilling to cede control of the remote, mountainous, western part of I Corps, the enemy built up its logistic bases near the Laotian border after the 1968 Tet Offensive. On May 11, 1969, a battalion of the 101st Division climbing Hill 937 in the A Shau valley far from any heavily populated areas collided with the entrenched NVA 29th Regiment. The division fought to capture the remote peak, later known as Hamburger Hill. Supported by artillery and air strikes, the Americans rooted out the enemy regiment, fighting hand to hand as they cleared out one fortified bunker after another. After ten days of unrelenting combat, the 101st captured the hill, sacrificing 70 dead and 372 wounded. Although the enemy suffered over 600 combat deaths, the operation achieved no lasting gains. The division abandoned the hill a few days after seizing it, allowing the enemy to return and reestablish its bases.

Hamburger Hill proved controversial. To many, the battle seemed to be a pointless use of men and equipment that did nothing to bring the allies closer to military victory. Critics regarded the engagement as epitomizing the futility of attrition. The operation seemed no different than many of those conducted under Westmoreland. The 101st Division departed from the A Shau valley in June 1970.

RUSSELL BEACH also made it difficult to argue that the forces under Abrams used a new strategy. The Viet Cong was so embedded in the Batangan Peninsula and parts of Quang Ngai that the government concluded it was necessary to relocate people in order to strike directly at the enemy's forces. This step had the advantage of minimizing civilian casualties, but since the operations were not meticulously carried out, the relocations imposed undue hardships on the supposed beneficiaries. The net result was counterproductive, as refugee adviser Wiesner made clear. The operations in Quang Ngai and the Batangan Peninsula offered little assurance that the South Vietnamese would be able to strengthen their political hold in enemy-controlled areas.

Abrams outlined a different approach to combat from Westmoreland. But under Abrams's broad operational framework, U.S. forces mounted operations as divergent as WASHINGTON GREEN, RUSSELL BEACH, and the assault on Hamburger Hill. It is difficult to discern a new or a unifying strategy at work. The carnage at Hamburger Hill for ephemeral gains in the remote A Shau valley and the undue suffering and political clumsiness of RUSSELL BEACH had little in common with the militarily restrained and politically focused one-war strategy of WASHINGTON GREEN. It is also difficult to call RUSSELL BEACH an example of a new approach or argue that subordinate commanders heeded Abrams's new operational precepts. Abrams viewed the war differently, but he was responding to changes in the nature of the war itself, just as Komer had when devising the APC. More than one analyst looking at military operations like RUSSELL BEACH felt that Abrams had failed to end the emphasis on search-and-destroy operations and that he had limited success in changing the ingrained operational practices of his commanders. According to this view, Abrams's plans and exhortations proved insufficient to change fundamentally the nature of army operations in South Vietnam.[47]

Both WASHINGTON GREEN and RUSSELL BEACH were intended to improve security. Yet the results were similarly disappointing. WASHINGTON GREEN exemplified Abrams's one-war approach, but the resilient Viet Cong came back in Binh Dinh. RUSSELL BEACH worked at cross-purposes with the spirit of the pacification program. U.S. intervention in these provinces did not lead to permanent improvement. Security problems in Quang Ngai and Binh Dinh proved intractable regardless of approach. Hard-core Viet Cong areas were likely to stay that way for much longer than the U.S. Army could afford to spend there, and the infrastructure remained strong enough to carry on the fight. The task of breaking the grip of the infrastructure remained an unavoidable and daunting challenge. If the joint efforts of the U.S. Army and the South Vietnamese government could not eliminate the insurgent threat where it was strongest, then the communists were likely to pose a continuing grave challenge to the Saigon government.

15

The Phoenix Program:
The Best-Laid Plans

The centerpiece of the allied effort to dismantle the Viet Cong infrastructure, the Phoenix program, officially began after President Thieu signed it into law in 1968. Based on South Vietnam's constitutional ban on membership in the Communist Party, Phoenix was the successor to earlier South Vietnamese efforts against the communist underground. Komer and Colby envisioned Phoenix primarily as a method for pooling intelligence from South Vietnamese agencies, enabling them to identify, arrest, and sentence specific leaders of the infrastructure.

Led by Komer, the Americans had long lobbied for a more vigorous program, and he ensured that Phoenix was a prominent part of the APC. In 1969, Abrams and Colby wanted the South Vietnamese to continue assigning high priority to the campaign. At the January 1969 commanders' conference, Abrams forcefully reiterated the requirement to "scarf up" the infrastructure because it supported the main force units and exercised political control at the village level. To the Americans, the Saigon government had little standing in areas where communist cadres could actively recruit, propagandize, and tax. To incapacitate the infrastructure would, the Americans believed, cripple the communists' ability to wage the counterpacification strategy outlined in COSVN Resolution 9.[1]

In practice, the program proved frustrating. Allegations of abuses embroiled it in controversy. As Colby later ruefully conceded, "The word 'Phoenix' became a shorthand for all the negative aspects of the war."[2] The South Vietnamese viewed the special anti-infrastructure effort as an American program, and numerous observers felt Saigon's officials carried it out ineffectively.[3]

The enemy, however, viewed the program with alarm. Nguyen Co Thach, Vietnam's foreign minister after 1975, admitted that Phoenix wiped out many bases in South Vietnam. A senior officer, Colonel Bui Tin, acknowledged that the program caused the loss of thousands of communist cadres.[4]

Procedures

The Phoenix program laid out clear steps for processing suspects. To pool information on persons belonging to the infrastructure, the government established intelligence operations and coordination centers at the provincial and district levels. The province and district chiefs, the police chief, and local intelligence officials all participated. Other South Vietnamese came from the Military Security Service (counterintelligence), the NPFF, the Special Branch, the *Chieu Hoi* program, the RD Cadre, and military intelligence. Under the Phoenix program, each constituent agency was supposed to share intelligence information with the others in order to compile dossiers on the party's operatives, identifying their aliases and functions in the infrastructure. Ideally, district officials would collate information from all sources and disseminate it quickly so authorities could make arrests.[5] District officials were empowered to detain a person when *three* reliable sources reported incriminating information. A number of government forces were to arrest suspects: the PRU, the NPFF, the National Police, the RF/PF, and, on occasion, regular military units.

Following initial questioning at the district level, suspects underwent more extensive examination at the province interrogation centers, the next step in processing. Usually one or two CIA advisers worked in the centers, participating in or observing interrogations.[6] The Special Branch had five days to build a case but could hold suspects for up to thirty days with the written permission of the province chief. Dossiers, the most important piece of written evidence, were compiled during the processing. In many instances, they were incomplete and poorly prepared.[7] Some marginally trained interrogators needed to refer to a checklist of written questions in order to perform their job.[8] Officials sometimes had to rely on confessions when the police failed to produce enough evidence to detain a suspect. When officials properly completed the dossier and it directly implicated a suspect, interrogators were supposed to seek information about other members of the infrastructure.

From the interrogation center, detainees next went to the Province Security Committee. Initially it consisted only of military, police, and administrative officials, but by 1971 it also included the province chief, who chaired the committee; the provincial police chief; the internal security chief; the provincial public prosecutor or judge; and one or two members of the elected Provincial Council. The provincial public prosecutor and the chairman of the provincial council served as advisers and did not make decisions. This committee met fairly regularly to review cases. Not surprisingly for a Third World country, South Vietnam had few legal professionals. Only twenty-eight prosecutors or deputy prosecutors could be found in the entire nation, and of these, seventeen served in Saigon. Thirty-three of forty-four provinces had no prosecutors.[9]

A shortage of legal professionals was not the only problem with the committees. Procedures were lax. The Province Security Committee was not bound, as one American adviser stated, "by any procedural rules or by quantums of proof or by any requirement to justify its decisions once rendered. The accused [had] no right of appearance, though in some places it is accorded, and no right to counsel."[10] CORDS legal adviser Gage McAfee characterized them as "administrative committees designed to temporarily detain individuals against whom there was inadequate evidence available for court conviction."[11] The lack of rigorous procedures was one reason the program had critics. Although the committees were not bound by rigorous legal procedures, the burden of proof still rested on the prosecution. Based on documents, eyewitnesses (at least three), intelligence reports, and confessions, the committee had to prove that a defendant belonged to the VC. Significantly, no one could be convicted solely on a confession or evidence obtained during interrogation.

The committee had authority to refer cases to a military court for trial or, under the *an tri* ("emergency") detention procedures, to sentence members of the VCI to a term of imprisonment based on the individual's position in the organization. These positions were divided into three categories: A was a leader; B, a cadre member; and C, a follower.[12] The intent was to concentrate on capturing A and B category VCI, the party's command-and-control elements. Category C might even be persons serving only part time.[13] VCI in categories A and B received a minimum sentence of one year and as high as two; and category C, a maximum of one year. These sentences could be renewed or extended. Almost all category A offenders, about one-half of the B, and about one-quarter of category C served extended sentences.[14] Despite guidelines prepared by the government and CORDS, Colby complained in 1969 that it was "unclear what amount of evidence was sufficient to guarantee *an tri* sentence from the Security Committees."[15]

Plans Gone Astray

I sometimes think we would have gotten better publicity for molesting children.

—George Jacobson, DepCORDS,
speaking about the Phoenix program at a CORDS conference
in MACV headquarters in February 1972

As head of CORDS, Colby found himself besieged. Some critics measured Phoenix against standards of American jurisprudence and the safeguards of the Bill of Rights and found the program wanting. Critics focused on the lack of due process in *an tri* detention procedures, excessive detention periods, inadequate prison facilities, the susceptibility of the program to abuse for political purposes, and allegations of torture and assassination. In congressional hearings in 1970 and 1971, Colby had to defend Phoenix from such charges.

Other critics supported the program's goals but argued that Phoenix had to be made more effective. In justification, they pointed out that Saigon was in a life-

or-death struggle with a adversary routinely using extralegal means—assassination and kidnapping—to advance its agenda.[16] Even the catalyst behind Phoenix, Robert Komer, urged an overhaul of the program. In 1970, he sent a closely held report to Colby and Defense Secretary Laird indicting Phoenix as a "fiasco." In Komer's view, South Vietnamese agencies gave the program low priority and poorly coordinated intelligence collection and dissemination. His chief complaint was that Phoenix had little impact on the infrastructure.[17]

Others saw the basic problem as the lack of a single South Vietnamese manager to oversee the agencies involved in the Phoenix program. The South Vietnamese agencies represented on the committees were reluctant to share their most sensitive intelligence with others, being more responsive to their parent organizations than to the needs of the district or province coordinating center.[18] At a time when the American withdrawal meant that the South Vietnamese would have to stand on their own, the cumulative weight of the criticism from all sides was too strong to deflect, eventually forcing CORDS to embark on a major study, *Phung Hoang Reexamination* (PHREEX), to reform the program.[19]

To provide a single manager for the program, the prime minister in May 1970 moved the Central *Phung Hoang* Permanent Office from the Prime Minister's Office to the Directorate General of the National Police, the first step toward complete control. The government gave several reasons. First, the police was already involved at every level both operationally and administratively and was in a position to centralize management of the program. Second, the anti-infrastructure campaign was essentially a police-type operation. Third, the National Police organically contained all the requisite intelligence and operational branches.[20] The influence of foreign advisers such as Sir Robert Thompson was evident. Thompson had long recommended that Phoenix be made a police responsibility, citing British experiences in Malaya, Palestine, and Cyprus in coping with insurgents.[21] Colby supported the change, arguing that the reorganization of Phoenix would be "the best way to accelerate the strengthening of the National Police." The government would give the police more assistance and attention, he believed, if it were responsible for a high-priority program.[22] To enhance police prestige, Colby supported upgrading the position of police director to brigadier general, and this was done in 1970.

On paper, the National Police may have been a logical choice to manage the Phoenix program, but a number of U.S. officials believed it was not up to the task. Making the police responsible for the Phoenix program would, AID administrator John Hannah concluded, not be

> prudent, given the jobs the police had yet to master adequately in nationwide civil law enforcement and support of other aspects of pacification. ... Some of our people are very concerned that the proposed change will overload the police and give them responsibility without adequate authority over the Provincial and District chiefs and para-military and intelligence elements who must play a central role in carrying out the program.[23]

In the military-dominated society of South Vietnam, the police had little status and a reputation for corruption. Policemen were poorly paid, inadequately trained, and understrength. The JCS also opposed the police takeover.[24] Captain Stuart Herrington, a member of a district advisory team in Hau Nghia province, later wrote that the impending change

> boded ill for the future of what had been a marginally effective Vietnamese effort in the first place. ... National Police personnel assigned to Hau Nghia were usually not the most competent and motivated men available. ... Military men made no secret of their contempt for the police, whom they saw as a lazy, corrupt bunch whose specialty was the acceptance of petty bribes at checkpoints. Hence our military counterparts told us openly that its transfer would be the death of the sickly Phoenix bird.[25]

To prepare the police for added responsibilities, Colby endorsed its rapid expansion, comparable to the sharp growth the RF/PF experienced in 1968–1969. The goal was 108,000 policemen by the end of 1970. The police failed to meet that target, growing from roughly 80,000 to 88,000 between 1968 and May 1970. Much of that increase resulted from the onetime transfer of ARVN personnel to the National Police to compensate for personnel turnovers and casualties. Police strength declined after May 1970 because recruiting failed to keep pace with attrition.[26] Cabinet ministers disagreed over how to increase police strength, and the JGS and the minister of defense were reluctant to provide additional ARVN officers for police duty.[27] The steep expansion of the police from 19,000 to 88,000 in the six previous years (1964-1970) had resulted in a shortage of middle- and upper-level managers that did little to enhance the capabilities of the police.[28] The goal of bringing in a 108,000-man police force by the end of 1970 proved too ambitious.

Of great concern to CORDS was the way the government's detention system operated. Police officers as well as district and province chiefs arbitrarily released many suspects without regard to official procedures. Government officials freed roughly 60 percent of the prisoners arrested in 1968, even many known members of the infrastructure or persons supporting the Viet Cong.[29] In other cases, district advisers believed that officials set free individuals with whom they had personal ties, even though those with incriminating dossiers.[30] People who were detained could languish in prisons for months before having their cases reviewed or their relatives notified. According to one estimate, a paltry 29 percent of the persons detained in the centers had been sentenced.[31] Bribery was a not uncommon way to supplement meager salaries. In the words of one adviser, "All the way up the chain of custody there were ample opportunities for an individual to buy his way out."[32] As for officials in detention centers, they extorted hundreds of thousands of piasters from prisoners as a condition for releasing them from jail.

The detention centers were seriously overcrowded. In May 1969, the provincial detention centers had an estimated capacity of around sixteen thousand persons but an actual population of over twenty-one thousand. With American funds, technical assistance, and supplies, the government renovated existing prisons and constructed additional detention centers and prisons to relieve overcrowding. By July 1971, the prison system had expanded to include four national prisons and thirty-seven provincial ones and was sufficient to handle the prisoner population.[33]

The government promulgated new detention policies. In April 1970, the prime minister reiterated the time limits for detention periods. Innocent people were to be released no later than forty-eight hours after their arrest. Total time for all procedures from arrest to sentencing was not to exceed forty-six days, still a lengthy period.[34] Although the decrees led to improvement, backlogs remained a problem, and many persons were not processed within the prescribed time. In February 1971, nearly a year after the government had passed the 1970 decree, John Paul Vann found widespread problems. On a preannounced visit, Vann toured detention centers in three delta provinces (Kien Hoa, Dinh Tuong, and Phong Dinh). He left appalled. Many in the centers did not know whether they had been sentenced or even the length of their imprisonment. One prisoner sentenced to twelve months had already served sixteen months at the time of Vann's inspection. Fearing that these problems characterized the entire system, Vann believed they lent "credence to the widespread mistrust and criticism of *Phung Hoang* activities on the part of the government. I got the distinct impression that any detainees not previously VC or VC sympathizers would almost assuredly become so after their period of incarceration."[35] This was damning evidence that the government system was not yet fixed.

Even more serious was the allegation that Phoenix engaged in assassination and torture. In testimony before the House of Representatives in 1971, former Army soldier Kenneth B. Osborn claimed to have seen prisoners murdered or tortured as part of the Phoenix program. Osborn served as an enlisted man in South Vietnam from September 1967 to December 1968 but was not directly assigned to the program. He remained on active duty until October 1969 and then served in the army reserves, attaining the rank of sergeant first class in 1971. Osborn was an uncooperative and unconvincing witness. He declined to provide the committee with the names of the individuals who allegedly committed the crimes.[36] The army had investigated his allegations in February 1971 prior to his congressional testimony, and at that time Osborn had refused to divulge specific information to support his charges. A separate Defense Department investigation by DOD counsel J. Fred Buzhardt, later one of Nixon's lawyers during Watergate, undertaken at the behest of the subcommittee after Osborn's testimony, also "failed to uncover evidences to support Mr. Osborn's allegations [and] revealed numerous disparities between the statements he made while testifying before the Committee and the factual evidence produced in the course of this investigation."[37] Although Osborn's undocumented charges were contradicted by other officials' testimony, and although he was not assigned to the Phoenix program, his allegations helped saddle the program with a well-nigh-unshakable image. The notoriety of the Phoenix program was forged in part in the crucible of congressional hearings.

Press accounts after the hearings seemed to accept Osborn's accusation that civilians were the targets of the Phoenix program. Some headlines were lurid: "Sterile Depersonalized Murder Plan," "Military Murders in Vietnam," "Political Killings in Vietnam."[38] Even in less inflammatory articles, the number of persons killed was usually mentioned first, implying that that held top priority in the program. A few articles characterized Phoenix the way many in the field perceived it, not as a ruthless murder campaign but as an inefficient operation seldom able to accomplish what it was meant to do: apprehend specific members of the infrastructure.[39]

The terminology of the program was, to put it mildly, infelicitous and undoubtedly contributed to Phoenix's problems. Officially sanctioned words such as *neutralized,* which designated party members who were captured, rallied, or killed in military or police operations, were ripe for misinterpretation. Neutralization was equated in the public's mind with killing and in the case of critics, with killing civilians.

In a bitter guerrilla war like Vietnam the term *civilian* could be misleading. Many communist combatants wore no military rank or uniform, fighting or engaging in acts of terrorism clad in the traditional black-pajama garb of the peasants. Many persons targeted for apprehension under Phoenix were only nominally civilians and under that rubric served the infrastructure as so-called legal cadres, overtly obeying South Vietnam's laws. Appearing to be farmers or shopkeepers, legal cadres nonetheless collected taxes from villagers, recruited and proselytized, assisted the movement of guerrilla and main force units, and helped execute and abduct village and hamlet officials. The National Liberation Front and its control apparatus, the infrastructure, were illegal political entities under South Vietnamese law and sought to topple South Vietnam's government. To equate persons who belonged to the NLF with true civilians was erroneous and discounted the violent and subversive purpose of the infrastructure. Given the way that the party prosecuted the war, there was no clear, bright line differentiating military and civilian.

The acts that Osborn alleged had occurred were totally inexcusable but also patently contrary to the program. No Phoenix directives or procedures authorized or condoned torture or assassination. Colby, Vann, and Major James Arthur, district senior adviser in Binh Chanh district, Gia Dinh province, had vigorously attested to this at a Senate hearing in 1970. Major Arthur, who had observed questioning in Binh Chanh, stated that when on one occasion he witnessed the forceful interrogation of a suspect, he complained to his counterpart and that afterward there was "not any more of this type of activity" in the interrogations he observed.[40] After the hearings, MACV issued another directive warning personnel assigned to Phoenix that assassinations and other violations of the rules of land warfare were illegal and that anyone with knowledge of such abuses had a responsibility to report it to his superiors.[41]

Unfortunately, the limited American presence in the interrogation centers and the paucity of firsthand testimony made it difficult to generalize about what occurred there. Major Arthur testified before Congress that he commonly observed interrogations.[42] Lieutenant John Cook, Phoenix adviser in Di An district, Bien Hoa province, lived next to the district interrogation center and routinely observed the questioning of suspects. Other advisers claimed they had little time to do so. Some CORDS personnel found it hard to learn what government officials actually did in the interrogation centers but were aware of rumors that the special police mistreated detainees. Advisers were sometimes excluded from the interrogation centers.[43] When advisers, such as Major Arthur, investigated, they usually did not observe any problems. The ability of advisers to monitor and moderate South Vietnamese procedures was limited. Advisers generally did encourage the South Vietnamese to adhere to a higher standard of conduct, but American admonitions could hardly eliminate abuses.

The CORDS leadership had other reasons to prohibit torture and assassination. It was an axiom of professional American intelligence agencies that coercion elicited little useful information, and it was American policy to try persuading the South Vietnamese that humane treatment was more likely to produce reliable information.[44] Suspects were more valuable alive than dead. They could provide intelligence information or be used as double agents against their former comrades. Captain Herrington related after the war how one informer's information snowballed to such an extent that the government apprehended almost the entire infrastructure in Trang Bang district. Nguyen Van Tung, village secretary of An Tinh, a communist stronghold, was interrogated in the fall of 1971. The district Phoenix adviser, Captain Tim Miller, had already compiled an extensive dossier on Tung and his role in the infrastructure. Using this detailed information, the interrogators were able to disarm him psychologically, confounding him with their knowledge of the local party. Tung provided the names of twenty-eight other communist agents, who were arrested, interrogated, and induced to identify still other party officials. By mid-1972, the original operation and its offspring had netted three hundred arrests.[45] If Tung had been killed, there would have been no rollup.

The program's results do little to support the charge that Phoenix was primarily an assassination campaign. Of the 10,444 members of the VCI killed between January 1970 and March 1971, over 9,000 died incidentally in firefights with military forces and were identified only posthumously as members of the underground. In other cases, party members, especially those of higher rank who were unlikely to surrender without a fight, were killed during police raids.[46] About 1,300 persons, less than 2 percent of all infrastructure members captured, rallied, or killed during this period, had been singled out for arrests. The available data on persons targeted and killed do not differentiate among persons resisting arrest, accidentally caught in a crossfire, or intentionally shot.[47]

Like other pacification programs, Phoenix relied on statistics to measure the anti-VCI effort. By subtracting the number of neutralized communists operatives from the estimated strength of the infrastructure, planners hoped to get an idea of Phoenix's impact on the VCI. Initially compiled to help manage the program, the numbers became quotas.[48] Advisers disagreed over this practice. One side argued that the pressure to meet quotas caused South Vietnamese officials to falsify data, sometimes by posthumously assigning Viet Cong soldiers killed in action to the ranks of the VCI. (Some VC soldiers killed during regular military operations were indeed correctly identified as members of the infrastructure.)[49] The other side claimed that without goals the South Vietnamese had little incentive to work hard; Americans needed to apply pressure on the South Vietnamese. One American officer noted that the number of ex post facto identifications increased toward the end of the month, when South Vietnamese officials were scrambling to meet targets,[50] indicating, depending on one's perspective, the motivational or the corrupting influence of quotas.

The F-6 and Binh Minh Campaigns

In a time of stress, such as the 1972 Easter Offensive, government authorities were tempted to streamline some procedural safeguards, as they did with the F-6 campaign, created by the chief of Chau Doc province in April. Alarmed that the local infrastructure was guiding NVA units, the province chief authorized the detention of suspects who were identified in only one report rather than the three normally required. To prevent abuse, the government issued strict guidelines that required the Special Branch police to list the VCI member on whom one or more credible reports were on file. The police would evaluate the reports and submit only those deemed highly credible to the province chiefs. The police was to consider only those reports on hand prior to April 24 and to establish a screening procedure and an appeal procedure, which would authorize the province chief to retain or release suspects. The commanding general of IV Corps, Lieut. Gen. Ngo Quang Truong, with the support of the prime minister, later authorized the special program for all delta provinces, but some did not participate because the directives were not specific enough.[51] Seeking to ensure that South Vietnamese officials strictly adhered to procedures, Wilbur Wilson, the IV Corps DepCORDS, cautioned General Truong and police officials in the delta to treat prisoners humanely and avoid arresting innocent people. Wilson was satisfied that the list of suspects was almost exclusively communist cadres living and operating in government-controlled areas.[52] The F-6 campaign lasted from April 1972 until January 1, 1973.

The campaign went smoothly for the most part. Phoenix advisers in IV Corps rated the screening of suspects in ten provinces as adequate but concluded that the centers in Dinh Tuong and Vinh Binh provinces were overtaxed by the large numbers of detainees. In two provinces, Bac Lieu and Kien Phong, the government inexplicably made no effort to establish the screening procedures that the special campaign required. By mid-May, government officials had detained about twenty-five hundred communist suspects in the delta, mostly low-level support personnel engaged in communications and liaison. The campaign's full effect was difficult to measure, but Wilson expected that the loss of communications and liaison personnel would at least disrupt the movement of enemy units and supplies and thus deter enemy attacks. He believed the F-6 campaign materially reduced the infrastructure's ability to support the Easter Offensive and concluded that the campaign was "remarkably free of reported abuses."[53]

Outside the delta, the reaction to the Easter Offensive occasioned serious abuses. Thieu apparently ordered the Capital National Police Command to make a list of "extremists, oppositionists, and leftists in the Saigon–Gia Dinh area." Persons on the list were subject to "scrutiny, detention, or arrest *as security dictates during the current national emergency.*" The categories of extremist, oppositionist, and leftist were broad enough for the government to put on the list retired General Duong Van Minh, a leader of the 1963 coup against Diem; several Buddhist notables; 7 senators; 10 Lower House members; 9 members of the Saigon City Council; 90 college and high school leaders; and 28 labor leaders. Of the 269 names on the list, less than half had some connection with the Viet Cong. The government was rightly apprehensive about possible subversion but apparently found the emergency a convenient pretext to try silencing critics.[54]

Unfortunately, the government went even further in I Corps, where, as one adviser noted, local officials sometimes stretched the term *infrastructure* to include their personal and political enemies.[55] Under the Binh Minh anti-infrastructure program in Thua Thien province, the police in May and June 1972 arrested about fourteen hundred people in Hue and its environs. The government's rationale was to prevent the recurrence of the communist mass political killings that had taken place in Hue during the 1968 offensive. But police chief Captain Lien Thanh, taking a broad view of what constituted Viet Cong activity, arrested leftist noncommunist radicals, intellectuals, and professors whose only known crimes were disaffection with the government and opposition to the war.

I Corps DepCORDS John Gunther Dean feared the police action had created a serious political problem. The provincial and Hue City Councils wanted the arrests stopped and called for quick hearings for those detained. Five deputies from the Lower House went to Hue to protest the police action. Dean believed that if the government did not end the campaign, quickly process those detained, and release the innocent, it would find itself in a divisive confrontation with the noncommunist Left. Antigovernment militancy would, in Dean's view, embarrass Saigon and destabilize the political situation in the midst of the enemy offensive.[56] Thanks in part to pressure from the five South Vietnamese deputies and the Americans, the police officially ended the campaign but continued to make selective arrests, to the dismay of CORDS officials.

In August, the Binh Minh campaign resumed in the Hue area. According to the new DepCORDS, Raymond G. Jones, the police planned to arrest about two hundred "subversives" and kill fifty of them "under the guise of VC handiwork." Jones was alarmed. He believed the program would intensify antigovernment sentiment and hand the enemy a propaganda windfall. "When news would inevitably leak out," he cabled George Jacobson, who had assumed the position of DepCORDS in 1971, "it could actually force the U.S. into a situation which could result in a rapid and complete exit with a rather complete close out of all types of aid. We have no knowledge that the program is confined only to MR I."[57] Jones raised the matter with General Truong, whom Thieu had sent to take over as I Corps commander, and American officials in the corps (Major General Howard Cooksey, Truong's counterpart, the Quang Tri province adviser, and the American counsel in Hue). Jones was concerned enough also to inform General Weyand (who had replaced Abrams as COMUSMACV) and George Jacobson.

On November 1, Cooksey wired the MACV chief of staff, Major General Gilbert Woodward, that the plans to assassinate "VC sympathizers and political opponents," which had alarmed Jones in August, would be carried out immediately. The police had a list of fifty persons, which included some well-known figures, who were slated to be killed.[58] The following day, Deputy Ambassador Charles S. Whitehouse took up the issue of stopping the plans with Prime Minister Tran Thien Khiem.[59] Although Phoenix was not intended as a program of terror or political retribution, American officials had to remain vigilant and exercise pressure to keep it from becoming one.

The Army's Involvement: A Matter of Ambivalence

For the U.S. Army, which provided the preponderance of personnel to CORDS as well as advisers to work on the anti-infrastructure program, Phoenix proved troublesome in two respects. First, it was difficult for the army's personnel system to obtain and train advisory personnel for an intelligence program that fell outside its traditional purview. Second, the army as an institution grew uncomfortable about its association with a controversial program.

As the war dragged on, many professional officers found themselves returning to South Vietnam for a second or third tour and under growing family pressure. Many career officers resigned rather than spend another year in combat. The ramifications affected the Phoenix program. By 1969–1970, many of the army's experienced intelligence officers had already served multiple tours in South Vietnam, forcing the army to assign to the Phoenix program low-ranking officers who were inadequately trained and inexperienced in military intelligence. The army designated advisory duty in the district coordinating centers a "branch immaterial" assignment, which meant officers with no background in military intelligence could be placed in this position. Adviser training was limited to a three-hour orientation at the U.S. Army Intelligence Training School, the Military Assistance Training Adviser Course, the Foreign Service Institute, or the Civil Affairs School at Fort Gordon, Georgia. A nine-day orientation course in South Vietnam followed. Instruction was hardly uniform and much too short to ready officers for the difficult work of advising the South Vietnamese on an untried program.

The military's policy of one-year tours in South Vietnam exacerbated the problem of inexperienced and inadequately trained officers and complicated staffing at the district intelligence centers. Regional Phoenix adviser Captain Harry Farmer made this point clearly: "It would take the adviser, perhaps, five or six months to begin to understand the program as it is quite complex. By the time the American adviser understands the program and has established a degree of rapport with his counterpart, it is the end of his tour."[60]

Low rank compounded the handicap of inexperience. A shortage of captains in the army, the rank authorized for the district centers, forced CORDS to accept as advisers some second lieutenants, the greenest of army officers. At the end of June 1970, Phoenix was authorized 305 captains; only 99 were actually assigned. The rest were lieutenants, 48 of whom were second lieutenants.[61] Under the army's personnel policy at the time, a second lieutenant could be routinely promoted to first lieutenant after one year of active duty and to captain after two years of active duty. CORDS complained but had to accept these junior officers without specialized training. After the basic officers' training course, there were only eighteen weeks to prepare second lieutenants for their tours in South Vietnam, barely enough time to impart rudimentary knowledge of military intelligence, let alone the simplest Vietnamese-language skills.[62] The necessity of accepting untried junior officers as district Phoenix advisers weakened the American presence at a critical level. One Phoenix adviser, a first lieutenant, griped that South Vietnamese officials were understandably reluctant to accept advice from such unseasoned "advisers."[63]

CORDS and the army recognized the need to prepare junior officers for assignments with the Phoenix program. Early in 1970, the Army established the military assistance security adviser (MASA) course at Fort Bragg. Twelve weeks long, the MASA provided six weeks of language training and six of academic instruction on the procedures of the Phoenix program. The first session started in September 1970.[64] The course came too late, however, to make an appreciable difference to the Phoenix program. The first graduates reached South Vietnam early in 1971, nearly three years after the program had begun. The course ran for little more than one year before it closed, in part owing to public controversy surrounding Phoenix. The drawdown of advisers under Vietnamization eliminated the need for sending new Phoenix advisers to South Vietnam after March 1972, so the training program was expendable.

The army's troubles in supplying qualified advisers were not its only problem with Phoenix. The army's association with the PRUs, which targeted individual members of the infrastructure, was an uneasy one. Chosen, paid, and trained by the Americans, the PRUs were often composed of Vietnamese minority groups or Viet Cong defectors. They were established with help from the CIA to provide province chiefs with a force trained specially to seek out the VCI and its leaders. The PRUs had a reputation for being tough, aggressive, and effective. This 4,000-man force killed or captured 1,683 members of the VCI in 1970, about 300 for every 1,000 men in the force.[65] Organized into 18-man teams, the PRUs were under the operational control of the province chief. Because the PRUs were effective, the Americans decided to provide more support. With the approval of General Abrams, support of the PRUs was transferred from CIA to MACV on July 1 1969, although the CIA continued to provide funds and a small number of advisers for the program.[66]

The PRUs were soon unwelcome in the Pentagon, largely because of allegations of atrocities. In October, Secretary of the Army Stanley Resor warned Secretary of Defense Laird that the army could suffer harmful publicity if it continued its association with the PRUs.[67] Laird, concerned with mounting adverse publicity about their role in the war and anxious to disengage the United States from Vietnam, requested the JCS in November 1969 to explore ways of ending advisory and funding support for the PRUs and having the South Vietnamese assimilate the program.[68] Because the PRUs were the most effective South Vietnamese force at capturing and killing members of the infrastructure, and because the CIA lacked the manpower to assume complete advisory responsibility,[69] the agency urged Laird to reconsider. The CIA hoped the secretary would be unwilling to relax an effort that was weakening the communists to assure what George Carver, the CIA's top specialist on the Vietnam War, called "Anglo-saxon morality criteria."[70] Carver lambasted the army's position, asserting that Resor's deputy, James Siena, author of a report critical of the Phoenix program, was "patently ill-informed about the nature of reality in Vietnam." Carver declared himself "disturbed by the emotionalism in Siena's study and even more disturbed by the emotional strain that permeates Resor's review request." In Carver's view, a discussion of the moral and social costs of the program "might be a stimulating topic for discussion over a decanter of port in the Harvard Fellows Common Room."[71]

Not wishing to clash with Laird and reluctant to be associated with the PRUs, over which MACV lacked operational control, Abrams decided in December not to replace army advisers when vacancies occurred.[72] This move in effect terminated the military advisory mission to the PRUs,[73] although army advisers continued to serve at least up to June 1971. American advisers to the Phoenix program were also being phased out during this period.

The army's differences with the CIA related to larger questions about ends and means. The CIA argued that abandoning the most effective weapon of anti-infrastructure operations in the midst of the war was irresponsible. The army agreed with the CIA that the PRUs were effective but believed the adverse publicity and possible damage to the army's reputation over the long run were not worth the PRUs' gains.

The issue became moot in July 1972 when the government dissolved the PRUs as a separate entity. The Special Branch of the police and the RF/PF absorbed the ex-members of the disbanded units. Then, with the conclusion of the F-6 campaign early in 1973, the Saigon government ended the Phoenix program. In mid-1972, all persons serving in the province and district intelligence centers were transferred to the command of the director of the National Police, who employed them in the police program to combat terrorism, newly named Protection of the People Against Terrorism. This effort, which lasted until the end of 1972, was the epilogue of what had been the Phoenix program. All American advisers had left

South Vietnam by June 30, 1972, although some administrative and financial support personnel remained.[74]

Results

Phoenix was unique and important. It was the major South Vietnamese operation aimed directly at the communist control apparatus, the "nerve center, the command post, of the enemy," in John Vann's words.[75] An intelligence and police program, Phoenix was designed to apprehend specific communist cadres critical to the infrastructure's operations. Phoenix was supposed to function as a central clearing house for information on the VCI; the underground was a primary, not an incidental, target. How effective was Phoenix in weakening the VCI and taking high-ranking members of the VCI out of action? Did the program's results make up for the negative publicity and erosion of support for the war?

On one level, it would be hard to judge the program as satisfactory. The forces specifically working on Phoenix (police, PRUs, etc.) accounted for perhaps 21 percent of the political cadres sentenced, captured, rallied, or killed. Only about 11 percent could be attributed to specific targeting as set forth in the program's procedures.[76] Relatively few operations were specifically targeted against known members of the VCI because of the scarcity of timely information on these persons, the very failing Phoenix was designed to remedy. Poor intelligence, a major flaw of the program, was related to the weak political support the government mustered in the countryside. If the South Vietnamese people remained unwilling to offer intelligence information on the infrastructure out of fear of communist reprisals or indifference to Saigon's cause, then the government operated under a severe handicap.[77]

Even if Phoenix had little success in targeting the infrastructure, that program combined with the government's other efforts did weaken the VCI. Military operations and the *Chieu Hoi* and Phoenix programs reduced the size of the communist political structure from an estimated eighty-four thousand in January 1968 to a little over fifty-six thousand in February 1972.[78] Collateral actions (military operations and *Chieu Hoi*) had a greater impact on the infrastructure than the Phoenix program, amounting to 80 percent of VCI losses. Military forces killed or captured roughly 50 percent of the VCI members taken out of action, and about 30 percent rallied through the *Chieu Hoi* program.[79]

The communists were particularly concerned with the program's effect in the villages and hamlets. Three-quarters of those captured, rallied, or killed operated at the village level or lower.[80] A document captured in December 1970 complained that Phoenix "espionage networks" destroyed the revolutionary movement in Long Khanh, eliminated hamlet agents, and controlled the people. Another lamented the program's efforts to disorganize the party's operations in hamlets and villages in VC subregion 5. An article published in Hanoi in March 1970 warned that Phoenix "agents" were detecting revolutionary cadres and were primarily responsible for controlling the local people. The article encouraged the annihilation of these agents. A Liberation Radio broadcast in October 1969 fulminated about how the Phoenix program was disrupting the lives of those in the movement, even those communist agents secretly serving in the ARVN and government administration.[81]

By weakening the communist organization at the lowest level, Phoenix created a gap in communication between village and hamlet cadres, on the one hand, and district and higher-level cadres, on the other. The provincial and district committees still functioned but had more difficulty managing lower-echelon committees. The expansion of pacification into contested and enemy-held hamlets and military operations against base areas often forced the low-level committees to move. It was the village and hamlet cadres who recruited new members, levied taxes, disseminated propaganda, and selected government officials for assassination. The government's actions dislodged VC cadres from populated areas, causing them to lose contact with the people.[82]

The shrinkage of areas under Viet Cong control and the expansion of government forces and programs into contested and enemy-held areas between 1969 and 1971 further hampered the VCI. HES data corroborated this conclusion. In December 1969, HES reported that 56 percent of the people of South Vietnam lived where the VCI (recruiters, tax collectors, and other cadres) could *not* freely move. By December 1972, that figure had reached 79 percent.[83]

Regarding Phoenix as a serious threat to village and hamlet organization, the party took countermeasures to protect its cadres. The communists stressed three defensive measures: compartmentalization, legal cadres, and tighter overall security. Compartmentalization served to isolate cadre groups from each other, making it more difficult for government intelligence agencies to exploit information. Legal cadres went under deeper cover. Security was tightened to prevent leaks of information and defections. As for offensive measures, the enemy undertook a persistent effort to find out how Phoenix worked and to identify its personnel. The party hoped to subvert Phoenix agents, plant communist cadres in the interrogation and coordinating centers, and stir up popular resentment against the program in the villages. It also tried to assassinate key directors. Issued in 1969, COSVN Directive 136 targeted all Vietnamese members of Phoenix. The more effective a Phoenix official was, the more likely it was that the communists would attempt to kill him. Viet Cong Armed Reconnaissance Units (ARUs) were charged with killing or kidnapping government officials. The communists also set up prison camps for communists the party accused of working for the Phoenix program.[84]

The communists also sought to discredit the campaign in the eyes of the South Vietnamese people and to capitalize on the adverse publicity Phoenix received in the United States. The quasi-judicial procedures of the province security committees, the arbitrary periods of presentencing detention, the questionable arrests, and the exaction of bribes constituted a bill of particulars ready for exploitation by communist propaganda. If the government sought to portray the infrastructure as a group of outlaws, the communists capitalized on the flaws of the Phoenix program, asserting that the Thieu regime was unfit to rule because it condoned corruption and perverted the program's procedures.

The government did try to strengthen the program, changing the annual goals to emphasize the apprehension and sentencing of high-level cadres rather than the mere detention of low-ranking suspects. Instead of counting all cadres, the 1969 goals concentrated on capturing, rallying, or killing only A and B levels. The goals were further refined in 1970 and 1971 to stress incarcerating A and B cadres, requiring that at least half of those captured be sentenced.[85] The government narrowed its criterion from the loose standard of counting the number captured to the more rigorous one of counting the number of communist operatives put behind bars.

Statistically, Phoenix came close to its goals. The number captured (whether sentenced or not), rallied, or killed was 15,800 in 1968 and 19,500 in 1969. With the more stringent criterion of sentenced, rallied, or killed, the result for 1970 was 21,000 and for 1971 was 18,000. The total was over 74,000 losses.[86] Of that number, 34,000 were political cadres who had rallied.[87]

But the infrastructure remained intact. Estimated strength declined by only about 20 percent because the communists compensated for losses by recruiting new members inside South Vietnam and bringing in replacements from North Vietnam. The government inadvertently assisted by releasing many of the persons apprehended; others slipped through the detention process and returned to the infrastructure. HES numbers for December 1972 suggested that only 29 percent of the population lived where no VCI existed. This finding roughly corresponded with Pacification Attitude Analysis System (PAAS) surveys in 1972. Only 23 percent of the survey respondents said that there were no communist cadres in the area or that, if present, they were ineffective.[88] The VCI was battered, but communist cadres remained active in the areas where over two-thirds of the population lived.

The Phoenix program was poorly understood even in South Vietnam.[89] To improve the program's image, the government undertook in October 1969 a public information campaign to enlist popular support. In Binh Dinh province, the government televised a nightly special explaining the program's procedures, showing photographs of the most-wanted VCI members, and offering rewards for information leading to arrests. Other provinces publicized the anti-infrastructure effort through wanted posters, radio and television broadcasts, and local loudspeaker systems. Despite these efforts, two-thirds of the rural people responding to a January 1970 PAAS survey were unaware of what the Vietnamese term *Phung Hoang* meant. Nor did popular understanding of the program significantly increase over time. Between 1971 and 1972, only 8 percent of the respondents to PAAS surveys said they understood the program, although 32 percent claimed at least "general understanding" and another 32 percent said they had heard the name.[90] The government's efforts to explain Phoenix to its own people had marginal success.

Two contrasting viewpoints emerged about Phoenix. One side claimed that the large number of VCI members neutralized represented permanent losses to the communists, cutting them off from many villagers and forcing them to find and train replacements. In this view, the government's expansion of territorial security shrank the pool of available VC recruits, making it more difficult for the communists to regain strength.[91] Dale Andrade, author of a comprehensive study supportive of Phoenix, concluded that by 1972, "the police were really chasing shadows." Of the VCI members remaining in the countryside, "only a small percentage were of any value to the communists."[92] In his view, American analysts, fixated on capturing high-ranking VCI members, failed to appreciate how seriously Phoenix wounded the underground at the hamlet and village level. Kolko, a critic of the war, essentially agreed. He contended that the "Phoenix program was certainly more successful than its organizers ever knew. It did round up sufficient low-level cadres to make an important difference to a highly decentralized political movement."[93]

Skeptics discounted these accomplishments. They believed that many who rallied or were captured were only temporary losses and eventually rejoined the Viet Cong. (No hard data are available to determine the numbers involved.) To this school of thought, rebuilding was not necessarily a sign of weakness since three-fourths of those killed, captured, or defected (according to Defense Department data) came from the lowest ranks, which were the easiest for the infrastructure to replace. Official figures strongly suggested the leadership structure remained intact. While conceding that Phoenix and other pacification endeavors had hampered the infrastructure's intelligence collecting, taxation, and recruiting, the skeptical concluded that the cadres still had access to the people for the purposes of propaganda or terror.[94]

The arguments over the Phoenix program revealed something of the indecisive results achieved by both sides. The government scored no knockout, allowing the communists to hold on for a long struggle. Phoenix disrupted the VCI but did not nullify its ability to regenerate. In that sense the program was unsuccessful. Surviving members were the core of the movement, and in areas such as Binh Dinh they had proved virtually impossible to uproot. These were the people whom the program had originally targeted for arrest and sentencing. According to the theory undergirding Phoenix, these leaders were indispensable to the growth and continued functioning of the infrastructure. Phoenix may have put them on the defensive, but by and large they survived.

Phoenix suffered from a mismatch of American managerial philosophy and South Vietnamese interests. The underlying purpose of Phoenix—to coordinate the efforts of diverse South Vietnamese intelligence and police units against the nerve center of their adversary—was eminently sensible by American standards. The program embodied an American managerial and organizational scheme that CORDS expected the South Vietnamese would carry out as the Americans intended. CORDS successfully applied the single manager principle, and the Americans hoped that the South Vietnamese would also use it to help rid the country of the VCI. But the South Vietnamese did not.

The army advisory effort was flawed, which helped weaken the program. CORDS found it difficult, with approximately five hundred Phoenix advisers, too many of whom were inadequately trained and too low in rank to influence their counterparts, to get the individual South Vietnamese agencies to cooperate, share information, and contribute qualified personnel to a combined anti-infrastructure effort.

The program had other defects. Arbitrary procedures and inequities of the judicial system in sentencing suspects, a shortage of detention facilities, bribery, and a use of the program to silence political opponents too frequently characterized the program, subverting its intended purpose. A willingness to tolerate political accommodation and strong family ties between government officials and VCI members also weakened the program,[95] helping explain why some persons identified as members of the infrastructure were not captured or, if captured, were quickly released from detention. One observer-participant, former CIA official Douglas Blaufarb, concluded, "Phoenix was not a viable concept in the Vietnam of the 1960s."[96]

There remains a profound ambivalence about the Phoenix program. Arguably, it was necessary to combat an entrenched insurgent political organization. But in the midst of a controversial war, Phoenix, with all its faults and its basis in subtle distinctions between infrastructure and guerrillas, leaders and rank and file, practically invited censure from American critics on legal and moral grounds. The results of the program were a frustrating mix of ineffectiveness in failing to target and capture the leadership and effectiveness in weakening the low-level infrastructure. The meaning of this program, like much of war, remains an enigma surrounded by controversy.

Phoenix proved to be a two-edged sword. The program hurt the enemy, which rightly feared it, but also hurt the cause of the United States and the government of South Vietnam. Charges of assassination and torture, though exaggerated, put South Vietnamese and CORDS officials on the defensive, forcing them to prove that they were not engaged in crimes. Such publicity only added to the American public's disenchantment with the war and its desire to disengage from Vietnam.

16

The Ambiguous Achievements
of Pacification

Between 1969 and 1972, the Americans and South Vietnamese continued the APC strategy of moving territorial forces into contested and enemy-controlled hamlets and further expanded Saigon's control of the countryside. According to MACV and the U.S. Embassy, security improved continually from the APC to the 1972 Easter Offensive. The gains inspired optimism in CORDS, especially at the top levels.

During the same period, President Thieu took steps to broaden participation in South Vietnam's political system, hoping to give more people a vested interest in supporting the Saigon government. The number of villages with local governments grew, and thanks to land reform, unprecedented numbers of South Vietnamese became landowners with an economic stake in South Vietnam's future. Yet other government actions in 1971 and 1972 cast doubt on the extent of Thieu's commitment.

Colby would later characterize the post-APC period as the time when pacification attained "victory" against the Viet Cong insurgency.[1] Other writers, not coincidentally also high-level participants in the war, reached comparable conclusions. General Davidson called pacification a big winner in 1971 because the VCI was demoralized and impotent. Westmoreland's deputy, General Palmer, called it a success, as did Komer.[2] Historians such as Gabriel Kolko, William Turley, and William Duiker took the opposing view, arguing that pacification failed to displace the NLF, which embodied the real rural revolutionary movement throughout the war.[3]

Because pacification's gains came while it enjoyed strong military support and a relatively quiescent enemy, which was nursing heavy losses, it is difficult to isolate the program's role in the war effort and conclude with any degree of certainty that pacification succeeded.[4] Nevertheless, given the context of the early 1970s, what did pacification accomplish? Was there substantive improvement in government implementation of the program? Was pacification profound enough to be lasting? On what evidence were claims of success based?

The Balance of Power in the Countryside

The continuing decline in the size of communist forces that began at Tet 1968 facilitated the expansion of pacification. The communists' casualties from 1968 to 1972 were enormous and may never be accurately known. According to Defense Department statistics, the communists suffered approximately 672,000 combat deaths in South Vietnam over the period.[5] Allied operations, from small police raids to sweeps by U.S. Army divisions, and the *Chieu Hoi* and Phoenix programs weakened Viet Cong guerrillas and infrastructure. The MACV J-2, Maj. Gen. William Potts, estimated that total Viet Cong strength in South Vietnam fell from around 189,000 in 1968 to 120,000 in 1972, a decline of over 36 percent, although the communists steadily infiltrated men and supplies from North Vietnam until the end of the war. Estimated strength of guerrilla units dropped by about 67 percent, from 77,000 in January 1968 to 25,000 in May 1972.[6] An infrastructure that in January 1968 had 84,000 members could count on its roll only around 56,000 in February 1972.[7] With good reason, CORDS and MACV argued that a smaller Viet Cong was less able to stop the erosion of communist-controlled areas or the expansion of government forces into contested hamlets.

Weakened by losses, the enemy decided against mounting large offensives and concentrated instead on economy-of-force military operations to stop the spread of pacification. The number of small-unit actions rose steadily from 1,374 in 1968 to 1,757 in 1970 and over 2,400 in 1972, while the number of battalion-sized attacks correspondingly dropped from 126 in 1968 to 34, 13, and 2 in each succeeding year.[8] This emphasis on small-unit actions, reflecting the enemy's desire to strike at what directly threatened it as well as what it was capable of attacking with minimal risk, persisted until the Easter Offensive of March 1972.[9]

A major goal of small-unit attacks was to wear down South Vietnam's internal security forces, principally the RF/PF. Data on combat fatalities revealed that these forces bore the brunt of Viet Cong– and North Vietnamese–initiated actions, enduring approximately 67 percent of all South Vietnamese combat fatalities in 1970 and 1971, up from 55 percent in 1969.[10] The number of raids against villages and territorial forces outposts rose above 1968 levels. As measured by combat deaths, service with the RF/PF was more dangerous than with ARVN or U.S. forces. With the exception of 1968, the Regional and Popular Forces had a higher combat death rate than the South Vietnamese or American armies. In 1970, for example, the rate was 11 per 1,000 for U.S. ground forces and 16 for ARVN. The RF/PF rate reached 22.[11]

Despite the unwelcome attention, Saigon's security forces continued to expand as Viet Cong strength waned. Regional and Popular Forces went from 300,000 at the end of 1967 to 520,000 at the close of 1972. Over that span, the police force grew from 74,000 to 121,000. The PSDF, a part-time, partially trained, and lightly armed militia, climbed from 1.4 million in June 1969 to about 3.9 million in September 1972.[12] In the delta, CORDS correlated the growth of the RF/PF with the expansion of government control. Between 1968 and 1970, South Vietnamese armed forces established over 800 new RF/PF units, paralleling a gain of eight hundred hamlets in the A and B security ratings. In the view of John Vann, senior pacification adviser in the region, the physical presence of these added units, some of which had existed only one year, made it unlikely that enemy forces then in the corps, about 44,000 Viet Cong and North Vietnamese, would be able to roll back the gains in pacification. By 1970, territorial forces accounted for over 60 percent of all military forces and over 50 percent of the enemy killed in action in the region.[13] Simply put, Saigon had more forces stationed in more villages providing security for more people. Effectiveness was another matter.

South Vietnam's Population Base

A weakened Viet Cong and numerically larger local forces undergirded the increase in the population under Saigon's control between 1969 and 1972. The communists acknowledged the government's gains and the Viet Cong's losses in documents later captured by the allies.[14] A sizable commitment of U.S. Army forces in support of the program and the continued efforts of General Abrams to focus his commanders on bolstering population security also contributed.

According to HES measurements, the population living in A or B hamlets rose by almost 25 percent in 1969, reaching a new high of 57 percent at the end of December. The relatively secure population (categories A, B, and C) rose above 93 percent, while contested fell to 4 percent and enemy-controlled to 2.7 percent, realizing Abrams's goal of achieving 90 percent relatively secure population eighteen months before the June 1972 target date.[15] The momentum toward greater government control of the countryside that began during the APC continued through 1970. The allied cross-border operation in May 1970 against enemy sanctuaries in Cambodia boosted pacification. The incursion caused large numbers of enemy soldiers and political cadres to rally and led to the capture of vast amounts of weaponry and rice. The operation also disrupted the communists' logistical system, preventing enemy forces from more vigorously contesting pacification in III Corps and the delta well into 1971.[16]

Between 1969 and 1972, a growing number of people, according to HES data, felt safe from the VC. The percentage who believed it was unnecessary for territorial forces to conduct security operations at night (when the Viet Cong normally taxed and recruited) rose from 2 to 19. By December 1972, some 40 percent of respondents said that security operations were not needed during daytime. On the basis of HES reports, people in more areas deemed that the police and militia were capable of dealing by themselves with the enemy's diminished threat to public order.[17] The police and PSDF in some government-controlled settlements assumed the local security mission from the RF/PF because of improved security. In December 1969, the territorials were responsible for protecting 63 percent of South Vietnam's population and the police and militia, 29 percent. By December 1972, the RF/PF's share had dropped to 46 percent, while that of the police and PSDF had climbed to 52 percent.

CORDS officials, especially those with long service in South Vietnam, were aware of how poorly pacification had fared in the past. Based on shared experiences, they were convinced that the situation had tangibly improved from the dark days following the Diem coup and that the numbers combined with staff evaluations, the periodic reports of advisers, and their own frequent visits to villages and hamlets indicated genuine progress in the countryside. Altogether this web of information encouraged CORDS. No one in CORDS denied the weaknesses in the administration of pacification—in fact, CORDS itself uncovered most problems—but in the judgment of men such as Jacobson, Colby, and Vann, the gains outweighed the shortcomings.

Looking back at the continual security gains of the previous four years and the concomitant decline in enemy strength, a confident Ambassador Bunker told President Nixon in January 1972 that the communists could not allow these unfavorable national trends to go unchallenged. Bunker believed the enemy would have to "mount a major military offensive ... to prove his public claims that Vietnamization and pacification are failures."[18] At the Nineteenth Plenum of late 1970 and early 1971, the Politburo had reached a similar verdict. Viewing with alarm the progress of pacification and Vietnamization and the declining military fortunes of communist forces, the leadership in Hanoi decided on a massive offensive to win the war militarily.[19] As in 1959–1960 and 1968, the communists changed strategy in an effort to reverse their fortunes.

Pacification Derailed: The 1972 Easter Offensive

The Easter Offensive began on Good Friday at the end of March 1972. Thirteen NVA divisions and some VC units heavily reinforced with fillers from the North invaded South Vietnam. This juggernaut of nearly two hundred thousand men, equipped with Soviet tanks, armored personnel carriers, long-range artillery, and heat-seeking SA-7 missiles, comprised virtually all of Hanoi's combat forces. Only one of North Vietnam's infantry divisions remained at home. The offensive was an unprecedented military step for Hanoi. Assaulting on four broadly separated fronts—across the demilitarized zone, into Pleiku and Kontum provinces, through Tay Ninh province in III Corps, and in the delta—the enemy pushed back Saigon's forces.

North Vietnam's Politburo, hoping to end the political and territorial losses sustained in South Vietnam, timed the offensive to coincide with the departure of Americans forces from South Vietnam. At the time of the attacks, the only U.S. Army units left in-country were the 196th Infantry Brigade at Phu Bai and two aviation groups. The army and marine corps still had advisers with South Vietnamese forces, but not as many as in 1970 or 1971. With American ground combat forces out of the way, the communists concentrated their attacks on the South Vietnamese. According to U.S. analysts, the communist leadership believed an offensive would compel Saigon to redeploy large numbers of its forces, leaving recently pacified areas vulnerable. Communist forces could return to their former strongholds and regain access to sources of manpower and supplies for their weakened guerrilla movement. In this respect, the offensive attempted to roll back pacification. The communists also hoped to secure a stronger position for a cease-fire and demonstrate dramatically that South Vietnam's forces were unable to stand alone, even with American equipment.[20]

The communists overran numerous RF/PF outposts in outlying areas. After making dramatic gains at the start, the NVA met stiffer opposition on the ground and had to contend with heavy U.S. Air Force bombing. The offensive lost its initial momentum. Most territorial forces units returned to their posts, but province advisers and other CORDS sources throughout South Vietnam observed considerable variation in RF/PF performance during the offensive. The RF/PF did well in Quang Tri and Binh Long but poorly in Binh Dinh and Kontum. In some areas, advisers asserted that the territorials were reluctant to risk casualties, but in other provinces advisers argued that the territorials outperformed ARVN units.[21]

From a national perspective, the offensive resulted in a limited setback for pacification. Prior to the offensive, government control as measured by HES categories A and B was slightly above 82 percent. Control fell sharply in April and reached bottom in October, when the population living in A and B hamlets hit 69.9 percent, the lowest reading since August 1970. By December 1972, A and B hamlets had risen to nearly 80 percent of the population, close to the preoffensive level. Looking at the country as a whole, CORDS believed that the offensive had not undone the national gains of 1968–1972. After an all-out invasion, the communists commanded about 25 percent of the hamlets they had controlled at their peak in March 1968.[22]

Not unexpectedly, population security fell sharply in areas where NVA divisions forced their way into South Vietnam. Between January and June, fourteen of South Vietnam's forty-four provinces saw secure population (HES categories A and B) drop 20 percent or more. Every province in I Corps suffered a serious decline: Quang Tri, nearly 95 percent; Thua Thien, 28 percent; Quang Nam, 30 percent; Quang Tin, over 34 percent; and Quang Ngai, 43 percent. Losses of secure population were of the same magnitude in some highland provinces: Kontum, nearly 83 percent; Phu Bon, 23 percent; Phu Yen, 27 percent; Phuoc Long, nearly 33 percent; and Binh Long, 100 percent. Of the provinces near Saigon or in IV Corps, only four witnessed a serious loss of secure population: Hau Nghia, about 30 percent; Kien Tuong, almost 43 percent; Bac Lieu, 21 percent; and An Xuyen, close to 23 percent.[23]

In other areas of South Vietnam, the offensive had a less dramatic impact. Three provinces in the delta (Go Cong, An Giang, and Sa Dec) reported no loss of population control; eight others suffered declines of 16 percent or less.[24] Because the delta faced less direct enemy pressure than other corps, the government redeployed RF/PF units from the delta to III Corps and upgraded PF platoons into RF companies to counter the enemy's invasion. The removal of PF platoons from their home stations was unpopular since PF members normally served close to their families. Moreover, the decision to redeploy RF/PF units left the countryside less well protected and forced postponement of operations against enemy bases in the delta. The incidence of civilian kidnapping also went up. Wilson reported that the Viet Cong in IV Corps resorted to ruthless methods of coercion to obtain recruits, some in their midteens. Elsewhere, the communists set up reeducation camps and pressed civilians into service as recruits, porters, and rice harvesters.[25]

The infrastructure had trouble helping NVA units because General Truong's special Phoenix campaign had swept up numbers of party cadre in the delta. Enemy prisoners complained that without local guides, outside forces wandered uncertainly through unfamiliar territory.[26]

The offensive increased the refugee population, especially in I and II Corps, as many civilians fled from their homes to escape the fighting. Contemporary estimates of the number of displaced persons were so varied that an accurate tally may never be known, but one authoritative account concluded that by May 5, the offensive had generated almost 700,000 refugees, over 500,000 from I Corps alone. When the offensive ended, over 1.25 million refugees had been driven into areas of government control that had shrunk during the fighting.[27] The enemy embarked on a campaign against the refugee camps, hoping, CORDS officials believed, to drive people from them into enemy-controlled territory.[28]

At this point in the war, the government had assumed complete responsibility for refugee care. The offensive disrupted ongoing refugee programs but did not overwhelm the government's capability to care for large numbers of newly displaced persons. Commodities were stockpiled in provincial and regional warehouses, and transport was available to distribute them. In May, the prime minister decided that he and the cabinet would take charge of the relief effort and appointed Maj. Gen. Cao Hao Hon, head of the CPDC, as executive agent. The U.S. Mission formed an ad hoc refugee relief committee that included executives from CORDS and engineers and officials from AID. The emergency relief effort was effective; temporary shelters were quickly erected, and food and supplies were promptly distributed. In mid-August, Nixon made available an additional $15 million for refugee assistance.[29]

Colby, who headed CORDS for much of the heyday of pacification, saw the Easter Offensive as vindicating the program. Pacification, he wrote in September 1972, "essentially did the job it was supposed to do—deprive the enemy of any population base. The last six months of attack have in my view been a recognition by Hanoi that they had lost the people's war and found it necessary to go into a soldier's war."[30] He reiterated that point in *Lost Victory*. A comparison of the enemy's 1968 and 1972 offensives buttresses Colby's point. In 1968, the government battled VC guerrillas and main forces. In 1972, South Vietnam faced the heavy firepower and massed formations of NVA regulars.

However, Colby's verdict was a partial one and, when placed in a larger context, was hardly reassuring. Intense bombing from the U.S. Air Force had stopped the enemy's advance in I, II, and III Corps; otherwise South Vietnam might have been totally defeated regardless of pacification's "success." Pacification suffered an irreplaceable loss when John Vann was killed in a helicopter crash during the offensive. The Easter attacks put South Vietnam at a disadvantage, causing enormous destruction and displacing over 1 million persons from their homes, many of them indefinitely. The enemy's invasion drove government forces from large parts of South Vietnam. At the end of the offensive, northern Quang Tri, most of Kontum, and much of Binh Long remained under communist control. By October, northwest Tay Ninh had become safe enough for the communists to reestablish COSVN headquarters there.[31] These gains in Kontum, Binh Long, and Tay Ninh made it easier for the enemy to resume infiltration and establish the logistical base for a subsequent offensive in 1975.

Underlying Doubts

The Easter Offensive brought to the surface the long-standing unease about pacification, serving as a reminder of the program's fragility. CORDS's own reports and documents on the status of pacification prior to the 1972 offensive brought to light numerous problems. Questions persisted about the ability of the South Vietnamese to end corruption and carry out an effective program to mobilize popular support. These were some of the same doubts Washington officials had voiced at the end of the APC. The Easter Offensive cast such questions into sharper relief.

The performance of RF/PF units was a major concern. South Vietnam's territorial forces were larger, but how good were they? Based on the TFES, CORDS knew that RF/PF units were, to put it charitably, uneven in quality. The system evaluated the number of men present for duty, the quality of training and equipment, and performance in the field. In March 1971, CORDS rated over half the units in South Vietnam as unsatisfactory. This finding forced CORDS to slow the withdrawal of the MATs that helped train the territorial forces. As part of Vietnamization, CORDS had planned to pull out all the teams by June 1972 but decided late in 1971, after the deputy assistant secretary of defense for systems analysis expressed his apprehension, to slow the phaseout in II and IV Corps.[32]

Desertions were a well-known and long-standing problem that contributed to disappointing RF/PF unit performance. Deserters cited separation from their families, low pay and benefits, dislike of military service, and discontent with their unit or commander as the primary reasons for leaving. In March 1967, before the buildup of equipment and advisers, the desertion rate per 1,000 of assigned strength was 12.5 for the RF and 17.7 for the PF.[33] By June 1971, after the buildup of arms and men for the RF/PF, desertion rates fell only slightly for the RF to 11.7 but dropped more dramatically for the PF to 9.1.[34] Continuing desertions epitomized the shortcomings of the territorial forces to many critics, who viewed them as marginally committed to the regime.

Even the RF/PF in I Corps, which the Systems Analysis Office in the Pentagon considered the most effective in the country, had serious deficiencies, as Colby noted.[35] The assistant commander for the RF/PF in the region complained that poor company and platoon leaders, a lack of direction from district chiefs, corruption, and the padding of payrolls with the names of fictitious soldiers eroded unit effectiveness. In his view, the higher echelons of the RF lacked experienced leaders who could coordinate several RF companies, calling into question the RF/PF's ability to step in for ARVN forces.[36]

The redeployment of American units cast further doubt on the provision of security in the most embattled part of South Vietnam, I Corps, which in 1970 had contained 42 percent of U.S. combat forces in the country. Even with the presence of so many Americans, the ratio of friendly to enemy strength was only 4.4 to 1, the lowest of any corps. As U.S. Army and Marine Corps forces withdrew, the government, if it hoped to consolidate its position, needed to station additional, locally recruited territorial forces in the region. But that step proved unfeasible because the government and the communists over the years had almost completely drained the pool of fighting-age men. The United States planned no further expansion of the RF/PF, leaving the Joint General Staff little choice save to enlarge the operational areas of existing RF/PF units.[37]

In II Corps, the performance of the territorial forces was even worse. RF/PF units conducted about as many operations as their cohorts in other corps but actually engaged the enemy fewer times. CORDS believed that political accommodations with the Viet Cong were one reason the RF/PF fought so infrequently. Inadequate training was another. Few territorial forces units even trained the recommended minimum of six hours a week, hardly an unreasonable standard. Without basic military skills, motivation, or confidence, it was not surprising that the twenty-two hundred territorial force companies and platoons in the corps generally managed in 1971 to make contact with the enemy only three to four times in a twenty-four-hour period, a figure CORDS found disappointing. Far too many RF/PF units were badly deployed, remaining in government-held areas instead of moving into contested villages where they could improve territorial security. A CORDS staff report bleakly concluded, "There has been no deterioration of the quality of RF/PF, but the quality is so low that this statement is somewhat irrelevant."[38]

The RF/PF were generally rated higher in III Corps, whose population benefited from the greatest concentration of territorial forces. Because of overwhelming friendly strength and the lack of enemy military pressure, the territorial forces were not severely tested in 1969 and 1970. Fewer RF/PF troops were killed in III Corps than in any other. Nevertheless, the government was reluctant to move forces from their current outposts to less secure areas where additional RF/PF might improve security, fearing separation from home and family would increase desertions.[39]

The territorial forces in the delta performed well overall. Systems analysts in the Pentagon concluded in 1969 that the region's RF/PF could cope with most enemy activity even without the U.S. 9th Division or ARVN battalions to conduct screening operations.[40] In Dinh Tuong and Kien Hoa provinces, where brigades of the

9th Division had operated, government forces raised an additional ninety-eight hamlets to relatively secure status after the division had left. Despite a resurgence of Viet Cong military activity and the reappearance of battalion-sized enemy formations in Dinh Tuong early in 1970, the government's territorial forces continued to do well, and according to province advisers, security continued to improve.[41]

The RF/PF remained an unknown quantity, yet in large measure Saigon had come to depend on the sheer size of its military forces to occupy the countryside and protect the people under its control. In 1971, the Regional and Popular Forces amounted to roughly half of South Vietnam's force structure of 1.1 million men. The government could afford to maintain a military establishment of that magnitude only with continued massive financial and material support from the United States. Yet in 1971 and 1972, the level of American assistance began inexorably to decline.[42] Desertions, infrequent military engagements with enemy forces, political accommodations with the Viet Cong, and the large number of units rated unsatisfactory in 1971 made it problematic that the RF/PF could sustain a high level of security over the long term. Government control of the countryside could regress. The communist movement, though weakened, had not faded away, and there was understandable concern that the government's forces might not be strong enough to stand alone.

Questions persisted about the value of the official statistics by which CORDS sought to certify "progress." The reports that spewed in great abundance from MACV and CORDS had long bred skepticism. Even well-meaning attempts to improve the accuracy of reporting could have potentially negative side effects. CORDS revised the HES criteria to make them more rigorous, unveiling a revised version of HES in January 1970 that it felt contained more objective criteria and measured functional areas of pacification, such as economics, education, and land reform, that had been previously omitted. The new HES questionnaire covered 139 items about events in each hamlet (compared with 37 in the original HES) and sought to elicit verifiable facts rather than the advisers' interpretative judgments about what had happened.[43]

CORDS revised HES again in 1971 to reflect the changing character of the war, giving greater weight to political factors (the infrastructure, terrorism, level of development) that affected security. Under the 1971 HES, over 84 percent of the population lived in hamlets rated A or B at the end of December 1971, roughly the results of the previous year, which were measured by less stringent standards.[44] How could CORDS project an image of progress if it continually had to make the measurement criteria more rigorous? Each iteration of HES seemed to raise questions about the validity of the previous version. Ultimately, it was hard to reconcile the changes in HES with the general notion that security was continually improving. The problems with HES stemmed from its inception, when U.S. officials yielded to the temptation to publicize HES data as evidence of progress. HES was designed as an internal management technique, which was a valid use. As a public relations tool, HES was disastrously misused.

HES was open to question on other grounds. A special assessment of HES in 1972 concluded that it generated anomalies, showing improvement, for example, "in cases where thousands of area residents are forced by tactical activity from their relatively insecure C villages into camps located in AB rated zones. In other words, although population has been uprooted, and territory lost, the HES will nevertheless show at least a temporary pacification advance in terms of AB population."[45]

The reliability of some reports declined after the South Vietnamese took responsibility for preparing them under Vietnamization. The Americans had compiled data on the number of enemy-initiated incidents as a rough measure of security: the lower the number, the greater the reason to view pacification optimistically. After the South Vietnamese assumed responsibility for compiling this report, CORDS advisers in the delta discovered just before the Easter Offensive significant discrepancies between the number of incidents that had been officially reported and the number that had actually occurred. From their sources, advisers had knowledge of over 100 incidents in one week; yet the government had reported less than 40. A CORDS survey in October 1972 showed similar results. Province advisers counted 240 incidents; the South Vietnamese, 91. Advisers advanced several reasons to explain the discrepancy: willful omissions, differences in reporting criteria, the absence of standard terminology, and suppression of information by higher authorities reluctant to cast local commanders or officials in a bad light. The underreporting of incidents gave a misleading portrayal of the enemy's activities and capabilities. Jacobson and Wilson, who were disturbed by the practice, believed that undercounting of the number of enemy-initiated incidents was common in other regions.[46]

The overall effect on the government's appreciation of the situation in the countryside was hard to gauge. American advisers were aware of the problem and could take into account the questionable reliability of South Vietnamese reporting. Unfortunately, with the withdrawal of American advisers, the actual state of affairs in the countryside would be more difficult to discern. South Vietnamese authorities apparently failed to heed Colby's warning to Thieu in 1969 that inaccurate reporting might lead the government to delude itself about its standing with its own people.[47]

HES data raised concern about the government's consolidation of control in secure areas. At the end of 1972, fifteen of the country's forty-four provinces reported a serious erosion of population living in secure areas (HES rating of A or B) during the year. Eleven of the fourteen provinces that saw over 20 percent of their secure population vanish between January and June had not recouped those losses by December. Phu Bon, Phu Yen, and Kien Tuong were the exceptions. In the ten least secure provinces in December, the percentage of the secure population ranged from a high of 58 in Hau Nghia to 0 in sparsely populated Binh Long. No A or B hamlets could be found in Quang Tri, which the North Vietnamese captured during the Easter Offensive. The ten worst provinces were long-standing enemy bulwarks; four were in the delta (Vinh Binh, Bac Lieu, An Xuyen, Chuong

Thien), one in III Corps (Hau Nghia), three in II Corps (Kontum, Binh Dinh, and Phu Yen), and two in I Corps (Quang Tri and Quang Ngai).[48]

The government could ill-afford to relax its anti-infrastructure efforts. In 1971, the delta provinces of Vinh Binh, Kien Hoa, Dinh Tuong, Vinh Long, Chuong Thien, Phong Dinh, Kien Giang, Ba Xuyen, and An Xuyen each had a communist infrastructure estimated at one thousand persons minimum. In many instances, Viet Cong legal cadres joined a PF platoon to subvert the unit's defenses.[49] In the first five months of 1971, enemy forces overran sixty-three outposts in IV Corps, compared to just six in the other three corps. The number of subverted outposts constituted only a small fraction of all outposts in the delta, but the 1971 total was double the number for the same period in 1970.[50] The Viet Cong, though weakened, remained capable of resisting the government's pacification efforts.

In II Corps, there were additional questions about security. CORDS attributed much of the security gains of 1970 and 1971 to the practice of relocating people from insecure to secure areas.[51] In mid-1970, General Ngo Ngi Dzu, the new commander of II Corps, relied heavily on involuntary relocations to reach his goal of eliminating all D and E hamlets from the region.[52] In February 1971, with little prior planning, General Dzu ordered over nine hundred people evacuated from a contested hamlet in Binh Dinh province to another settlement with marginal security. In March, again with minimal planning, Dzu ordered the relocation of the population of another three hamlets in the province to a more easily defended site, where they received inadequate care. The people, largely Viet Cong dependents, resented the move. The acting province adviser, Daniel Leaty, concluded that the relocations may have deprived the enemy of some fighters and laborers, but, he sadly noted, "the results were considerable hardships inflicted upon the people and an even more embittered group of VC and dependents."[53] Other hamlet relocations met with resistance. The government's policy also contributed to a dramatic increase in the number of contested hamlets abandoned in the province between March and May 1971.[54] Dzu's relocations in Binh Dinh apparently continued until July, when General Hon met with province officials and disapproved, at least temporarily, any additional forced moves of hamlet residents.[55]

In addition to the relocations in Binh Dinh, General Dzu moved hamlet populations elsewhere in II Corps and resettled numerous Montagnard tribespeople in the central highlands.[56] By April 1971, Dr. Gerald Hickey, an American authority on the Montagnards, was estimating that Dzu had relocated forty thousand persons from 100–150 villages throughout the region.[57] When queried by American officials in II Corps, General Dzu made it clear, in the words of one adviser, "that he does not want political interference with his operations."[58] He took exception to Hickey's outspoken protest against this policy. According to Hickey, pressure from Colby and John Vann, who had assumed the duties of senior American adviser in II Corps, restrained Dzu. In June 1971, his plans to move ten thousand highlanders came to naught because, as he put it, "American sensitivity" prevented him from doing so.[59]

On balance, CORDS was guardedly optimistic about pacification. In its view, the national trend for the period 1969–1972 was unmistakable: dramatically improved security as measured by the HES and the VSSG. To CORDS, the best confirmation of these gains came from the enemy. After the APC, the enemy had embarked on a campaign of protracted warfare but had failed to stop pacification. This failure deprived the guerrillas of their population base. With guerrilla forces stymied, the communists had little choice but to resort to a conventional invasion of South Vietnam. Even that effort did not roll back the government's gains.

In retrospect, the CORDS assessment does not hold up well. The Easter invasion underscored the fragility of pacification. Territorial forces and militia were no match for large conventional units, nor were they designed to be, and the process of pacification ceased when the NVA entered an area. The invasion forced the government to spread its forces thinly, reducing the protection provided to the rural populace. The departure of American units and advisers meant the South Vietnamese by themselves would have to deal with the communists in the important provinces where they remained traditionally strong and government control habitually weak. The infrastructure continued to threaten Saigon's control in parts of the countryside. Significantly, the Easter Offensive demonstrated that even if the enemy no longer expected to win an insurgency, it was prepared to wage all-out war to gain victory. Thanks to cross-border sanctuaries and political pressure to withdraw U.S. forces, the communists would have another opportunity for a decisive offensive.

Building a Political Community

Lasting security required a solid political foundation. Between 1969 and 1972, the Saigon government, behind the security shield of U.S. and South Vietnamese forces, concentrated on strengthening its political ties to the rural population. Land reform and elections would, pacification officials hoped, nurture the growth of a broadly based political community and give the average citizen a political and economic stake in South Vietnam's future.

The land reform act of 1970, entitled Land to the Tiller, represented the most successful government attempt to improve the lot of citizens. The law granted full title to the current tillers of the land, regardless of political allegiance or even lack of a legal claim. The law did not exclude those persons who had received grants of land from the Viet Cong and recognized them as owners. Under the law, all government-owned rice land and communal land were deeded to cultivators. The law allowed owners to retain thirty-seven acres of land that they themselves cultivated and compensated landlords for expropriated property. By offering to compensate landowners, Thieu ended their long-standing opposition to reform and ensured passage of the legislation.

The Thieu administration set a goal of distributing 2.5 million acres to tenants in three years. Although the program started slowly, by April 1973 the government had issued titles for 2.5 million acres and distributed about 75 percent of this land to new owners.[60] The 1970 law affected people in nearly all rural areas and, taken in conjunction with the modest distributions made under Diem's restricted land reform of the 1950s, amounted to a major change in the pattern of rural landholding. Between 1956 and 1973, 65 percent of the rice land in South Vietnam, about 5.7 million acres, was redistributed. Land tenancy dropped from 60 to 10 percent between 1970 and 1973. The government continued the Land to the Tiller program after the 1973 cease-fire.

Benefiting from extensive publicity and a high degree of public awareness, land reform succeeded for other reasons as well. President Thieu gave it unwavering support and placed able leaders in charge. Village committees decided who should receive land, an example of the regime successfully encouraging local political involvement. The central government acted with vigor, using aerial surveys to locate plots to be distributed rather than the more time-consuming method of cadastral surveys. Computers sped up the process of registering landownership and issuing titles, thus bypassing the customarily dilatory South Vietnamese bureaucracy.[61]

Not all observers deemed the government's land reform of 1970 a success. Historian Gabriel Kolko dismissed the significance of land reform. He held that the land problem had been "transformed" by 1970. The war had changed the rural economy, forcing farmers to abandon much land and creating serious rural labor shortages. The peasant's need for land was therefore less pressing, and reform was no longer a critical issue. Moreover, rents and land prices had fallen, and land reform was a boon to landlords, enabling them to make profits by selling devalued land to the government. In Kolko's interpretation, land reform came ten years too late and did not eliminate the economic basis of peasant radicalism.[62]

Undeniably, land reform would have been more effective sooner, but when it did happen, it was sweeping and fundamental. The program wrought significant social and economic changes in rural South Vietnam, helping create a middle class of small landowners for whom communist collectivized agriculture had scant appeal. Land redistribution stimulated agricultural productivity, giving the new owners clear incentives to invest capital and increase their harvests. More rice to sell on the market meant the possibility of higher incomes for farmers. Landlords lost influence and could no longer demand menial services and exact high rents. An AID study based on interviews and studies conducted in the countryside in the first half of 1972 concluded, "The Land to the Tiller Program is a splendid means to pacification. ... It is helping turn a once-disaffected, politically neutral mass of potential and sometimes actual revolutionaries (formerly providing rice, information, labor and military manpower to the enemy) into middle class farmers in support of the regime."[63]

Kolko's interpretation also fails to consider the fierce opposition of landowners and Thieu's skill and persistence in overcoming this opposition and seeing his plan enacted into law. Land reform was no bailout of the landowners, as Kolko alleged. Bergerud, author of a study of Hau Nghia province, was on the mark. In his judgment, land reform was the most ambitious effort on the part of the government to build political support in the war and served to counter the NLF's argument that a government victory would allow the landlords to return.[64]

From the government's perspective, the reform had a major flaw: Political loyalty was not a condition for receiving land. Thieu hoped the reform would induce loyalty among Viet Cong supporters receiving titles. The problem, as others have shown, was that reform in some areas ratified the land redistribution previously carried out by the NLF and did not penalize those continuing to support the communists. Under these circumstances, land reform was likely to have little success in developing loyalty among the politically disaffected. Moreover, party propaganda and cadres attacked Thieu's grants, pointing out that the peasants should feel no gratitude to a thief (the government) returning stolen property.[65]

Another goal of pacification was to involve more people in local politics. The government envisioned locally elected governing bodies as the foundation of a political order loyal to the Saigon regime, as the primary political link between the capital and the people of the countryside. The number of hamlets and villages with elected governments remained essentially at about 98 percent between 1970 and 1972.[66] Most of the rest had appointed governments. In most instances voter turnout for local elections was fairly high, although no authoritative figures exist. Most elections went well; province advisers reported few instances of voting irregularities. In a few areas, however, communist harassment discouraged candidates from running.[67]

The electoral process operated to ensure loyalty. The district chief, an appointed representative of the central government, exerted considerable influence in the selection of candidates for village and hamlet elections, seeking competent local people loyal to Saigon. He would enlist support for candidates whom he and the local elite found acceptable. In the absence of suitable candidates, the chief might offer the name of a PF platoon leader or a member of the RD Cadre—who might be an outsider—in hopes of encouraging the village to find a home-bred alternative. In the government's eyes, the district chief's involvement provided stability, but critics saw the process as manipulative, helping elect to local office candidates whom the local elite could support.[68]

Saigon worked to improve the caliber of locally elected officials, many of whom lacked formal education, providing training in government programs and procedures at the Vung Tau National Training Center and provincial schools. The government established a four-week training program for key village and hamlet officials at the Vung Tau Center and an in-province training program for lower-ranking local officials. Supported by American military and civilian advisers from AID and the CIA, the Vung Tau Center trained nearly sixteen thousand village and hamlet officials in 1969, over seven thousand in 1970, and more than thirteen thousand in 1971. In the latter year, provincial centers trained over forty-six thousand South Vietnamese elected officials and cadre members in technical matters such as local budgeting, taxation, and administration. Vung Tau also provided political indoctrination and instruction in mobilizing the people politically but provided much less instruction in these subjects than members of the Viet Cong typically received. The various training centers helped develop a base of leadership talent that was popularly elected and loyal to Saigon. At the end of June 1971, American advisers were no longer assigned to Vung Tau. The government assumed complete responsibility for funding the training center at the end of 1971.[69]

Despite training programs, numerous local elections, and sweeping land reform, the Thieu government remained uncertain about how much power should devolve to the provinces and districts. During the Easter Offensive, Saigon reversed its long-standing policy on local elections on grounds of internal security. The government claimed to discover during the offensive that a number of hamlet chiefs were actually communists who assisted enemy forces, a clear indication of the infrastructure's continuing influence. Ostensibly in reaction, Prime Minister Khiem issued Decree 120 in August 1972 suspending the 1966 law authorizing hamlet elections. The decree authorized province chiefs to dismiss those hamlet officials they deemed unfit. Village chiefs, however, continued to be elected.

Saigon's rationale can only be viewed as a pretext. The regime had known since the start of the war that some hamlet officials were sympathetic to or belonged to the Viet Cong, and yet the government had sanctioned local elections and even distributed weapons to the local militia. Political considerations played a large part in the government's decision. Thieu wanted to consolidate his government's grip. Complaints from district chiefs about hamlet officials were particularly prevalent in I and II Corps, where the strength of lawful opposition political parties (i.e., noncommunist) was heavily concentrated. The new procedure for selecting hamlet officials helped ensure that officials loyal to Thieu would be in power at the time of a possible cease-fire.[70] The popular reaction to these changes was hard to discern, and CORDS declined to investigate. Jacobson instructed the four military regions to "not attempt to determine the attitude of any segment of the population relative to GVN Circular 120."[71] Jacobson apparently regarded the government's decision as a sensitive matter and did not wish to stir up trouble. But the decree represented a clear retreat from the policy of broadening the base of the Saigon government and blemished the image of the government as conciliatory and democratic.

The 1971 Presidential Election

South Vietnam's constitution mandated a presidential election in 1971. Intended to show South Vietnam as a functioning democracy, the electoral process, close to farce, exacerbated criticism of the regime. In August, a three-man panel of the Supreme Court disqualified Ky, Thieu's most serious rival. An election law enacted in June required candidates to have endorsements from a minimum of either 100 provincial councilors or 40 assemblymen.[72] Ky received only sixty-one endorsements, and the court disallowed the later endorsements he received from councilors who switched their support from Thieu to him.[73] A number of councilors had endorsed Thieu's candidacy before the law was promulgated. General Duong Van

"Big" Minh dropped out of the race on August 20,[74] believing he would lose against Thieu. Although the full Supreme Court later reversed the earlier decision and allowed Ky to run, Minh, other opposition leaders, and American officials failed to persuade Ky to enter the race.[75]

Over 6 million voters in South Vietnam, or 87.7 percent of those registered, went to the polls on October 3, 1971. Of that total, over 94 percent cast ballots for Thieu, the only candidate. About 5 percent of those participating cast blank or defaced ballots in protest.[76] Thieu's was a hollow victory, undermining the credibility of his attempts to create a broad-based democratic government in South Vietnam. Thieu's manipulations cast serious doubt on his commitment to democratic rule and embittered his rivals. Critics saw the election as confirmation that the Saigon government was unrepresentative and authoritarian. Thieu's restrictions on the autonomy of local government and his blatant maneuvering in the 1971 election were pieces in a pattern of trying to consolidate his rule by eviscerating his opposition. The election failed to broaden Thieu's base.

South Vietnam's president retreated from democratic rule on other fronts. He curtailed operations of the nongovernment press, raising the price of newsprint 125 percent in March 1972 and requiring each paper to post a $47,000 bond to cover legal costs if the government charged the paper with violating the press code. Promulgated in August, the new law forbade criticism of the government or armed forces and allowed authorities to seize any newspaper that was in violation. The effect was to shut down fourteen antigovernment newspapers and fifteen of the eighteen periodicals published in the capital.

During the Easter Offensive, Thieu suspended the constitution and ruled by decree for six months. While Thieu's decree powers were in effect, he signed a statute establishing stringent new regulations requiring all political parties to establish branches in at least one-quarter of the villages in one-half of South Vietnam's provinces and in every city. The regulations also required that each branch register at least 5 percent of the voters in each area and win at least 20 percent of the vote in any national election or be dissolved. Leaders of opposition parties believed that only Thieu's party would be able to meet these criteria.[77]

At the end of 1972, basic questions about pacification still lacked answers. More South Vietnamese lived in a secure environment than before, but the permanence of the gains was unknown because they depended to a large extent on special and perhaps transitory conditions: the massive buildup of South Vietnam's forces occupying the countryside, American matériel and military support, and the inability of the Viet Cong to mount effective resistance. Although South Vietnam's forces had staved off the North Vietnamese invasion in 1972, they did not do it alone. Without U.S. airpower, it was unlikely that Saigon's forces would have turned the tide in I, II, and III Corps. The ability of South Vietnam's forces by themselves to provide security for the countryside remained unproven.

To what extent did the Thieu government enjoy the allegiance of the people in the countryside? Even the leadership of CORDS was unsure, debating at the beginning of 1973 the issue of how many would remain loyal.[78] Widespread improvements in rural economic conditions were no guarantee of popular allegiance, especially at a time when President Thieu was taking steps to suppress the expression of legitimate political dissent in order to consolidate his rule. The ultimate political goal of pacification, winning hearts and minds, was largely intangible, making a clear verdict difficult to reach. But it appeared doubtful that the program had helped established a strong political community before the last American soldier went home.

17

The End of an Experiment

CORDS was a singular organization, unique in structure, unique in goals. Formed at President Johnson's behest, it came into being to meet security and development problems that no single U.S. agency by itself could satisfactorily address. CORDS attempted to help South Vietnam halt an insurgency that posed a political and military threat to its existence, furnish economic assistance, and aid the government in developing a political foundation. An ad hoc organization melding U.S. soldiers and civilians, CORDS had no real precedent. Its existence ended in January 1973 when the Paris Accords went into effect. An entirely civilian operation headed by George Jacobson, special assistant to the ambassador for field operations (SAAFO), assumed CORDS's functions and programs. Jacobson, an ex-army officer whose Vietnam experience began in 1954, had long served in CORDS.

The army played a major role in CORDS, providing the bulk of the personnel for headquarters and field advisory positions. Over 95 percent of the 6,464 military advisers assigned to CORDS in September 1969 came from army rolls. The relatively few from other services tended to be assigned to CORDS's headquarters staff. CORDS also included 1,137 American civilians from DOD, AID, and other U.S. government agencies as well as 7,038 South Vietnamese and 223 third-country nationals, who served primarily as analysts, translators, and secretaries. Of the total, 5,812 military advisers served in the field, and 652 were stationed in regional and national headquarters.[1] Support of CORDS may have been a minor aspect of the army's role in the war, but the army as an institution struggled to adapt its customary personnel policies to meet the requirements of a hybrid organization whose mission extended beyond the military's normal charge.

Advisers: Seeking the Best and Brightest

When the United States first began withdrawing combat units from South Vietnam late in 1969, the work of U.S. advisers—preparing the South Vietnamese to rely to a greater extent on their own efforts—became more important. Despite a clear need for truly outstanding advisers, Secretary of Defense Melvin Laird, who was responsible for the management of Vietnamization, believed that the army's personnel policies discriminated against advisers because they were not accorded the same importance as combat commanders in matters of promotion and selection for higher military schooling. In December 1969, Laird asked Secretary of the Army Stanley Resor to take corrective action and ensure that the army assigned "only the most highly qualified personnel to advisory duty."[2]

Resor responded by taking strong steps to enhance the status of pacification advisory assignments. He strengthened the ongoing incentive program for province senior advisers initiated in 1967 by Undersecretary McGiffert and Army Chief of Staff General Johnson by adopting in April 1970 additional incentives for outstanding officers, mainly majors, to serve the normal twelve-month tour as district advisers. The inducements included a personal letter signed by the chief of staff (which became part of the officer's permanent record) attesting to the importance of the assignment, a chance for the district adviser to select his next assignment, consideration for civilian schooling, and an offer of family quarters at posts in the continental United States. Officers signing up for an eighteen-month tour as district senior advisers received in addition thirty days special leave, an offer of family quarters in posts in Hawaii, a five-year exemption from additional short tours, and, most significantly, guaranteed early consideration by a selection board for promotion to lieutenant colonel. Resor directed a senior officer promotion board to equate service as an adviser with command of an army unit in combat. In addition, he designated, when possible, at least one former adviser as a member of field officer promotion boards. Resor hoped the incentives would not only encourage promising officers to seek advisory positions but also ensure that "no officer's future should suffer in any way from the fact that he served as an adviser instead of in some other assignment."[3]

In public appearances, Resor was emphatic about the importance of pacification advisers and their contributions in South Vietnam, hoping to persuade army audiences to share the high value he personally attached to pacification assignments. "I know of no assignment of greater importance to achieving our objectives in Vietnam ... than that of province or district senior adviser," Resor told the graduates of the district adviser training course in May 1970. "Ultimately our whole effort in Vietnam will succeed or fail depending on what the Vietnamese do. ... In the advisory program, there are only 300 province and district senior adviser positions at the local level to provide the crucial leverage point on which the Vietnamization program turns."[4]

Although Resor hoped his measures would help ensure that officers selected to advise would be the equals of officers assigned to command,[5] many prospective advisers resisted. They remained skeptical that the program would change ingrained personnel practices or that the army would ever regard advising as commensurate for promotion purposes with commanding. The *Christian Science Monitor,* which published a series of articles on army advisers in 1970, concluded, "Military officers do not look on jobs advising the Vietnamese as a way up. Young officers of the sort one expects to have a great future ... generally shun advisory duty."[6] Resistance to advisory assignments was nothing new. In 1968, only 38 of the 105 officers invited to participate in the province adviser program accepted.[7] The problem for the army was the difficulty of changing the institution to reward officers interested in important but somewhat unorthodox assignments.

In trying to attract high-caliber advisers, the army confronted a basic conflict between the goals of officers seeking advancement along traditional career paths and its requirement to supply the best possible personnel for special assignments like advising; between the army's traditional role of fighting a conventional war and its responsibility for providing officers for an ad hoc multiagency effort to advise South Vietnamese officials. The conflict proved nearly irreconcilable. The kind of officers the army incentives targeted, those aspiring to become general officers, preferred assignments that yielded rapid promotions. In the eyes of most officers, advising would never substitute for command. They perceived advising as a lost opportunity. It bears repeating that command of a unit remained the most desirable army assignment and that as an institution the army could not afford to have too many of its most promising future leaders choosing to advise and not to command. The mentors of many up-and-coming officers counseled them against serving as advisers.[8]

The incentives could not compete with the institutional emphasis on combat command. A survey taken after the war found that almost 65 percent of the province and district advisers who had served between July 1967 and January 1970— that is, after the army issued its initial command equivalency guidance in 1967— believed that army promotion boards gave less weight to advisory duty than to combat command. "More than six out of ten of the officers who received these repeated assurances of equity still felt that the matter of command equity was substantially a myth."[9] A majority of advisers serving between 1962 and 1967 also believed that promotion boards and senior service college selection boards regarded advisory duty as less significant than time in command. This was true prior to 1965, when no army officers commanded troops in battle and advisers served in a war zone, and it was also true after the army put in place its various incentive packages. The same survey also discovered that nearly fifty percent of those polled who had served as district or province senior advisers between October 1965 and January 1970 felt that their service as advisers would prejudice their future career prospects. That figure was unaffected by the army's incentives.[10] It is unlikely that any incentive program could have been attractive enough to change basic perceptions about the inadvisability of advising.

Unfortunately for pacification advisers, they were not the only officers receiving equivalent credit for command time. The army decided to extend this benefit to other officers in special assignments to enhance their prestige and attract officers on the fast track. Project managers with the Army Matériel Command; area, district, and division engineers; and Army Security Agency battalion commanders were also recognized as "commanding" a combat unit. Overuse of this incentive could only debase its value with promotion boards.

Even with the incentive program, pacification advisers faced severe career handicaps. Promotion boards found it difficult to evaluate an adviser's work and compare it to what an officer in a traditional army assignment did. The adviser produced nothing measurable and exercised little control over what his counterpart accomplished. The adviser's duties varied from district to district, making it difficult to establish uniform measures of performance. Few superiors writing the efficiency reports of advisers had daily contact with them; weekly contact or less was the norm. Pacification advisers perceived that they were not rated accurately or fairly, placing them at a disadvantage with their peers.[11]

The army had trouble persuading many of its truly superior officers to serve as advisers, although a number of promising officers signed up knowing the possible risks to their careers. In addition, CORDS had difficulty obtaining enough officers of the grade it wanted as province and district advisers and sometimes had to settle for captains instead of majors as district senior advisers and lieutenant colonels instead of colonels as province senior advisers. The army personnel system, under stress from a long war that required it to send some soldiers with critical skills or training again and again to South Vietnam, did not fully satisfy CORDS's needs. With American involvement in the war winding down and the army's role in CORDS also getting smaller, it would have been surprising if CORDS had gotten what it asked for. By the time Resor's incentives were in place, the war had become controversial, further decreasing the chances that the cream of the officer corps would risk working for an unconventional outfit such as CORDS.

CORDS Under Siege

The problems in obtaining advisers were not the only challenge to CORDS. From its inception, CORDS had to fend off efforts to weaken it. Late in 1967, AID tried to regain control of some programs from CORDS, and a frustrated Komer temporarily ended CORDS's involvement in land reform because he felt that AID was dragging its feet in developing American policy.[12] Under Vietnamization, CORDS, like other elements of MACV, was forced to reduce, but CORDS also faced additional pressure from U.S. agencies anxious to get back their personnel and programs. In 1970, Colby had to repel Washington's attempt to pull the territorial security mission out of CORDS, and he had to defend CORDS from its critics in Congress. Colby believed that the appearance of key members of CORDS before the Senate Foreign Relations Committee in February and March 1970 was helpful in holding political support for the organization.[13]

Vietnamization steadily lowered personnel ceilings on MACV, mandating the withdrawal of district teams. From a peak of 6,464 in September 1969, the number of military advisers assigned to CORDS declined as MACV began to reduce the number of district advisers in the latter half of 1970. The cuts were deep. Between June 1970 and June 1971, CORDS's military advisory strength dropped nearly 24 percent, to 4,924. Over the same period, civilian advisers declined from 1,127 to

744, a reduction of more than 33 percent.[14] General Abrams, desiring an orderly phaseout, hoped to retain an advisory team in a district until it was "no longer a trouble spot."[15] This rule allowed MACV to eliminate entire teams in some secure districts, replacing them with a provincial liaison officer. In other cases MACV left a one- or two-man team in the district. The reductions had the effect of lessening the close involvement of advisers with local officials and changing their role to a broader one of managerial advice on program administration.

Vietnamization reopened old debates about the role of advisers. Those wanting to cut district advisory teams argued that they had a limited capability to provide developmental assistance, inhibited the development of South Vietnamese initiative and self-reliance, and had become increasingly unnecessary in secure areas. This group did not believe that monitoring South Vietnamese officials and their expenditure of U.S. funds justified maintaining an American presence in the countryside. Ignoring the costly lessons of the early 1960s when poor information on the countryside masked the Viet Cong's virtual control of large rural areas, these observers also saw little need for extensive field reporting.[16]

CORDS worked to hold onto its district advisers, the Americans nearest to developments in the field, as long as personnel ceilings allowed. The regional DepCORDS argued that district advisers were needed to monitor the conduct of government programs and administer American aid. John Dean, DepCORDS for Military Region I, felt that the "presence of resident U.S. advisors—even one man—has a beneficial psychological effect on not only the district chief and other GVN officials, but the general populace as well."[17] Dean and Robert Paxette, assistant DepCORDS for Military Region 4, also held that district advisors facilitated the transfer of excess U.S. property to the GVN and provided U.S. policymakers with reliable "grass-roots" information,[18] which was one reason the United States had stationed advisers in the first place. General Dzu, II Corps commander, concurred, noting that advisers would "tell him what the situation is really like."[19] Without advisers, U.S. officials would have to rely more on South Vietnamese sources for information, as they had in the past.

Despite CORDS's pleas, MACV continued to withdraw district teams even during the Easter Offensive. At the beginning of the offensive, MACV knew little of the situation in northern I Corps, in part because it had no district advisers on the scene and South Vietnamese forces were in retreat. Despite CORDS's hopes for a reprieve, MACV did not augment the CORDS advisory effort during the offensive, not even in territorial security or in refugee work, both areas of prime importance. The underlying policy was to continue the withdrawals of advisers on schedule, no matter what the circumstances. In September 1972, President Nixon ordered further cuts, accelerating the reduction of district advisers and mobile advisory teams.

Additional pressure on CORDS came from another quarter when civilian agencies in Washington tried to carve up CORDS. In planning for withdrawal, the State Department, Department of Defense, and AID asked the embassy in 1971 to examine CORDS's projected personnel requirements, civilian and military, for the coming years and submit a proposal for reducing the number of advisers. Deputy Ambassador Samuel D. Berger, at the direction of William Sullivan, head of the Vietnam Task Force of the NSC, led a study on whether CORDS should be continued and, if so, in what form.[20]

In November, Berger's study group issued its findings, recommending retention of a CORDS organization until FY 1973, but one that was broken into component parts. Under the proposal, CORDS would retain control over territorial security functions and war victims programs, but political, economic, social, and psychological programs would return to their parent agencies. Specifically, the Directorates of Community Development, Municipal Development, and Management Support would be moved out of CORDS. The *Chieu Hoi* and Phoenix Directorates would be phased out. The report also urged that the deputy for CORDS, at that time General Weyand, who had replaced Ambassador Colby, be made a civilian position.[21] The findings were hardly surprising from a civilian-dominated panel (four of the six members came from nonmilitary agencies) working for the embassy.

The embassy also wanted to phase out district advisers and MATs first and then the province teams. Province teams (half military and half civilian) would include a senior adviser and a deputy, a senior operations adviser, a police adviser, a development adviser, and a clerk-typist. CORDS would shrink from 3,205 in 1972 to 1,782 in the following year and fall to 750 at the end of FY 1974. Civilians, who made up less than 40 percent of CORDS personnel in FY 1972, would constitute over 58 percent by FY 1974.[22] What remained of CORDS would be subject to further personnel reductions. Such steps would have been the coup de grâce.

The MACV and CORDS members of the task force objected. General Abrams and General Weyand (who was then both deputy MACV commander and DepCORDS) opposed Berger's study on grounds that State and AID wanted to reduce CORDS faster than MACV considered appropriate. Ambassador Bunker supported MACV, and the report had little effect.[23] MACV and CORDS viewed the report as an attempt to weaken CORDS by reclaiming programs and personnel, a renewal of the bureaucratic fighting over CORDS.

The signing of a cease-fire agreement in late January 1973 made the issue moot. The terms required the withdrawal of all American armed forces, save for a handful assigned to the Defense Attache's Office in the embassy. Stripped of remaining military personnel, CORDS no longer had a rationale for existence and ceased operations on February 27, 1973. It was succeeded by the Office of the Special Assistant to the Ambassador for Field Operations. At the headquarters level, staff management functions were transferred from CORDS to SAAFO. The Territorial Security Directorate was dissolved, and SAAFO took on the *Chieu Hoi* program. The Directorates for Community Development, War Victims (Refugees), and Public Safety (Police) all returned to AID.[24] Graham Martin replaced Bunker as U.S. ambassador. Jacobson served as the American liaison officer to the prime minister and the Central Security and Development Council and oversaw four regional directorates. The directorates advised the military region commander and the regional security and development council. Only seventeen province representatives remained to assist the forty-four province chiefs and province security and development councils.

The Heritage of CORDS

As an organization created to bring civilian and military programs under a single manager, CORDS was largely successful. Thanks to its efforts, civil pacification programs received support from U.S. Army engineers and civil affairs companies. CORDS also helped make available to South Vietnamese officials and American advisers working on development projects military matériel, transportation, and communications. As an integral part of MACV, CORDS obtained assistance from U.S. Army units that provided local security. Although some civilians objected, especially in the early days, that CORDS was unworkable, a "nonfusible mixture of military and civilian aptitudes, attitudes, skills, and procedures," according to one AID official,[25] most Americans working on pacification came to acknowledge the necessity of merging civil and military programs under one manager and felt that CORDS successfully coordinated military and civilian programs.[26]

As an organization to support South Vietnamese programs, CORDS also achieved success. The growing numbers of South Vietnamese working on pacification programs after 1967 tells a significant story. To cite one example, CORDS was primarily responsible for the growth of the territorial forces. Prior to CORDS, the RF/PF were small in size, a poorly equipped force of about 300,000 in mid-1966. By the end of 1969, the territorials were better equipped and trained, reaching a strength of 470,000. The police also grew over that period from 60,000 to over 82,000; the RD Cadre, from 35,000 to 58,000. Funding for pacification also showed remarkable growth, in large part because of CORDS's insistence on more resources for the other war. U.S. and South Vietnamese support of pacification, which amounted to $582 million in 1966, climbed to over $1.5 billion in 1970, most of which went for equipping and paying the RF/PF.[27] Unfortunately, the increase in resources did not completely eliminate the RF/PF's deficiencies, and a significant but probably unknowable percentage of the money spent on the RF/PF paid the salaries of ghost soldiers who existed only on the rolls.

In a number of areas, CORDS's strong voice enhanced American influence with the South Vietnamese. Partly thanks to CORDS, South Vietnamese planning for pacification gradually improved. If the Americans had played a dominant role in preparing the combined national pacification plans of the mid-1960s, that changed under CORDS's tutelage. The government's ability to formulate the plans steadily improved, most notably with the APC. The community defense and local development plan of 1972, the last one, represented a totally South Vietnamese effort.[28] CORDS pushed the government long and hard to reform its top-level organization for pacification and got results. In late 1968, the government formed the CPDC, which embodied the single manager principle, placing one organization in charge of the efforts of the many separate ministries responsible for different aspects of pacification. With the continual urging of Komer and Colby, President Thieu became more involved in pacification and, beginning with the APC, incorporated the program into his political strategy. Thieu took advantage of General Thang's groundwork in reviving pacification and became an active proselytizer for the program.

Where CORDS registered perhaps its most significant success in influencing the South Vietnamese was the APC. In the aftermath of Tet, a cautious Thieu initially was content to protect the areas the government already controlled from further attack. The Americans, especially Komer, convinced the president that it would be a strategic mistake to remain on the defensive. Thieu's acceptance of the special campaign was significant, marking the beginning of a steady period of expansion of the population under government control. Without a single, authoritative voice speaking for all U.S. agencies involved in pacification, it would have been much more difficult, perhaps impossible, to persuade Thieu, the ultimate authority on pacification, to challenge the Viet Cong in contested areas after the Tet Offensive.

Another area where the Americans had a measurable impact was in influencing the government to replace corrupt or ineffective officials. Although some Americans believed it was inappropriate for CORDS to interfere with South Vietnamese appointments or, as one adviser put it, to look for crooks and have them fired,[29] Colby and then General Weyand and Jacobson recognized that pacification required able and dedicated South Vietnamese leaders and managers to carry it out. So they continued Komer's system of removing poorly performing province and district officials. This represented the major American effort to improve the caliber of the South Vietnamese leaders carrying out pacification programs. No other element of MACV adopted the procedure, despite Secretary Laird's pointed suggestion to MACV that it might prove useful in improving the level of ARVN leadership.[30]

The numbers of officials replaced for cause (corruption, dishonesty, or incompetence) clearly showed American influence. According to CORDS's data, CORDS sought and obtained the removal of 14 of the 20 province chiefs the government replaced for prejudicial reasons in 1968, 1969, and 1971. Over the same time span, the government removed 124 district chiefs for cause. Of that number, the United States had sought and obtained removal of 84.[31] John Vann, regional DepCORDS for IV Corps during those years, felt that the complaints of advisers accounted for 70 percent of those removed for cause.[32]

The removal of corrupt and ineffective officials was only a first step. The key point was whether their replacements would prove more honest or able. Although CORDS suggested names, it did not select replacements; the South Vietnamese government did. In some cases the replacement was a significant improvement; in others the new official was not. After a discreet interval, Saigon might reassign an individual to a different post in another part of the country. Information on the subsequent reassignments of relieved officials was sketchy. Not all were penalized. As a consultant to the State Department described the process, if the South Vietnamese were forced to replace someone because of blatant American pressure, they would promote the man or send him to another good job.[33] Of the thirty-odd province chiefs the government relieved from January 1968 to mid-1969, five whose performance CORDS considered poor rose in rank. Most of the rest remained at the same rank or were demoted. CORDS influenced the removal of numerous officials, but it would be hard to argue that the process resulted in a net improvement on a national basis. That the Saigon government retained dishonest or inept officials was one indication that it still relied on a closed, entrenched political system whose bedrock principle was loyalty, not competence, and that it had the means to deflect U.S. pressure to reform.

In other ways CORDS's influence was also limited. Its ability to get the government to improve the implementation of pacification programs in the provinces and districts remained circumscribed for the simple reason that the government, not CORDS, issued directives to the field. Komer, Vann, Colby, and other CORDS leaders had no intention of arrogating Saigon's authority and accepted the fact that the government's guidance took precedence over the counsel of American advisers. Province and district advisers were frequently and understandably frustrated at the slowness with which government ministries carried out programs in settlements that U.S. and South Vietnamese forces had secured. CORDS also had limited success in curtailing the government's counterproductive policy of relocating thousands of persons in I and II Corps against their will. CORDS failed to get a wholehearted South Vietnamese commitment to the Phoenix program. CORDS did not succeed in getting the South Vietnamese to produce reliable reports on pacification, despite repeated admonitions, and persuaded Saigon to use HES to measure the APC only after repeated admonitions. Nor did CORDS have much success in getting the Thieu government to eliminate corruption. At the last CORDS conference held in January 1973, Jacobson complained that South Vietnamese corruption was worse than ever, running out of control.[34]

In evaluating CORDS, one should remember the ambiguous relationship of the U.S. agencies and the South Vietnamese government. The American government held CORDS to a difficult, deliberately restricted role. CORDS exercised limited influence over the conduct of programs approved and administered by a sovereign nation, yet pacification was supposed to be a catalyst to get the entire governmental apparatus to work. In supporting pacification, CORDS was to concentrate resources and influence in order to push the South Vietnamese civil and military structure into doing the right things. The ultimate objective of the program was to transform the government structure into a system that could achieve popular support. Paradoxically, CORDS's limited charter meant that it could not force the government to transform itself.

At face value, America's strength as a military and economic superpower should have given Washington the ability to dictate terms to Saigon, but that was not the case, for Washington did not seek to reinstitute colonial dominion. Nor did it wish to take charge of pacification. The restricted U.S. role in pacification support led to tensions between the allies. Because American prestige was linked to South Vietnam's survival, Washington could ill-afford to abandon the Saigon government in the middle of a war. South Vietnamese authorities knew from experience that the United States would provide aid even when Saigon strayed from joint goals. They felt they were in a position to resist American initiatives. Saigon thus exercised considerable independence of action from its powerful patron.

Although the army's participation in CORDS was the sine qua non of CORDS's existence, pacification remained a minor part of army activities in South Vietnam. The army concentrated on fighting a conventional war. Data from FY 1969 and FY 1971, the period of Abrams's one-war strategy, indicate that ground fighting consumed about 30 percent of the total cost of the war to the Americans and that logistics, administration, communications, and other types of support consumed about 19 percent. Only about 2 percent of U.S. funds were spent directly on police and Regional and Popular Forces. In FY 1969, artillery support alone cost more than five times as much as the territorial forces that were protecting the villages from the Viet Cong.[35] Pacification was not accorded the resources commensurate with its importance in countering a communist threat that was directed heavily against the RF/PF.[36]

The army's record in providing combat support in South Vietnam was mixed. The improved local security that stemmed from operations such as WASHINGTON GREEN was offset by CEDAR FALLS, RUSSELL BEACH, and other operations in populated areas that destroyed homes and crops, displaced people, and allowed the Viet Cong to reclaim an area as soon as American soldiers departed. Nor could it be said that all army commanders adhered to Abrams's one-war policy. To some commanders, pacification was merely a variant of civic action: digging wells, repairing damaged buildings, distributing rice, and the like. It was window dressing, and these commanders concentrated on using firepower to wear down enemy forces.

Even though CORDS brought much-needed coordination and unity of command to an important program, only the intervention of a strong-willed president, Lyndon Johnson, accomplished the merger of civilian and military support. The president overcame the resistance of civilian agencies reluctant to cede funds, programs, and personnel to an entity that they did not run. In essence, CORDS came about because Johnson wanted the military to run the pacification support effort and by stages maneuvered the civilian agencies and the military into accepting a new arrangement. He made this decision after realizing that interagency coordination was inadequate to handle a complex, wartime, multiagency program. A forceful president pushed the departments and agencies under him to acknowledge their inability to manage separately a matrix of programs that did not neatly fit the charter of any single one of them.

CORDS resolved the organizational problem of American support but was constrained by bureaucratic politics (agencies trying to regain control of programs) and a lack of resources. One observer compared CORDS to a beggar: "CORDS, as such, is an organization in name only. It has no assets of its own; it has no authority; it can't buy or sell anything. Everything we did out there in the administrative operation of CORDS was done through some agency."[37] CORDS had to obtain supplies, equipment, and personnel through other agencies, which had an understandable reluctance to provide another organization with funds for which they were accountable. How far could AID, for example, go in hiring people and then loaning them to CORDS? Could AID relieve itself of responsibility for those people?

CORDS was founded on the assumption that pacification needed better management to succeed, but that assumption, based on good intentions, may have been taken too far. The danger for CORDS as an organization was that it could equate the projects and methods it supported with the process of pacification. The projects in turn created pressure to show results that could be reported quantitatively, and such reports sometimes produced misleading conclusions about what had been accomplished. Pacification was in danger of becoming bureaucratic and mechanical. So many projects completed in an area equaled success. The danger of this approach was that the pacification program became a kind of surrogate, trying by its own devices to achieve popular support on behalf of the government by bringing more and more villages and hamlets under Saigon's authority. Reducing a complicated and difficult process, the transformation of South Vietnam into a viable nation, to a collection of bureaucratic programs had an insidious effect. It may have kept the Americans from recognizing the intractable nature of South Vietnam's political, social, and military problems. Statistics, programs, and other management tools created a way to make sense of pacification and to manage the overall effort, but they provided an inaccurate gauge for measuring the transformation of South Vietnam.

Although CORDS provided a model for the South Vietnamese to centralize their direction of pacification, the limited influence of its advisers could not compensate for the flawed execution of pacification plans and programs, the ubiquitous corruption, and the failure of the South Vietnamese government to build a broad, self-sustaining political base. Nor could those Americans involved in the other war compensate for the misconceptions that characterized allied military operations. Would the eventual outcome of the war have possibly been different had the United States actually run pacification programs, directly hired and fired South Vietnamese officials, and commanded South Vietnamese paramilitary forces? Given the iron determination of the communists to unite Vietnam, their patience and resilience, their strategic and tactical flexibility, on the one hand, and the systemic problems of the Saigon government, on the other, the answer is no. The advocates of pacification hoped it would cause a fundamental transformation of South Vietnam. But even if that transformation had occurred, it would most likely have taken too long and would in any case have exhausted the patience of the American people, inevitably eroding political support in the United States.

A Note on Sources

In writing this book, I used several collections of documents. The U.S. Army Center of Military History (CMH) currently houses unique materials on the Vietnam war and pacification that historians, political scientists, and students have mined before me. The papers at CMH fall into three groups. First and of foremost importance for the subject of pacification are the documents of the office of the Deputy (to the U.S. military commander) for Civil Operations and Revolutionary Development Support, or DepCORDS. Spanning the period of CORDS's existence, 1967–1973, the DepCORDS files include documents on organization and management, the operations of various pacification programs, CORDS's liaison with South Vietnamese officials, relations with U.S. military commanders and units, the Viet Cong, as well as reports from CORDS's evaluators and province and district advisers. Documents from this collection are labeled DepCORDS files in the endnotes. Second, a larger set of documents at CMH are the materials opportunistically and informally collected by CMH historians during the war from a myriad of sources. Covering more than just pacification, these documents include material on relations between MACV and various Washington departments and agencies, logistics, forces, and operations. This assemblage is eclectic and cannot be considered a single, coherent corpus of records. Therefore, documents cited from this group are simply designated by their current location, CMH. The third group of Vietnam materials, the papers of the American military commander General William Westmoreland, help place pacification in the larger context of the ground war. CMH has a duplicate set of Westmoreland's papers; the originals are in the Lyndon Baines Johnson Library in Austin, Texas.

The LBJ Library houses invaluable materials for the story of the revitalization of pacification and the movement to put support of pacification under the military. The "National Security File, Country File, Vietnam" is the general classification for documents on the war. The country file on Vietnam is rich in documents on decisionmaking and the roles and views of the government agencies involved in support of pacification. It contains countless analyses of the situation in Vietnam from the Department of Defense, the Joint Chiefs of Staff, the Department of State, the Central Intelligence Agency, the American embassy, and MACV headquarters as well as from a legion of government consultants. "National Security File, Memos to the President" also includes much material on Vietnam. "The Presidential Diary" and "Diary Backup" are a daily record of the president's appointments and meetings. The National Security Files of President Johnson's two national security advisers, McGeorge Bundy and Walt Rostow, are filled with memorandums and letters to the president on the status of pacification and the managerial and organizational changes under consideration. The most important collections for pacification at the LBJ

Library are the "National Security Files of Robert Komer" and the "Komer-Leonhart File (1966–1968)."

Oral history interviews are an important part of the primary source documentation. The extended, detailed interview Robert Komer granted to CMH historians Charles Mac-Donald and Thomas Scoville in 1970, covering his involvement in pacification from 1966 to 1968, is used here with Mr. Komer's permission. In addition, William Colby and Robert Komer made themselves available on numerous occasions to answer with patience the author's many questions. Under the U.S. Army Senior Officer Debriefing Program, general officers leaving Vietnam were interviewed on their wartime experiences. Copies of these interviews are located at CMH and the U.S. Army Military History Institute in Carlisle, Pennsylvania. The Agency for International Development conducted its own debriefing program of departing officials at its Asia Training Center in Hawaii. Many of the interviews, which deal with pacification, were printed, and copies of some interviews can be found at CMH. In addition, CMH has a collection of over one thousand oral histories, the Vietnam Interview Tapes, conducted by U.S. Army military history detachments on duty in Vietnam. Many interviewees served with CORDS in various capacities and gave detailed accounts of their assignments. Unfortunately, many are still untranscribed.

The secondary literature on Vietnam continues to grow. The most valuable works for this book were Dale Andrade's *Ashes to Ashes,* Eric Bergerud's *Dynamics of Defeat,* William Colby's *Lost Victory,* Robert Komer's *Bureaucracy at War,* Thomas Scoville's *Reorganizing for Pacification Support,* and Louis Wiesner's *Victims and Survivors.* A number of studies written by American advisers have illuminated the village war from a local perspective: John Cook, *The Adviser;* Orrin DeForest, *Slow Burn;* David Donovan, *Once a Warrior King;* Stuart Herrington, *Silence Was a Weapon;* Jeffrey Race, *War Comes to Long An;* and F. J. West, *The Village.* Thomas Thayer's *War Without Fronts* remains the best overall statistical analysis of the costs and nature of the Vietnam war. The endnotes cite the other books and articles that I used.

Notes

Introduction

1. Lloyd Gardner, *Approaching Vietnam* (New York: Norton, 1988), p. 12.

2. William Colby, *Lost Victory: A Firsthand Account of America's Sixteen-Year Involvement in Vietnam* (Chicago: Contemporary Books, 1989); Robert Komer, *Bureaucracy Does Its Thing: Institutional Constraints on U.S.-GVN Performance in Vietnam*, R-967-ARPA (Santa Monica, Calif.: Rand, 1972 [reissued in 1986 as *Bureaucracy at War*]); and Edward Lansdale, *In the Midst of Wars* (New York: Harper and Row, 1972).

3. Louis Wiesner, *Victims and Survivors: Displaced Persons and Other War Victims in Vietnam, 1954–75* (New York: Greenwood Press, 1988); and Dale Andrade, *Ashes to Ashes: The Phoenix Program and the Vietnam War* (Lexington, Mass.: Lexington Books, 1990).

4. Eric Bergerud, *The Dynamics of Defeat: The Vietnam War in Hau Nghia Province* (Boulder: Westview Press, 1991).

5. See David Donovan, *Once a Warrior King: Memories of an Officer in Vietnam* (New York: Ballantine Books, 1986); Stuart Herrington, *Silence Was a Weapon: The War in the Villages* (Novato, Calif.: Presidio Press, 1982); John Cook, *The Advisor* (New York: Bantam Books, 1987); and Orrin DeForest and David Chanoff, *Slow Burn: The Rise and Bitter Fall of American Intelligence in Vietnam* (New York: Simon and Schuster, 1990), for examples of this literature.

6. Charles Osgood, *Limited War: The Challenge to American Strategy* (Chicago: University of Chicago Press, 1957).

7. Douglas Blaufarb, *The Counterinsurgency Era* (New York: Free Press, 1977), p. 206.

8. Thomas C. Thayer, *War Without Fronts* (Boulder: Westview Press, 1985), pp. 14–15, 207.

Chapter 1

1. See Joseph J. Zasloff, "Origins of the Insurgency in South Vietnam, 1954–1960: The Role of the Southern Vietminh Cadres," RM 5163 (Santa Monica, Calif.: Rand, March 1967); and Joseph J. Zasloff, "Political Motivation of the Viet Cong: The Vietminh Regroupees," RM 4703 (Santa Monica, Calif.: Rand, May 1968.

2. Jeffrey Race, *War Comes to Long An* (Berkeley and Los Angeles: University of California Press, 1973), pp. 72–80; and Robert F. Turner, *Vietnamese Communism: Its Origins and Development* (Stanford: Hoover Institution Press, 1975), p. 169.

3. William J. Duiker, *The Communist Road to Power in Vietnam* (Boulder: Westview Press, 1981), p. 183.

4. Ibid., pp. 183–184.

5. Ibid., pp. 188–189.

6. See "A Party Account of the Situation in the Nam Bo Region of South Vietnam from 1954–1960" and "A Party Account of the Revolutionary Movement in South Vietnam from 1954 to 1963," which were captured by American forces and later translated and reprinted by the State Department, both in the U.S. Army Center of Military History (CMH); and Colby, *Lost Victory*, pp. 53–54.

7. Douglas Pike, *Viet Cong: The Organization and Techniques of the National Liberation Front of South Vietnam* (Cambridge, Mass.: MIT Press, 1968), pp. 80–82; Turner, *Vietnamese Communism*, pp. 174–175; information report, CIA, sub: Structure of National Front for Liberation, 28 October 1966, LBJ Library, Austin, Texas, National Security Files (NSF), Vietnam, vol. 71.

8. Duiker, *The Communist Road to Power*, pp. 198–199.

9. Scholars are divided in their interpretation of the period 1956–1960. Sansom and Race stressed the communists' reforms in explaining their strength. Pike's *Viet Cong;* William R. Andrews, *The Village War* (Columbia: University of Missouri Press, 1973); and W. Phillips Davison, "Some Observations on Viet Cong Operations in the Villages," RM 5267 (Santa Monica, Calif.: Rand, May 1968), argued that communist success in the villages derived less from the social benefits bestowed than from coercive actions, which Pike labeled the "violence program," and the communists' superior organization.

10. Russell Betts, *Viet Cong Village Control: Some Observations on the Origins and Dynamics of Modern Revolutionary War* (Cambridge, Mass.: Center for International Studies, August 1969); Andrews, *The Village War;* and Denis Warner, *The Last Confucian* (New York: Macmillan, 1963), Chap. 8.

11. Andrews, *The Village War*, pp. 55–56.

12. Bernard Fall, *The Two Vietnams*, rev. ed. (New York: Praeger, 1964), p. 359.

13. Andrews, *The Village War*, pp. 61, 70.

14. Paul Berman, *Revolutionary Organization* (Lexington, Mass.: D. C. Heath, 1974), pp. 68–69, 77.

15. Andrews, *The Village War*, pp. 104–106.

16. Pike, *Viet Cong*, pp. 92–102.

17. Colby, *Lost Victory*, pp. 53–55.

18. Robert Scigliano, *South Vietnam: Nation Under Stress* (Boston: Houghton Mifflin, 1964), p. 11.

19. Their autonomous character was epitomized in the traditional Vietnamese proverb "The laws of the emperor yield to the customs of the village." Gerald Hickey, *Village in Vietnam* (New Haven: Yale University Press, 1964), p. 276.

20. Scigliano, *South Vietnam*, p. 10; and Pike, *Viet Cong*, pp. 47–48.

21. Unless otherwise noted, this section on rice and rubber growing is based on the following works: Joseph Buttinger, *Vietnam: A Dragon Embattled* (New York: Praeger, 1966), vol. 1, pp. 162–171; Charles Robequain, *The Economic Development of French Indochina*, trans. by Isabel Ward (London: Oxford University Press, 1944) Chaps. 6 and 8; Robert Sansom, *The Economics of Insurgency in the Mekong Delta* (Cambridge, Mass.: MIT Press, 1970), Chaps. 2, 3; and Philippe Devillers, *Histoire du Vietnam de 1940 á 1952* (Paris: Editions du Seuil, 1952), pp. 39–40.

22. Robequain, *The Economic Development*, p. 22.

23. Memo, Lansdale to Bunker, sub: Historical Note, 13 May 1967, Hoover Institution, Stanford University, Palo Alto, California, Lansdale Papers, Box 58.

24. For an account of the buildup and training of South Vietnam's armed forces, see Jeffrey J. Clarke, *Advice and Support: The Final Years* (Washington, D.C.: GPO, 1988).

25. Until November 1962, South Vietnam was divided militarily into three corps areas (I, II, and III). Afterward, it was divided into four corps tactical zones (I, II, III, and IV).

26. The following section draws on Chester Cooper et al., *The American Experience with Pacification*, 3 vols. (Washington D.C.: Institute for Defense Analysis, March 1972); William Nighswonger, *Rural Pacification in Vietnam* (New York: Praeger, 1966); and *The Pentagon Papers: The Defense Department History of United States Decisionmaking on Vietnam*, Senator Mike Gravel edition (Boston: Beacon Press, 1971), vol. 2, cited as PPG 2.

27. Douglas C. Dacy, *Foreign Aid, War, and Economic Development: South Vietnam, 1955–1975* (Cambridge: Cambridge University Press, 1986), pp. 68, 200. The average for American aid is derived from Table 10.2. The dollar value of South Vietnam's GNP comes from Table A3.5.

28. Scigliano, *South Vietnam*, pp. 111, 112; and Ronald H. Spector, *Advice and Support: The Early Years* (Washington, D.C.: GPO, 1983), p. 120. Scigliano described how import subsidies worked.

29. *United States–Vietnam Relations, 1945–1967: Study Prepared by the Department of Defense*, 12 vols. (Washington D.C.: GPO, 1971), cited as *US-VR;* and Dennis J. Duncanson, *Government and Revolution in Vietnam* (New York: Oxford University Press, 1968), pp. 281, 289–293.

30. Special report 411, Hq., USARPAC, G2, *Military and Security Forces of Southeast Asia*, 2 November 1959, CMH; and Scigliano, *South Vietnam*, pp. 47, 164.

31. Spector, *Advice and Support*, p. 378.

32. Interview with Donald Blackburn (U.S. Army Ret.), adviser to William Yarborough, Washington, D.C., May 1984; and Francis Kelly, *U.S. Army Special Forces, 1961–1971* (Washington, D.C.: GPO, 1973), p. 5.

33. PPG 2, pp. 23–25; and Colby, *Lost Victory*, pp. 82–83.

34. PPG 2, pp. 24–25.

Chapter 2

1. Ltr., Kennedy to Taylor, 13 October 1961, reprinted in Maxwell Taylor, *Swords and Plowshares: A Memoir* (New York: Norton, 1972), pp. 225–226.

2. A detailed analysis of the Taylor mission is found in PPG 2, pp. 84–98, as well as in Taylor, *Swords and Plowshares*, Chap. 18.

3. For an account of the first province advisers, see James W. Dunn, "Province Advisers in Vietnam, 1962–1965," in *Lessons from an Unconventional War*, ed. Richard A. Hunt and Richard H. Shultz Jr. (New York: Pergamon Press, 1982), pp. 1–22.

4. Ltr., Jacobson to Yarborough, 4 October 1962, Yarborough Papers, Fort Bragg, North Carolina. Colonel George D. Jacobson, who would later play a prominent role in CORDS, in 1962 was the chief of the Operations and Training Division of the MAAG.

5. Advisers first appeared at the district level in 1964.

6. *US-VR*, IV B. 3. p. 133.

7. Ibid., p. 126.

8. Decker's comments were cited in Lloyd Norman and John B. Spore, "Big Push in Guerrilla Warfare," *Army* (March 1962): 34.

9. Memo, Stilwell to the secretary of the army, sub: Army Activities in Underdeveloped Areas Short of Declared War, 13 October 1961, Washington National Records Center (WNRC) 64A2207/6, Suitland, Maryland; and memo, chief of staff to the secretary of the army, sub: Army Activities in Underdeveloped Areas, 8 December 1961, WNRC 64A2207/6. Decker made his comments when forwarding this report to Secretary of the Army Elvis J. Stahr Jr.

10. Memo, Lemnitzer to Taylor, sub: Counterinsurgency Operations in South Vietnam, 12 October 1961, reprinted in PPG 2, pp. 650-651. On the tendency of government agencies to play their strong suits, see Komer, *Bureaucracy Does Its Thing.*

11. For more information, see Spector, *Advice and Support,* pp. 320–325, 378; Charles A. Cannon, "The Military Industrial Complex in American Politics," (Ph.D. diss., Stanford University, 1974), pp. 172–173; Thayer, *War Without Fronts,* Chap. 14; and David Halberstam, *The Making of a Quagmire* (New York: Random House, 1965).

12. This argument is developed in Blaufarb, *The Counterinsurgency Era,* Chap. 3 and esp. p. 82.

13. *Field Manual 100-5* (Washington, D.C.: Department of the Army, 1962), p. 139.

14. Andrew F. Krepinevich Jr., *The Army and Vietnam* (Baltimore: Johns Hopkins University Press, 1986), pp. 38–42, contained an account of the halting development of counterinsurgency doctrine. *The Advisory Handbook* (Washington, D.C.: Department of the Army, April 1965).

15. Memo, Lansdale to Bunker, 13 May 1967; and Colby, *Lost Victory,* p. 62.

16. Cooper et. al., *The American Experience,* vol. 3, pp. 120–126, 140; Nighswonger, *Rural Pacification,* pp. 37–39; and Joseph J. Zasloff, "Rural Resettlement in South Vietnam: The Agroville Program," *Pacific Affairs* 25, no. 4 (Winter 1962–1963): 327–340.

17. Cooper et al., *The American Experience,* vol. 3, pp. 141–159.

18. PPG 2, pp. 139–140; and Robert Thompson, *Defeating Communist Insurgency* (New York: Praeger, 1966), esp. Chap. 11.

19. Colby, *Lost Victory,* p. 100.

20. PPG 2, p. 129; Cooper et al., *The American Experience,* vol. 3, pp. 164, 180. This section on the strategic hamlet program relies on Thompson, *Defeating Communist Insurgency;* and Milton E. Osborne, *Strategic Hamlets in South Vietnam,* Data Paper 55, (Ithaca: Cornell University Southeast Asia Program, April 1965), unless otherwise noted.

21. Krepinevich, *The Army and Vietnam,* Chap. 3.

22. PPG 2, pp. 128–129, 146–148.

23. Ltr., minister of the interior to Trueheart, counselor of the U.S. Embassy, 6 August 1962, copy in CMH.

24. Komer, *Bureaucracy Does Its Thing,* p. 133.

25. See Cooper et al., *The American Experience,* vol. 3, p. 167; and Carl W. Schaad, "The Strategic Hamlet in Vietnam" (Student thesis, U.S. Army War College, May 1964).

26. Rpt., CIA, TDCS-3/529, 667, 29 November 1962, copy in CMH.

27. Stanley Karnow, *Vietnam: A History* (New York: Viking Press, 1984), claimed that Nhu's chief lieutenant, Col. Pham Ngoc Thao, a secret communist agent, duped Nhu into accelerating the program, thereby estranging the peasants. The basis for Karnow's information was "communist sources," a term that offers other researchers no way to evaluate his evidence. In any event, the effect of building hamlets too quickly was not merely that the peasants were estranged but that the hastily constructed hamlets offered no real security (see p. 257).

28. Colby, *Lost Victory,* p. 115.

29. Msg., COMUSMACV to AIG 924, sub: Province Rehabilitation Program 081020z, September 1962, copy in CMH.

30. Osborne, *Strategic Hamlets*, pp. 32–39.

31. Race, *War Comes*, pp. 131–134.

32. Rpt., CIA, TDCS 3/516, 14 July 1962, CMH.

33. Race, *War Comes*, pp. 192–193.

34. Airgram, A-88, Saigon to Washington, 9 August 1962, CMH.

35. Ltr., Harkins to Palmer, British Advisory Mission, 15 May 1963, CMH.

36. Record of special meeting on RVN held at Headquarters CINCPAC, Camp Smith, on 20 November 1963, dated 23 November 1963, CMH.

37. Rpt., Earl Young, province representative, Long An province, 31 July 1964, CMH.

38. Thayer, *War Without Fronts*, p. 198.

39. Jeanette Koch, *The Chieu Hoi Program* (Santa Monica, Calif.: Rand, 1972) pp. 22–24; and Thayer, *War Without Fronts*, pp. 195–203.

40. Presidential decree, Republic of Vietnam, 146/PTT/NV, 27 June 1962; and msg., Saigon 1600, 9 October 1964, both in CMH.

41. Colby, *Lost Victory*, pp. 83, 116.

42. Memo, Office of the Special Assistant to the Ambassador to the secretary of state, sub: Police Assistance Program, 24 January 1963, CMH; and Blaufarb, *The Counterinsurgency Era*, p. 213.

43. Fact sheet, MAC J-21, sub: Methods of Attack on the VC Political Infrastructure, 5 March 1965; fact sheet, MAC J-29, sub: Sector Operations intelligence Center, 1 March 1965; and memo MAC J-21, sub: Coordinated Intelligence Center Concept, 28 December 1963, all in CMH; and Joseph McChristian, *Role of Military Intelligence, 1965–1967* (Washington D.C.: Department of the Army, 1974), pp. 19, 21, 26.

44. Blaufarb, *The Counterinsurgency Era*, pp. 211–212.

45. Memo, McNamara to the president, sub: Vietnam, 16 March 1964, CMH.

46. MACV, *Command History, 1964* (MACV, 1964), pp. 64–68; and Nguyen Khanh, "Policy and Program of the Government of the Republic of Vietnam," 7 March 1964, CMH.

47. Paul Supplizio, "A Study of the Military Support of Pacification in South Vietnam, April 1964–April 1965" (Master's thesis, Command and General Staff College, 1966), pp. 208–217. The French resident-general of Morocco, Marshall Lyautey, developed the oil spot concept between 1912 and 1925 and used it to pacify Morocco. Paul A. Jureidini, *Case Studies in Insurgency and Revolutionary Warfare: Algeria, 1954–1962* (Washington, D.C.: Special Operations Research Office, 1963), pp. 92–93.

48. MACV, *Command History, 1964*, pp. 64–68.

49. Msg., Saigon 2331, DAIN 303886, 28 May 1964, CMH.

50. Memo, to DCSOPS, sub: RVN National Pacification Plan, 23 April 1964, CMH.

51. Memo, DePuy to Collins, liaison officer to the JGS, Sub: Review and Revision of the *Chien Thang* Plan, AB 139, and Associated Matters, 20 September 1965, DePuy Papers, U.S. Army Military History Institute (MHI), Carlisle Barracks, Pennsylvania.

52. Cooper, et al., *The American Experience*, vol. 3, pp. 218–219.

53. William C. Westmoreland, *A Soldier Reports* (New York: Doubleday, 1976), pp. 82–85.

54. Ltr., ASD-ISA, Bundy to Nes, 16 January 64, CMH.

55. Msg., Westmoreland to Taylor, MAC J005423, 2515017Z, January 1964; and memo, to Westmoreland, sub: *Hop Tac* Secretariat, 24 October 1964, both in Westmoreland Papers, LBJ Library, Austin, Texas.

56. In 1964, the Civil Guard was renamed the Regional Forces, and the Self-Defense Corps became the Popular Forces.

57. Cooper et al., *The American Experience,* vol. 3, p. 228.

58. Memo, Throckmorton, deputy commander MACV, to Lodge, sub: *Hop Tac* Evaluation, 24 October 1964, CMH; and memo, to Westmoreland, MAC J03, sub: Strength of Combat Units Committed to *Hop Tac,* 16 October 1964, Westmoreland Papers.

59. Airgram, Saigon to Washington, A-339, sub: *Hop Tac* Planning, 2 November 1964, CMH.

60. Memo, Richards to Westmoreland, sub: Major *Hop Tac* Problems, 30 November 1964, Westmoreland Papers.

61. Memorandum for record (MFR), sub: Meeting on Vietnam, 30 May 1964; and MFR, sub: White House meeting on Vietnam, 25 July 1964, both in CMH.

62. Memo, to the chairman, JCS, sub: Population Control in South Vietnam, 23 July 1965, LBJ Library, NSF, NSC history, vol. 7.

63. Memo, sub: Verbatim Record of Conference with Secretary McNamara, Ambassador Lodge, General Taylor, General Harkins, and Others, 12 May 1964, CMH.

64. Talking paper, OPS/OD FE, sub: Attack on *Chau Hiep,* copy in CMH.

65. William Westmoreland, *Report on the War in Vietnam* (Washington, D.C.: GPO, 1969), p. 84.

66. Memo, Johnson to Taylor, sub: Instructions from the President, 3 December 1964, CMH.

67. Memo, DePuy to Westmoreland, sub: Conversation with General Thang, 29 January 1965, DePuy Papers, MHI.

68. Memo, DePuy to Westmoreland, sub: The Revolutionary Spirit, 6 February 1965, DePuy Papers, MHI.

69. Memo, DePuy to Westmoreland, 23 February 1965, DePuy Papers, MHI.

Chapter 3

1. Lyndon Baines Johnson, *The Vantage Point: Perspectives of the Presidency, 1963–1969* (New York: Holt, Rinehart and Winston, 1971), p. 233. Thayer, *War Without Fronts,* p. 33, calculated that 55 NVA battalions were inside South Vietnam in addition to 105 VC battalions.

2. Msg., Westmoreland to Wheeler, MACV 20055, sub: Concept of Operations—Force Requirements and Deployments, South Vietnam, 14 June 1965, Westmoreland Papers; and J. D. Coleman, *Pleiku: The Dawn of Helicopter Warfare in Vietnam* (New York: St. Martin's Press, 1988) pp. 27–28.

3. PPG 3, p. 483.

4. Harold Moore and Joseph Galloway, *We Were Soldiers Once ... and Young* (New York: Random House, 1992), pp. 338–339.

5. PPG 3, p. 453.

6. Westmoreland, *A Soldier Reports,* p. 130.

7. Msg., COMUSMACV to CINCPAC, 260242Z, sub: Concept of Operations, August 1966, CMH; Mission Council action memo 84, 15 June 1966, CMH; and Westmoreland,

Report on the War, p. 100. The statistics on population control are from msg., Saigon to Washington, Saigon 3458, 20 April 1965, CMH.

8. Vincent Demma, "The U.S. Army in Vietnam," in *American Military History,* ed. William Stofft (Washington D.C.: GPO, 1989), p. 643.

9. Mission Council action memo 41, 24 January 1966, CMH.

10. Mission Council action memo 106, 10 August 1966, CMH.

11. After the war, Thomas Thayer, who helped write the reports, analyzed these data and published them in *War Without Fronts.*

12. Westmoreland, *Report on the War,* Chap. 5; Cooper et al., *The American Experience,* vol. 3, pp. 247–248; and Thayer, *War Without Fronts,* p. 163.

13. MFR, DePuy, sub: Conversation with Generals Thang and Phong, 23 July 1965, dated 24 July 1965, DePuy Papers, MHI.

14. Memo, M. Bundy to the president, sub: Current and Future Strategy in Vietnam—An Exchange of Views Between Washington Principals and Lodge, 23 September 1965, LBJ Library, NSF, Memos to the President, McGeorge Bundy, vol. 15.

15. Memo, Mock, DCSOPS, to chief of staff of the army, sub: U.S. Operations in South Vietnam and Rural Construction, 5 October 1965, CMH; and Westmoreland, *Report on the War,* p. 100.

16. PPG 2, pp. 475–478.

17. Memo, W. Bundy to M. Bundy, 26 October 1965, LBJ Library, NSF, VN, vol. 41.

18. Memo, secretary of defense to the Joint Chiefs of Staff and secretary of the army et al., sub: Role of U.S. Forces, 3 November 1965, ISA Papers, WNRC 70A3717/44.

19. Msg., joint State Defense White House to the ambassador and Westmoreland, 26 October 1965, LBJ Library, NSF, VN, vol 41; memo, Taylor to McNamara and Wheeler, sub: Concept of Employment of U.S./GVN Ground Forces, 19 November 1965, LBJ Library, NSF, VN, vol. 42; and msg., Wheeler to Westmoreland, JCS 4500-65, 21 November 1965, Westmoreland Papers.

20. Memo, M. Bundy to the president, sub: History of Recommendations for Increased U.S. Forces in Vietnam, 24 July 1965, LBJ Library, NSF, Bundy Memos to the President, vol. 12; and memo, W. Bundy, sub: A "Middle Way" Course of Action in South Vietnam, 1 July 1965, CMH.

21. Msg., M. Bundy to the president, 3 December 1965, LBJ Library, NSF, Bundy Memos to the President, vol. 17.

22. Bundy, memo for discussion, 16 March 1965, LBJ Library, NSF 31, Memos A; and memo, Cooper to Bundy, sub: Vietnam, 1 March 1965, LBJ Library, NSF 30, Memos, conveyed the president's concerns.

23. Memo, director of intelligence and research to secretary of state, sub: The Balance Sheet in South Vietnam, 21 December 1965, CMH.

24. Msg., Saigon 3063, 22 February 1966, CMH.

25. Memo, Central Revolutionary Development Council, 4946/XD/411, sub: Administration of RD Cadres, 1 August 1966; and msg., Saigon 3063, 220535Z February 1966, both in CMH.

26. Memo, Hq. MACV J33, sub: Comments of General Thang on 1966 RD Program, 28 March 1966, CMH. The first director, Lieutenant Colonel Tran Ngoc Chau, turned out to be a poor administrator and resigned in August 1966 under pressure from Thang and the Americans. Major Nguyen Be, Chau's replacement, instituted a training regimen that stressed national ideology. R. W. Apple Jr., "Dispute Hinders Pacification Program in Vietnam," *New York Times,* 10 February 1966.

27. Memo, Joint Operations Center, JGS, to deputy chief, RD Division, CORDS, sub: Survey of Backgrounds of RDC, 30 October 1967, copy in CMH. Some of these projects came under the new life program, a corollary of the RD effort, also run by General Thang.

28. Msg., Saigon A-627, sub: Viet Cong Attacks Against RD Teams, 4 May 1967; and intelligence memo, CIA, sub: Communist Counteraction Against the RD Program, 20 November 1967, both in CMH.

29. Memo, CIA, sub: Revolutionary Development Cadre Attrition, 3 March 1967, copy in CMH.

30. Ibid.

31. "Roles and Missions Study," part 2, copy in CMH. Daniel Ellsberg, then working in Lansdale's liaison office, was the author of a section of "Roles and Missions Study." He later published his analysis in *Papers on the War* (New York: Simon and Schuster, 1972), pp. 156–170.

32. Thang's comments are relayed in memo, Lansdale to Lodge, sub: South Vietnamese Needs, 21 March 1966, CMH.

33. Robert W. Chandler, *War of Ideas: The U.S. Propaganda Campaign in Vietnam* (Boulder: Westview Press: 1981), p. 82; and Koch, *The Chieu Hoi Program*, pp. 26–28.

34. Koch, *The Chieu Hoi Program, p. 28.*

35. Memo, MAC J-14, sub: Regular Force Strength as of 31 October 1964, dated 28 November 1964, Westmoreland Papers; and MACV, *Command History, 1966*, p. 108.

36. Msg., CINCPAC to chairman, Joint Chiefs of Staff, 190645Z October 1965, CMH. For information on ARVN and PF casualty rates, see Thayer, *War Without Fronts,* Chaps. 10, 14.

37. Msg., Saigon 16543, 26 January 1967, CMH.

38. Memo, Bell, administrator, AID, to Komer, sub: Report on Pacification and Other Non-Military Programs in Vietnam, 7 June 1966, LBJ Library, NSF, Komer Memos, vol 15.

39. Wiesner, *Victims and Survivors*, p. 59.

40. Ibid., p. 75.

41. Ibid., p. 346.

42. Gunter Lewy, *America in Vietnam* (New York: Oxford University Press, 1978), pp. 107–114, contained an overview of the refugee problem based on official and unofficial sources. Msg., USOM, regional director, I Corps, to acting associate director for field operations, Danang 1550, 29 October 1966, CMH.

43. Briefing paper, sub: Refugee Situation in I Corps; and memo, Vann to O'Neill, USOM refugee coordinator, Saigon, sub: Refugee Situation Binh Dinh Province, 25 September 1965, both in CMH.

44. Memo, Nelson, USOM field representative, to O'Neill, sub: Refugee Support in Several Province of Regions I and II, 13 September 1965, CMH; memo, MACV, ACS J-3 to COMUSMACV, sub: Comments of USOM Proposal, 12 September 1965, CMH; rpt., Senate Judiciary Committee, 1058, sub: Refugee Problem in South Vietnam, 4 March 1966, copy in CMH.

45. Msg., Saigon to Washington, sub: Monthly Report, 071210Z January 1966; and briefing paper, USAID, sub: Refugee Situation in I Corps, 20 August 1966, written by Richard C. Holdren, AID regional refugee officer, both in CMH.

46. Wiesner, *Victims and Survivors*, p. 87.

47. Briefing, Refugee Relief in I Corps, rpt., Senate Judiciary Committee; memo, MACV, ACS J3 to COMUSMACV, 12 September 1965; and bulletin, USOM refugee coordinator to regional directors, sub; Establishment of the ... SCR, 9 April 1966, all in CMH.

48. The elections, which made Thieu president and Ky vice president, were held in September 1967.

49. Allan E. Goodman, *Politics in War: The Bases of Political Community in South Vietnam* (Cambridge, Mass.: Harvard University Press: 1973), pp. 2, 34, 36, 37.

50. Decree, Republic of Vietnam, 199-SL/DUHC, sub: Governing the Election of Village Council Members, 24 December 1966, CMH.

51. Decree, RVN, 198-SL/DUHC, sub: Governing the Reorganization of Village, Hamlet Administration, 24 December 1966, CMH.

52. Village briefing, ACS, CORDS-PSG, April 1969, CMH.

53. Cooper et al., *The American Experience,* vol. 3, pp. 251–252; and Ellsberg, Special Liaison Office, backup notes to 31 March Evaluation of 1966 Prospects for RD, 30 March 1966, CMH.

54. Msg., Saigon 1594, November 1965; and msg., Saigon 4208, 26 April 1966, both in CMH.

55. Ellsberg, backup notes.

56. MFR, Ellsberg, sub: The Day Loc Tien Was Pacified, 16 December 1966, CMH. Ellsberg published his account in *Papers on the War,* pp. 174–190.

57. Msg., from Lodge for Komer, Saigon 16455, 25 June 1967, LBJ Library, NSF, Komer Memos, vol. 27.

58. Memo, to the president, sub: Second Komer Trip to Vietnam, 23–29 June 1966, 1 July 1966, CMH; Mission Council action memo 116, 31 August 1966, CMH; and interview, Jeffrey Race with Walter Deyerle, 23 November 1967, microfilm reel 1 of Race document collection located at the Center for Research Libraries, Chicago, Illinois.

Chapter 4

1. The section on army civil affairs teams and companies is based on Jeffrey J. Clarke, "A Survey History of Civil Affairs Units and Teams in South Vietnam, 1960–1971," January 1974, CMH.

2. For an idea of the variety of engineer civil affairs projects, see the operational reports of the 34th Engineer Group, the 45th Engineer Group, the 46th Engineer Battalion, and the 159th Engineer Group and the unit history of the 1st Engineer Battalion, CMH. Two monographs in the Vietnam Studies series cover the engineers: Carroll H. Dunn, *Base Development in South Vietnam: 1965*–1970 (Washington, D.C.: Department of the Army, 1974), p. 99; and Robert R. Ploger, *U.S. Army Engineers: 1965*–1970 (Washington, D.C.: Department of the Army, 1974), pp. 166–167.

3. Spurgeon Neel, *Medical Support of the U.S. Army in Vietnam: 1965*–1970 (Washington, D.C.: Department of the Army, 1973), pp. 164–165.

4. Ibid., pp. 162–163.

5. John H. Hay Jr., *Tactical and Matériel Innovations* (Washington, D.C.: GPO, 1974), Chap. 12, described an example of such an operation in Tan Phuoc Khanh, Binh Duong province. Rpt., "Debrief of a Military Sub-Sector Advisor, Ben Cat, Binh Duong Province Vietnam, 1966–1967," published by AID Asia Training Center, p. 12, CMH.

6. Hay, *Tactical and Matériel Innovations*, p. 142.

7. Special joint rpts., Binh Duong, July–September 1966, copies in CMH.

8. Rpt., MACCORDS, sub: Completed *Ap Doi Moi*, Khanh Loc, Binh Duong Province, 4 February 1968, copies in CMH. *Ap doi moi* was the Vietnamese term for a new life hamlet.

9. Information briefing, Hau Nghia province, 1969, CMH.

10. Special joint rpts., Hau Nghia province adviser, 1965, CMH.

11. Tom Mangold and John Penycate, *The Tunnels of Cu Chi: The Untold Story of Vietnam* (New York: Random House, 1985), Chap. 12.

12. Boyd Bashore, "The Name of the Game Is Search and Destroy," *Army* (February 1967):56–59. Bashore commanded the 2d Battalion, 27th Infantry, 25th Division in late 1966.

13. Pfeiffer, "Evaluation of Pacification Techniques of the 2d Brigade, U.S. 25th Infantry Division," 20 December 1968, CMH. Dale B. Pfeiffer was a field evaluator for MACV.

14. Rpt., Young, operations officer, Long An, sub: Long An Province Policy Review, 31 July 1964, copy in CMH.

15. Mission Council action memo 122, 17 September 1966, CMH.

16. Province rpts., JUSPAO, January, May 1966, and province rpt., AID, March 1966, both in CMH.

17. Mission Council action memo 84, 15 June 1966, CMH.

18. Ibid.; and Westmoreland history notes, June 1966, Westmoreland Papers.

19. Mission Council action memo 120, 12 September 1966, CMH.

20. Westmoreland, *A Soldier Reports*, p. 258.

21. Mission Council action memo 122; and Westmoreland, *A Soldier Reports*, p. 208.

22. Bergerud, *The Dynamics of Defeat*, p. 162.

23. Mission Council action memo 122.

24. Msg., Saigon 9245, 11 November 1966; and msg., Saigon 9648, 22 November 1966, both in CMH.

25. Mission Council action memo 140, 28 November 1966, CMH; and msg., Lodge to Komer, Saigon 16455, 25 January 1967, LBJ Library, NSF, Komer Memos, vol. 27.

26. Msg., Lodge to Rusk, Saigon 10600, 10 November 1966, CMH.

27. Rpt., CORDS, sub: The Long Huu Village Study, December 1967, CMH. Written by Captain David Pabst, the report was based on the visit of CORDS evaluators to Long Huu and interviews with local officials after the operation.

28. The story of the Long Huu operation is based on the reports (dated 20 March, 23 March, 27 March, and 2 April) that Calvin Mehlert, an AID officer assigned to III Corps, sent to John Vann.

29. Rpt., CORDS, The Long Huu Village Study.

30. MFR, Scotton, OCO/Eval, sub: Long Huu: Follow-Up Evaluation, 12 June 1967, CMH. This MFR was excerpted from a longer memo prepared on 29 May 1967, CMH.

31. Ibid. and CORDS, The Long Huu Village Study.

32. Ibid.

33. Memo, AID director, MR III, to Naughton, assistant AID director for field operations, sub: Regional Director Monthly Report October 1966, 10 November 1966, CMH.

34. Memo, State Dept., Teare to Habib, sub: Long An, 26 January 1967; memo, OCO, Lathram, director, to the deputy ambassador, sub: Long An and the Single Manager Concept, 20 April 1967; and msg., Lodge to Komer, Saigon 16455, 25074Z January 1967, all in CMH.

35. "Interview, Robert W. Komer, Organization and Management of the New Model Pacification Program, 1966–1969" (Santa Monica, Calif.: Rand, May 7, 1970), p. 42.

36. The five nets were run by the Special Branch, the district chief, the census-grievance cadre, the PRUs, and the Military Security Service. The district chief did not consider any of these effective.

37. Quoted in memo, Burnham and Holbrooke, Office of Civil Operations, to Komer, 24 May 1967, CMH.

38. Quote from memo, OCO to Komer, sub: Binh Chanh, 24 May 1967, copy in CMH; Msg., Eckhardt, senior advisor, IV Corps, to Abrams, 28 November 1967, Hoa 1729, Abrams Papers, CMH.

39. Bernard W. Rogers, *Cedar Falls–Junction City: A Turning Point* (Washington, D.C.: Department of the Army, 1974) Chaps. 1–7; MFR, Vann, director, Office of Civil Operations, III Corps, sub: Complaints of Major General DePuy Relative to OCO/GVN Performance on Handling Refugees During Operation Cedar Falls, 14 January 1967, CMH; msg., Saigon 15790, sub: Refugee Handling in Cedar Falls, 17 January 1967, CMH; and memo, MACCORDS-RE, sub: Evaluation of Lai Thieu Refugee Resettlement Project, 26 September 1967, CMH.

40. Wiesner, *Victims and Survivors,* pp. 128–129.

41. MFR., Vann, 14 January 1967.

42. See Johnathan Schell, *The Village of Ben Suc* (New York: Knopf, 1967), for the most widely known account. His report first appeared in *The New Yorker.* William M. Hammond, *The Military and the Media* (Washington, D.C.: GPO, 1988), pp. 301–302, discussed media coverage.

43. MFR, sub: General Westmoreland Meeting with General Thieu on 13 January 1967, dated 17 January 1967, Westmoreland Papers.

44. Phillip B. Davidson, *Vietnam at War: The History, 1946–1975* (Novato, Calif.: Presidio Press, 1988), p. 430.

45. Rogers, *Cedar Falls–Junction City,* p. 158.

46. Statistics on military advisers come from *US-VR,* Book 3, IV. B. 3., p. 133.

47. Krepinevich, *The Army in Vietnam,* pp. 207–208; and Peter M. Dawkins, "The United States Army and the 'Other War' in Vietnam: A Study of the Complexity of Implementing Organizational Change" (Ph.D. diss., Princeton University, 1979), p. 79.

48. Gerald Hickey, *The American Military Adviser and His Foreign Counterpart: The Case of Vietnam,* ARPA 189-61 (Santa Monica, Calif.: Rand, March 1965).

49. A sector was the military equivalent of a province: a subsector, the equivalent of a district.

50. Coordination suffered also at the Saigon level. The Mission Council had responsibility for managing American support and coordinating civil and military programs. Located in the American Embassy, the Mission Council consisted of the senior representatives of the embassy, MACV, USOM, USIA, and CIA, who could appeal directly to their Washington headquarters. Clearly, the council did not always have the last word in resolving disputes.

51. Quoted in Krepinevich, *The Army and Vietnam,* p. 222.

52. Memo, Rostow to the president, 29 August 1966, with Westmoreland's message 29797, LBJ Library, NSF, VN, Rostow Memos, vol. 11.

53. Memo, Rostow to the president, 31 August 1966, LBJ Library, NSF, VN, Rostow Memos, vol. 11.

Chapter 5

1. Memo, M. Bundy to Johnson, 3 February 1966, CMH.

2. Executive Order 10575, sub: Administration of Foreign Aid Functions, 8 November 1954. President Dwight D. Eisenhower had codified that arrangement in the 1950s with an executive order giving the ambassador in each country authority to manage and coordinate the U.S. Mission in all matters that did not involve merely internal agency affairs.

3. Cooper et al., *The American Experience,* vol. 3, p. 221; Westmoreland, *A Soldier Reports,* p. 69; and ltr., Westmoreland to Nes, 27 February 1964, Westmoreland Papers. Nes's correspondence indicates that Lodge's other deputies may have resented his role as chair. Part of this section is based on Thomas W. Scoville, *Reorganizing for Pacification Support* (Washington, D.C.: GPO, 1982).

4. Cooper et al., *The American Experience,* vol. 3, p. 223; draft rpt., Bohannon, 11 February 1965, Hoover Institution, Bohannon Collection, Box 2. See also Box 1 for more information on Killen and AID.

5. Ltr., Johnson to Taylor, 2 July 1964, quoted in full in msg., JCS, CINPAC and COMUSMACV, 7217, 2 July 1964, CMH; and memo, M. Bundy to the president, sub: Letter for Cabot Lodge, 28 July 1965, LBJ Library, NSF, Bundy Memos, vol. 12.

6. This was Komer's comment on the draft manuscript.

7. George Eckhardt, *Command and Control, 1950–1969* (Washington, D.C.: GPO, 1974), p. 48; and Scoville, *Reorganizing for Pacification,* p. 9.

8. "Interview, Komer," p. 23. Robert Montague, Westmoreland's special assistant for pacification, drafted the plans for the experiment. Westmoreland raised the notion with the ambassador in 1964 after a visit to Malaysia with Robert Thompson (ltr., Westmoreland to Maynard, 29 September 1970, CMH). See also memo, Herfurt to Taylor, sub: Appointment of U.S. Team Chief in Selected Provinces, 7 May 1965; and memo, MACV J-3 to Westmoreland, sub: Team Chief Experiment, both in CMH.

9. Memo, M. Bundy to the president, sub: The Situation in Vietnam, 7 February 1965, CMH.

10. Memo, Cooper to M. Bundy, sub: Vietnam Revisited, 10 March 1965, LBJ Library, NSF 30, Memos.

11. Memo, Anthis to Goodpaster sub: RVN Pacification, 24 February 1965; and msg., draft joint State/Defense/AID/USIA/CIA to Saigon, 24 February 1965, both in CMH.

12. Memo, Cooper to M. Bundy, sub: Vietnam: Policy vs. Implementation in the Pacification Field, 13 March 1965, LBJ Library, NSF, Komer Memos, vol. 32. Given the relatively small size of Bundy's NSC staff, it is surprising that he did not push Cooper's proposal. Bundy's staff numbered forty-eight people, some of whom he shared with the Office of Science and Technology and the Foreign Intelligence Advisory Board. Bundy had a single assistant for Vietnam (Cooper), who in turn had two assistants to help him. See memo, M. Bundy to the president, sub: Organization of the NSC, 2 August 1965, LBJ Library, NSF, Bundy Memos, vol. 13; and memo, Cooper to M. Bundy, 21 July 1965, LBJ Library, NSF, VN, vol. 37.

13. Memo, M. Bundy to the president, sub: Contingency Planning, 30 June 1965, LBJ Library, NSF, Bundy Memos, vol. 11.

14. Ibid.

15. Memo, M. Bundy to the president, sub: ... An Exchange of Views Between Washington Principals and Lodge, 23 September 1965, LBJ Library, NSF, Bundy memos, vol. 15.

16. Memo, M. Bundy to the President, 23 September 1965.

17. PPG 2, pp. 527–531.

18. Quoted in PPG 2, p. 528.

19. Ltr., Johnson to Lodge, 28 July 1965. Taylor had agreed to serve one year.

20. Msg., Lodge to the president, Saigon 694, 31 August 1965, LBJ Library, NSF, vol. 13.

21. Memo, MAC J33, DePuy, J-3, to Westmoreland, sub: RC Cadre, 6 December 1965, CMH.

22. Memo, Lansdale to Lodge, 24 June 1966; and Memo, MAC J33, sub: Operational Guidelines for Advisory Support of RDC, 13 June 1966, CMH. This memo reproduced Lodge's and Porter's guidance. Only after the Honolulu conference of February 1966 did the Johnson administration, faced with congressional pressure against a CIA-funded expansion of the RD Cadre, decide to have AID gradually assume responsibility from the CIA for funding and logistical support of the program.

23. Memo, Lodge to Lansdale, sub: Roles of Different U.S. Agencies in the Three Phases of Rural Construction, That Is, Military Clearing, Pacification, and Development, 15 December 1965, Hoover Institution, Lansdale Collection, Box 59.

24. Ltr., Johnson to Lodge, 28 July 1965; Ltr., Lansdale to Williams, 27 April 1967, Hoover Institution, Lansdale Collection, Box 54; and "Interview, Komer," p. 22.

25. Memo, Cooper to M. Bundy, attachment: draft memo, sub: Organization Arrangements for Vietnam Affairs, 29 October 1965, LBJ Library, NSF, vol. 41.

26. Msg., M. Bundy to Jacobson for the president, 8 November 1965, LBJ Library, NSF, Bundy Memos to the president, vol. 16. Jacobson was one of Johnson's aides.

27. Memo, White House, sub: Possible Items for Discussion, 22 July 1965, LBJ Library, NSF, VN, vol. 37; and memo, M. Bundy to the president, sub: Current and Future Strategy in Vietnam, 23 September 1965, LBJ Library, NSF, Bundy Memos to the President, vol. 15. The quote is from msg., Bundy to Johnson, CAP 65828, 7 December 1965, LBJ Library, NSF, VN, vol. 43.

28. Dacy, *Foreign Aid*, p. 200.

29. Draft memo, McNamara to the president, sub: Military and Political Actions Recommended for South Vietnam, 4 December 1965, CMH; draft memo, McNamara to the president, sub: Courses of Action in Vietnam, 3 November 1965, LBJ Library, NSF, vol. 42; memo, McNamara to the president, 30 November 1965, LBJ Library, NSF, vol. 75; and memo, McNamara to the president, sub: Military and Political Action Recommended for South Vietnam, 6 December 1965, LBJ Library, NSF, vol. 75.

30. Rpt., Porter and Unger, to the principals and Lodge, sub: Warrenton Meeting on Vietnam, 13 January 1966, CMH; MACV, *Command History, 1966*, p. 504; and memo, Porter and Unger to the acting secretary, sub: Highlight of Warrenton Meeting, 13 January 1966, LBJ Library, NSF, vol. 45.

31. Quotes from memo, M. Bundy to the president, sub: Possible Topics for Your Talk with Porter, 17 January 1966, LBJ Library, NSF, Memos to the president, 6, McGeorge Bundy, vol. 18. Additional information on the Porter appointment is found in memo, M. Bundy to the president, 14 January 1966.

32. Scoville, *Reorganizing for Pacification*, pp. 18–19.

33. Johnson, *The Vantage Point*, pp. 249, 258–259.

34. Msg., M. Bundy to Smith, Saigon 24182, 11 February 1966, State Department, Pol. 27 Viet S.

35. Scoville, *Reorganizing for Pacification*, p. 22.

36. "Interview, Komer," pp. 20–21.

37. Memo, Mock to acting chief of staff, sub: Comments on Message from CG, FMFPAC to CMC, 1 October 1965, CMH.

38. Interview, Paige Mulholland with Chester Cooper, 17 July 1969, LBJ Library, Oral History Project, p. 12.

39. PPG 2, p. 543; and George C. Herring, *LBJ and Vietnam: A Different Kind of War* (Austin: University of Texas Press, 1994), p. 67.

40. Rpt., sub: Honolulu Meeting: Record of Conclusions and Decisions for Further Action, 23 February 1966, CMH.

41. Memo, White House press secretary, sub: Text of Joint Communique, 8 February 1966; and memo, sub: Declaration of Honolulu, 8 February 1966, copies of both in CMH.

42. PPG 2, p. 552.

43. Memo, M. Bundy to the president, sub: Notes on the Pacification Problem in Vietnam, 5 February 1966, LBJ Library, NSF, McGeorge Bundy files, 17, Organization.

44. Ibid.

45. Memo, M. Bundy to the president, 11 February 1966, LBJ Library, NSF, Memos to the president, 6, McGeorge Bundy, vol. 20.

46. Memo, M. Bundy to the president, sub: Non-Military Organization for Vietnam—in Saigon and in Washington, 16 February 1966, LBJ Library, NSF, Memos to the president, 6, McGeorge Bundy, vol. 20. Johnson wrote at the end of the five-page memo, "This is excellent—"

47. Msg., Lodge to the president, Saigon 2959, 15 February 1966, LBJ Library, NSF, vol. 46, Nodis, vol. 3.

48. Memo, M. Bundy to the president, 16 February 1966.

49. Memo, M. Bundy, to the president, sub: The Kintner Job, 27 February 1966, LBJ Library, NSF, Memos to the president, 6, McGeorge Bundy, vol. 20.

50. Memo, M. Bundy to the president, 16 February 1966, LBJ Library, NSF, Bundy Memos, vol. 20; and memo, Cooper to the President, sub: Management of Vietnam Policy, 3 March 1966, LBJ Library, NSF, Bundy Memos, vol. 21.

51. "Interview, Komer," p. 27.

52. National Security action memo 343, drafted by Komer, cited in PPG 2, p. 568.

53. Memo, Komer to the president, 26 March 1966, LBJ Library, NSF, Komer Memos, vol. 31.

54. "Interview, Komer," pp. 28–29; and memo, Ungar to members of the Vietnam Coordinating Committee, sub: Future Functioning of the VNCC, 19 April 1966, CMH. Ungar proposed disbanding his own group.

55. Msg., Komer to Porter, 30 April 1966, LBJ Library, NSF, Komer files, 3, 4, Backchannel cables, Komer-Porter.

56. Memo, Komer for the president, 24 May 1966, LBJ Library, NSF, Komer Memos, vol. 31.

57. Memo, Porter to Komer, sub: Proposal for Rapid Increase in RD Groups, 6 April 1966; and memo, Komer to secretary of defense et. al., sub: Expansion of RD Cadre Program, 21 April 1966, both in CMH.

58. Ltr., McNaughton, assistant secretary of defense (ISA), to Komer, 27 April 1966; memo, chairman, JCS, to secretary of defense, sub: Expansion of RD Cadre Program, 25 April 1966; and msg., Westmoreland to Wheeler, sub: Expansion of RD Cadre Program, MACV 14162, April 1966, all in CMH.

59. Memo, Jacobs to de Silva, sub: RDC Expansion and Manpower Availability, 1 July 1966, copy in CMH.

60. Msg., TOAID 8288, sub: Revolutionary Development Cadre, 29 May 1966, CMH; and msg., Lodge and Porter to Komer and Helms, Saigon 003, 230456Z, 23 July 1966, LBJ Library, NSF, Komer Memos, vol. 30.

61. MACV, *Command History, 1966*, p. 523.

62. Mission Council action memo 106, 10 August 1966, CMH.

63. Rpt., CIA, sub: Objection of Some Vietnamese Army Officers to the New Role to Be Played by the ARVN in the Pacification Program, date of information December 1966, LBJ Library, NSF, Komer Papers, vol. 36b.

64. PPG 2, pp. 576–577.

65. Memo, Komer to McNamara, 1 September 1966, LBJ Library, NSF, Komer Memos, vol. 27. Among the other studies that Komer mentioned was the "Roles and Missions" report submitted in August 1966 by an interagency task force based in South Vietnam and headed by Mission Council coordinator George Jacobson.

66. Memo, Leonhart for Komer, sub: Visit to Vietnam: May 17–29, 31 May 1966, copy in CMH.

67. Memo, Komer to the president, 9 August 1966, LBJ Library, NSF, Komer Memos, vol. 31.

68. Ibid.

69. Numerous memoranda in the LBJ Library (NSF, Komer Memos) contain his recommendations to the president. For Komer's early assessment, see memo, Komer to the president, sub: Komer Report on Saigon Trip, 19 April 1966.

70. Ltr., Komer to Porter, 30 April 1966; memo, Komer to Porter, 1 May 1967; and memo, Komer to Johnson, 9 May 1966, all in LBJ Library, NSF, Komer files 3, 4, Backchannel cables, Komer-Porter.

71. Msg., Porter to Komer, 21 July 1966, LBJ Library, NSF, Komer files, 3, 4, Backchannel cables.

72. Ltr. 9 and ltr. 10, Komer to Porter, 27 July 1966, LBJ Library, NSF, Komer files, 3, 4, Backchannel cables.

73. The memo is dated 7 August 1966. See PPG 2, p. 589.

74. Memo, Komer to the president, 17 August 1966, LBJ Library, NSF, Komer Memos, vol. 32.

75. Rostow's and McNamara's views were contained in several memos from Rostow to the president that are located in the NSF files of the LBJ Library: 29 August 1966, vol. 57; 30 August 1966, vol. 58; and 31 August 1966, vol. 47. See also PPG 2, p. 589.

76. Ltr., Komer to McNamara, 1 September 1966, CMH.

77. Memo, Johnson to Rusk, sub: McNamara's Proposal for Placing Pacification Under COMUSMACV, 1 October 1966, CMH.

78. Memo, Ungar, FE, to Rusk, sub: Porter's Views on McNamara's Proposal, October 2, 1966, CMH.

79. Memo, Unger to Rusk, sub: Ambassador Porter's Views, 2 October 1966; and msg., Porter to Lodge, 6 October 1966, both in LBJ Library, NSF, vol. 60.

80. Interview, Scoville with Komer, Washington, D.C., 6 November 1969.

81. Westmoreland's history notes, 17 October 1966, Westmoreland Papers.

82. Memo, McNamara to the president, 14 October 1966, CMH.

83. Msg., Katzenbach to Rostow and the president, State 68390, 18 October 1966, LBJ Library, NSF, vol. 60, contained the proposal. Rostow's agenda for the meeting with Secretary Rusk, 26 October 1966, same location in the LBJ Library, presented his reactions.

84. Msg., Rusk, McNamara, and Komer to Lodge, State 78865, 4 November 1966, State Department.

85. Ltr., Johnson to Lodge, 16 November 1966, LBJ Library, NSF, Komer Memos, vol. 31.

86. Ibid.

87. Msg., Rusk, McNamara, and Komer to Lodge, 15 November 1966, LBJ Library, NSF, vol. 61; and msg., Rusk, McNamara, and Komer to Lodge, State 83699, 12 November 1966, State Department Pol. 27 Viet S.

88. Msg., Lodge to Rusk, Saigon 11125, 17 November 1966, State Department Pol. 27 Viet S.

89. Lansdale, memo for the record, sub: Talk with Lodge, 11 November 1966, Hoover Institution, Lansdale Papers, Box 58.

90. Msg., Wheeler to Westmoreland, 2139Z, 17 October 1966; and msg., Johnson to Westmoreland, 22 October 1966, both in Westmoreland Papers.

91. Msg., Porter to Komer, 10 November 1966; and msg., Komer to Porter, CAP 66949, 11 November 1966, both in LBJ Library, NSF, Komer Memos, vol. 30.

92. Ltr., Johnson to Lodge, 16 November 1966, LBJ Library.

Chapter 6

1. Parts of this chapter make use of Scoville, *Reorganizing for Pacification,* pp. 31–73.

2. Memo, Holbrooke to Komer, sub: Vietnam Trip Report: October 26–November 18, 1966, dated 1 December 1966, LBJ Library, NSF, Komer files, 5, Gaud.

3. Memo, deputy ambassador to USAID, sub: U.S. Mission's Office of Civil Operations, 1 December 1966, CMH.

4. "Interview, Komer," p. 37.

5. Memo, deputy ambassador to USAID, 1 December 1966.

6. Airgram, Saigon A-43, sub: OCO Progress Report, 22 March 1967, CMH.

7. Memo, Komer to the secretary of state et al., sub: Ambassador's Porter's Urgent Request for Personnel, 5 December 1966; MFR, sub: Interagency Meeting on Personnel for Civil Operations, 8 December 1966, both in CMH.

8. Memo, Leonhart to Komer, sub: Accelerating Pacification: Talking Points, 24 January 1967, LBJ Library, NSF, Komer Memos, Katzenbach 6a.

9. Ibid.

10. Memo, Komer to the president, 23 January 1967, LBJ Library, NSF, Komer files 1, 2, Memos to the president.

11. Ibid.; and memo, Rostow to the president, 4 February 1967, LBJ Library, NSF, Rostow Memos, vol. 20.

12. Memo, Komer to the president, 26 January 1967, LBJ Library, NSF, Komer Memos, vol. 31. The president's instructions were written in the margin.

13. Memo, Katzenbach to the president, sub: Taylor's Letter on Appointing General Westmoreland as Ambassador, 11 February 1967, LBJ Library, NSF, Rostow Memos, vol. 20; and ltr., Lodge to the president, 21 January 1967, LBJ Library, NSF, Rostow Memos, vol. 19.

14. Ltr., Johnson to Rusk, 2 March 1967, LBJ Library, NSF, vol. 67. Bunker was already ambassador at large, but not in Saigon.

15. Correspondence, Dean Rusk with author, 9 June 1981.

16. Correspondence, Ellsworth Bunker with author, 22 June 1981.

17. Scoville, *Reorganizing for Pacification,* Chap. 4.

18. Ltr., Johnson to Locke, 13 March 1967, LBJ Library, NSF, Rostow Memos, vol. 23. The *New York Times* reported on March 16 that Komer would expand his operation and spend more time in Saigon than Washington, clearly implying that he would divide his time between Washington and Saigon, an idea that Komer squelched. Hedrick Smith, "New Envoy Named," *New York Times,* p. 1.

19. Memo, Komer to the president, 18 March 1967, LBJ Library, Presidential Diary Backup file.

20. Memo, Rostow to the president, 25 March 1967, LBJ Library, NSF, Rostow Memos, vol. 24; and Smith, "New Envoy," *New York Times,* 16 March 1967. Abrams's predecessor as deputy COMUSMACV, Lieut. Gen. John A. Heintges, also was charged with improving South Vietnam's military.

21. Quote from memo, Komer to the president, 27 April 1967, LBJ Library, NSF, Komer Memos, vol. 31; Johnson, *The Vantage Point,* pp. 369–370; and Davidson, *Vietnam at War,* p. 431.

22. Komer, memo to the president, 19 April 1967, LBJ Library, NSF, Komer files 1, 2, Memos to the president.

23. Westmoreland, *A Soldier Reports,* p. 215.

24. Memo, Komer to McNamara, 29 March 1967, LBJ Library, NSF, Komer Memos, vol. 27.

25. Msg., Rusk to Bunker, State 184979, 29 April 1967, State Department Pol. 27 Viet S.

26. NSAM 362, sub: Responsibility for U.S. Role in Pacification, 9 May 1967, CMH. Bunker and Komer had collaborated on the new arrangements before leaving Washington. See memo, Komer to Bunker, 6 May 1967, CMH.

27. Chaisson correspondence, Hoover Institution, esp. the letters of 24 March and 25 May 1967.

28. Davidson, *Vietnam at War,* pp. 457–458.

29. Author interview with Komer, Washington, D.C., 29 November 1990.

30. Directive, MACV, 10-12, sub: Organizations and Functions of CORDS, 28 May 1967, CMH; msg., Abrams to Johnson, MAC 5307, 4 June 1967; and msg., Abrams to Johnson, MAC 8312, 2 September 1967, both messages in Abrams Papers.

31. "Interview, Komer," p. 62.

32. Memo, Westmoreland to Komer, 24 June 1967; memo, Komer to Westmoreland, sub: Organization for CORDS in CTZs [corps tactical zones], 25 June 1967; memo, Komer to Westmoreland, 13 September 1967; and memo, Westmoreland to Komer, 14 September 1967, all in DepCORDS files, CMH.

33. Directive 10-12, Hq. MACV, sub: Organizations and Functions for Civil Operations and Revolutionary Development Support, 28 May 1967, CMH. MACCORDS was a shortened form of MACV, CORDS; Komer's title was usually abridged to DepCORDS.

34. "Interview, Komer," p. 63.

35. Handbook, sub: Territorial Forces Evaluation System III Reports Handbook, CORDS, January 1971, CMH; and "Interview, Komer," pp. 202–203.

36. Memo, Culbertson, associate director for local development, to MacDonald, AID director, sub: Revolutionary Development and "National" Programs, 7 August 1967, DepCORDS files.

37. Memo of understanding, DOD-CIA, sub: Revolutionary Development Cadre Program, 29 March 1968, CMH.

38. Memo, Forsythe to MACV chief of staff, sub: Civil Affairs Companies, 15 July 1967; disposition form (DF), J-3 to chief of staff, 23 August 1967; DF, ACS, CORDS, to chief of staff, sub: Transfer of Civic Action Responsibilities, 30 August 1967, all in DepCORDS files; and draft rpt., sub: 1967 MACV Civic Action Projects, 27 December 1967, CMH.

39. "Interview, Komer," pp. 122–124; memo, Komer to PSA, An Giang province, 25 March 1968; and memo, 9 April 1968, both in CMH.

40. Scoville, *Reorganizing for Pacification,* p. 68.

41. Directive, MACV, 10-12, 28 May 1967.

42. Memo, Komer to all district senior advisers, sub: Functioning of District Advisory Teams, 23 May 1968, CMH.

43. Memo, 2d Regional Assistance Group, sub: Policy Guidance and Information Memorandum 1, 5 June 1971, CMH. This document in effect reiterated the guidance that Vann had issued in earlier years.

44. Briefing, Knowlton to Army Policy Council, sub: Army Advisory Effort in Vietnam, 22 January 1969, CMH.

45. Albert C. Bole Jr. and K. Kobata, "An Evaluation of the Measurements of the Hamlet Evaluation System," Project–118 (Newport, R.I.: Naval War College Center for Advanced Research, 1975), pp. 18–19.

46. Fact sheet, DCSOPS to army chief of staff, sub: Hamlet Evaluation System, 16 August 1967, CMH.

47. Msg., State 54020, 14 October 1967, DepCORDS files; and Peter Braestrup, *The Big Story* (Garden City, N.Y.: Anchor Books, 1978), p. 406. On HES as a management tool, see Thayer, *War Without Fronts.*

48. Ltr., Komer to Westmoreland, 11 August 1967, DepCORDS files.

49. Westmoreland, *A Soldier Reports,* pp. 215–216; and "Interview, Komer," p. 192.

50. Memo, Gaud for Katzenbach, sub: Responsibility and Accountability for U.S. Support of Revolutionary Development, 22 June 1967, CMH; and ltr., Komer to Gaud, 30 June 1967, DepCORDS files.

51. Memo, Rostow to the president, 15 September 1967, LBJ Library, NSF, Komer Memos, Presidential Memos.

52. Memo, Komer to the president, 29 April 1967, LBJ Library, NSF, Komer files 1, 2, Memos to the President.

Chapter 7

1. Memo, Komer to Bunker, sub: Completing the Transition, 5 May 1967, DepCORDS files.

2. Memo, Komer to Westmoreland, sub: How to Get Our Case Across, 19 June 1967, DepCORDS files. Takeoff was named in honor Walt W. Rostow, who had employed the term to characterize one part of the process of economic development in his book *The Stages of Economic Growth* (Cambridge: Cambridge University Press, 1960).

3. Quotes from "Interview, Komer," p. 64. Takeoff's objectives are found in memo, MACJO1R, sub: Project Takeoff, 19 July 1967, DepCORDS files.

4. Memo, Komer to Bunker and Westmoreland, sub: Pacification Discussion with GVN Top Level, 30 July 1967, DepCORDS files.

5. Memo, Komer to Bunker, sub: Pacification Discussion with GVN Top Level, 30 July 1967; and draft memo, Komer to Bunker, sub: Project Takeoff, 20 June 1967, both in DepCORDS files.

6. Rpt., MACV, Project Takeoff, 11 August 1967, vol. 2, pp. III-1–III-4, CMH.

7. AB 143 Combined Campaign Plan 1968, CMH.

8. Memo, ACS, CORDS, to DepCORDS, sub: Project Takeoff Year-End Wrap-Up, 1967, 10 January 1968, DepCORDS files.

9. Rpt., sub: Chieu Hoi Program 1967 Year End Report, DepCORDS files; and memo, ACS, CORDS, 10 January 1968.

10. Memo, ACS, CORDS, 10 January 1968.

11. Memo, MACCORDS-CH, Williams to Komer, sub: Returnee Ratios in Binh Duong Province, 17 October 1968, DepCORDS files; and rpt., MACV, Project Takeoff, vol. 2, p. VII-16.

12. Memo, ACS, CORDS, 10 January 1968.

13. MFR, MACCORDS-PP, sub: Meeting with Col Lac, 25 November 1967, DepCORDS files.

14. Memo, ACS, CORDS, 10 January 1968.

15. Memo, Montague to Komer, sub: Mr. Quang, 15 December 1967, DepCORDS files.

16. Wiesner, *Victims and Survivors,* p. 89.

17. Ibid., pp. 97–98.

18. Memo, ACS, CORDS, 10 January 1968.

19. Memo, Komer to MACV chief of staff, sub: Evaluation of Refugee Handling in Quang Ngai, 16 September 1967, DepCORDS files; and msg., Saigon 8577, 141210Z October 1967, CMH.

20. Memo, ACS, CORDS, 10 January 1968.

21. Memo of conversation, sub: Meeting with the Minister of Interior on Police Matters, 31 October 1968; and memo, Parker to Forsythe, sub: Upgrading NPFF Capabilities, 2 April 1968, both in DepCORDS files.

22. Memo, Sansom, AID land reform adviser, to Komer, sub: Land Reform, 25 August 1967; and memo, Lowman, CORDS land reform adviser, to Komer, sub: Project Takeoff Land Reform, 23 August 1967, both in DepCORDS files.

23. Memo, Komer to Bunker, sub: Land Reform Responsibility, 3 October 1967; and msg., Saigon 7521, 3 October 1967, both in DepCORDS files.

24. Memo, Komer to Bunker, sub: Items to Raise in Washington, 7 November 1967, DepCORDS files; "Interview, Komer," p. 66; and memo, Komer to Westmoreland, sub: 1968 Pacification Program, 10 January 1968, DepCORDS files.

25. Memo, Komer to McNamara and Vance, 24 April 1967, copy in CMH.

26. MACV, *Command History, 1967;* MACV, 1967, p. 590; and memo, Komer to chief of staff, MACV, sub: RF/PF Advisory Effort, 25 May 1967, CMH.

27. Memo, Komer to secretary of defense, 30 August 1967, CMH.

28. DF, chief, RDS to chief P&P, sub: Additional Advisory Structure, 16 June 1967, CMH.

29. Msg., McNamara to Komer, 3 September 1967; chief of staff of the army, "Daily Information Summary," 8 September 1967; and fact sheet, JCS (SACSA), all in CMH.

30. MACV, *Command History, 1966,* pp. 452–455; MACV, *Command History, 1967,* vol. 1, p. 245; PPG 2, pp. 547–548; and msg., Abrams to Johnson, MACV 6716, 18 July 1967, Abrams Papers.

31. Memo, McGiffert to Resor, 26 July 1967, CMH.

32. Msg., Johnson to Abrams, 15 July 1967; msg., DA to COMUSMACV, 29 November 1967; and msg., COMUSMACV to CG, USARV, 6 December 1967, all in CMH.

33. Msg., CJCS to CINCPAC, DAIN 224833, CMH.

34. MFR, MACCORDS PP-RDS, sub: IV Corps Advisers, 28 September 1967, DepCORDS files.

35. MACV, *Command History, 1967*, p. 591.

36. Memo, Forsythe, Asst. DepCORDS, to Kerwin, MACV chief of staff, sub: Meeting with General Thang, 29 November 1967, DepCORDS files. See also MFR, sub: Weekly Meeting with Vice Chief of Staff, JGS, 2 December 1967, DepCORDS files.

37. Msg., COMUSMACV to deputy COMUSMACV, sub: Requirements IV Corps, 120613Z October 1967; DF, MAC J-3, to chief of staff, sub: Concept of Deployment of MATs, 8 November 1967; and msg., COMUSMACV to commanding general, USARV, MAC38651, 280845Z November 1967, all in CMH.

38. Daily log, Mobile Advisory Team III 34, Mo Cong village, Tay Ninh province, 1–31 March 1969, CMH.

39. MACV *Command History, 1967*, p. 591; and Clarke, *Advice and Support*, p. 236.

40. Douglas Pike, *War, Peace, and the Viet Cong* (Cambridge, Mass.: MIT Press, 1969), pp. 9–10; rpt., MACV J-2 (Strategic Reports and Analysis), sub: North Vietnamese Presence in the Viet Cong Infrastructure, 16 September 1969; and fact sheet, chief of staff of the army, sub: VCI, 16 August 1967, both in CMH.

41. D.W.P. Elliott and C.A.H. Thomson, *A Look at the VC Cadres: Dinh Tuong Province, 1965–1966*, RM 5114-ISA/ARPA (Santa Monica, Calif.: Rand, March 1967), Chap. 4.

42. Rpt., MACV J-2 (Strategic Research and Analysis), sub: VCI Newsletter 11, VCI Functional Element Description, 27 February 1969; and rpt., MACV J-2, sub: Summary of VCI Activities, 19 April–9 May 1970, dated May 1970, both in CMH.

43. Thayer, *War Without Fronts*, pp. 14, 207.

44. Memo, CIA, sub: The Erosion of the Communist Cadre Structure, 17 March 1967, CMH.

45. U.S. military personnel were used mostly for interrogating pows.

46. Andrade, *Ashes to Ashes*, p. 61.

47. Ibid., pp. 58–59, stated that the CIA responded to Komer in June, but, according to Komer, actually it had sent Komer a memo on the collection, collation, and exploitation of intelligence at the province and district level at the end of April prior to his leaving Washington. See "Interview, Komer," pp. 160–161.

48. Memo, Komer to Kerwin, sub: Attack on the VCI, 5 June 1967; memo, Komer to J-2, sub: Attack on the VCI, 3 June 1967, both in DepCORDS files; and "Interview, Komer," pp. 160–161.

49. Scoville, *Reorganizing for Pacification*, Chap. 6; and memo, Komer to Westmoreland, 15 June 1967, DepCORDS files.

50. Memo, Westmoreland to Komer, 16 June 1967, DepCORDS files.

51. Scoville interview with Komer, 6 November 1969, cited in Scoville, *Reorganizing for Pacification*, Chap. 6; and Westmoreland, *A Soldier Reports*, p. 216.

52. Directive, MACV, 381-41, sub: Military Intelligence: Intelligence Coordination and Exploitation for Attack on VC Infrastructure, Short Title: Phoenix, 9 July 1967; memo, Parker to DepCORDS, sub: Attack on the VCI, 30 October 1967; and handwritten notes, Parker, June 22, 1967, in DepCORDS files.

53. Komer's request for active-duty FBI agents to serve as police advisers for the Phoenix program was politely but firmly denied by J. Edgar Hoover. Ltr., Hoover to Komer, 16 May 1968, DepCORDS files.

54. Lewy, *America in Vietnam*, p. 287; and Andrade, *Ashes to Ashes*, pp. 133–134.

55. Memo, Nickel, director, JUSPAO, to Komer, sub: Phoenix Policy Paper, 29 March 1968, DepCORDS files.

56. Memo, Parker to Komer, sub: First ICEX Coordinator Course, 10 September 1967; and memo, Parker to Komer, sub: Combined Intelligence Staff Training Course, 14 September 1967, both in DepCORDS files.

57. Directive, MACV, 381-42, sub: Military Intelligence Reporting on Elimination of Viet Cong Infrastructure, 25 November 1967, CMH.

58. MFR, Komer, sub: Attack on the Infrastructure, 22 August 1967, CMH; MFR, Komer, sub: Meeting with Minister of Interior, 11 December 1967, "Interview, Komer," pp. 158–168; and memo, Parker to Komer, sub: Attack on the VCI: A Progress Report, 30 October 1967, CMH.

59. Quotes are from directive, GVN, 89ThT/VP/M, sub: Annihilation of VC Infrastructure, 20 December 1967; msg., Saigon to Washington, Saigon 13737, 200845Z December 1967; and msg., COMUSMACV to CINPAC, sub: Phoenix Directive, 020908Z January 1968, and in CMH.

60. Memo, Komer to Parker, 22 September 1967; and memo, Parker to Komer, sub: Manpower Requirements, PSB, 17 September 1967, both in DepCORDS files.

61. MFR, sub: Conversation Between Ambassador Komer and BG Loan on 16 April 1968, dated 18 April 1968; memo, Parker to Komer, sub: Talking Paper for Meeting with Director General National Police Loan, 4 January 1968; ltr., Westmoreland to Vien, 26 February 1968; and memo, Komer to Westmoreland, 17 March 1968, all in DepCORDS files.

62. Msg., COMUSMACV to CINCPAC, sub: Phoenix Program, 251134Z April 1968, CMH.

63. "Interview, Komer," pp. 165–167.

64. Rpt., CORDS-Eval, sub: Evaluation of *Phung Hoang* in Khanh Hoa and Pleiku Provinces, 13 November 1968, CMH.

65. Memo, Colby to Komer, sub: Legal Processing of VC Suspects, 26 June 1968, DepCORDS files.

66. Memo, Komer to Hai, director general, National Police, sub: VC Techniques of Escaping Capture, 21 July 1968; and memo, Hai to Saigon police precincts, sub: VC Documents, 18 July 1968, both in DepCORDS files. At official exchange rates, 118 piasters = $1. The black market rate was in the range of several hundred piasters per dollar.

67. Msg., COMUSMACV to CINCPAC, sub: Request for Funds for Detention Facilities, 061127Z January 1968, CMH; memo, Harper, legal counsel, ICEX, to DepCORDS, sub: Expansion of Military Field Courts, 3 October 1967; memo, Harper to Komer, 8 November 1967; Decree, Republic of Vietnam, 49/67, 30 October 1967; and memo, Locke to Westmoreland, sub: Trying and Imprisoning the Infrastructure, August 1967, all three in DepCORDS files.

68. Memo, Parker to Komer, sub: I Corps *Phung Hoang* Developments, 22 May 1968; memo, Parker to Komer, sub: Misc Notes on Current Activities, 26 February 1968; rpt., sub: Survey—Recent GVN Actions; and memo, Vann to Komer, sub: Attack on the VCI, 5 March 1968, all in DepCORDS files.

69. Memo, Komer to Parker, sub: Analyzing the Size of the VC Infrastructure, 27 April 1968; memos, Parker to Komer, same subject, 4 May 1968, 22 June 1968, and 14 July 1968,

all in DepCORDS files; and memo, CIA, sub: The Erosion of the Communist Cadre Structure, 17 March 1967, copy in CMH.

Chapter 8

1. Fact sheet, Shea, to chief of staff, sub: Leverage and Its Uses, 24 July 1967, CMH.

2. Memo, Cottrell to all province senior advisers, 9 October 1967, DepCORDS files.

3. Operations memo, U.S. Operations Mission, 190-66, 26 November 1966, CMH.

4. Operational memo, Office of Field Operations, 93-66, sub: MACV Subsector Fund, 1 May 1966; directive, MACV, 37-11, sub: Financial Administration Subsector Fund; 20 April 1966; and memo, MACV comptroller to chief of staff, MACV, sub: USOM Proposal for Local Currency CY 1966, 8 October 1965, all in CMH.

5. PPG 2, p. 479.

6. Memo, AID, sub: Joint Sign-Off Authority, 22 September 1967, CMH.

7. PPG 2, pp. 393–394; and MFR, Wilson, province adviser, Long An province, 3 December 1966, CMH.

8. American dissatisfaction with Chinh may have had something to do with his reassignment in the fall of 1967. He then became deputy for territorial forces in III Corps, which would involve him in pacification. Neither Komer nor Thang was pleased. Thang believed that the decision had been made at a "very high level and that he was stuck with it" (MFR, sub: Meeting with General Thang, 5 September 1967, DepCORDS files).

9. Since Hunnicutt was within one month of completing his normal tour of duty in Vietnam (which would have ended January 7, 1967), his removal in December 1966 may have been, as MACV insisted, routine rather than punitive. But his reassignment did not go unnoticed by other advisers, who could construe Hunnicutt's transfer as a form of censure.

10. PPG 2, pp. 393–394.

11. Circular, JUSPAO, reprinted in circular, MACV, 4 March 1967, CMH. JUSPAO came under the authority of the American ambassador.

12. The quotation is from msg., AIDTO 4370, sub: Provincial Joint Sign-Off Authority, 28 October 1967, LBJ Library, NSF, Komer Memos, vol. 11; and fact sheet for chief of staff of the army, sub: Leverage, 27 July 1967, CMH.

13. Msg., Rusk to Bunker, State 30023, 310159Z August 1967; and msg., Sharp to Westmoreland, 081917Z September 1967, both in CMH.

14. Memo, Komer to Thang, 23 May 1967, DepCORDS files.

15. Memo, Komer to Lathram, 22 June 1967, DepCORDS files.

16. Memo, Lathram, ACofS, CORDS, Sub: Leverage Briefing, 29 May 1967, DepCORDS files. Warner later rose to the rank of general.

17. Komer's marginal notes were on a draft chapter ("Interview, Komer," p. 144).

18. Memo (draft), Komer to McNamara, sub: Giving a New Thrust to Pacification, 10 August 1966, PPG 2, pp. 570–572; and "Interview, Komer," pp. 144–145.

19. Ibid.

20. "Interview, Komer," pp. 144, 155–156.

21. Memo, Lansdale to Komer, sub: Corruption, 21 July 1967; and memo, Calhoun to Komer, sub: Coping with Corruption, 27 July 1967, both in CMH.

22. Directive, MACV, 381-9, sub: Military Intelligence and Biographic Reporting, 25 July 1967, CMH.

23. Memo, Komer to Westmoreland and Bunker, sub: Removal of Corrupt and/or Incompetent Officials, 20 September 1967, DepCORDS files.

24. DF, ACS, CORDS, to MACV chief of staff, sub: *Chieu Hoi* in the Delta, 19 October 1968, CMH.

25. Interview, author with Clay McManaway, former director of plans, programs, and policies, CORDS, Washington, D.C., October 1973; and memo, Komer to Westmoreland, 19 August 1967, DepCORDS files.

26. Memo, Komer to Bunker, 25 September 1967, CMH.

27. Ltr., Komer to Ky, 21 September 1967, DepCORDS files.

28. Ltr., Komer to Thang, 22 September 1967; ltr., Komer to Thang, 26 September 1967; and MFR, sub: Meeting with General Thang, 28 September 1967, all in DepCORDS files.

29. AIK funds were drawn from the imprest funds allocated to district advisers to deal with emergencies.

30. "Interview, Komer," p. 148.

31. MFR, sub: Conversation with Minister Tri, MRD, 18 November 1967, DepCORDS files. Forsythe and Huss were the American representatives at the meeting.

32. In later guidance Vann presented his views on advising and leverage in more detail. See memo, 2d Regional Assistance Group, sub: Policy Guidance and Information Memorandum 1, 5 June 1971, CMH.

33. Memo, Komer to all province senior advisers, sub: Exchange of Ideas on Pacification, 7 September 1967.

34. Memo, Cottrell, DepCORDS, IV CTZ, to Komer, 8 November 1967, CMH. Komer's judgments appeared on the margin of the memorandum.

35. Memo, Lathram to Komer, 8 November 1967; msg., Komer to Cottrell, 140526Z November 1967; and memo, Vann to Lathram, 11 November 1967, DepCORDS files. Komer's comments were on the draft.

36. Memo, Komer to Bunker and Westmoreland, Sub: Leverage, 30 January 1968, DepCORDS files.

37. "Interview, Komer," p. 144.

38. Memo, Komer to Corps DepCORDS, 4 January 1968, DepCORDS files.

39. Memo, Lathram to Komer, sub: Liaison Report, 29 September to 27 October 1967, dated 30 October 1967; and memo, Huss, liaison officer, MORD, to chief, Plans and Programs, sub: A Worm's Eye View of the Big Picture, 15 October 1967, both in DepCORDS files.

40. Msg., Saigon to Washington, 070115Z October 1967, Saigon 07861, copy in DepCORDS files.

41. Msg., MACV to CINCPAC, sub: Pacification in South Vietnam During 1967, 030250Z February 1968, CMH; rpt., MACCORDS, sub: NLD Programs, CMH; and "Interview, Komer," p. 122.

42. MFR, DePuy, SACSA, to Wheeler, CJCS, sub: Conversations with Ambassador Komer and Major General Forsythe, 17 January 1968, CMH; msg., Bunker to Rusk, Saigon 16850, 24 January 1968, CMH; memo, Komer to Bunker, 11 January 1968, DepCORDS files; memo, Komer to Westmoreland, 19 January 1968, DepCORDS files. President Thieu was inaugurated on October 31, 1967. Thieu organized a new cabinet under Prime Minister Nguyen Van Loc in November 1967.

43. MFR, addendum to MFR, sub: Meeting with Vice Chief of Staff, JGS, 28 December 1967, DepCORDS files.

44. Memo, Komer to Westmoreland, 19 January 1968, DepCORDS files. For an idea of the high esteem in which the Americans held General Thang, see John Mecklin, "The Struggle to Rescue the People," *Fortune* (April 1967): 126–133.

45. Msg., Saigon 16940, sub: Thieu's Address and the National Assembly, 25 January 1968; and MFR, Forsythe's visit, both in DepCORDS files.

46. Memo, DePuy to Wheeler, 17 January 1968.

Chapter 9

1. Thayer, *War Without Fronts*, p. 34.

2. "Southeast Asia Statistical Summary" (Washington, D.C.: Office of the Assistant Secretary of Defense [Comptroller], April 1979). See also Thayer, *War Without Fronts*, p. 104, for estimates on enemy killed.

3. Rpt., CIA, sub: Current Viet Cong Problem, Policies, and Solutions, 26 July 1967, CMH; Also see Thayer, *War Without Fronts*, p. 200, for statistics on defections.

4. Westmoreland, *Report on the War*, p. 195.

5. Rpt., sub: VC Loss of Population Control, 1967, CMH. For estimates on enemy killed, see Thayer, *War Without Fronts*, Chap. 10.

6. Msg., Rostow to Bunker, 27 September 1967, LBJ Library, NSF, vol. 59; and memo, Rostow to Johnson, 3 November 1967, LBJ Library, Rostow Memos, vol. 49.

7. Memo, Rostow to the president, 10 November 1967, LBJ Library, Rostow Memos, vol. 50. See also memo, Rostow to Johnson, 2 August 1967, LBJ Library, Rostow Memos, vol. 1; and memo, Rostow to Johnson, 13 September 1967, LBJ Library, Rostow Memos, vol. 4.

8. Neil Sheehan, *A Bright Shining Lie: John Paul Vann and America in Vietnam* (New York: Random House, 1988), pp. 698–699. See Westmoreland, *A Soldier Reports*, pp. 228, 315, for the general's own account.

9. Duiker, *The Communist Road to Power*, pp. 261–263.

10. Captured document, sub: VC Strategy and Objectives in 1967–68, captured 23 October 1967 by the ARVN 21st Infantry Division, IV Corps, pp. 8–10. The document was received at the Combined Document Exploitation Center, 5 November 1967, and was summarized and published in *CDEC Bulletin* 7884, 6 November 1967. MACV translated and published the entire document on 22 November 1967, as translation rpt., Log 11-1209-67, CMH.

11. Westmoreland, *A Soldier Reports*, pp. 312–314.

12. Msg., CIA, sub: Papers on the VC Winter-Spring Offensive, 15 December 1967, CMH.

13. Memo, Komer to Westmoreland, sub: 1968 Pacification Program, 10 January 1968. See also ltr., Komer to Alsop, 4 January 1968; and ltr., Komer to Owen, chief, Policy Planning Council, State Dept., 3 January 1968, both in DepCORDS files.

14. Rpt., MACCORDS, sub: Slow Progress in Expanding Local Security During 1967, 10 January 1968, DepCORDS files.

15. Msg., Westmoreland to Momyer, Palmer, Cushman, and Veth, MAC 01307, 280153Z January 1968, CMH. In 1968, the cease-fire was scheduled to be in effect from 6 P.M. on 29 January to 6 A.M. on 31 January, but owing to allied expectations that the communists were likely to make an unprecedented move, allied military forces did not stand down in I Corps, and the demilitarized zone and air interdiction continued against roads in North Vietnam south of the city of Vinh.

16. Don Oberdorfer, *Tet!* (Garden City, N.Y.: Doubleday, 1971), p. 116. Oberdorfer made extensive use of official as well as unofficial sources to compile his account.

17. Ibid., p. 232; rpt., CIA, sub: Situation Appraisal of Problems in Hue City, 18–21 Feb 1968; rpt., MACCORDS-RE, 25 March 1968; and briefing, Mission Council 26 April 1968, all in CMH.

18. Wiesner, *Victims and Survivors,* p. 160.

19. Intelligence memo, CIA-DIA, sub: The Effect of the Tet Offensive on the Economy of South Vietnam as of 15 February 1968; and information memo, AID, administrator to Grant, assistant administrator for Vietnam, sub: Vietnam Bureau's Fortnightly Report, 27 March–9 April, dated 24 April 1968, periodic CORDS situation rpt., 212400–282400 March 1968, both in CMH.

20. Ibid.

21. Wiesner, *Victims and Survivors,* p. 161.

22. Msg., COMUSMACV to CINCPAC, 290740Z March 1968, CMH.

23. Intelligence memo, CIA, sub: Spot Report on the Situation in Vietnam, 019070Z February 1968; and CIA msgs., 2 February 1968, 1800 hours; and 2 February 1968, 1500 hours, all in CMH.

24. Fact sheet, DCSOPS, sub: Assessment of Post-Tet Pacification, 5 April 1968, CMH. See Chapter 10 for more details.

25. Survey, JUSPAO, sub: Provincial Popular Attitudes on the Tet Attacks, 4 March 1968; and memo, Office of the Special Assistant for Vietnamese Affairs, CIA, sub: Effect of Tet, 7 February 1968, both in CMH.

26. CIA rpt., sub: Operations to Clear VC from Saigon, 3 February 1968, CMH.

27. Msg., Johnstone to ACS, CORDS, 083007 February 1968, CMH. Johnstone's account reached Komer, Abrams, and Westmoreland, who pressured the government to punish the commander of the Ranger Battalion and the province officials who had permitted such an outrage to occur. Johnstone also alleged that the unit's behavior had been just as atrocious before Tet. See memo, Komer to Westmoreland and Abrams, sub: 43d Ranger Battalion, 9 February 1968, DepCORDS files.

28. Memo, Komer to Westmoreland, sub: Progress in Phoenix, 24 April 1968, DepCORDS files.

29. Memo, Parker to Komer, sub: Security of SVN Prisons from VC Attack, 23 March 1968; memo, sub: Attack on VC Infrastructure—Highlights of Phoenix Activities During February 1968; and memo, Berkeley, ICEX staff, to Komer, 9 February 1968, all in DepCORDS files.

30. Memo, ICEX coordinator Hoa to ICEX coordinator, II CTZ, sub: Attack on VCI, 5 February 1968; memo, sub: Attack on VCI, 6 February 1968; ltr., Parker to Loan, 6 February 1968; memo, Parker to Phoenix committee, sub: Status of DIOCCS and PIOCCS as of 23 February 1968, dated 28 February 1968; and memo, Greenwalt to Komer, sub: Report on Visit to I and II Corps, 9 February 1968, all in DepCORDS files.

31. Oberdorfer, *Tet!* pp. 154–155; and Duiker, *The Communist Road to Power,* p. 269. Duiker referred (p. 367, note 60) to a CIA report, Joint Office of Current Intelligence and Office of Economic Research memo, dated March 1, 1968, that put communist losses at thirty-eight thousand.

32. MFR, CORDS, sub: Narrative Assessment Post-Tet Pacification Status, I CTZ, 14 February 1968; rpt., Puckett, field evaluator, to Koren, 7 February 1968; and trip rpt., CORDS-RE, sub: Visit to I CTZ, 28 February 1968, all in CMH.

33. Handwritten overview of II CTZ as of 12 February 1968; MFR, sub: Narrative Assessment of II CTZ Pacification Status, 15 February 1968; and msg., senior advisor II CTZ to COMUSMACV, sub: CORDS SITREP as of 041800H February 1968, all in CMH.

34. Trip rpt., Dodson, CORDS evaluator, sub: Status of Pacification in Binh Dinh, 27 March 1968, CMH.

35. Rpt., CORDS-RD, sub: Report on Phu Yen and Quang Duc, 11 March 1968, copy in CMH.

36. Trip rpts., CORDS-RE, 1 March and 4 March 1968, CMH.

37. Trip rpt., CORDS-RE, IV Corps, 29 March 1968, CMH.

38. Herbert Y. Schandler, *The Unmaking of a President* (Princeton: Princeton University Press, 1976), p. 82.

39. Assessment cited in PPG 4, pp. 551–552.

40. Intelligence memo, sub: Pacification in the Wake of the Tet Offensive in South Vietnam, 19 March 1968, CMH.

41. Schandler, *The Unmaking of a President*, p. 216.

42. PPG 4, p. 556.

43. *Southeast Asia Analysis Report* (February 1968): 48, CMH.

44. PPG 4, p. 548; see also pp. 547–552.

45. Memo, Rostow to the president, sub: The Clifford Committee, 4 March 1968, LBJ Library, NSF, Rostow Memos, vol. 65. The agenda of the 28 February meeting (Rostow Memos, vol. 64) indicated that the question of the strategic use of the reinforcements was scheduled to be discussed.

46. Memo, Rostow to the president, 12 February 1968, LBJ Library, NSF, Rostow Memos, vol. 61; notes of meeting, 27 February, attended by Rusk, McNamara, Clifford, Katzenbach, Bundy, Rostow, Califano, and McPherson, LBJ Library, NSF, March 1970, vol. 1; and msg., Rostow to the president, 27 February 1968, LBJ Library, NSF, March 1970, vol. 1.

47. Notes of the president's meeting with senior foreign policy advisers, 4 March 1968, LBJ Library, NSF, March 1970, vol. 1.

48. Quote from ltr., Komer to author, 11 June 1974, CMH; *Southeast Asia Analysis Report* (March 1968): 33; and msg., Komer to Enthoven, MAC 4188, 271245Z March 1968, all in CMH. As time went on, officials in Washington grew more optimistic about the allies' prospects. Even Enthoven conceded in April that pacification was "more alive and kicking than previously thought." See msg., Enthoven to Komer, ASD/SA 04015, 12234Z April 1968, CMH.

Chapter 10

1. Rpt., CIA, sub: Roles of Thieu, Ky, and Loc in Present Crisis, 2 February 1968, CMH.

2. Msg., Saigon 17480, 2 February 1968, 021125Z, CMH.

3. "Interview, Komer," p. 85.

4. MFR, MACJO1R, sub: Initial US/GVN Meeting for Project Recovery, 3 February 1968; and msg., COMUSMACV to corps senior advisors, MACV 03682, sub: GVN Organization for Relief of Destruction, 050210Z February 1968, both in DepCORDS files.

5. Memo, Komer to MacDonald et al., 25 March 1968, DepCORDS files. Clayton McManaway, head of the CORDS planning staff, coordinated the work of the various task forces.

6. Memo, Komer to Bunker, sub: Performance of GVN Officials During the Tet Offensive, 29 March 1968, DepCORDS files. See Chapter 8 for a fuller discussion of the question of American leverage. To carry out programs in the field, the Central Recovery Committee established subordinate committees at corps, province, and district that included both the South Vietnamese corps commanders and the U.S. Army Field Force commanders. Those committees, like the central one, brought together officials from civilian agencies and the military (MACV, *Command History, 1968*, vol. 1, pp. 536–537).

7. Memo, MACCORDS-PP to DepCORDS and province advisers, sub: 1968 Pacification Planning, Project Recovery, Emergency Use of Resources, 2 March 1968, copy in CMH.

8. MFR, sub: Project Recovery, 19 February 1968; memo, Montague to Komer, 19 February 1968; and memo, ACS, CORDS to assistant DepCORDS, sub: Availability for Provincial Use, 8 February 1968, all in DepCORDS files.

9. "Interview, Komer," p. 83; and Wiesner, *Victims and Survivors*, p. 163.

10. Msg., COMUSMACV to corps senior advisers, Saigon 04586, 131517Z February 1968, DepCORDS files.

11. Msg., Saigon 17601, 3 February 1968, 031135Z, copy in CMH.

12. Msg., Saigon 18269, 6 February 1968; ltr., Komer to Ky, 4 February 1968; ltr. of transmittal, Vann to ACS, CORDS, 7 February 1968; memo, Komer to Cang, 9 February 1968; memo, Lathram to Forsythe, sub: Commercial Operations, 10 February 1968; memo, Forsythe to Thang, 17 February 1968; DF, J-4 to chief of staff, sub: Status of POL Support of Project Recovery, 16 February 1968; memo, Komer to Westmoreland, sub: Reducing and Standardizing Curfews, 20 February 1968; and memo, Komer to Westmoreland, 25 February 1968, all in DepCORDS files.

13. Memo, Vann to ACS, CORDS, sub: High Impact Assistance to Victims of the VC Tet Campaign, 7 February 1968; memo, Montague to Forsythe, same subject, 10 February 1968; memo, Komer to Bunker, sub: Project Recovery Losing Steam, 22 February 1968, all in DepCORDS files; and "Interview, Komer," p. 83.

14. MACV, *Command History, 1968*, pp. 539–540; handwritten notes, Komer, CRC meeting, 15 February 1968; memo, Komer to Bunker, sub: Project Recovery Losing Steam, 22 February 1968; and ltr., Komer to Ky, 22 February 1968, all three in DepCORDS files.

15. Msg., Bunker to Rusk, 151113Z March 1968; msg., Bunker to Rusk, Saigon 24247, 0612001 April 1968; MFR, sub: Conversation with Ngoc, 20 April 1968; memo, Lansdale to Bunker, 19 April 1968; and msg., Bunker to the president, 23 April 1968, all in CMH.

16. Field overviews, CORDS, May, I, II, III, and IV Corps; msg., Komer to Cushman, MAC 6462, 17 May 1968; and msg., Komer to Cross, MAC 6215, May 1968, all in CMH.

17. Memo, special assistant to the ambassador to the deputy ambassador, sub: Damage Assessment and Public Reactions, 12 May 1968; memo, Komer to Westmoreland, sub: Popular Reaction; and memo, Mason, executive secretary, IV Corps, to Montague, sub: Assessment of Recent Incidents on Pacification, 12 May 1968, all in DepCORDS files.

18. MACV, *Command History, 1968*, pp. 132, 540.

19. Msg., Saigon 27133, sub: Project Recovery Situation Report as of 12 May 1968, dated 13 May 1968, DepCORDS files.

20. Msg., Saigon 27133, CMH.

21. MACV, *Command History, 1968*, pp. 675–676, 542.

22. For a full account of this point, see Braestrup, *The Big Story.*

23. MFR, sub: Conversation with Thieu, 15 March 1968, DepCORDS files.

24. MFR, Forsythe, sub: Trip with President Thieu to Hue, 9 March 1968, DepCORDS files.

25. Msg., Westmoreland to all PSAs, 12105Z March 1968; and talking paper, Komer to Weyand, 8 March 1968, both in DepCORDS files.

26. Since Vietnam is approximately twelve hours ahead of Washington time, the conference occurred before Johnson announced on television that he would not seek reelection.

27. MFR, commanders' conference, 31 March 1968, CMH.

28. MFR, commanders' conference, 19 May 1968; memo, U.S. Embassy, sub: Status of VC Liberation Committees as of Mid-June, 16 June 1968; msg., Bunker to Rusk, Saigon 29468, 080910Z June 1968, all three in CMH; and Pike, *War*, pp. 18–32.

29. Ltr., Komer to Rostow, 28 May 1968; and memo, Komer to Bunker, sub: The Washington Scene and What to Do Next, 8 April 1968, both in DepCORDS files.

30. Quoted in memo, Clifford to the president, sub: Trip to SVN, 13–18 July 1968, dated 18 July 1968, copy in Westmoreland's Papers.

31. MFR, commanders' conference, 20 July 1968, CMH.

32. General Westmoreland left South Vietnam at the end of June to become army chief of staff. Although this reassignment had been in the offing since the previous fall, his departure, so soon after the Tet attacks, seemed hardly a coincidence. In March, he had been rebuffed on the issue of additional troops, and his entire strategy for conducting the war had been discredited by influential members of the president's inner circle.

33. The reasons and the timing of Westmoreland's departure were not altogther clear. Lewis Sorley's biography of Abrams *Thunderbolt, from the Battle of the Bulge to Vietnam and Beyond: General Creighton Abrams and the Army of His Times* (New York: Simon and Schuster, 1992), pp. 194–196, claimed that Abrams went to South Vietnam specifically to replace Westmoreland as commander but did not know why the president waited fourteen months to do it. Westmoreland in his memoir, *A Soldier Reports*, pp. 361–362, downplayed any connection with Tet, noting that he had discussed a new assignment with Wheeler in November 1967. The president, however, notified Westmoreland of his selection as chief of staff in March 1968.

34. Estimate of enemy offensive, Abrams, 6 September 1968, CMH.

35. Field Overviews, CORDS, August and September 1968, CMH.

36. Memo, Montague to Komer, 28 September 1968, DepCORDS files.

37. Msg., Bunker to Rusk, 15 March 1968, Saigon 22205, 151113Z March 1968, CMH. For more information on mobilization, see Clarke, *Advice and Support*.

38. Komer specifically asked President Johnson to appoint Colby as deputy (Colby, *Lost Victory*, p. 221).

39. Decree, 280-a/TT/SL, 1 July 1968, CMH. Colby became the ACS, CORDS in March 1968. See Chapter 7 for the origins of the Phoenix program.

40. Memo, Parker to Komer, sub: I Corps Phung Hoang Developments, 22 May 1968; memo, Parker to Komer, sub: Misc. Notes on Current Activities, 26 February 1968; rpt., sub: Survey—Recent GVN Actions; and memo, Vann to Komer sub: Attack on the VCI, 5 March 1968, all in DepCORDS files.

41. Standard operating procedure 1, 23 July 1968; decree, 280-a/TT/SL; and ltr., Khiem to Komer, sub: Comments on Phoenix Committee and DIOCC, 28 June 1968, all in DepCORDS files.

42. Decree, 280-a/TT/SL; and ltr., Khiem to Komer, 28 June 1968.

43. Category A included all persons who belonged to the People's Revolutionary Party and exercised command or leadership positions. Category B comprised all trained communist cadres who did not hold significant positions but were capable of doing so. Category C covered all persons engaging in activities beneficial to the communists who were

not counted in categories A or B. See memo, Gould, legal adviser, to Colby, sub: Classification Guidelines, 12 November 1968, DepCORDS files.

44. Phoenix memo, MACV, 1, sub: Missions and Functions of the Phoenix Staff, 20 May 1968, DepCORDS files. The Phoenix staff was prohibited from managing order-of-battle intelligence or infringing on CIA intelligence activities.

45. "Interview, Komer," p. 220,

46. For more details on the buildup of the South Vietnamese military, see Clarke, *Advice and Support*.

47. Memo, Komer to chief of staff, 31 July 1968, DepCORDS files. CORDS had to beat back army proponents of conventional military forces who opposed building up the territorial forces during July and September. See memo, Komer to Abrams, 4 September 1968; and DF, J3 to MACV chief of staff, sub: Review of Goals in AB 143, 1 September 1968, both in DepCORDS files.

48. Memos, Komer to Bunker, 15 August 1968 and 21 August 1968, DepCORDS files; and DF, MACJ03, sub: J-3 Historical Summary, August 1968, dated 21 September 1968, CMH.

49. Memo, Montague to Maynard, 3 September 1968; and memo, all members of the Mission Council, sub: Liberation Committees, 26 August 1968, both in DepCORDS files.

50. Memo, Komer to Abrams, 15 September 1968, DepCORDS files. The question was hardly phrased objectively.

51. MFR, MACV commanders' conference, 20 September 1968; and rpt., Colby, sub: Proposal for a Counteroffensive, which he drafted and delivered at the conference, both in CMH.

52. Ibid.

53. MFR, MACV commanders' conference, 20 September 1968.

54. Memo, Komer to Abrams, sub: Counteroffensive, 27 September 1968, DepCORDS files.

55. Msg., Bunker to Rusk, sub: Pacification Counteroffensive—Joint Meeting with GVN, 1 October, dated 2 October 1968, DepCORDS files. See also "Interview, Komer," pp. 86–88.

56. Msg., COMUSMACV to senior commanders, MAC 3580, sub: Operational Guidance, 4th Quarter, 2 October 1968, DepCORDS files. Colby drafted this message.

57. Memo, Komer to Abrams, 3 October 1968; and memo, Komer to La, sub: Feasibility Study for APC, 3 October 1968, both in DepCORDS files.

58. Rpt., Vien to Thieu, 9 October 1968, DepCORDS files.

59. Msg., MACV chief of staff to commanding generals and senior advisors of corps tactical zones, 12 October 1968, DepCORDS files.

60. MACCORDS guidelines for using the PSDF in the APC; rpt., MACCORDS to minister of the interior, 4 October 1968; and msg., MACV chief of staff to corps senior advisors, 180319Z October 1968, all in DepCORDS files.

61. Directive, chief JGS to corps commanders, 13–14 October 1968. *Neutralize* was the official term denoting death, wounding, defection, or apprehension of infrastructure members.

62. Memo, Montague to Komer, 20 October 1968; and memo, Montague to Quang, both in DepCORDS files.

63. Msg., CRDC to RD councils at corps and province, 25 October 1968, DepCORDS files. When Eckhardt alerted Komer to the mixup, he consulted General Quang, who reaf-

firmed the second option (msg., Eckhardt to Komer, 251240Z October 1968, DepCORDS files).

64. MFR, sub: Meeting of Komer and Minister Dao, 21 October 1968, DepCORDS files. McManaway reiterated the same proposal several days later (MFR, sub: Meeting of McManaway and Minister Dao, 25 October 1968, DepCORDS files).

65. Ltr., W. Bundy to Berger, 7 October 1968, CMH.

66. Msg., Saigon 39602, 061200Z October 1968; and ltr., Komer to Grant, 19 October 1968, DepCORDS files.

67. Komer, talking paper.

68. Memo, Colby to MACCORDS, sub: Planning memo 807—Special Pacification Campaign, 23 October 1968, DepCORDS files.

69. Memo, Komer to MACV chief of staff, sub: Draft on the Counteroffensive, 24 October 1968, DepCORDS files.

Chapter 11

1. Msg., Abrams to senior commanders, MAC 14143, 20032Z October 1968, Abrams Papers; msg., Abrams to senior commanders, MAC 14710, 1 November 1968, LBJ Library, NSF, Rostow Memos, vol. 103; msg., Rostow to the president, CAP 82681, 4 November 1968, LBJ Library, NSF, Rostow Memos, vol. 103 (this message relayed Abrams's guidance); and msg., Abrams to Wheeler, MAC 14936, 6 November 1968, Abrams Papers.

2. Msg., Abrams to Wheeler, MAC 14329, 24 October 1968, LBJ Library, NSF, Rostow Memos, vol. 101. In mid-November, the 1st Cavalry Division redeployed to III Corps. The Republic of Korea was one of several countries allied to South Vietnam that sent combat forces to help Saigon fight the communists. The other nations were Australia, New Zealand, and Thailand. For more information on this aspect of the war, see Stanley Larsen and James Collins, *Allied Participation in Vietnam* (Washington, D.C.: Department of the Army, 1975).

3. Ibid.; and memo, Montague to Colby, sub: Talking Points for Meeting with President Thieu, December 1968, DepCORDS files.

4. This was the finding of the South Vietnam Special Studies Group indicator, a Washington-based evaluation derived from field data. Most officials considered it a more conservative estimate of population security than the HES. MACCORDS-Eval, APC Sitrep 18, Thua Thien province, 021200 December 1968, CMH.

5. Msg., Stilwell to Abrams, PHB 1365, 132024Z September 1968, Abrams-MACV Papers; and Tolson, *Airmobility*, pp. 205–206. The South Vietnamese called the operation Lam Son 260.

6. CORDS, corps overview, I CTZ, December 1968, CMH files.

7. John J. Tolson, *Airmobility* (Washington, D.C.: GPO, 1973), p. 206; and Hay, *Tactical and Matériel Innovations*, pp. 163–168.

8. After action rpt. (AAR), Hq, 2d Brigade, 101st Airborne Division, sub: Combat After Action Report, Operation Vinh Loc, 30 October 1968, CMH.

9. Tolson, *Airmobility*, pp. 208, 209; and msg., Stilwell to Abrams, September 1968.

10. Province study, VSSG, Quang Nam, CMH. See also F. J. West, Jr., "U.S. Strategy and Policy: The Danang Case" (Santa Monica, Calif.: Rand, 1968), CMH.

11. MACCORDS-Eval, APC SITREP 28, Dien Ban district, Quang Nam, 170022 December 1968. CMH.

12. Memo, Wetherill to senior advisor, I CTZ, CG III MAF, sub: Trip Report, 15 November 1968, DepCORDS files.

13. Unless otherwise stated, information on the operation comes from the following sources: MACV, *Command History, 1968*, pp. 383–384; msg., Hq., III MAF to MACV, 23084Z November 1968; and msg., COMUSMACV to CINCPAC, sub: Phoenix Spot Report, MAC 40576, 080100Z December 1968, both in CMH.

14. See memo, National Police Field Force advisor, Quang Nam, to province adviser, Quang Nam, sub: Operation Meade River, 2 December 1968, CMH files.

15. Msg., Abrams to Cushman, MAC 42600, 190900Z December 1968; and msg., Cushman to Abrams, sub: Meade River Follow-on, 231602Z December 1968, both DepCORDS files.

16. Province study, VSSG, Quang Nam; West, "U.S. Strategy"; and memo, Colby to Chief of Staff, 1 December 1969, CMH.

17. Memo, Colby to ACS CORDS, 19 January 1969, DepCORDS files; DF, ACS, CORDS to C/S, sub: Meade River Follow-on, 4 March 1969, DepCORDS files; and memo, Parker, Quang Nam province adviser, to DepCORDS, III MAF, sub: Current Evaluation of 2d ROKMC Brigade, CMH.

18. Larsen and Collins, *Allied Participation*, Chap. 6; memo, Colby to Townsend, sub: ROK TAOR, 22 December 1968, DepCORDS files; msg., Peers to Abrams, 091145Z December 1968, Abrams Papers; and memo, Colby to Corcoran, MACV C/S, 16 January 1969, CMH.

19. Rpt., AVFA-CG-OT, HQ, IFFV, sub: Operational Report Lessons Learned for the Quarter Ending 31 January 1969, dated 28 February 1969, pp. 1, 11, WNRC.

20. Msg., Corcoran to Abrams, NHT 0610, 141430Z April 1969, DepCORDS files.

21. Msg., CG I Field Force South Vietnam to COMUSMACV, 150320Z November 1968; and memo, Montague to regional DepCORDS, sub: Critique and Evaluation of APC in II Corps, 29 March 1969, both in CMH.

22. Rpt., AVDDH-GC-MH, HQ 4th Infantry Division, sub: Operational Report Lessons Learned for Period Ending 31 January 1969, dated 15 February 1969, pp. 1, 11, CMH.

23. Senior officer debriefing rpt., Stone, CG, 4th Infantry Division, 4 January–30 November 1968, dated 15 November 1968, pp. 1–3, 17, CMH.

24. Ibid., pp. 4–5, 36; Martin Blumenson and James L. Stokesbury, *Masters of the Art of Command* (New York: Da Capo Press, 1990), p. 354.

25. Memo, to regional DepCORDS, sub: Critique and Evaluation of APC in II Corps, 20 March 1969; msg., Peers to Abrams, 091145Z December 1968; rpt., MACCORDS-Eval, sub: Evaluation of ROK Army Involvement in the APC, 1 January 1969; and memo, Wetherill to senior adviser, II CTZ, sub: Trip Report, 18–20 November 1968, dated 24 November 1968, all in DepCORDS files. See also senior officer debriefing rpt., I Field Force commanders, Collins, March 1971, Peers, 7 June 1969, and Brown, 14 May 1971, CMH. Larsen and Collins, *Allied Participation*, pp. 134–35, 146, 159, assessed the South Korean role.

26. Larsen and Collins, *Allied Participation*, pp. 151–154.

27. Ibid., pp. 157–159; and ltr., AVFA-CG, Peers to COMUSMACV, 15 December 1968, DepCORDS files.

28. Memo, chief evaluation branch to ACS, CORDS, 4 January 1969, DepCORDS files.

29. Ltr., Peers to Komer, sub: Command Relations, 30 August 1968, DepCORDS files.

30. Msg., Peers to Abrams, NHT 1329, 150530Z September 1968, Abrams Papers.

31. Ltr., Peers to Abrams, 29 December 1968, DepCORDS files.

32. Directive, MACV, 10-12, sub: Organization and Functions for CORDS, 28 May 1967, CMH; emphasis added.

33. For insight into the tense relations between Abrams and Komer, see Kerwin, senior officer oral history transcript, 1980, pp. 350–354, MHI.

34. Ltr., Montague to Komer, 1 May 1969, Montague Papers, MHI.

35. Ibid.; and ltr., Peers to Wetherill, 29 December 1968, DepCORDS files.

36. Ltr., Colby to Peers, 12 February 1969; and ltr., Peers to Colby, 2 March 1969, both in DepCORDS files.

37. CORDS, overview, II Corps, 13 November 1968; overview, II Corps, 13 January 1969; msg., Luan to II CTZ commander, 24 December 1968, 977/V2CT/BDXD/BTV/NG, all three in CMH; and talking points, MACJO1R, for Thieu, December 1968, DepCORDS files.

38. MACJO1R, APC Sitrep 19, 061500 December 1968; and memo, Colby to ACS, CORDS, sub: Evaluation of APC in II Corps, 6 December 1968, both in CMH.

39. Memo, sub: Province Senior Advisors' Conference, 14–15 December 1968, dated 6 January 1969, CMH.

40. Ibid.

41. Rpt., CORDS, I Field Force South Vietnam, sub: Critique and Evaluation of II Corps APC, 17 March 1969, CMH.

42. CORDS, corps overview, 14 January 1969, CMH; memo, Montague to Colby, sub: Talking Points for Colby to Raise with President Thieu, December 1968; and msg., DepCORDS IV Corps to COMUSMACV, 031634Z December 1968, both in DepCORDS files.

43. CORDS, corps overview, 14 December 1968; and memo, HQ II FFV, to COMUSMACV, sub: Forces in Support of APC Hamlets, 28 December 1968, both in CMH.

44. Msg., Abrams to Wheeler, MAC 14329, 24 October 1968, Abrams Papers.

45. Memo, Mehaffey, USMC, Dep ACS, CORDS, to Colby, sub: APC Summary Extracts from Province Reports for November 1968, 16 December 1968; and memo, AVFBG-PPR, to COMUSMACV, sub: Forces in Support of APC Hamlets and Related Matters, 28 December 1968, both in DepCORDS files.

46. Memo, OCO, for Komer, sub: Binh Chanh, 24 May 1967, CMH.

47. Ibid., and PPG 4, pp. 512, 513.

48. Field survey rpt., CORDS Rural Technical Team, sub: The APC in Binh Chanh District, 23 January 1969, DepCORDS files.

49. Michael E. Pearce, *Evolution of a Vietnamese Village* RM 4552-M (Santa Monica, Calif.: Rand, April 1965), p. 4. See also memo, Komer to Forsythe, 25 June 1967, CMH. See Chapter 8 for details on the Chinh-Hunnicutt affair.

50. Msg., province senior adviser, Hau Nghia, to ACS, CORDS, 241645Z February 1968; msg., Saigon 20451, sub: Hau Nghia Province, April 1968, 10 April 1968; and rpt., MACCORDS-RE, sub: A Study of Pacification and Security in Cu Chi District, 29 May 1968, Cook and Pabst, III CTZ field evaluators, all in CMH.

51. Msg., province adviser, Hau Nghia, to DepCORDS, III CTZ, 190445Z May 1968, CMH; memo, Montague to Forsythe and Komer, sub: Pacification in Hau Nghia, 27 May 1968; and memo, Komer to PSA, Hau Nghia, 30 May 1968, in DepCORDS files.

52. Memos, Komer to DepCORDS, III CTZ, 19 July, 19 August, and 8 September 1968, CMH; rpt., MACCORDS, sub: Provincial Administration in Hau Nghia, 17 August 1968, CMH; author interview with Michael Lynch, commander of 2d Brigade, 25th Infantry Di-

vision from September 1968 to February 1969, Washington, D.C., 24 April 1975; ltr., Meyers, Deputy PSA, Hau Nghia, CMH; memo, Bernard to Komer, sub: Intelligence Program in Hau Nghia, 13 July 1968, CMH; rpt., province adviser, November 1968; and memo, Wetherill to senior advisor, III CTZ, sub: Observations During Visits to Tay Ninh and Hau Nghia, 27 November 1968, DepCORDS files.

53. Rpt., MACCORDS, sub: A Study of Pacification and Security in Cu Chi District, Hau Nhgia, 29 May 1968, CMH.

54. Operational rpt. lessons learned (ORLL), 25th Infantry Division, 1 November 1968–31 January 1969, dated 1 February 1969, WNRC; and rpt., MACCORDS-Eval, sub: Evaluation of Pacification Techniques of the 2d Brigade, U.S. 25th Infantry Division, 20 December 1968, Pfeiffer, III CTZ field evaluator, CMH.

55. Memo Montague to Cushing, sub: Phuoc Tuy, 31 March 1969, CMH; and memo, to COMUSMACV, 28 December 1968.

56. Memo, Wetherill to senior adviser, III CTZ, sub: Observations During Visits to Tay Ninh and Hau Hghia, 27 November 1968, DepCORDS files.

57. Rpts., province senior adviser, Hau Nghia, November 1968 and January 1969, CMH.

58. Memo, HQ 25th Infantry Division, sub: Upgrading of Hamlets to GVN Control, 16 December 1968; and memo, Montague to Colby, sub: 25th Division Problems, 23 December 1968, both in DepCORDS files.

59. Author interview with Williamson, Arlington, Virginia, April 1975; rpt., MACCORDS-Eval, 20 December 1968; David Hoffman, "Pacification: Merely a 'Numbers Game'?" *New York Times,* 28 January 1969, p. A12; and MFR, MACCORDS-PP&P, sub: Visit to the 25th Infantry Division, 24 March 1969, CMH.

60. Memo, Montague to Colby, 14 January 1969, CMH; and author interview, with Lynch, Washington, D.C., 24 April 1975.

61. Msg., Wetherill to Freund, SACSA, 30 January 1969, CMH.

62. Hoffman, "Pacification," *New York Times* and msg., U.S. Embassy to State Department, sub: Political Development in III CTZ, 10 February 1969, DepCORDS files.

63. Arno Ponder, "Trang Bang," *Army* (January 1976): 34–35.

64. Msg., USARV to DA, sub: Congressional Inquiry—25th Infantry Division, 021008Z June 1969, CMH; and Roger Williams, "Pacification in South Vietnam" *Ramparts* (May 1969): 22.

65. ORLL, 25th Infantry Division, 1 November 1968–31 January 1969, dated 1 February 1969, CMH.

66. Memo, Davidson, district senior adviser, Trang Bang, to Bernard, sub: Operation in An Thinh, 9 December 1968, CMH.

67. Bergerud, *The Dynamics of Defeat*, p. 234. Bergerud offered incisive analysis of the impact of the APC in Hau Nghia.

68. Msg., USARPAC to DA, June 1969; and Williams, "Pacification."

69. Rpt., province senior adviser, Hau Nghia, January 1969, CMH.

70. Ibid.

71. Bergerud, *The Dynamics of Defeat*, pp. 237–239.

72. ORLL; 9th Infantry Division, 1 November 1968–31 January 1969, dated 15 February 1969, WNRC 70A 1436/3.

73. Memo, MACCORDS-RE, sub: Operation of the U.S. 9th Division in Dinh Tuong, 25 June 1968, CMH. Quotes are from memo, HQ, II FFV, sub: Impressions of a Division Commander in Vietnam, March 1969, CMH. General Ewell wrote this memo after he assumed command of II Field Force.

74. Julian Ewell, and Ira Hunt, *Sharpening the Combat Edge: The Use of Analysis to Reinforce Military Judgment* (Washington, D.C.: Department of the Army, 1974), pp. 190, 194.

75. ORLL, 9th Infantry Division, 1 November 1968–31 January 1969.

76. Ewell and Hunt spelled out their conception in *Sharpening the Combat Edge*, pp. 160–161, 164.

77. Memo, MACCORDS-RE, to Chief Reports and Evaluation Division, sub: Operation of the U.S. 9th Division in Dinh Tuong, 25 June 1968, copy in CMH. Cf. Ewell and Hunt, *Sharpening the Combat Edge*, Chaps. 4, 6, 8, 11.

78. Kevin Buckley, "Pacification's Deadly Price," *Newsweek*, June 19, 1972, pp. 42–43; rpt., MACCORDS-PSG, sub: Impact of the Redeployment of the U.S. 9th Division from Dinh Tuong and Kien Hoa, 3 August 1969, CMH; Ewell and Hunt, *Sharpening the Combat Edge*, p. 152; rpt., MACCORDS-PSG, sub: Attitudes of the Vietnamese in Dinh Tuong and Kien Hoa Provinces Toward the U.S. 9th Division Relocation, 22 October 1969, CMH; and memo, Colby to Abrams, 13 December 1969, DepCORDS files. The memo referred to a translation of an article on the 9th Division that had appeared in a South Vietnamese newspaper on 2 December 1969.

79. Province rpt., Kien Hoa, December, 1968, CMH.

80. Unless otherwise stated, information on Kien Hoa comes from the Briefing Folders for Kien Hoa and the Kien Hoa Province Study prepared for the VSSG province study, CMH.

81. Rpt., Kien Hoa, province senior adviser, January 1969, CMH.

82. Province study, VSSG, Kien Hoa, CMH. These figures are the VSSG indicators, which were derived from the HES.

83. Cease-fire paper, VSSG, Dinh Tuong, 16 April 1970; and province study, VSSG, Dinh Tuong, both in CMH.

84. Rpt., MACCORDS-Eval, sub: RF/PF in Dinh Tuong, 12 July 1968, CMH.

85. Rpts., province senior adviser, Dinh Tuong, November 1968–January 1969, CMH; and province study, Kien Hoa.

86. The analysis of ARVN support is based on a CORDS rpt., sub: Evaluation of ARVN Support of Pacification in IV CTZ, 12 December 1968, CMH.

87. Rpt., province senior adviser, Dinh Tuong, January 1969, CMH, contained Amos's remarks. See also province study, VSSG, Dinh Tuong, and APC Sitrep, 23, 17 December 1968, both in CMH.

88. Ibid.

89. Ltr., Komer to Dao, minister of state, 22 October 1968, DepCORDS files.

90. Rpt., sub: CORDS Overview for IV Corps for Month Ending January 1969, CMH.

91. Ltr., Wilson to Komer, sub: Current Assessment of 1968 RD Program, 27 September 1968; and U.S. Embassy airgram A-17, sub: Political Development in IV Corps, 21 January 1968, both in CMH.

92. *Southeast Asia Analysis Report* (February 1969); 40, CMH. See Chapters 11 and 12 for a detailed treatment of U.S. Army support of the APC.

93. *Southeast Asia Analysis Report* (June 1969): 33–35.

Chapter 12

1. Rpt., MACV commanders' conference, 11 January 1969, CMH.

2. Meaningful talks seemed likely on October 31 when President Johnson announced the cessation of all air, naval, and artillery bombardment of North Vietnam in the expecta-

tion of imminent, substantive negotiations among the United States, North Vietnam, South Vietnam, and the National Liberation Front.

3. Memo, Komer to Thieu, Bunker, Abrams, and Colby, 5 November 1968, DepCORDS files. Thieu's decision increased his support among the South Vietnamese, who feared that the Americans might abandon South Vietnam.

4. Memo, Ruhr to McManaway, sub: Secure Target Hamlets Selected for APC, 12 November 1968, DepCORDS files.

5. Memo, Colby to ACS, CORDS, 19 December 1968, DepCORDS files.

6. Msg., Central Pacification and Development Council to all provinces, 050/PTHT/BDXD, 10 January 1969, DepCORDS files.

7. Memo, Colby to ACS, CORDS, sub: APC Dinh Tuong, 28 January 1969, DepCORDS files.

8. Memo, Colby to ACS, CORDS, sub: Province Chief Use of Obsolete Hamlets, 10 January 1969, DepCORDS files.

9. Ltr., Colby to Lac, 14 November 1968, DepCORDS files.

10. Msg., minister of revolutionary development to Corps Pacification and Development Councils, 2411 XD/31/CD, 25 November 1968, DepCORDS files.

11. Directive, Thieu to prime minister and deputy ministers, prefects, province chiefs, and mayors, sub: Changes in the Utilization of the Terms ABCDE and V Hamlets or Areas, 098/T.T, 16 January 1969, DepCORDS files.

12. Ltr., Colby to Thieu, 2 February 1969, CMH.

13. MFR, sub: Briefing for COMUSMACV on MACV Joint Strategic Objectives Plan, 23 November 1968, chief, Long-Range Planning Task Group, CMH. Abrams's words were paraphrased in this document.

14. Memo, Wetherill to Goodpaster, sub: Optimum Coordinated Use of ARVN Resources, 30 November 1968, DepCORDS files.

15. William Colby and Peter Forbath, *Honorable Men: My Life in the CIA* (New York: Simon and Schuster, 1978), p. 261.

16. Colby, *Lost Victory,* p. 256.

17. *Southeast Asia Analysis Report* (February 1969): 34–37, CMH.

18. DF, ACS, CORDS, to MACV chief of staff, sub: Profile of APC Hamlets, 18 January 1969, CMH.

19. Summary of APC, MACCORDS, 1 November–31 January, dated 28 February 1969; MACCORDS-Eval, sub: Accelerated Pacification Campaign Sitrep 27, 22170 December 1968, both in CMH; and MACV, *Command History, 1969,* vol. 2, p. viii-6.

20. Msg., COMUSMACV to CINCPAC, sub: Accelerated Pacification Campaign Wrap-Up, 120440Z February 1969; memo, MACCORDS, to Quang, sub: Information for the President's Press Conference, 6 February 1969, both in CMH; and summary of APC, MACCORDS, 1 November–31 January.

21. Gabriel Kolko, *Anatomy of a War* (New York: Pantheon Books, 1985), p. 330.

22. MACCORDS-Eval, December 1968.

23. Msg., Bunker to Rusk, 1612000Z January 1969, DepCORDS files. Nevertheless, the government had to do more. Appointed officials outnumbered elected ones in the APC hamlets, and a great number of hamlets not specifically targeted in the campaign were devoid of local officials loyal to Saigon.

24. Msg., Abrams to corps senior advisers, 241018Z November 1968; msg., COMUSMACV to CINCPAC, sub: Pacification in SVN, 16–22 November 1968, 261130Z November 1968; and memo, Colby to MACV C/S, sub: Enemy Counteraction to the APC, 29 January 1969, all in DepCORDS files.

25. *Southeast Asia Analysis Report* (February 1969): 38; and MACCORDS-Eval, December 1968.

26. Msg., Abrams to senior advisers, 2410187Z November 1968, copy in DepCORDS files.

27. Duiker, *The Communist Road to Power*, pp. 269, 277; and Kolko, *Anatomy of a War*, pp. 329–330.

28. Kolko, *Anatomy of a War*, pp. 371–373. Kolko made extensive use of North Vietnamese oral and written sources.

29. Tran Van Tra, *History of the Bulwark B-2 Theater*, vol. 5, *Concluding the 30-Years War*, Southeast Asia Report 1247 (JPRS, February 2, 1983), pp. 35–36.

30. Duiker, *The Communist Road to Power*, pp. 270, 274.

31. Rpt., sub: Profile of the VC Liberation Committees Identifiable in the HES (as of 15 January 1969), DepCORDS files; and *Southeast Asia Analysis Report* (June 1969): 35–36, CMH.

32. See also Robert Thompson, *Peace Is Not at Hand* (New York: David McKay, 1974), pp. 61–72.

33. Ltr., Colby to Seigneous, military representative at Paris, 3 January 1969; memo, Colby to C/S MACV, sub: Information for Paris, 14 November 1968, both in DepCORDS files; and memo, Colby to ACS, CORDS, sub: Population Control, 15 November 1968, CMH.

34. Msg., Colby to Rostow, 22 November 1968, CMH.

35. Msg., Rostow to Colby, 22 November 1968, DepCORDS files; and memo, Rostow to the president, 25 November 1968, LBJ Library, NSF, vol. 60.

36. Msg., Bunker to the president, 161200Z January 1969, CMH.

37. Msg., Freund, SACSA, to Colby, JCS 03461, 2012148Z March 1969; and memo, Montague to Colby, sub: Pacification Status, 16 January 1969, both in CMH. The latter memo discussed the ISA evaluation that discredited 1968 pacification gains.

38. Msg., Freund to Colby, March 1969.

39. Msg., Abrams to JCS, MAC 509, 13 January 1969, CMH.

40. Summary and evaluation of enemy post–Tet Offensive, 1969; and msg., COMUSMACV to CINCPAC, sub: Effect of Current Enemy Attacks on the GVN Overall Pacification Program, 040320Z March 1969, CMH.

41. Rpt., CIA, sub: Viet Cong Reaction to APC and Phoenix, 12 May 1969, CMH.

42. See, for example, John V. Tunney, "Measuring Hamlet Security in Vietnam," Report to the House of Representatives, 91st Cong., 1st sess. (Washington, D.C.: GPO, 1969). See also Thayer, *War Without Fronts*, pp. 145–152; and Albert C. Bole Jr. and K. Kobata, "An Evaluation of the Measurements of the Hamlet Evaluation System," (Naval War College Center for Advanced Research, Newport, R.I., 1975) for a discussion of the validity of HES.

43. Bernard Weinraub, "Saigon's Authority Believed to Be in Critical Stage," *New York Times*, 11 February 1968; Weinraub, "U.S. Admits Blow to Pacification," *New York Times*, 25 February 1968; Ward Just, "Guerrillas Wreck Pacification," *Wasthington Post*, 4 February 1968; Lee Lescaze, "Saigon Is Returning to Normal Pattern," *Washington Post*, 9 February 1968; and MFR, Ellsberg, sub: Impact of the VC Winter-Spring Offensive, 28 February 1968, CMH, used HES data as evidence for their pessimism about the fate of pacification after the Tet Offensive.

44. Thayer, *War Without Fronts*, p. 144.

45. Colby, *Lost Victory*, p. 259.

46. Ibid., p. 225.

47. Ibid., p. 271.

Chapter 13

1. For an account of the origin of the term *Vietnamization,* see Henry Kissinger, *White House Years* (Boston: Little, Brown, 1979), pp. 270–273.

2. For a discussion of NSSM 1, see Clarke, *Advice and Support,* pp. 341–346.

3. See the responses to questions 5–10 of NSSM 1 for a fuller critique of the attrition strategy (NSSM 1, Kissinger to secretary of state, secretary of defense, and director of Central Intelligence, sub: The Situation in Vietnam, 20 January 1969, CMH). A number of these conclusion were further developed by the Department of Defense's Systems Analysis Office and were later published by Thayer, *War Without Fronts.*

4. Hazel Erskine, "The Polls: Is the War a Mistake?" *Public Opinion Quarterly* 34, no. 1 (Spring 1970): 134–150. On criticism of attrition, see Alain Enthoven and Wayne Smith, *How Much Is Enough?* (New York: Harper and Row, 1971), pp. 298–299.

5. Clarke, *Advice and Support,* pp. 347–348.

6. Ibid., p. 348.

7. Richard Nixon, *The Memoirs of Richard Nixon* (New York: Grosset and Dunlap, 1978), pp. 391–393; and Kissinger, *White House Years,* pp. 272–273.

8. Henry Kissinger, "The Vietnam Negotiations," *Foreign Affairs,* 47, no. 2 (1969): 213.

9. Ibid., pp. 214–215.

10. VSSG also produced two comprehensive studies—"The Situation in the Countryside" (1969) and the "Ceasefire Study" (1970), both in CMH—to help the Nixon administration assess South Vietnam's long-term prospects.

11. Msg., Abrams to McCain, 130945Z October 1968, MAC 13840; and msg., Abrams to regional commanders, 200328Z October 1968, MAC 14143, both in CMH.

12. Davidson, *Vietnam at War,* pp. 571–572.

13. Msg., Abrams to regional commanders, October 1968.

14. Abrams to general officers in South Vietnam, 010158Z November 1968, MAC 14710, CMH.

15. Msg., COMUSMACV to senior advisers, sub: Operational Guidance, 170308Z January 1969, CMH.

16. MFR, sub: MACV Commanders' Conference, 11 January 1969, MACV HIMS Collection, reel 11, MHI.

17. Quoted in MACV, *Command History, 1969,* vol. 2, p. VIII-22.

18. Davidson, *Vietnam at War,* p. 571.

19. Ibid., p. 613. See Chapter 5 for a discussion of the PROVN study.

20. Strategic objectives plan, MACV, copy in CMH. See also Richard Shultz, "The Vietnamization-Pacification Strategy of 1969–1972: A Quantitative and Qualitative Assessment," in *Lessons from an Unconventional War,* ed. Hunt and Shultz, pp. 54–55; and Samuel Lipsman, Edward Doyle, and the editors of Boston Publishing Company, *Fighting for Time* (Boston: Boston Publishing, 1983), p. 54.

21. Quoted in Lipsman et al., *Fighting for Time,* p. 54.

22. Ltr., Zais to Colby, 1 January 1970, CMH.

23. Ltr., Zais to Wright CG, 101st Airborne Division, 18 December 1969, copy in CMH. In the summer of 1969, Zais was promoted to lieutenant general and elevated to com-

mander of the XXIV Corps. Yet Abrams's message to his commanders was not without ambiguity. Abrams praised Ewell for his conduct of Operation SPEEDY EXPRESS, an operation in the delta that resulted in extraordinarily high claims of enemy casualties, and he was promoted to lieutenant general and commander of II Field Force.

24. Msg., Wheeler to McCain, JCS 09134, July 1969, CMH. The message relayed Wheeler's conversation with Defense Secretary Laird.

25. Davidson, *Vietnam at War*, pp. 596–597.

26. Memo, Colby to Goodpaster, 10 March 1969, DepCORDS files.

27. Memo, Komer to Bunker, 3 July 1968; ltr., Komer to Abrams, 28 July 1968; ltr., Komer to Rostow, 30 September 1968, all in DepCORDS files; and msg., Abrams to Wheeler, MAC 3996, 290954Z March 1969, CMH. See also Chapter 11 for an account of Komer's disagreements with General Peers.

28. See the Kerwin interview for an account of this uneasy relationship; and Sorley, *Thunderbolt*, pp. 196–197.

29. Statistics on RF/PF strength come from Thayer, *War Without Fronts*, p. 157. Information on the improvement and modernization program comes from MACV, *Command History, 1969*, pp. 134–135.

30. Ltr., Colby to Thieu, 2 February 1969; and memorandum of conversation, MACJO1R, Thieu and Colby, 9 December 1968, dated 10 December 1968, both in DepCORDS files.

31. Ltr., Colby to Blanchard, director, Vietnam Task Force, 21 March 1970, DepCORDS files.

32. Ltr., Colby to Khiem, 23 December 1968, DepCORDS files; and MFR, sub: Meeting on 15 November 1968 with Minister of Interior Khiem, Ambassador Colby, and Mr. James L. Culpepper, CORDS Liaison Officer, dated 22 November 1968, DepCORDS files.

33. Memo, Warner to Westmoreland, sub: Comments on *The Nature of Revolutionary War*, 3 December 1971, copy in CMH.

34. Memo, Colby to chief, OCO, sub: Problems of Province Teams, 21 October 1968, DepCORDS files.

35. Press interview of Thieu, 25 March 1969; and Lipsman et al., *Fighting for Time*, pp. 31–32.

36. Fact sheet, CORDS, sub: 1969 Pacification and Development, 30 January 1969, CMH. The 1969 pacification and development plan set forth eight major objectives: (1) bring security to 90 percent of the population and extend government control over the entire land; (2) reduce the infrastructure by thirty-three thousand through a combination of Phoenix, *Chieu Hoi*, police, and ARVN operations; (3) establish local government in all villages in the land; (4) organize 2 million persons in the PSDF and arm four hundred thousand; (5) convince twenty thousand members of the Viet Cong to defect; (6) decrease the number of refugees to less than 1 million, and resettle three hundred thousand persons in their home villages; (7) increase the information and propaganda effort; and (8) stimulate the rural economy, including the increase of rice production from 5 to 6 million tons. MACV, *Command History, 1969*, pp. VIII-8–VIII-10; and Colby, *Lost Victory*, p. 277.

37. MACV, *Command History, 1969*, p. VIII-14.

38. See Chapter 15 for a discussion of some military operations that resulted in the forced relocation of South Vietnamese.

39. William S. Turley, *The Second Indochina War* (New York: Mentor, 1987), p. 135.

40. Decree, GVN, 45, sub: Composition and Authority of Village Administrative Committees, 1 April 1969; and fact sheet, MACCORDS-RAD, sub: Local Government, copies of both in CMH.

41. Charles Stuart Callison, *Land to the Tiller in the Mekong Delta* (Boston: University Press of America, 1983), p. 81. Callison provided an extensive analysis of the 1970 land reform.

42. Davidson, *Vietnam at War,* pp. 590–591.

43. For an account of Operation LIBERTY CANYON, the move of the 1st Cavalry Division to III Corps, see Shelby Stanton, *Anatomy of a Division: 1st Cav in Vietnam* (Novato, Calif.: Presidio Press, 1987), Chap. 8.

44. Ibid., pp. 160–167.

45. Msg., Bunker to Nixon, Saigon 5423, 210845Z March 1969; and msg., Bunker to Nixon, Saigon 8757, 6 May 1969, both in CMH.

46. Summary and evaluation of enemy post–Tet Offensive, 1969; and msg., COMUSMACV to CINCPAC, sub: Effect of Current Enemy Attacks on the GVN Overall Pacification Program, 040320Z March 1969, CMH.

47. Captured enemy document, Viet Cong counter-pacification plan, SR 5, COSVN, 12 December 1968, CDEC 6 028 0472 69, CMH.

48. Msg., Abrams to McCain, MAC 5636, 030933Z May 1969, CMH.

49. Resolution, COSVN, 9, Kolko, *Anatomy of a War,* pp. 368–371; and Davidson, *Vietnam at War,* p. 597.

50. Intelligence rpt., CIA, sub: Vietnamization in the Delta—Two Years Later, no. 1714, 28 June 1971, CMH; and Davidson, *Vietnam at War,* p. 610.

51. Memo, Colby to chief of staff, 5 January 1971, DepCORDS files. A report by the Systems Analysis Office in the Defense Department, based on statistical data reported from the field from a variety of official sources and on the reports filed by the provincial senior advisers, is attached. Intelligence rpt., CIA, 28 June 1971; and MACV, *Command History, 1970,* vol. 1, pp. III-185–186.

52. Memo, Colby, 5 January 1971; and intelligence rpt., CIA, 28 June 1971.

53. Field information rpt., CIA, sub: Effects of Pacification on the Viet Cong in Tay Ninh, 11 July 1970, CMH.

54. Rpt., OASD-SA, sub: Terrorism in SVN, 16 October 1972; and memo, Baldwin, director of international and civil affairs, DCSOPS, to chief of staff, sub: Assessment of VC/NVA Assassinations/Abductions/Recruitments in RVN, 27 June 1970, both in CMH.

55. Memo, secretary of defense to secretaries of the military departments, sub: Incidence of Assassinations and Abductions in the Republic of Vietnam, 6 July 1970, CMH.

56. Msg., Abrams to Wheeler, 271124Z March 1969, MAC 3910, Abrams Papers.

Chapter 14

1. Davidson, *Vietnam at War,* p. 614.

2. Sorley, *Thunderbolt,* p. 245.

3. Author interview with Whitehouse, Marshall, Virginia, 10 December 1987. Whitehouse left III Corps in October 1970. Rpt., CORDS-PSG, sub: Effects of the Redeployment of the 1st Infantry Division, 31 March 1970, CMH. The division departed from Vietnam in April 1970.

4. MFR, HQ IFFV, sub: U.S. Commanders' Conference, 28 March 1969, CMH.

5. Personal memoir, Barnes, June 1990, pp. 26–27, CMH.

6. Rpt., MACCORDS-PSG, sub: 173d Airborne Brigade Participation in Pacification in Northern Binh Dinh Province, enclosure 1, comments by Barnes, 28 July 1969, CMH; press briefing, Barnes, sub: Operation WASHINGTON GREEN, 10 October 1969, CMH; and Orr Kelly, "General Tells of Pacification Sucess," *Washington Star,* 11 October 1969. Barnes also briefed the Army Policy Council on the operation on 1 October 1969.

7. Rpt., Pike, sub: Binh Dinh: The Anatomy of a Province, October 1972, p. 7, CMH.

8. Cease-fire study, VSSG, Binh Dinh, 1970, p. 1, CMH.

9. Rpt., MACCORDS-PSG, 28 July 1969, p. 4; and press briefing, Barnes, 10 October 1969.

10. Rpt., MACCORDS-PSG, 28 July 1969, pp. 5–6.

11. Ibid., and AAR, 173d Airborne Brigade, Operation WASHINGTON GREEN, 15 April 1969–31 December 1970, WNRC 319-71A-6880, Box 17.

12. Rpts., province senior adviser, Binh Dinh, April–November 1969, CMH.

13. Memo, IFFV DepCORDS to chief of staff, sub: Pacification in Binh Dinh Province, 27 March 1969, CMH.

14. AAR, Operation WASHINGTON GREEN, p. 17; and press briefing, Barnes, 10 October 1969.

15. Press briefing, Barnes, 10 October 1969; and memo, CIA, Carver to Shepard, regional director, ISA, sub: Pacification in Binh Dinh Province, 22 October 1969, CMH.

16. Rpt., MACCORDS-PSG, 28 July 1969; AAR, Operation WASHINGTON GREEN; and press briefing, Barnes, 10 October 1969.

17. Ltr., Barnes to CG, IFFV, 6 July 1969, CMH.

18. AAR, Operation WASHINGTON GREEN; information rpt., CIA, sub: Summary of Viet Activity in II Corps for the Week Ending 16 May 1970, dated 20 May 1970, CMH; and memo, CIA, sub: Pacification in Binh Dinh.

19. Press briefing, Barnes, 10 October 1969. This copy was incomplete and unsigned. According to Barnes's autobiographical note, he gave the briefing over one hundred times in a sixteen-month period.

20. Memo, U.S. Embassy, sub: Developments in Military Region II During 1970 and Early 1971, 20 July 1971, p. 7, CMH.

21. Rpt. MACCORDS-PSG, 28 July 1969, p. 10.

22. Rpt., province senior adviser, Binh Dinh, December 1970, CMH.

23. Rpt., ACS, CORDS, sub: Status of Pacification, Republic of Vietnam, 19 September 1971, CMH; rpt., Pike, October 1972, p. 9; memo, U.S. Embassy, 20 July 1971; p. 12; memo, CIA, sub: Pacification in Binh Dinh; and rpt., CORDS MR II, sub: Pacification Profiles and HES Summary, 10 February 1972, CMH.

24. RUSSELL BEACH was the code name for the army part of the operation; BOLD MARINER was the tag for the marine portion.

25. Thayer, *War Without Fronts,* p. 116. Over three-fourths of American combat deaths occurred in ten provinces, of which Quang Ngai was one; over one-half the American combat deaths occurred in I Corps.

26. Memo, Jacobson to Rosson, sub: Possible Points, Trip to I CTZ, 1 May 1969, CMH; MACV, *Command History, 1969,* pp. VIII-21–22; and rpt., Fleet Marine Force Pacific, sub: Operation of U.S. Marine Forces, Vietnam, January 1969, USMC Historical Center, Washington, D.C.

27. Wiesner, *Victims and Survivors,* pp. 168–169.

28. ORLL, 23d Division, 1 May–31 July 1969, CMH; and rpt., CORDS, sub: I CTZ Refugee Field Program, 21 November–20 December 1969.

29. Wiesner, *Victims and Survivors*, p. 229.

30. Ibid., p. 230.

31. See Chapter 4 for the treatment of an earlier county fair operation.

32. Details of the operation come from the operational reports of the American units involved, the monthly reports of the province senior adviser, and the reports of Louis Wiesner, head of the CORDS refugee program in I Corps at the time of RUSSELL BEACH, as well as his book on the refugee program in Indochina, *Victims and Survivors*.

33. ORLL, Americal Division, 1 May–31 July 1969; and msg., Saigon to Washington, Saigon 7455, sub: Communist Propaganda, 18 April 1969, both in CMH; Lewy, *America in Vietnam*, pp. 139–140, contained a brief account of the operation.

34. Ltr., Firfer, DepCORDS, I Corps, to Colby, 16 September 1969, DepCORDS files. A report of the activities of the 29th Civil Affairs Company dated 15 September 1969 was attached.

35. ORLL, 23d Division, 1 February–30 April 1969, CMH.

36. Ltr., inspector, social welfare, I CTZ, to minister of social welfare, sub: Living Conditions of the Repatriated People in the Batangan Campaign, Quang Ngai, 23 January 1970; msg., inspector, social welfare, to province chief, Quang Ngai, 73/XH/TT/VI, 28 January 1970; rpt., chief, Refugee Division, III MAF, sub: Shortage of Food on Batangan Peninsula, Quang Ngai, 29 January 1970; and msg., I Corps Headquarters to 2d Infantry Division, 135/BTL/QD/I/VICT, 4 February 1970, all in CMH.

37. Author interview with Wiesner, Washington, D.C., 19 August 1987.

38. Rpt., I Corps, sub: Corps Field Refugee Programs, 21 November–20 December 1969, CMH.

39. Ltr., Jacobson, acting DepCORDS, to Lazar, DepCORDS, I Corps, 11 September 1971, DepCORDS files.

40. Rpt., I Corps CORDS, Refugee Division, 21 March–20 April 1970, CMH. Louis Wiesner wrote the report.

41. Rpt., Fleet Marine Force Pacific, USMC Historical Center.

42. ORLL, 23d Division, 1 February–30 April 1970, CMH.

43. Rpt., province senior adviser, Quang Ngai, January 1971, CMH.

44. Memo, Colby to PSAs, sub: Relocation of Civilians in Province; and memo, prime minister to province chiefs, sub: Relocation of Civilians in Provinces, 1412-PThT/BDPT/KH11, 12 May 1971, both in CMH.

45. Author interview with Cushing, Washington, D.C., 24 November 1987; Wiesner, *Victims and Survivors*, p. 245; rpts., province senior adviser, Quang Ngai, January–October 1971; and MFR, Johnson, chief, CPDC Liaison Group, sub: Action Taken by CPDC/CC to Resolve the Problems Concerning the Relocations of Montagnards and Vietnamese (March–April), 4 May 1971, both in CMH. Cushing was transferred to IV Corps, where he held several assignments and was eventually promoted to deputy consul general. During the summer of 1971, the Americal Division and U.S. Army Engineer units were in the process of withdrawing from Vietnam. By October, they had completed their departure.

46. See Chapter 8 for details.

47. Blaufarb, *The Counterinsurgency Era*, pp. 268–269; Lewy, *America in Vietnam*, p. 138; and Krepinevich, *The Army and Vietnam*, pp. 254–255.

Chapter 15

1. See Chapter 13 for details on these resolutions and Abrams's views.

2. Colby and Forbath, *Honorable Men,* p. 272.

3. I am unaware of any formal survey of Phoenix advisers, but much of the literature written by participants stresses the theme of inefficiency. Wayne L. Cooper, "Operation Phoenix: A Vietnam Fiasco Seen from Within," *Washington Post,* 18 June 1972. Cooper was a Foreign Service officer who spent eighteen months in Vietnam, mostly as a Phoenix adviser in Can Tho. Stuart Herrington, *Silence Was a Weapon* (New York: Ivy Books, 1987). Herrington served as a district adviser and was closely associated with Phoenix. Memo, Stofft, field evaluator, to chief, Pacification Studies Group, sub: General Observation, Vinh Long, 18 February 1972, DepCORDS files. Robert S. Hallock, Phoenix adviser, Gio Linh district, Quang Tri province, interview with 20th Military History Detachment (MHD), 11 August 1970, transcript, CMH.

4. Stanley Karnow, *Vietnam: A History* (New York: Viking Press, 1984), p. 602.

5. The "Green Book," published in 1970, formally known as "The Current Breakout of VCI Executive and Significant Cadres," catalogued the functions of the infrastructure. "Standing Operating Procedures" set forth the missions of the various echelons of the Phoenix hierarchy. Both in CMH.

6. See the *Congressional Record,* 22 April 1971, pp. E3329–E3334, for Representative Jerome R. Waldie's report on Phoenix; and memo, Colby to ACS, CORDS, sub: Speech Made by Rep. Waldie (Calif.) on Phoenix, 14 May 1971, CMH.

7. Robert C. Nalley, Phung Hoang legal officer, Delta Military Assistance Command, interview with 45th Military History Detachment, Can Tho, Vietnam, 5 December 1970 and 2 March 1971, transcript, pp. 7–8, CMH.

8. Msg., Vann, Deputy for CORDS MR 4, to Colby, sub: Training of National Police Interrogators and Investigators, 080955Z October 1970, DepCORDS files.

9. Information on prosecutors was compiled from data in DepCORDS files; Nalley interview, p. 13; and Colby and Forbath, *Honorable Men,* p. 274.

10. Nalley interview, p. 5.

11. End-of-tour rpt., McAffee, CORDS legal adviser, August 1971, DepCORDS files.

12. Lewy, *America in Vietnam,* p. 288; and Colby and Forbath, *Honorable Men,* p. 268.

13. Colby and Forbath, *Honorable Men,* p. 268.

14. Lewy, *America in Vietnam,* p. 290, the data for which came from U.S. House, Committee on Government Operations, *U.S. Assistance Programs in Vietnam,* Hearings, 92nd Cong., 1st sess. (Washington, D.C.: GPO, 1971), p. 196; and Colby and Forbath, *Honorable Men,* p. 274.

15. Memo, CORDS-PSD, sub: Proposals to the Ministry of Interior for Improvements in the Processing of Communist and Political Detainees, 1969, pp. 9–10, DepCORDS.

16. Colby and Forbath, *Honorable Men,* p. 275. See also DeForest and Chanoff, *Slow Burn.*

17. Robert Komer, "The Phung Hoang Fiasco," 30 July 1970, CMH.

18. Nalley interview, p. 9; briefing, MACCORDS-PHX, sub: Phung Hoang Reexamination Study (PHREEX), 23 October 1971, p. 8; and Colby, "Internal Security in South Vietnam—Phoenix," 12 December 1970, pp. 6, 8, both in CMH.

19. Begun in the middle of 1971, PHREEX was completed in October.

20. Decree, prime minister, 069-SL/Th.T/BDPT, 26 May 1970, as related in msg., COMUSMACV to CINCPAC, sub: Phung Hoang/Phoenix Program, 13 June 1970, CMH.

21. Robert Thompson et al., "Report on the National Police, Republic of Vietnam" (Saigon, March 1971). For an example of this kind of thinking in the years preceding the change, see Julian Paget *Counter-Insurgency Operations: Techniques of Guerilla Warfare* (New York: Walker, 1967).

22. Ltr., Colby to Laird, sub: Komer's "Phung Hoang Fiasco," 8 October 1970, p. 5, CMH.

23. Ltr., Hannah to Bunker, 23 April 1970, CMH.

24. Memo, Herbert, chief, Current Operations Directorate, SACSA, OJCS, to Blackburn, sub: Transfer of Phung Hoang Responsibility to the National Police, 8 April 1970, CMH.

25. Herrington, *Silence,* pp. 239–240.

26. Information brief, sub: GVN National Police, 22 September 1970, CMH.

27. Fact sheet, DOD, sub: National Police Manpower Problems in South Vietnam, 8 January 1971; and msg., COMUSMACV to CINCPAC, sub: Support of GVN National Police Project, 131722Z February 1971, both in CMH.

28. Fact sheet, DOD, 8 January 1971.

29. Data compiled from information on detainees in CMH.

30. Harry F. Farmer, Phung Hoang Regional Center advisor, HQ, DRAC, interview with 45th MHD, 17 May 1971, transcript, p. 9, CMH.

31. Msg., Bunker to SECSTATE, sub: Corruption: (A) Huynh Khac Dung Case, (B) Nationwide Judicial Police Shake-up, (C) Phung Hoang, 201000Z September 1972, CMH.

32. Nalley interview, p. 8.

33. Public Safety Division, sub: Prison Rehabilitation and Detention Centers, Action Program, CY-1968; and rpt., State Department, Bureau of Public Affairs, sub: Civilian Prisons in South Vietnam, 1 July 1971, both in CMH.

34. Decree, Ministry of the Interior, 757, March 1969; decree, Ministry of the Interior, 2212, August 1969; cable, 19217/LS/U/KH/K, 15 September 1969; and decree, 1206/PtHt/BDPT/HC, 24 April 1970, all in CMH.

35. Memo, Vann to Jacobson, sub: Visit to Correction and Detention Centers, MR4, 26 February 1971, CMH.

36. U.S. House, *U.S. Assistance Programs,* pp. 315 ff.

37. Ltr., Buzhardt, Office of the General Counsel for the DOD, to Moorhead, chairman, Foreign Operations and Government Information Subcommittee, 2 November 1972, CMH.

38. See Mary McGrory's column in the *Washington Star,* August 3, 1971; Daniel Rappaport's story in the *Washington Post* on the same day; and "House Panel Criticizes Pentagon on Political Killings in Vietnam," *New York Times,* October 4, 1972.

39. See, for example, Cooper, "Operation Phoenix"; and Robert G. Kaiser, "U.S. Aides Scorn Phoenix Program," *Washington Post,* 17 February 1970.

40. U.S. Senate, Committee on Foreign Relations, *Vietnam: Policy and Prospects, 1970 (CORDS),* 91st Cong., 2d sess., February 17–20 and March 3, 14, 17, and 19, 1970 (Washington, D.C.: GPO, 1970) pp. 196–197.

41. Colby and Forbath, *Honorable Men,* pp. 270–271; and Nalley interview, pp. 4–5.

42. Colby, Vann, and other CORDS officials, including Arthur, returned to Washington early in 1970 to testify. See U.S. Senate, *Vietnam.*

43. Cushing interview; Nalley interview, p. 11; author interview with Cook, Washington, D.C., 24 November 1987; and Lewy, *America in Vietnam,* p. 287.

44. Nalley interview, pp. 3–4, 8–9; and Colby and Forbath, *Honorable Men,* p. 230. Colby was quoted in Lewy, *America in Vietnam,* pp. 287–288.

45. Herrington, *Silence,* pp. 134–140. See also DeForest and Chanoff, *Slow Burn,* pp. 155–159, for another account of Captain Miller's operation.

46. Cook interview; and John L. Cook, *The Adviser* (New York: Bantam Books, 1987), Chap. 13.

47. Thayer, *War Without Fronts,* pp. 211–212.

48. Farmer interview, p. 8.

49. U.S. Senate, *Vietnam,* and testimony of Vann, p. 120. See also Peter R. Kann, "The Invisible Foe," *Wall Street Journal,* 5 September 1968; and Kaiser, "U.S. Aides Scorn Phoenix." Both articles were included in U.S. Senate, *Vietnam.*

50. Nalley interview, p. 15.

51. The F-6 campaign was discussed in Andrade, *Ashes to Ashes,* pp. 246–253. See also, msg., Saigon to Washington, Saigon 6019, sub: Special Phung Hoang Campaign in the Delta, 270905Z April 1972; and msg., COMUSMACV to CINCPAC, sub: Special Anti-VCI Operations, 182315Z May 1972, both in CMH.

52. Msg., Wilson to Jacobson, assistant DepCORDS, sub: Acceleration of Phung Hoang Program, 290140Z April 1972, DepCORDS files.

53. Ibid.

54. Intelligence information cable, CIA, sub: Results of the National Police Special Branch Roll-up Campaign in GVN Military Region 3 During the Period 8 April–7 July 1972; intelligence information cable, CIA, sub: Difficulties Encountered by Police Special Branch in Arresting Known or Suspected Viet Cong in Tay Ninh Province, 24 May 1972; and intelligence information cable, CIA, sub: Capital National Police Command Watch List of Politically Suspect Persons, 26 May 1972, emphasis added, all in CMH.

55. Hallock interview.

56. Msg., Dean to Jacobson, sub: Request for Rapid Processing of Thua Thien Detainees, 120725Z June 1972, CMH.

57. Msg., Jones to Jacobson, sub: New Binh Minh Type Operations in Hue, 020426Z August 1972, CMH.

58. Msg., Cooksey to Woodward, 011120Z November 1972, CMH.

59. Memo, sub: Operations in Hue, 2 November 1972, DepCORDS files; and Whitehouse interview.

60. Farmer interview, p. 3.

61. Ltr., director, CIA, to deputy secretary of defense, 1 July 1970, CMH.

62. DF, DCSPER, to DCSOPS, sub: Training of Phoenix Advisers; and msg., COMUSMACV to CINCPAC, sub: Training of Phoenix Advisers, 220842Z July 1969, both in CMH.

63. Hallock interview.

64. Fact sheet, DCSPER, sub: Military Assistance Adviser Course (MASA), 29 June 1970, CMH.

65. Thayer, *War Without Fronts,* p. 210.

66. Action memo, MACCORDS, chief of staff 69-31, sub: Phoenix Transfer, 11 March 1969, CMH. Support involved matters of personnel, force structure, airlift operations (both passengers and cargo), supply and maintenance, construction (including facilities maintenance), communications, and funding. See also memo, Wheeler to Laird, sub: U.S. Military Involvement in the Provincial Reconnaissance Unit Program in the Republic of Vietnam, 8 December 1969, CMH.

67. Memo, Resor to Laird, sub: The Phoenix and Provincial Reconnaissance Unit Programs in Vietnam, 20 October 1969, CMH.

68. Memo, Laird to Wheeler, sub: Evaluation of U.S. Involvement in the Provincial Reconnaissance Unit Program in the Republic of Vietnam, 28 November 1969, CMH.

69. Thayer, *War Without Fronts*, p. 210; Peter R. Kann, "The Invisible Foe," *Wall Street Journal*, 5 September 1968; and Blaufarb, *The Counterinsurgency Era*, p. 245.

70. Memo, Hand, OSD, to Carver, 23 October 1969; and memo, Carver, special assistant for Vietnamese affairs, to director, CIA, sub: Army Secretary Resor's Request to Secretary Laird for a Review of the Phoenix and PRU Programs, 23 October 1969, both in CMH.

71. Memo, Carver to director, 23 October 1969. Carver's first response on this topic was in a memo to Laird, sub: Comments on the 6 October 1969 Paper Entitled "The Phoenix Program," 22 October 1969, CMH.

72. Msg., Abrams to Moorer, acting CJCS, sub: PRU, 3 December 1969, CMH.

73. Memo, Shackley, special assistant to the ambassador, to Jacobson, ACS, MACCORDS, sub: Military Personnel Assigned to OSA, 1 November 1969, CMH.

74. Andrade, *Ashes to Ashes*, p. 250.

75. U.S. Senate, *Vietnam*, p. 321.

76. Thayer, *War Without Fronts*, p. 211.

77. Lewy, *America in Vietnam*, pp. 281, 283; and end-of-tour rpt., Fleigh, PSA, Binh Duong, 9 November 1970, CMH.

78. Thayer, *War Without Fronts*, p. 206. The 1972 figure comes from the Combined Intelligence Center, Vietnam's order-of-battle summary, vol. 2, for June 1972, CMH, and was the last combined (American and South Vietnamese) estimate. Subsequent estimates were purely South Vietnamese figures and were considered less reliable. Estimates of the enemy's order of battle proved controversial during the war and were the subject of a major lawsuit between General Westmoreland and CBS after the war. Consequently, the estimates are primarily useful to show gross changes in the size of the infrastructure and guerrilla forces.

79. Thayer, *War Without Fronts*, p. 211.

80. Ibid., p. 209.

81. Karnow, *Vietnam*, p. 602. Resolution, COSVN, 9; Viet Cong radio broadcasts; articles in North Vietnamese publications; and captured enemy documents ("Military Activity Plan of Sub-Region 5 from July to September 1970" and "Report on Enemy and Friendly Situation During the First Six Months of 1970 [Long Khanh Province]), both in CMH, described in general terms how Phoenix disrupted the communist movement at the local level. See also Nayan Chanda, "The Phoenix Programme and the Ashes of War," *Far Eastern Economic Review*, 2 May 1988, p. 40.

82. Rpt., CIA, 28 June 1971. Kolko, *Anatomy of a War*, pp. 330, 397–398, asserted that the CIA and other government agencies, fooled by the limitations of their own data, did not understand how seriously Phoenix had hurt the infrastructure.

83. Thayer, *War Without Fronts*, p. 215.

84. Andrade, *Ashes to Ashes*, pp. 256 ff; captured enemy document, CDEC 6 028 0816 70, sub: Establishment of the GVN Phung Hoang Intelligence Organization in Villages, 25 August 1970; and memo, Phoenix coordinator, I Corps, to PCS/S, sub: Phoenix Security, 12 December 1969, both in DepCORDS files.

For wartime assessments by the enemy, see the following: msg., Detachment 6, 1021st USAF FAS/AFE Team B, Bien Hoa AB, to MACV J-2, sub: VC Concept and Evaluation of the Phung Hoang Program, 011030Z February 1972; daily intelligence review, Intelligence and Security Division., ODCSOPS, HQ USARV, sub: Interrogation of a Former VC Commander of a Security Company for VC My Tho Province, 21 January 1971; msg., DISUM,

COMUSMACV to AIG 7051, 180326Z January 1971 (another *hoi chanh* interrogation); and intelligence memo, CIA, sub: The Viet Cong Infrastructure: Its Status and Effectiveness, 15 June 1971, all in DepCORDS files.

85. Nalley interview, p. 16.

86. Thayer, *War Without Fronts*, p. 209.

87. Ibid., p. 200.

88. Ibid., p. 216.

89. DF, MACCORDS, ACS CORDS, to chief of staff, MACV, sub: Phoenix Program Evaluation, 13 November 1969, CMH.

90. Thayer, *War Without Fronts*, pp. 213–214; and DF, CORDS-PHD, ACS, CORDS, to chief of staff, sub: Spot Report No. 3, 1 March 1971, DepCORDS files.

91. The hardships of the VC during 1969–1972 are related in the memoir of a former Viet Cong official, Truong Nhu Tang, with David Chanoff and Doan Van Toai, *A Vietcong Memoir: An Inside Account of the Vietnam War and Its Aftermath* (New York: Harcourt Brace Jovanovich, 1985).

92. Andrade, *Ashes to Ashes*, p. 252.

93. Kolko, *Anatomy of a War*, p. 397.

94. Memo, Colby to Askew, sub: Can We "Neutralize" the VCI? 24 May 1971, memo of personal view by Sizer of the embassy's political staff was attached, DepCORDS files. Sizer's memo was an insightful contemporary summation of the pros and cons of the Phoenix program.

95. Farmer interview, p. 4; and Colby, "Internal Security," p. 15.

96. Blaufarb, *The Counterinsurgency Era*, p. 247.

Chapter 16

1. Colby developed this argument at some length in Parts 5 and 6 of *Lost Victory*.

2. See Colby, *Lost Victory;* Davidson, *Vietnam at War;* Bruce Palmer Jr., *The 25-Year War: America's Military Role in Vietnam* (New York: Touchstone, 1984); and Komer, *Bureaucracy Does Its Thing.* Thayer, *War Without Fronts*, also argued for the success of pacification.

3. See, for example, Kolko, *Anatomy of a War;* Turley, *The Second Indochina War;* and Duiker, *The Communist Road to Power.*

4. Interestingly, Komer conceded this point in a letter to Thayer, 24 October 1969, CMH.

5. Statistical summary, OSD-Comptroller, Southeast Asia, December 1973, CMH. This report did not separate Viet Cong from North Vietnamese deaths.

6. Rpt., Combined Intelligence Center Vietnam, sub: Order of Battle Summary, June 1972, 2 vols., copy in CMH. See also Turley, *The Second Indochina War*, p. 131. The figures in this section are intended to indicate the relative decline in the size of communist forces, not to assert absolute strength. Even the most carefully prepared estimates were often based on imprecise parameters. Although the CIA and military intelligence agencies disagreed during the war over the estimated size and composition of the enemy's order of battle, there was little argument that communist forces had suffered serious losses. After the war, the conflicting intelligence estimates of the enemy order of battle were the focus of a lawsuit, *Westmoreland* v. *Columbia Broadcasting System* (1982).

7. Thayer, *War Without Fronts*, p. 206.

8. Ibid., p. 48; and Turley, *The Second Indochina War*, p. 132. Much of the statistical information in this chapter comes from Thayer's authoritative account. As director of the Southeast Asia Division in the Defense Department's Office of Systems Analysis from 1967 to 1972, he helped compile operational data on many aspects of the war. After the war, Thayer further analyzed the DOD data and published his findings in a single volume, *War Without Fronts*, which remains the basic source on the long-term statistical trends of the Vietnam War.

9. Ibid., p. 46.

10. Ibid., p. 163; and Peter Braestrup, ed., *Vietnam as History: Ten Years After the Paris Peace Accords* (Washington, D.C.: University Press of America, 1984), p. 43.

11. Data from Thayer, *War Without Fronts*, pp. 119, 161–163. See also Blaufarb, *The Counterinsurgency Era*, p. 267; and Richard A. Hunt, "On Our Conduct of the Vietnam War: A Review Essay of Two New Works," *Parameters* 16, no. 3 (1986): 56–57.

12. Thayer, *War Without Fronts*, p. 157.

13. Memo, Colby, to chief of staff, 5 January 1971; memo, Wilson, director of intelligence production, J-2, to Abrams, sub: To Provide an Assessment of an Enemy Document Captured in the U Minh Forest, 8 February 1971, DepCORDS files; and memo, Vann to ACS, CORDS, 15 March 1970, CMH.

14. See, for example, Tra, *Concluding the 30-Years War;* and memo, Wilson, to Abrams, 8 February 1971.

15. Abrams's goals for pacification are discussed in Chapters 12 and 13.

16. MACV, *Command History, 1970,* vol. 1, pp. I-2–I-5; and msg., COMUSMACV to CINCPAC, sub: Status of Pacification—Looking Back at 1970, 090326Z February 1971, depCORDS files. Colby drafted this message.

17. Thayer, *War Without Fronts*, pp. 156–158.

18. Msg., Bunker to Nixon, Saigon 1175, 260758Z January 1972, CMH. Bunker's messages to the president have been published: Douglas Pike, ed., *The Bunker Papers: Reports to the President from Vietnam, 1967*–1973 (Berkeley: University of California, Institute of East Asian Studies, 1990), 3 vols. Bunker's reports were critically reviewed by Wallace J. Thies, "How We (Almost) Won in Vietnam: Ellsworth Bunker's Reports to the President," *Parameters* 22, no. 2 (Summer 1992): 86–95.

19. Davidson, *Vietnam at War*, p. 673.

20. Msg., Saigon to Washington, sub: Further Assessment of the Political and Anti-Pacification Efforts of the Communists During the Current Offensive, Saigon 7962, 300225Z May 1972, CMH; Ngo Quang Truong, *The Easter Offensive of 1972* (Washington, D.C.: U.S. Army Center of Military History, 1984); and Turley, *The Second Indochina War*, p. 143.

21. Rpt., assistant secretary of defense, systems analysis, sub: The Vietnam Conflict—1972 and Beyond, February 1973; and rpt., Pacification Studies Group, sub: Impact of the Enemy Offensive on Pacification, both in CMH.

22. Msg., Saigon to Washington, May 1972; rpt., assistant secretary of defense, February 1973; and fact sheet, CORDS, sub: HES, 19 February 1973, CMH.

23. Rpt., assistant secretary of defense, February 1973.

24. MACV-Eval, sub: Impact of the Enemy Offensive on Pacification, CMH; and msg., Saigon to Washington, May 1972.

25. Msg., Wilson to Jacobson, 29 April 1972; and msg., Saigon to Washington, May 1972.

26. Msg., Saigon to Washington, May 1972. Truong's campaign is discussed in Chapter 15.

27. Wiesner, *Victims and Survivors*, pp. 256, 258. Other estimates can be found in Lewy, *America in Vietnam*, p. 198; Nguyen Duy Hinh, *Vietnamization and the Cease-fire* (Washington, D.C.: Army Center of Military History, 1984), p. 91; rpt., PSG, sub: Evaluation of the Impact of the Enemy Offensive on Pacification, 5 October 1972; and corps overviews, March–September 1972, both in CMH.

28. Msg., Jones, DepCORDS, MR I, to Jacobson, sub: Weekly Report, 22 October 1972, CMH; and Wiesner, *Victims and Survivors*, p. 265.

29. Wiesner, *Victims and Survivors*, pp. 263–264.

30. Ltr., Colby to Jacobson, 29 September 1972, CMH.

31. Wiesner, *Victims and Survivors*, p. 256; and Tang et al., *A Viet Cong Memoir*, pp. 219–220.

32. Ltr., Jacobson to McManaway, 27 September 1971; and ltr., McManaway to Jacobson, 2 September 1971, both in DepCORDS files. McManaway had served in CORDS as head of the Plans and Programs Directorate until 1970.

33. Fact sheet, MAC J14, sub: RVNAF Desertions, March 1967.

34. Rpt., MACV, sub: ARVN Improvement and Modernization, 22 August 1971, CMH; and ltr., McManaway to Jacobson, 2 September 1971. The desertion figures are gross rates, which do not take into account the number of soldiers eventually returning to their units.

35. Memo, Colby to chief of staff, 5 January 1971.

36. Rpt., CIA, sub: Views of I Corps Assistant Commander for RF/PF on His Territorial Forces, 18 March 1970, CMH.

37. Memo, Colby to chief of staff, 5 January 1971; and rpt., ACS, CORDS, sub: Status of Pacification, 19 September 1971, CMH.

38. Rpt., ACS, CORDS, 19 September 1971.

39. Ibid.

40. Memo, Colby, to chief of staff, 5 January 1971; memo, Vann to ACS, CORDS, 15 March 1970; and Hunt and Shultz, *Lessons from an Unconventional War*, p. 89.

41. Rpts., province senior adviser, Kien Hoa and Dinh Tuong, provinces, 1969–1972, CMH.

42. Dong Van Khuyen, *The RVNAF* (Washington, D.C.: Army Center of Military History, 1980), pp. 219–220; and Ngo Quang Truong, *Territorial Forces* (Washington, D.C.: Army Center of Military History, 1981), p. 102.

43. Bole and Kobata, "An Evaluation of the Hamlet Evaluation System," pp. 22–24.

44. *Southeast Asia Analysis Report* (November 1971–January 1972): 2–4; and Thayer, *War Without Fronts*, p. 141.

45. Quoted by Shultz, "The Vietnamization-Pacification Strategy," in *Lessons from an Unconventional War*, p. 65. Shultz dated the assessment in the latter half of 1972.

46. Memo, Wilson to Jacobson, sub: ARVN Reporting in MR 4, 30 March 1972; and memo, Wilson to Jacobson, sub: Validity of the ARVN Reporting System, 6 October 1972, DepCORDS files.

47. Ltr., Colby to Thieu, 2 February 1969, DepCORDS files. This letter is also mentioned in Chapter 13.

48. *Southeast Asia Analysis Reports* (November 1971–January 1972): 1–6, CMH.

49. Memo, Vann to Colby, sub: Utilization of Territorial Forces in Pacified Areas, 3 May 1971, DepCORDS files.

50. Rpt., CIA, sub: Vietnamization, 28 June 1971, CMH.

51. Rpt., ACS, CORDS, 19 September 1971.

52. Gerald C. Hickey, *Free in the Forest: Ethnohistory of the Vietnamese Central Highlands, 1954*–1976 (New Haven: Yale University Press, 1982), pp. 221–223.

53. Rpt., province senior adviser, Binh Dinh, March 1971, CMH.

54. Shultz, "The Vietnamization-Pacification Strategy," p. 76.

55. Rpts., province senior adviser, Binh Dinh, February, March, and July 1971, CMH.

56. DF, ACS, CORDS, to chief of staff, sub: Relocation of Population, 20 July 1971, with enclosures, DepCORDS files.

57. Hickey, *Free in the Forest.*

58. Memo, Taft, acting senior military adviser, to DepCORDS, sub: Meeting with General Dzu on 26 February, 26 February 1971, CMH.

59. Quoted in Hickey, *Free in the Forest,* p. 223.

60. This discussion of land reform is based on Callison, *Land to the Tiller;* Thayer, *War Without Fronts,* Chap. 19; and information from the DepCORDS files. The provisions of the law are discussed in Chapter 4.

61. Thayer, *War Without Fronts,* pp. 240–241.

62. Kolko, *Anatomy of a War,* pp. 389–393.

63. Henry C. Bush, Gordon H. Messegee, and Roger V. Russell, *The Impact of the Land to the Tiller Program in the Mekong Delta* (Washington, D.C.: Control Data Corporation, December 1972): p. 88. AID Vietnam contracted for the study. See also Callison, *Land to the Tiller,* p. 328; and Thayer, *War Without Fronts,* p. 242.

64. Bergerud, *The Dynamics of Defeat,* pp. 298–299.

65. Ibid., p. 299.

66. MACV, *Command History, 1970,* vol. 2, p. vii-102; MACV, *Command History, 1971,* vol. 1, p. vii-29; and MACV, *Command History, 1972–73,* Vol. 1, p. D-18.

67. Howard R. Penniman, *Elections in South Vietnam* (Washington, D.C.: American Enterprise Institute, December 1972), pp. 50, 115, 147; and Thayer, *War Without Fronts,* p. 50. According to Penniman (p. 47), voter participation in village council elections in 1970 was 85 percent. According to the *World Almanac* for 1985, 55.2 percent of those eligible cast ballots in the U.S. presidential election in 1972, and that was one of the heaviest turnouts in American history.

68. Airgram, Saigon to Washington, A-181, sub: District Chiefs' Control of Village and Hamlet Elections, 10 June 1970, DepCORDS files. The duties of hamlet and village officials are discussed in Chapter 4.

69. MACV, *Command History, 1970,* p. VIII-64; and MACV, *Command History, 1971,* p. VII-28.

70. From a supplement to the local government branch weekly rpt., CORDS, 2 September 1972, p. 4, which dealt with decree 120; ltr., Dean, DEPCORDS for MR 1, to Jacobson, 22 March 1972, both in DepCORDS files; Edward W. Knappman, ed., *South Vietnam: U.S.-Communist Confrontation in Southeast Asia* (New York: Facts on File, 1973), vol. 7, p. 294; and Penniman, *Elections,* p. 46. See Chapter 4 for information on the 1966 law.

71. His order was dated 1 October 1972.

72. Penniman, *Elections,* p. 130; and memo, Quinn, administrative assistant to DepCORDS, to chief, PSG, sub: Recent Developments and Possible Outcomes in the Presidential Elections, 1 October 1971, DepCORDS files.

73. Memo of conversation between Bao, chairman of the Gia Dinh Province Council, eleven other provincial councilmen from Saigon, Gia Dinh, and Bien Hoa, with Thompson, second secretary of the embassy, held 31 July 1971 at Ky campaign headquarters; and

telegram from U.S. Embassy Saigon to the secretary of state, sub: Ky Files for Presidential Candidacy, 4 August 1971, both in CMH.

74. Penniman, *Elections,* pp. 128, 131; and "U.S. Inhibits Fair Vote, Minh Says," *Washington Post,* 16 July 1971.

75. Penniman, *Elections,* p. 131; and memo, Quinn to chief, 1 October 1971.

76. Results are from the Washington Embassy of South Vietnam, *Vietnam Bulletin,* 4 October 1971.

77. Information on the press laws, Thieu's emergency powers, and the restrictions on political parties comes from Knappman, *South Vietnam,* vol. 7, pp. 291–296.

78. Transcript, DepCORDS conference, January 1973, CMH.

Chapter 17

1. Information on the strength of CORDS was compiled from data in the DepCORDS files; MFR, Watts, military assistant to the secretary of the army, sub: Officers assigned to CORDS, 1 December 1969; and memo, MACV J12, sub: District Senior Advisor Program, 16 April 1971, both in CMH.

2. Memo, secretary of defense to secretary of the army, sub: Quantity and Quality of U.S. Advisors in Vietnam, 16 December 1969, CMH.

3. Memo, Resor to Laird, sub: Quantity and Quality of Advisers in Vietnam, 2 February 1970, CMH.

4. Stanley Resor, "An Assignment of Great Importance," *Army Digest* (July 1970): 48–49.

5. Memo, Resor to Laird, 2 February 1970.

6. George Ashworth, "U.S. Fails to Sell Officers on Vietnam Advisory Jobs," *Christian Science Monitor,* 12 February 1970.

7. Memo, McRae, chief, RD Division, JCS, to DePuy, SACSA, sub: Military Advisor Training at the Vietnamese Training Center of FSI, 7 August 1968, CMH.

8. Peter Dawkins, "The United States Army and the Other War in Vietnam: A Study of the Complexity of Implementing Organizational Change" (Ph.D. diss. Princeton University, 1979), p. 71. A West Point graduate and Rhodes scholar, Dawkins was once touted as a possible chief of staff of the army. He served in South Vietnam and later rose to the rank of brigadier general before leaving the army.

9. Ibid., pp. 79–80.

10. Ibid., pp. 68, 79–80.

11. Ibid., pp. 84, 107, 119–122.

12. See Chapter 7.

13. Author interview with Colby, Washington, D.C., August 1985. Along with Colby, several other prominent CORDS officials testified at the hearings: William Hitchcock, director of refugee programs; John Vann, the DepCORDS for IV Corps; Hawthorne Mills, provincial adviser for Tuyen Duc; and Clayton McManaway, director of plans, policy, and programs. U.S. Senate, *Vietnam.*

14. The numbers come from MACV *Command History, 1971,* pp. VII-4–5.

15. Msg., Abrams to Hollingsworth, commanding general, Third Regional Assistance Command (TRAC), sub: Joint Table of Distribution, 27 February 1972, CMH.

16. The arguments against keeping district advisers were set forth in rpt., Special Interagency Task Force to the Mission Council, sub: The Future of CORDS in Viet-Nam, 1

November 1971, pp. 4–5, CMH. Unfortunately, this document does not identify the persons articulating these views.

17. Msg., Dean, DepCORDS, MR-1, to Jacobson, sub: Rationale for Keeping District Teams, 9 March 1972, DepCORDS files.

18. Ibid.; and msg., Paxette, assistant DEPCORDS, MR-4, to Weyand, sub: Why Have District Advisory Teams? 4 March 1972, DepCORDS files.

19. Msg., Barnes, DEPCORDS, MR-2, to Jacobson, ACS, CORDS, sub: Retention of District Advisors, 10 March 1972, DepCORDS files. See also msg., Funkhouser, DepCORDS TRAC, to Weyand, 8 March 1972, DepCORDS files.

20. Msg., State/Defense/AID, to embassy Saigon, State 051712, sub: Study of Future of CORDS Advisory Program, 27 March 1971, CMH.

21. Rpt., Special Interagency Task Force, 1 November 1971. AID official John Heileman chaired the task force.

22. Msg., Saigon to Washington, sub: Study of Future CORDS Advisory Program, 6 May 1971; and msg., State/Defense, Saigon to Washington, sub: Study of Future CORDS Advisory Program, 4 June 1971, both in CMH.

23. Trip rpt., Singer, SACSA, sub: Future Organization of CORDS, 1 December 1971, CMH.

24. MACV, *Command History, 1972*–73, vol. 1, pp. D-43, 44.

25. AID province representative, Kien Phong and Dinh Tuong provinces, 1965–1967, interview 126712, Asia Training Center, AID, Honolulu, Hawaii. This is one of an extensive series of debriefing interviews that AID did with its officials after they left South Vietnam. To encourage candor, the transcripts were left anonymous.

26. Provincial refugee adviser, Binh Dinh, 1967–1969, interview 26695; district senior adviser, Ninh Hoa, 1966–1968, interview 27682; and debrief of a brigade commander, MR III, 1967–1968, interview 17682, Asia Training Center, AID, are some of the officials attesting to the efficacy of CORDS.

27. "Interview, Komer," pp. 219–222.

28. Memo, Weyand, DepCORDS, to Bunker, sub: Four Year Community Defense and Local Development Plan, 29 February 1972, DepCORDS files.

29. Interview with AID province representative, Kien Phong.

30. Thayer, *War Without Fronts*, pp. 69–70.

31. Information was compiled from the following documents: memo, Woods, sub: List of Province Chiefs Replaced Since Tet, August 1969; fact sheet, CORDS, sub: Thieu Improvements (Province and District Personnel), February 1970; memo, Sweet, director, Plans and Programs, to Allitto, executive assistant, sub: Thirty-six Questions, 28 August 1971; fact sheet, sub: Province Chief and District Chief Removal, no date; and ltr., Montague to Pickering, sub: Removed GVN Officials, 28 August 1968, all in CMH.

32. Memo, Vann to ACS, CORDS, 15 March 1970, CMH.

33. Senior State Department consultant, 1961–1968, interview, 25687, Asia Training Center, AID.

34. Taped proceedings, DepCORDS conference, MACV HQ, 5 January 1973, CMH.

35. Thayer, *War Without Fronts*, Chap. 3.

36. RF/PF casualties and the enemy's targeting of the territorial forces are discussed in ibid., Chap. 16.

37. CORDS management consultant, Saigon, 1967–1968, interview 23682, Asia Training Center, AID.

About the Book and Author

During the Vietnam War, the United States embarked on an unusual crusade on behalf of the government of South Vietnam. Known as the pacification program, it sought to help South Vietnam's government take root and survive as an independent, legitimate entity by defeating communist insurgents and promoting economic development and political reforms. In this book, Richard Hunt provides the first comprehensive history of America's "battle for hearts and minds," the distinctive blending of military and political approaches that took aim at the essence of the struggle between North and South Vietnam.

Hunt concentrates on the American role, setting pacification in the larger political context of nation building. He describes the search for the best combination of military and political action, incorporating analysis of the controversial Phoenix program, and illuminates the difficulties the Americans encountered with their sometimes reluctant ally. The author explains how hard it was to get the U.S. Army involved in pacification and shows the struggle to yoke divergent organizations (military, civilian, and intelligence agencies) to serve one common goal. The greatest challenge of all was to persuade a surrogate—the Saigon government—to carry out programs and to make reforms conceived of by American officials.

The book concludes with a careful assessment of pacification's successes and failures. Would the Saigon government have flourished if there had been more time to consolidate the gains of pacification? Or was the regime so fundamentally flawed that its demise was preordained by its internal contradictions? This pathbreaking book offers startling and provocative answers to these and other important questions about our Vietnam experience.

Richard A. Hunt received his Ph.D. in history from the University of Pennsylvania. After completing a tour of duty in Vietnam as a U.S. Army Captain at the Headquarters of the Military Assistance Command, Vietnam, he joined the Center of Military History in Washington, D.C. He lives in Alexandria, Virginia, with his wife and daughter.

Index

Abrams, Creighton W., 87, 88, 89, 149, 157, 158, 167, 176, 179, 211, 217, 220, 227, 234, 254, 273, 274
accelerated pacification campaign, 172, 182, 193, 195–196, 203, 205–207
change in strategy, 212–213, 221, 223–233
CORDS reporting, 180
Komer and, 151, 154–155, 180, 214
military operations and pacification, 192, 233
Nixon's mission statement, 213
Operation WASHINGTON GREEN, 222–224
PRU advisers and, 245–246
replaces Westmoreland, 151
strategic objectives plan, 212–213, 221, 232
Tet offensive (1968) effects, 149
Accelerated Pacification Campaign (APC), 157, 159, 233
Abrams's views, 193
achievements, 197–202, 204, 205–206
components, 157
CORDS effects, 276
goal, 172
GVN directive problems, 158
Hamlet Evaluation System, 158–159, 194, 195, 197, 198(table)
I Corps, 172–177
II Corps, 177–181
III Corps, 182–188
IV Corps, 188–192
military support, 192, 203
Operation SPEEDY EXPRESS, 189
Operation VINH LOC, 173–175
See also Le Loi campaign
Advisers, 17, 18, 26, 48, 53, 54, 62, 64, 65, 91, 95, 100, 122, 123, 126, 159, 179, 224, 265
AIK program, 127–128
Chieu Hoi program, 101–102
civilian advisers, 60
incentives, 107, 109, 269–272
leverage, 129, 130
pacification vs. military assignments, 270–271
Phoenix program and, 244–246, 251

piaster fund allocations, 145
recommended relations with the Vietnamese, 123, 124
responsibilities, 59–60
RF/PF, 106–107
training programs, 17–18, 108, 115, 244–245
See also Agency for International Development; Central Intelligence Agency
Agency for International Development (AID), 13, 18, 24, 40, 42, 45, 46, 55, 59, 72, 82, 93, 96, 101, 103, 104, 105, 115, 117, 122, 145, 257, 264, 265, 269, 272, 274, 279
Komer's views, 73
responsibilities, 63
South Vietnamese National Police training, 38–39
Agrovilles, 6
purpose, 20
Viet Cong resistance, 20
AID. See Agency for International Development
AIK. See Assistance in Kind
Allied military power (1967), 133
American press, 63, 104, 132, 134
Phoenix program and, 240
reaction to Tet offensive (1968), 141
Amos, Harry, 191
An Thinh village, 192, 241
pacification and military operations, 186–187
Andrade, Dale, 250
Anti-infrastructure campaigns, 25, 199, 244, 262
CIA participation, 113
communist political group guidelines, 153
F-6, 243
ICEX program, 113–114
mobile advisory teams, 109
NPFF responsibilities, 116
organizations, 139
Project Takeoff, 99–101
shortcomings, 117–118
South Vietnam efforts, 112
APC. See Accelerated Pacification Campaign

Ap Cho village, 54
Armed propaganda teams, 38, 102
Armed Reconnaissance Units (ARUs), Viet Cong,
    248
Army, United States. *See* United States Army
Army of the Republic of (South) Vietnam
    (ARVN), 5, 11, 12, 14, 17, 19, 21, 24, 41, 45, 48,
    49, 51, 52, 54, 83, 102, 140, 149, 231
    corruption charges, 138
    Gia Dinh province, 55–56
    guerrilla warfare, 34, 87
    Hop Tac program, 27, 28
    II Corps, 177
    military advisers, 190–191
    military strength, 27
    pacification support, 75, 85, 89, 102, 172, 178, 196,
        225
    peasants, 34, 187
    support to RD cadre, 74, 131, 147, 151
    Saigon rebuilding efforts, 148
    transfer of people to the National Police, 238
    treatment of Viet Cong defectors, 102
Arthur, James, 240–241
ARVN. *See* Army of the Republic of (South)
    Vietnam
Assistance in Kind (AIK), 127–128
Attrition concept, 212
    criticism of, 209
    in Long An, 51–52
    provisions, 33

Ball, George, 68
Barnes, John, 223–226
Bashore, Boyd, 50
Bell, David, 68
Ben Suc village, evacuation, 57–58
Berger, Samuel D., 274
Bergerud, Eric, 188, 264
Bernard, Carl, 184, 185, 187
Binh Chanh district, 43, 56, 183, 240
Binh Dinh province, 3, 139, 226, 227
    allied offensive, 223–224
Binh Minh campaign, 243–244
Bissell, Richard, 18
Blaufarb, Douglas, 251
Brigham, Irwin, territorial forces evaluation
    system creation, 93
British Advisory Mission, 21
Buddhists, 10
    rebellion, 41
Bui Tin, 234
Bundy, McGeorge, 28, 35, 66, 70, 71, 164(photo)
    decision-making influence, 72

    pacification program, 63, 65, 67, 68, 73, 80
    views on Henry Cabot Lodge, 71
Bundy, William, 35, 141, 159
Bunker, Ellsworth, 86, 87, 88, 97, 99, 100, 105, 126,
    131, 134, 144–145, 147, 156, 158, 165(photo), 212,
    213, 255, 274
    accelerated pacification campaign, 202, 205
Buzhardt, J. Fred, 239

Calhoun, John, 125
Ca Mau peninsula, 5
Cambodia, 35, 57, 142, 143, 219
Cao Dai sect, 6, 10, 53, 139
Cao Hao Hon, 232, 257, 262
Cao Van Vien, 116, 149, 157
CAP program. *See* Combined Action Platoon
    program
Carver, George, 246
CEDAR FALLS. *See* Operation CEDAR FALLS
Central Committee, 8
Central Intelligence Agency (CIA), 2, 11, 18, 22, 24,
    82, 265
    accelerated pacification campaign, 202, 203, 205
    ICEX, 113
    OCO funding, 82, 83, 93
    Phoenix program and, 154, 235
    provincial reconnaissance units, 245–246
    RD cadre teams, 74
    VCI intelligence information, 113, 119
    views on Tet Offensive, 141
Central Intelligence Office (CIO), 24, 113
Central Office for South Vietnam (COSVN), 110,
    258
    counterpacification strategy, 234
    directive 136, 248
    purpose, 8
    Resolutions 9 and 14, 218–219
Central Pacification and Development Council
    (CPDC)
    purpose, 196, 216, 227, 228, 257, 274, 275
    refugee relocations, 231, 232
Central Recovery Committee, 144–145, 148, 196.
    See also Project Recovery
Central Revolutionary Development Council, 36,
    101, 130, 147, 158
CG. *See* Civil Guard
Chaisson, John R., 89
Chien Thang
    provisions, 25–26
    weaknesses, 26, 27
Chieu Hoi program, 24, 26, 30, 53, 54, 63, 105, 116,
    126, 180
    accelerated pacification campaign, 198
    advisers, 101–102

communist defectors, 101, 168(photo)
origin, 23
Project Takeoff, 101–102
reorganization, 38
Chinh-Hunnicutt affair, 123, 183
Churchill, Winston, 65
CIA. *See* Central Intelligence Agency
CIDG camp. *See* Civilian Irregular Defense Group
CINCPAC. *See* Commander in Chief Pacific
  Command
CIO. *See* Central Intelligence Office
Civil Guard (CG)
  Chien Thang plan, 26
  purpose, 11–12
  reorganization, 13–14
Civilian, wartime definition, 240
Civilian Irregular Defense Group (CIDG), 178
Civil Operations and Revolutionary Development
    Support (CORDS), 3, 119, 263
  achievements, 275–279
  advisers, 107, 108(table), 244–246, 251, 271–273
  civilian agencies, 273–274
  civilian role in CORDS, 88
  creation, 3, 86–88, 89–90
  dissolution, 274
  field reporting system, 115–116
  HES, 185, 186, 194–195, 204, 211, 260
  II Corps, 180
  III Corps, 185, 187, 188
  IV Corps, 189–192
  ICEX, 113, 114, 115
  Komer's role, 90–91, 99–100
  leverage strategies, 121–124, 125, 128, 129–130
  opening roads, 94
  Operation SPEEDY EXPRESS, 189
  organization, 94–95
  pacification reporting system, 179–180
  pacification support, 93, 119, 134, 149, 159, 258,
    263, 277, 279
  Phoenix program, 154, 198, 241, 251
  programs, 93–94
  Project Recovery, 145
  Project Takeoff, 100–106
  PSDF views, 199
  purpose, 98, 269, 277
  RD cadre support, 102–103
  reductions, 274
  refugees, 103–104
  relocation of people, 176, 228, 229, 230–232, 277
  replacement of government officials, 276–277
  review of GVN budget planning, 127, 128
  role after Tet Offensive, 143, 145, 149
  South Vietnamese government and, 277–278

South Vietnamese officials, 126
staff, 92(fig.)
United States Army, 269
VINH LOC Operation, 174–175
Clark, Robert, 94
Clifford, Clark, 155, 211
  views on strategy, 141–143, 150–151, 211
Colby, William, 2, 8, 24, 113, 118, 153, 156, 158,
    168(photo), 171(photo), 172
  accelerated pacification campaign, 158, 159, 176,
    188, 193, 194, 195, 196, 197, 206, 207, 262, 272
  CORDS evaluation of Koreans, 179
  CORDS leadership, 214, 236
  counteroffensive strategy, 155
  Easter Offensive, 257
  evaluation of pacification, 252, 255, 257
  forced relocations, 231, 232
  ICEX, 113
  pacification goals, 193, 214–215
  Paris peace talks, 202
  Phoenix, 118, 153, 234, 236, 237, 240
  replaces Komer, 193, 214–215
  responsibilities, 206
Colonial rule, French, effect on South Vietnam,
    10, 11
Combined Action Platoon (CAP) program, 108,
    229
Combined campaign plan (1967), 85, 101
Combined campaign plan (1968), 101, 128
Commander in Chief Pacific Command
    (CINCPAC), 14, 17
Communists
  anti-infrastructure efforts, 153
  cadre units, 7
  in countryside, 198
  defectors, 168(photo)
  killings in Hue, 136
  liberation committee formation, 150, 201
  losses, 253
  National Liberation Front, 6
  Phoenix program, 247, 248–249
  political moves, 150
  presence in Hau Nghia, 49
  propaganda campaigns, 23
  revenue for VC, 134
  South Vietnam, 2, 111(fig.)
  Tet Offensive (1968), 136–140
  Tet Offensive (1969), 217–220
  See also North Vietnam; Viet Cong; Viet Cong
    infrastructure
Cook, John, 241
Cooksey, Howard, 244
Cooper, Charles, 73

Cooper, Chester
  Honolulu meeting, 70
  pacification recommendations, 65–68
Corcoran, Charles A., 222–223
CORDS. *See* Civil Operations and Revolutionary
    Development Support
Corruption, 39, 42, 277
COSVN. *See* Central Office for South Vietnam
Cottrell, Sterling, 122
  pilot leverage plan, 129
Counterinsurgency
  development, 2–3
  doctrine, 20
  Kennedy administration support, 16–18
  plan, 14
  special group, 18–19
County fair operations
  example, 48, 228
  purpose, 47–49
CPDC. *See* Central Pacification and Development
    Council
Crittenberger, Willid D., 83
Cross, Charles, 147
Cu Chi, 49
Cushing, Henry B., refugee relocations, 231, 232
Cushman, Robert E., Jr., 173, 176

Dang Lao Dong, 110. *See* Indochinese Communist
    Party
Davidson, Ollie, 187
Davidson, Phillip, 58, 113–114, 212, 221, 222, 252
Dean, John Gunther, 243, 273
Decker, George, 19
Defense Intelligence Agency (DIA), 119
Department of Defense (DOD), 3, 18, 108, 202, 269
DePuy, William E., 26, 29, 30
  Ben Suc evaluation, 57–58
Detention centers, provincial, 118, 238–239
DIA. *See* Defense Intelligence Agency
Diem. *See* Ngo Dinh Diem
Dien Ban district, 175–177
DIOCCs. *See* District Intelligence Operations
    Coordinating Centers
District advisory teams, 94, 95
District Intelligence Operations Coordinating
    Centers (DIOCCs), 116–117, 153
Do Cao Tri, 182, 184
DOD. *See* Department of Defense
Dodson, Jerry, 139
Dolvin, Welborn, 232
Dong Tam. See Operation *Dong Tam*
Dong Van Quang, 214
Duiker, William, 6, 252

Duong Van Minh, 243, 265–266

Easter Offensive, 255–258
  effect on pacification, 263
  RF/PF performance, 258–260
  strategy, 255–256
Eckhardt, George, 155, 191
Economic aid, 68
Economic development, 67, 80
Eisenhower, Dwight D., 13
Elections
  local elections, 265–266
  1971 South Vietnam presidential race, 266–268
Enthoven, Alain, 141
Ewell, Julian, 61, 189, 192
  views on strategic objectives plan, 213

FAIRFAX. *See* Operation FAIRFAX
Fall, Bernard, 7
Farmer, Harry, 245
FBI. *See* Federal Bureau of Investigation
F-6 campaign, purpose, 242–243
Federal Bureau of Investigation (FBI), 115
Felt, Harry, 14
Field reporting system, anti-VCI efforts, 115
Forsythe, George, 91, 108, 128, 131, 132, 145, 147, 173,
    214
  mobile advisory teams, 108
Fort Bragg, 108, 245
  Special Warfare Center, 17
Fowler, Henry, 142
Fulbright, William, 70

Gates, Mahlon E., 94
Gaud, William, 83, 96–97
Gia Dinh province
  accelerated pacification campaign, 183
  pacification efforts, 55
  Tet Offensive effects, 139–140, 147, 148
  VCI presence, 56
  See also Binh Chanh district; Operation
      FAIRFAX
Goodpaster, Andrew, 214
Great Society, 2, 70, 80
Greenwalt, William, 117
Guerrillas, 19, 151
  COSVN Resolutions 9 and 14, 218–219
  rebuilding, 210
  reduction, 253
  support from Hanoi, 28–29, 177
  types, 7–8
  U.S. response, 19–20
  Viet Cong, 7, 99, 219

Habib, Phillip, 51
Hamburger Hill, 232–233
Hamlet Evaluation System (HES), 197, 201, 248
  accelerated pacification campaign, 158–159, 194,
    195, 197, 198(table), 204
  CORDS revisions, 260
  data interpretation disagreements, 204, 210, 211,
    261
  Easter offensive, 256
  effect offensive (1969), 203
  effect of Tet offensive (1968), 137, 152
  hamlet security, 254
  III Corps, 185–186
  Kien Hoa province, 190
  measurement of progress, 96
  Nixon administration and, 210, 211
  Paris peace talks, 193, 202
  problems associated with, 194
  structure and origin, 95–96
  VCI and, 248, 249
Hannah, John, 247
Hanoi, 4, 5, 209, 219–220
  change in operations, 211
  new military strategy, 135
  troop increases, 28–29
  Viet Cong infrastructure, 110
  See also Communists; North Vietnam; Viet
    Cong; Viet Cong infrastructure
Harkins, Paul D., 17, 18, 23, 28
Harriman, Averill, 202
Hau Nghia province
  accelerated pacification campaign, 183–188
  communist presence, 49, 61
  pacification efforts, 48–50
  United States 25th division, 49–50
Helms, Richard, 53
Herrington, Stuart, 241
  views of National Police, 238
HES. *See* Hamlet Evaluation System
Hickey, Gerald, 262
Hoa Hao sect, 6, 10, 126, 139
Hoang Ngoc Du, 176
Hoang Van Lac, 158, 194
Hoang Xuan Lam, 173, 176, 177, 229–230, 231, 232
Ho Chi Minh, 4, 5, 183
Hoi Chanh, 54. *See also* Chieu Hoi
Holbrooke, Richard, 73, 82
Hop Tac program, 28, 50, 73, 183
  American support, 26–27, 28
  Gia Dinh, 55
Hospitals, U.S. assistance, 46–47
Hue
  Binh Minh campaign, 243

civilian mass killing, 136
  Tet Offensive damage, 136, 137
Huks, 1, 2
Humphrey, Hubert, 208
Hunnicutt, Cecil, 123, 232
Huss, Mark, 67, 125

Ia Drang, 32, 33
ICEX. *See* Infrastructure Coordination and
    Exploitation
I Corps
  accelerated pacification campaign, 172–177
  refugee population, 257
  RF/PF performance, 258–259
  security forces, 177
  strategic hamlets, 22
  U.S. troop presence, 259
II Corps
  accelerated pacification campaign, 177–181
  military forces, 177
  RF/PF performance, 259
  security concerns, 262
  strategic hamlets, 22
III Corps
  accelerated pacification campaign, 182–188
  RF/PF performance, 259
  strategic hamlets, 22
III Marine Amphibious Force (MAF), 173, 175
Indochinese Communist Party, 4, 5, 10
  unification of Vietnam, 5
Infrastructure Coordination and Exploitation
    (ICEX), 113–116
  responsibilities, 113–114
  origin, 113
  structure, 114
  See also Phoenix program
Intelligence
  Phoenix program, 235
  South Vietnam, 24–25, 56
  types, 112
  VCI information, 112–113
  See also specific agencies
Inter-Agency Committee for Province
    Rehabilitation, 22
Interrogation centers, province, 113, 235
Iron Triangle, 57, 58
  pacification efforts, 57–58, 58–59
IV Corps
  accelerated pacification campaign, 188–192
  Viet Cong presence, 200, 219

Jacobson, George, 181, 236, 243, 244, 255, 261, 266,
    269, 271, 276, 277
JCS. *See* Joint Chiefs of Staff

JGS. *See* Joint General Staff
Johnson, Harold K., 33, 75, 80, 107, 270
Johnson, Lyndon, 1, 16, 29, 31, 35, 55, 97, 134, 135–
    136, 142, 143, 163–166(photos), 206, 269, 278
    change in U.S. policy, 29
    combat engagement restrictions, 31–32
    Honolulu meeting, 70–71
    land reform, 104–105
    military objectives, 79
    military strength increases, 142
    pacification program, 1, 67–68, 75–76, 80, 85, 86,
        87, 88
    reelection attempt, 134–135
    Tet Offensive effects, 143, 149
    U.S. combat troops, 31–32
Johnstone, Craig, 138
Joint Chiefs of Staff (JCS), 18, 28, 68, 74
    accelerated pacification campaign, 203, 204, 238,
        246
    enemy strength, 209
    U.S. withdrawal, 209
Joint General Staff (JGS), 12, 39, 108, 128, 131, 132,
    196, 238, 259
Joint United States Public Affairs Office
    (JUSPAO), 101
    psyops techniques, 115
Jones, Raymond G., 243, 244
Jordan, Pendleton A., 148
J-2 intelligence office, purpose, 113
JUSPAO. *See* Joint United States Public Affairs
    Office

Katzenbach, Nicholas, 78, 86, 97, 124
Kennedy, Edward, refugee problems, 103
Kennedy, John F., 19
    administration, 25
    counterinsurgency plan, 16–18
    South Vietnam reforms, 14
Kerwin, Walter, 107, 113, 114, 155, 182, 186, 221
Khmers, 10
Kien Hoa province, pacification efforts, 140, 190
Kieu Cong Cung, pacification attempts, 20
Killen, James, 64
Kissinger, Henry, 202
    pacification criteria, 210
Knowlton, William A., 80, 91, 128
Kolko, Gabriel, 198–199, 206, 250, 252
    land reform, 264
Komer, Robert W., 2, 43, 55, 82, 87, 131, 132, 134,
    164–166(photos), 211, 212, 252, 272
    Abrams and, 151, 154–155, 180, 214
    accelerated pacification campaign, 158–159, 205,
        206, 233, 276
    AID and, 93

APC role, 158–159
    appointment to MACV, 87
    CORDS leadership, 90, 99–100, 214
    CORDS reporting, 179–180
    counteroffensive proposal, 150, 156
    decision-making power, 73
    effect of Tet offensive (1968) on pacification,
        140, 141, 143, 149
    "Giving a New Thrust to Pacification," 76–77
    ICEX program, 113–114, 115, 116
    leverage, 121, 126, 185
    MACV relationship to, 89, 91
    management style, 105–106
    memo to Bunker, 133
    Nguyen Duc Thang and, relationship, 124–125,
        127, 130, 132
    OCO and, 82, 83, 85
    pacification efforts, 75–76, 77, 85, 87–88, 97, 125,
        135, 143, 197
    peers and, 179
    Phoenix program, 116, 117, 118, 153, 234, 237
    post-Tet strategy, 150, 151, 152, 155, 156, 157
    presidential special assistant, appointed as, 72,
        73
    Project Recovery, 145
    Project Takeoff, 99–101, 103, 105, 130
    recommendation from McGeorge Bundy, 72
    review of GVN budget, 126, 127, 128, 129
    RF/PF advisers, 106–109
    single manager, Long An province and, 86
    support for United States Army, 76
    Westmoreland and, relationship, 87–88, 89, 96
Koren, Henry, 78
Kotzebue, Albert, 190
Ky. *See* Nguyen Cao Ky

Laird, Melvin, 209, 213, 237, 246, 270, 276
Land reform, 11, 14, 15, 216, 252, 263, 264
    Project Takeoff, 104–105
    South Vietnamese support, 104–105
Land to the Tiller Law, 217, 263
    flaws, 265
    Thieu's provisions, 263–264
Lansdale, Edward, 2, 11, 20, 67, 72, 79, 80, 125
    pacification program, 67
Laos, 32, 142, 143
Lathram, L. Wade, 83, 100, 125, 128
League for the Independence of Vietnam. *See*
    Vietnam Doc Lap Dong Minh Hoi
Leaty, Daniel L., 226–227, 262
Le Loi (emperor), 194
Le Loi campaign, 157. *See also* Accelerated
    Pacification Campaign
Lemnitzer, Lyman, 19, 66

Le Nguyen Khang, 55, 102, 118, 123, 153
Leonhart, William, 73, 83
  succeeds Komer, 97
Le Tri Tin, 176
Le Van Than, 174
Leverage
  CORDS strategies, 100, 121, 122, 128
  definition, 121
  replacement of government officials, 276–277
  State Department views, 124
  Vann's strategy, 129
Liberation committees, 150, 154, 198, 200–201
  advantages to communists, 201
Lien Thanh, 243
Linh Quang Vien, 116
Locke, Eugene, 87
Loc Tien hamlet, 43
Lodge, Henry Cabot, 29, 50, 51–52, 65, 68, 71, 72,
    73, 75, 76, 77, 78, 81, 83, 165(photo)
  decision-making influence, 69
  Johnson's admonitions, 79
  pacification support, 66–67
  RD cadre program, 67
  See also Office of Civil Operations; Porter,
    William
Long An
  Communist presence, 61
  pacification efforts, 50–53
  single manager, 53, 55, 86
  strategic hamlet program, 22–23
  United States 25th division, 52–53
Long Huu village, 56, 92
  military operation, 54
  pacification efforts, 53–55
Long-Range Planning Task Group (LORAPL),
    purpose, 212
LORAPL. *See* Long-Range Planning Task Group
Lu Mong Lan, 177, 180
Lu Van Tinh, 127
Lynch, Eugene, 186

MAAG. *See* Military Assistance Advisory Group
MACCORDS. *See* Military Assistance Command,
    Civil Operations and Revolutionary
    Development Support
MACDC. *See* Military Assistance Command,
    Vietnam, Directorate of Construction
MacDonald, Donald, 103
MACV. *See* Military Assistance Command,
    Vietnam
Magellas, James, 180, 181
Magsaysay, Ramon, 11
MALTs. *See* Mobile advisory logistics teams
Manila Conference (October 1966), 74

Mao Zedong, 4
Marshall, Donald, 212
Martin, Graham, 274
MASA course. *See* Military assistance security
    adviser course
Ma San Nhon, 184
MATs. *See* Mobile advisory teams
Matteson, Robert, 151
May 1968 offensive, 147
McAfee, Gage, 236
McCarthy, Eugene, 134
McCone, John A., 27
McGarr, Lionel, 21
McGiffert, David E., 107, 270
McManaway, Clayton, 147
McNamara, Robert, 27, 28, 34, 35, 52, 166(photo)
  pacification program, 61, 68, 72, 73, 77, 78, 79,
    80, 85, 86, 97, 106–107, 141
McNaughton, John, 74, 77
MEADE RIVER. *See* Operation MEADE RIVER
MEDCAP. *See* Medical Civil Affairs Program
Medical Civil Affairs Program (MEDCAP),
    outpatient care provisions, 46
Mekong Delta, 140. *See also* IV Corps
  development program, 1
  French cultivation, 11
  RF/PF performance, 259–260
  security measures, 197
  Viet Cong control, 5, 188, 219
Mendheim, Billy, 226
Military assistance
  costs, 68
  in South Vietnam, 11, 15
Military Assistance Advisory Group (MAAG), 13,
    27
Military Assistance Command, Civil Operations
    and Revolutionary Development Support
    (MACCORDS), 90–91
Military Assistance Command, Vietnam,
    Directorate of Construction (MACDC), 93,
    148
Military Assistance Command, Vietnam (MACV),
    31, 39, 45, 63, 65, 67, 72, 76, 77, 79, 83, 126, 128,
    135, 200, 209, 252
  accelerated pacification campaign, 203–204
  adviser behavior recommendations, 123, 124
  advisory teams, 273
  Chien Thang program, 25–26
  formation, 17
  HES review, 211
  Hop Tac program, 26–27, 28
  J-2 intelligence office, 33, 113, 114, 119
  Phoenix and, 154
  refugee policy, 104

Revolutionary Development Support
Directorate, 80, 91
staff principals, 167(photo)
strategic hamlets, 22
strategic objectives plan, 212–213
Military Assistance Program (MAP), purpose, 13
Military assistance security adviser (MASA)
course, 245
Military Assistance Training Adviser (MATA)
course, 244
Military Provincial Health Assistance Program
(MILPHAP)
purpose, 46–47, 229
Military Security Service, 112, 114, 235
Miller, Tim, 241
MILPHAP. *See* Military Provincial Health
Assistance Program
Ministry of Defense, 127
Ministry of Public Works, 93
Ministry of Psychological Warfare, 23
Ministry of Refugees, 145, 227
Ministry of Revolutionary Development, 67, 102,
125, 127, 145
RD cadre support, 130
Ministry of Rural Reconstruction, 40–41
Ministry of Social Welfare, 40–41
Ministry of Social Welfare and Relief, 229
Mission Council, 33, 43, 52, 53, 95, 144
objectives, 65
piaster imprest fund, 122–123
Mobile advisory logistics teams (MALTs), 109
Mobile advisory teams (MATs)
purpose, 108
responsibilities, 109
rural presence, 204
withdrawal, 258
Mobile Riverine Force, 181, 188–189, 191
Mobile training team, 59
Mobilization bill, objectives, 152
Mock, Vernon P., 69
Montagnards, 10, 139, 181, 262
Montague, Robert, 26, 73, 82, 91, 114, 173, 180, 186,
214
Moorsteen, Richard, 73
Myung Shin Chae, 177

NANTUCKET BEACH. *See* Operation
NANTUCKET BEACH
Nathan, Robert, 164(photo)
National Assembly, 14, 152
National Liberation Front (NLF), 109, 193, 217, 240
purpose, 6
views of peasants, 7

National Police, 11, 19, 24, 38, 113, 137, 138, 154, 176,
235
expansion, 238, 253, 254, 275
Special Branch, 24, 112, 113, 116, 138, 225, 235, 242,
246
National Police Field Force (NPFF), 56, 57, 69, 137,
154
anti-infrastructure responsibilities, 112, 113, 116,
178
corruption charges, 138
expansion, 104, 238
Phoenix program, 235, 237–238
Project Takeoff, 104
purpose, 39
Viet Cong, 225
weaponry, 154
National Security Action Memorandum (NSAM),
288
provisions, 29, 61, 213
National Security Action Memorandum 362, 88
National Security Council (NSC), 18
National Security Study Memorandum (NSSM),
36, 209
National Security Study Memorandum 1, 210,
319(n3)
National Training Center (at Vung Tau), 36, 103,
265–266
NCOs. *See* Noncommissioned officers
Nes, David G., 64
Ngo Dinh Diem, 4, 5, 8, 12, 14–15, 17, 20, 122, 264
coup, 25
Hau Nghia province, 184
pacification program, 11
police and security forces, 13–14
political base, 12
strategic hamlet program, 21–22, 23
Ngo Dinh Nhu, 20
strategic hamlet program, 21–22
Ngo Ngi Dzu, refugee relocation efforts, 262, 273
Ngo Quang Truong, 173, 174, 242, 244, 257
Nguyen Bao Tri, 128
Nguyen Cao Ky, 36, 41, 54, 116, 123, 144, 145, 146,
153, 163(photo), 266
military increases, 74
Nguyen Chanh Thi, 34, 41
Nguyen Co Thach, 234
Nguyen Duc Thang, 34, 38, 41, 67, 79, 103, 108, 122,
145, 146
Komer and, relationship, 124–125, 127, 130, 132
orders ARVN offensive, 140
pacification program, 29, 36, 42–44
RD cadre program, 131
reasons for South Vietnam disunity, 131–132
resignation, 132

Nguyen Huu Co, 34
Nguyen Khanh, 50
    pacification plans, 25–26, 27
Nguyen Ngoc Loan, 116, 117, 118, 138, 153
Nguyen Phuc Que, 41
Nguyen Ton Nghia, 118–119
Nguyen Van Hieu, 224
Nguyen Van La, 157
Nguyen Van Loc, 146
    ICEX program, 116
Nguyen Van Thieu, 36, 41, 58, 70, 91, 116, 126, 131,
        132, 156, 163(photo), 252
    accelerated pacification campaign, 157, 196, 206
    anti-VCI efforts, 116
    authoritarian actions, 267, 268
    Ben Suc evacuation, 58
    cease fire, 193
    Four "Noes," 215
    hamlet evaluation system, 195
    HES use, 195
    II Corps, 181–182
    land reform, 263–265
    mobilization, 152
    national unity, 144
    1971 presidential elections, 266, 267
    pacification efforts, 132, 154, 215–217, 252
    pacification strategy, 149, 150, 156, 157, 193
    peasant relocations, 181–182
    Phoenix program, 117, 118–119, 153, 234, 243
    rural support, 267
    suspension of local elections, 266
    Tet offensive (1968) and, 144–146, 147, 148
Nguyen Van Toan, 173, 231
Nguyen Van Tung, 241
Nguyen Viet Thanh, 188
Nixon, Richard M., 193, 206, 207, 210, 255, 257
    accelerated pacification campaign, 203
    condition for withdrawal, 210
    election and Vietnam, 208–209
    mission statement to Abrams, 213
    troop withdrawal policy, 209–210, 220
    Vietnamization policy, 208, 211–212, 220
    WASHINGTON GREEN, Operation, 226
NLF. *See* National Liberation Front
Nolting, Frederick, 22, 23
Noncommissioned officers (NCOs), 17
    training, 109
North Vietnam
    army. *See* North Vietnamese Army
    COSVN Resolutions 9 and 14, 218–219
    creation, 4
    Easter Offensive, 255–256, 257
    goals, 4
    Johnson's military restrictions, 31–32

    military hierarchy, 8
    National Liberation Front support, 6
    Tet offensive planning, 135
    VCI control, 110
    See also Communists; Hanoi; Politburo; Viet
        Cong
North Vietnamese Army (NVA), 27, 29, 30, 174, 177
    II Corps accelerated pacification campaign, 180
    IV Corps, 188, 200, 219
    1968 Tet casualties, 223
    strength in South Vietnam, 31, 134
NPFF. *See* National Police Field Force
NSC. *See* National Security Council
NSSM. *See* National Security Study Memorandum
NVA. *See* North Vietnamese Army

OCO. *See* Office of Civil Operations
Office of Civil Operations (OCO), 58, 80, 88, 90
    civilian operations, 83
    funding, 82
    pacification support, 85
    problems associated with, 85
    program divisions, 82–83
    purpose, 57
    responsibilities, 79, 82
    structure (December 1966–April 1967), 84(fig.)
Operation CEDAR FALLS, pacification effort, 56–
        59, 90, 227
Operation COLORS UP, 184
Operation *Dong Tam,* 148
Operation FAIRFAX, 183
    effect on Viet Cong infrastructure, 55–56
Operation MEADE RIVER
    accelerated pacification campaign, 175–177
    corps and province officials, 176
Operation NANTUCKET BEACH, 231
Operation RUSSELL BEACH/BOLD MARINER,
        222, 227–231
    logistics, 227
    plan deployment, 228–229
    purpose, 228
    relocations, 227–230
Operation SPEEDY EXPRESS, 189
Operation VINH LOC, 173–175
Operation WASHINGTON GREEN, 222–227
    achievements, 226
    purpose, 223
    strategy, 224, 233
Osborn, Kenneth B., 239–240
Osgood, Charles, 2

PAAS surveys. *See* Pacification Attitude Analysis
        System surveys
Pacific Architects & Engineers, 148

Pacification
    absence of a single manager, 64, 65, 69, 72, 75
    advisers' role, 59–60
    agrovilles, 20
    ARVN support, 75, 102, 196
    basic concepts, 2–3, 69, 211
    Chien Thang program, 25–26
    civil affairs teams, 60–61
    Colby's approach, 214–215
    CORDS support, 93, 119, 130, 134, 149, 159
    Diem coup, 25–26
    Diem's strategies, 20–25
    Easter Offensive effects, 256–257, 263
    funding, 275, 278
    Gia Dinh, 55
    goals, 1, 2, 85
    hamlet program, 21–22
    Hau Nghia, 48–50
    Honolulu meeting, 70–71, 72, 80
    Hop Tac program, 28–29
    Kissinger's criteria, 210
    Komer's support, 91, 135, 143
    Long An, 50–55
    military and civil programs, 64
    need for military's resources, 69, 97
    OCO support, 85
    Operation CEDAR FALLS, 56–59
    origin of term, 11
    political effects, 265
    problems associated with, 42–43
    progress under Nguyen Duc Thang, 42–44
    Project Takeoff, 99–101
    reporting system, 179–180
    revival, 35–42
    roles of U.S. and South Vietnamese forces, 34
    setbacks, 28
    shortcomings, 131
    single manager trial (Dinh Tuong, Bin Thuan,
        Darlac), 65
    South Korean forces, 178–179
    South Vietnam support, 11, 36, 43(table), 147,
        154, 156, 216–217, 279
    Tet Offensive (1968), effects, 141
    Tet Offensive (1969), effects, 217–218
    Thieu's efforts, 215–217
    U.S. support, 68–69, 76, 222
    Westmoreland's concept of operations, 32–33
Pacification Attitude Analysis System (PAAS)
    surveys, 249
Pacification Studies Group, responsibilities, 96,
    226
Palmer, Bruce, 76
Paramilitary forces, 39
    Civil Guard, 11–14, 26

    See also People's Self-Defense Force; Regional
        Forces and Popular Forces
Paris peace talks, 193, 195, 201, 202, 210
Parker, Evan, 115, 117
Parker, Warren, 176
Paxette, Robert, 273
Peasants
    Chien Thang plan, 25–26
    civil affairs assistance, 48
    colonial rule effects, 10
    Easter Offensive effects, 256
    HES statistics, 197
    land reforms, 263
    political and economic affairs, 41–42
    refugees, 40–41
    relocation of villagers, 20, 58, 181–182, 227–229
    security reforms, 216
    strategic hamlet program, 22
    Viet Cong influences, 6–7
    views on South Vietnamese government, 37–38
    See also Refugees; Rural population; Villages
Peers, William, 68, 155, 177, 178, 179–180
    II Corps acceleration pacification campaign,
        178–179
People's Revolutionary Party (PRP), 109–110, 158.
    See also National Liberation Front; Viet
    Cong; Viet Cong infrastructure
People's Self-Defense Force (PSDF), 170(photo),
    218, 254
    accelerated pacification campaign, 199
    growth, 253
    II Corps, 181
    III Corps, 182, 185
    purpose, 152
    strength, 253
    training goals, 199
    weapons, 154
Pham Truong Chinh, 123, 126
Phan Van Quang, 103
Philips, Rufus, 22
Phoenix program, 2, 101, 116, 118
    achievements, 249, 250
    accelerated pacification campaign and, 158, 198–
        199
    an tri procedures, 236
    assassination and torture allegations, 236, 239–
        241, 251
    casualty statistics difficulties, 241–242
    communist reaction, 247–248
    CORDS involvement, 154, 180, 198, 250
    criticisms, 239
    defects, 238, 247, 251
    detention system, 238–239, 249

District Intelligence Operation Coordinating Center, 116–117
effectiveness, 247, 248, 249, 250
interpretations of, 250
management by National Police, 237
procedures, 235–236
promulgation, 152–153
public awareness of, 249
purpose, 250
sentencing guidelines, 236, 249
South Vietnam, 237
structure, 117
terminology, 240
Tet Offensive effects, 138
U.S. Army advisers, 244–246, 251
Viet Cong infrastructure, 234, 247, 249–250
See also Detention centers; Infrastructure Coordination and Exploitation (ICEX); *Phung Hoang* program; VCI
Phong Dinh province, 22
Phung Hoang program, 116, 153, 158, 237. *See also* Infrastructure Coordination and Exploitation (ICEX); Phoenix program
Phu Yen province, Tet Offensive effects, 139
Piaster imprest fund
appropriations, 145
establishment by Mission Council, 122–123
Plain of Reeds, 5
Police. *See* National Police
Police Field Force. *See* National Police Field Force
Politburo, 8, 138, 211, 255
Porter, William, 51–54, 67, 164(photo)
and Komer, 73, 74, 75, 76, 80
and OCO, 80, 82, 83
role in pacification program, 71–72, 73, 74, 75, 77, 78, 79, 81
views on military involvement in pacification, 76
Warrenton Conference, 68, 69
Potts, William, 253
Program for the Pacification and Long-Term Development of Vietnam (PROVN), 75, 212
Project Recovery, 144–147
achievements, 148
shortcomings, 146
structure, 146
ten/ten/five program, 146
Tet Offensive aid, 144–145
Viet Cong attacks, 147
See also Central Recovery Committee
Project Takeoff, 99–106, 119, 121, 130
armed propaganda teams, 102
eight action programs, 100
ICEX development, 113

police force increases, 104
refugee care, 103–104
Protection of the People Against Terrorism, 246–247. *See also* Phoenix program
Province advisory teams, 90, 126, 184
importance, 273
leverage role, 128–129
responsibilities, 94–95
Province Intelligence Coordination Committees, 24
Province interrogation centers, 112–113
Province Security Committee, 248
problems associated with, 235–236
structure, 235
Provincial Coordinating Committee, 60, 64
Provincial Reconnaissance Units (PRUs), 56, 112, 113, 235
advisers, 245–246
allegations of atrocities, 246
CIA, 245–246
structure, 245
PROVN. *See* Program for the Pacification and Long-Term Development of Vietnam
PRP. *See* People's Revolutionary Party
PRUs. *See* Provincial Reconnaissance Units
PSDF. *See* People's Self-Defense Force
Psyops, 26
techniques, purpose, 115

Race, Jeffrey, views on strategic hamlet program, 23
RD cadre teams. *See* Revolutionary Development cadre
Refugees, 2, 39–41, 60, 61, 134
CEDAR FALLS, Operation, 57
civil affairs teams, 45–47, 69
CORDS involvement, 103, 104
Easter Offensive effects, 257
forced relocation, 57, 58, 103, 104, 181, 216, 262
fund allocation, 127
growth of, 40–41
I Corps, 257
Project Takeoff, 103–104, 105
RUSSELL BEACH, Operation, 229–230
Saigon's role, 40, 41, 46
ten/ten/five program, 146
See also Peasants; Relocation of villagers; Rural population
Regional Forces and Popular Forces (RF/PF), 18, 27, 48, 59, 63, 74, 91, 93, 114, 131, 134, 162(photo)
accelerated pacification campaign, 182, 197, 218, 225, 235, 246
adviser increases, 106–107

casualty rates, 253
CORDS efforts, 89, 275
desertions, 258
Dinh Tuong province, 190
Easter Offensive performance, 256, 257, 258
growth, 154, 253, 254, 275
hamlet security, 157
III Corps strength, 185
Long Huu, 54
mobile advisory teams, 108, 109, 204, 258
operations, 102
performance, 258–260
strength increases, 39
territorial forces evaluation system, 93, 258
Tet Offensive effects, 137
training programs, 74, 89, 225
Viet Cong attacks, 253
weaponry, 214
Relocation of villagers, 58, 227–232
CORDS influence, 277
justifications, 230
problems associated with, 262
See also Refugees
Republic of Korea forces (South Korean), 75, 173,
177, 178, 179
pacification support, 178, 179
Resor, Stanley, 246
pacification advisers, 270, 272
Resurrection City, 228
Revolutionary Development (RD) cadre, 36, 37,
39, 41, 44, 48, 53, 63, 72, 91, 229
advisers, 59
ARVN support, 42, 74, 102–103, 131, 137
assistance program, 83
attrition, 37–38
change in team size, 216
CIA and, 83, 93
Colby and, 168(photo)
growth, 154
hamlet security, 157
Long An, 52
Project Takeoff, 102, 103, 105
responsibilities, 36–37
support, 130
Tet Offensive effects, 137, 139, 140, 147
training, 74, 102–103, 169(photo)
U.S. support, 101
weaponry, 154
RF/PF. *See* Regional Forces and Popular Forces
Richards, Daniel, 28
Rogers, Bernard W., 58–59
Roles and Missions Study, 37
Rollins, Andrew P., 148

Roman Catholics, 139
migration to South Vietnam, 10
Rosenblatt, Peter, 73
Rosson, William, 19, 104
Rostow, Walt W., 16, 61, 72, 77, 79, 85, 87, 134, 142,
165(photo), 202
Rowan, Carl, 83
Rung Sat Special Zone, 53
Rural population
extension of security, 216
guerrilla attacks, 119
HES statistics, 197, 254
relocation of villagers, 20, 181–182
South Vietnam, 20, 193
Tet Offensive (1968) effects, 136–137
See also Peasants; Refugees; Villages
Rusk, Dean, 35, 83, 86, 72, 79, 166(photo)
RUSSELL BEACH/BOLD MARINER. *See*
Operation RUSSELL BEACH/BOLD
MARINER

SAAFO. *See* Special Assistant to the Ambassador
for Field Operations
SACSA. *See* Special Assistant for
Counterinsurgency and Special Activities
Saigon
accelerated pacification campaign, 191, 203, 205
civil servants, 20
colonial rule effects, 10
government problems, 126, 132
government succession, 1
HES population estimates, 137–138, 254
pacification efforts, 67, 75
peasants, 7
political legitimacy, 29–30
port of, 73, 146
rebuilding efforts, 148
refugee assistance, 46
Tet Offensive damage, 136
U.S. aid, 30
Viet Cong infiltration, 5–6
See also South Vietnam
SDC. *See* Self-Defense Corps
Seaman, Johnathan, 55–56
pacification efforts in Iron Triangle, 57–58
Security committee, 114
Self-Defense Corps (SDC)
Chien Thang plan, 26
purpose, 11–12, 39
Self-defense groups, 39
Self-help projects, 46
Sharp, Ulysses S. Grant, 63
Shea, Leonard, 121
Siena, James, 246

SLO. *See* Special Liaison Office
Small-unit attacks, 253
Sorley, Lewis, 221, 222
Southeast Asia Analysis Reports, 141
Southeast Asia Treaty Organization, 13
South Korea, pacification efforts, 75, 178–179
South Korean Army units
    Capital Division, 177, 224
    9th Infantry Division, 177
South Vietnam
    accelerated pacification campaign, 158, 196, 199
    administrative divisions, 9(map)
    budget review, 127
    CEDAR FALLS, 58
    census grievance teams, 25
    Chieu Hoi program, 23–24
    command-and-control agreements, 34–35
    communist organization, 111(fig.)
    CORDS purpose in, 121, 275
    corrupt officials, 276
    counterinsurgency plan, 14, 18–19
    county fair operations, 47–49
    demographics, 10
    detention policies, 239
    Easter offensive, 256
    economic aid, 13
    GNP, 13
    HES misuse, 194–195
    history, 8, 10
    Honolulu meeting results, 70–71
    ICEX program, 116
    intelligence agencies, 24–25, 112
    land reform, 104–105
    leadership disunity, 131
    leverage strategies, 128–129
    local elections, 265–266
    management inefficiencies, 132
    MEADE RIVER, 175
    medical civil affairs assistance, 46–47
    military advisers and, 59–60
    military and civilian involvement, 80–81
    mobilization legislation, 152
    national police, 24
    1967 presidential election, 116, 124, 134
    1971 presidential election, 266–268
    pacification efforts, 20–24, 34, 36, 43(table), 61–
        62, 88, 147, 154, 156, 216–217, 279
    paramilitary forces, 11–12
    Phoenix program, 234, 237, 249
    piaster imprest fund, 122–123
    police and security forces, 13, 15, 38–39
    population base, 254–255, 261–262
    Project Recovery, 144–147
    Project Takeoff, 100

    refugees, 39–40
    reliability of reports, 261
    response to Tet Offensive (1968), 143
    security forces, 69, 91, 278
    Taylor-Rostow mission, 17–18
    terrorist acts, 6–7
    Tet counteroffensive objectives, 150–151
    U.S. military support, 12–15, 18, 31, 50, 63–64
    Viet Cong, 196–197
    village development, 103, 105
    WASHINGTON GREEN, Operation, 225–226
    See also individual provinces; Saigon
South Vietnamese units
    1st ARVN Division, 173
    2d ARVN Division, 173, 229–230, 231
    5th ARVN Division, 48, 57
    7th ARVN Cavalry, 174
    7th ARVN Division, 190, 191
    22d ARVN Division, 38, 224
    25th ARVN Division, 51, 123, 232
    43d Ranger Battalion, 138
Special Assistant for Counterinsurgency and
    Special Activities (SACSA), 18, 68
Special Assistant to the Ambassador for Field
    Operations (SAAFO), 269, 274
Special Commisariat for Refugees, 41
Special Liaison Office (SLO), 79, 125
SPEEDY EXPRESS. *See* Operation SPEEDY
    EXPRESS
Stalemate doctrine, 134
State Department, 18, 72, 73, 78
    accelerated pacification campaign, 202, 203, 205
    leverage concept, 124
    pacification efforts, 77–78, 86
Staum, Vernon, 109
Stilwell, Richard, 173, 174
Stone, Charles, accelerated pacification campaign
    support, 178
Strategic Hamlet program, 23, 40, 194, 195
    data, 22
    effect on refugee relocation, 40
    failure, 30
    origin, 21
Strategic objectives plan, 221
    goals, 212–213
Sullivan, William, 274

Tactical area of responsibility (TAOR), 35
Tan Phuoc Khanh village
    county fair operation, 48
    pacification efforts, 48–49
TAOR concept. *See* Tactical area of responsibility
Task Force OREGON, 104
Taxes, VC revenues, 134

Taylor, Maxwell, 16, 23, 28, 29, 33, 66, 67, 80, 81, 85
  appointment as ambassador, 65
  views on Westmoreland's military strategies, 35
Taylor-Rostow mission, in South Vietnam, 17–18
Templar, Gerald, 65
Territorial Force Evaluation System (TFES), 93, 258
Territorial security, 18
Territorial security forces, 99, 149, 172. *See also* People's Self-Defense Force; Regional Forces and Popular Forces
Terrorism, 200, 201, 218
  South Vietnamese officials, 6–7, 20, 131
  U.S. classifications, 219
  villages and hamlets, 219
Tet holidays, 135
  cease-fire agreement, 136
Tet Offensive (1968)
  damage to Saigon, 136
  effect on pacification, 141, 143
  Phoenix program, 138
  planning, 136
  Project Recovery, 144–148
  urban effects, 136–137
  Viet Cong strength, 138–140, 143, 200, 223
Tet Offensive (1969), 203, 217–218
  losses, 218
TFES. *See* Territorial Force Evaluation System
Thang. *See* Nguyen Duc Thang
Thieu. *See* Nguyen Van Thieu
Thompson, Robert, 23, 28, 237
  strategic hamlet program and, 21
Throckmorton, John, 28
Tolson, John, 175
Tran Thien Khiem, 153, 215, 216, 244, 266
Tran Van Huong, 156, 157
Troika signoff, 64, 122
Truman, Harry S., 12
Truong Chinh, 4
Truong Tan Thuc, 176
Turley, William, 252

Ungar, Leonard, 68
United States
  accelerated pacification campaign, 172–177, 192
  anti-Diem coup, 25
  Chien Thang plan, 25–26
  Chieu Hoi program, 23–24, 38
  civil affairs teams, 45–47
  civil and military operations, 69
  command-and-control arrangements, 34–35
  Hamlet Evaluation System, 194–195
  Hop Tac program, 26–27
  military strength, 31, 133

  pacification support, 3, 34, 222
  political objective of war, 61
  South Vietnam, 12–15, 29, 41
  terrorist action classifications, 219
  troika signoff, 122–123
  troop withdrawal policy, 209–210, 220
United States Air Force (USAF), 1, 256, 257
United States Army, 16, 17, 18, 19, 20, 21, 46
  advisers, 269–272
  civil affairs, 45–47, 60, 93
  combat style, 50
  CORDS, 269, 278
  counterinsurgency preparations, 19
  county fair operations, 47–49
  excessive firepower use, 187
  Field Manual, 19, 100–105
  ground operations, types of, 47
  guerrilla warfare, 19–20
  Komer's support, 76
  pacification responsibilities, 69
  pacification support, 60, 61, 76, 127, 131, 172, 192, 222, 225, 229, 254
  Phoenix program, 244–246
  port of Saigon, 73
  Project Recovery support, 146
  reserve forces, 31, 142
  South Vietnam objectives, 79
  Special Forces, 14, 17, 19
United States Congress, 64, 134–135
United States Embassy, 25, 124, 126, 145, 252, 274
United States House of Representatives, 239
United States Information Agency (USIA), 18, 22, 64, 73
United States Marine Corps (USMC), 1, 31, 95, 108, 176, 227, 228, 230
United States Mission, 69, 75, 257
United States Navy, 174, 176, 188
United States Operations Mission (USOM), 13, 20, 60, 66. *See also* AID
United States Seabees (Construction Battalions), 94, 102, 148
United States Senate
  Foreign Relations Committee hearings, 70, 240, 272
  Subcommittee on Refugees, 103
USAF. *See* United States Air Force
USIA. *See* United States Information Agency
USMC. *See* United States Marine Corps
USOM. *See* United States Operations Mission
U.S. units
  1st Cavalry Division, 32, 173, 174, 182, 217
  1st Civil Affairs Company, 93
  1st Infantry Division, 48, 57, 58, 217, 222
  2d Civil Affairs Company, 45–46

3d Marine Division, 173
4th Infantry Division, 177, 178, 224, 226
5th Mechanized Division, 173
9th Infantry Division, 61, 94, 188–192, 219, 259–260
23d Infantry Division (Americal), 173, 227, 228, 229, 231
25th Infantry Division, 49, 50, 51, 52, 57, 80, 183, 184, 186, 217
29th Civil Affairs Company, 45, 93, 229
41st Civil Affairs Company, 45, 93
46th Engineer Battalion, 148
82d Airborne Division, 182
101st Airborne Division, 173, 182, 232
173d Airborne Brigade, 33, 185, 222–226
196th Infantry Brigade, 255
199th Infantry Brigade, 53, 54

Vann, John Paul, 57–58, 83, 85, 90, 114, 118, 155, 185, 197, 239, 240, 247, 254, 255, 258, 262, 276
   expectations of advisers, 94–95
   leverage concept, 129
VC. *See* Viet Cong
VCI. *See* Viet Cong infrastructure
Viet Cong (VC), 3, 5, 6, 14, 16, 18, 23, 27, 28, 29, 30, 31, 41, 43, 44, 48, 69, 131, 219
   accelerated pacification campaign, 191, 197, 200, 204
   agroville destruction, 20
   An Thinh, 186–187
   August 1968 offensive, 151–152
   casualties, 133–134, 172, 223, 253
   casualty rate control, 209
   CEDAR FALLS, Operation, 59, 134
   control in South Vietnam, 25
   counterattacks, 147–148
   defections, 101–102, 161(photo), 191
   detention centers, 238–239
   Easter Offensive, 255–256, 257
   guerrilla forces, 7
   Hau Nghia province, 49–50, 184, 186, 187
   II Corps, 177, 180
   III Corps, 182–183
   infrastructure. *See* Viet Cong infrastructure
   insubordination, 134
   IV Corps, 200
   Kien Hoa province, 190
   land reforms, 15
   liberation committee formation, 201
   Long An province, 51, 52
   Long Huu, 54
   losses (1964–1967), 133–134
   MEADE RIVER, Operation, 175–177
   Mekong delta, 5, 188, 189
   military hierarchy, 8
   mobile advisory teams, 109
   pacification attacks, 131
   political activity, 150, 200–201
   population base decreases, 254–255
   propaganda campaigns, 37
   recruiting campaigns, 15, 226
   revenue sources, 134
   RF/PF targeted by, 218
   rural control, 196–197
   sanctuaries, Laos and Cambodia, 142, 143, 177, 182, 219, 254
   small-unit attacks, 253
   Tet (1968) losses, 138, 143, 198
   Tet Offensive (1968), 136, 138–140, 143, 200, 223
   Tet Offensive (1969), 203, 217–218
   villages, 43, 210–211
   Vinh Loc district, 174
   Westmoreland's strategy, 33–34
   See also Communists; North Vietnam
Viet Cong infrastructure (VCI), 3, 6, 24, 47, 48, 257, 262, 263
   anti-infrastructure campaigns, 99–101, 113–114, 172, 198, 199
   assassination and torture allegations, 239–241
   CEDAR FALLS, Operation, 61
   Diem's programs and, 24
   dismantling attempts, 109–110
   functions and organization, 109–112
   Gia Dinh, 56
   GVN classification of, 153
   Hamlet Evaluation System and, 248, 249
   hierarchy, 110–111
   identification methods, 117
   imprisonment classifications, 236
   intelligence information, 112
   "legal" cadre, 110, 240, 248, 262
   losses, 253
   North Vietnam and, 110
   Phoenix program, 117–118, 234, 247, 249–250
   province strength, 112
   RUSSELL BEACH, Operation, 228–229, 233
   size, 119
   South Vietnam, 3, 150–151
   structure, 109–110
   VINH LOC, Operation, 174
   WASHINGTON GREEN, Operation, 224, 225–226, 233
Viet Minh, 5, 12, 30, 49
   destruction of colonial rule, 4
   See also Viet Cong
Vietnam, 1
   division, 4
   influence of Indochinese Communist Party, 5

North. *See* North Vietnam
South. *See* South Vietnam
Vietnam Coordinating Committee, 65, 73
Vietnam Doc Lap Dong Minh Hoi. *See* Viet Minh
Vietnamese Alliance of National, Democratic, and
    Peace Forces, purpose, 150, 158
Vietnam Information Service, propaganda, 54
Vietnamization policy, 211–212, 213, 220, 255, 272
Vietnam Quoc Dan Dang, 10
Vietnam Special Studies Group (VSSG), 175, 210–
    211
Village administrative committee, 41
Village council, 41–42, 215, 216, 217
Villages
    colonial rule effects, 10–11
    development programs, 103, 105, 131, 216
    elections, 265–266
    government authority attrition, 61
    See also Peasants; Refugees; Rural population
VINH LOC. *See* Operation VINH LOC
Vo Nguyen Giap, 4
    views on U.S. military efforts, 135
VSSG. *See* Vietnam Special Studies Group

Warner, Volney, 125, 215
Warrenton Conference, 68–69, 71
War Zone C, 57, 186, 217
War Zone D, 5, 21, 33, 48, 57, 186, 217
WASHINGTON GREEN. *See* Operation
    WASHINGTON GREEN
Westmoreland, William C., 30, 31, 43, 49, 63, 72,
    79, 85, 86, 87, 88, 90, 123, 134–135, 163(photo)
    ambassador appointment, 86
    appointment as army chief of staff, 151
    CEDAR FALLS, Operation, 57, 58
    Chien Thang plan, 26–27
    CORDS reporting, 179–180

CORDS support, 106–107, 108, 109, 119
counteroffensive objectives, 150–151
Hop Tac, 26–28, 29, 73
ICEX and, 114, 116
joint commanders' conference, 149
Komer and, 87–88, 89, 96
Long An, 51–52
military strategy, 32–35
military strength increases, 142
operations concept, 33–34
pacification support, 32, 61, 74, 77, 78, 80
post-Tet troop request, 141–143
Project Takeoff, 100
single manager support, 65
Tet Offensive (1968) and, 135, 140, 144, 148, 149,
    150
Viet Cong, 43
Wetherill, Roderick, 176, 179
Weyand, Frederick, 52, 217, 244, 274, 276
Wheeler, Earle, 28, 74, 78, 80, 107, 141–142
Whitehouse, Charles, 222, 244
Wiesner, Louis, 228, 230, 232
Williams, Al, 73
Williams, Ogden, 38
Williams, Samuel, 14
Williamson, Ellis, 33, 184, 185, 186
Wilson, Samuel V., pacification effort in Long
    Huu, 53, 55
Wilson, Wilbur, 151, 242–243, 257, 261
Woodward, Gilbert, 244

Yarborough, William P., 17–18
Young, Earl, 51
Youngdale, Carl A., 176

Zais, Melvin, 174
    views on strategic objectives plan, 213